# Flourishing

A clinical psychologist by profession, Dr Maureen Gaffney is currently Adjunct Professor of Psychology and Society at University College Dublin. For many years she was Director of the Doctoral Programme in Clinical Psychology at Trinity College Dublin. Over the past ten years she has divided her time between consultancy and a number of state and other boards. She has served as Chair of the National Economic and Social Forum, Chair of the Council of the Insurance Ombudsman of Ireland, board member of the Health Service Executive and the Law Reform Commission, and council member of the Economic and Social Research Institute.

She advises many kinds of organizations and businesses, helping them to develop programmes on leadership, emotional intelligence, gender and diversity, and building positive organizational cultures. She has worked with major international companies in Ireland, the UK, Israel and the USA. She is a well-known broadcaster, writer and *Irish Times* columnist.

An enduring theme in her work has been the effort to understand what enables people to function at their best, to be resilient in the face of problems and setbacks, and to flourish under fire.

Her primary degree is in Psychology from University College Cork. She has an MSc in Behavioural Sciences from the University of Chicago and a PhD from Trinity College Dublin. She is a member of the Women's Leadership Board of Harvard University's Kennedy School and serves on its executive committee.

She lives in Dublin with her husband, John. They have two grown-up children, Elly and Jack.

# Flourishing

*How to achieve a deeper sense of well-being, meaning and purpose – even when facing adversity*

MAUREEN GAFFNEY

PENGUIN IRELAND

Published by the Penguin Group
Penguin Ireland, 25 St Stephen's Green, Dublin 2, Ireland
(a division of Penguin Books Ltd)
Penguin Books Ltd, 80 Strand, London WC2R 0RL, England
Penguin Group (USA) Inc., 375 Hudson Street, New York, New York 10014, USA
Penguin Group (Australia), 250 Camberwell Road, Camberwell, Victoria 3124, Australia
(a division of Pearson Australia Group Pty Ltd)
Penguin Group (Canada), 90 Eglinton Avenue East, Suite 700, Toronto, Ontario, Canada M4P 2Y3
(a division of Pearson Penguin Canada Inc.)
Penguin Books India Pvt Ltd, 11 Community Centre,
Panchsheel Park, New Delhi – 110 017, India
Penguin Group (NZ), 67 Apollo Drive, Rosedale, Auckland 0632, New Zealand
(a division of Pearson New Zealand Ltd)
Penguin Books (South Africa) (Pty) Ltd, 24 Sturdee Avenue,
Rosebank, Johannesburg 2196, South Africa

Penguin Books Ltd, Registered Offices: 80 Strand, London WC2R 0RL, England

www.penguin.com

First published 2011
005



Set in Bembo 11.75/14.25pt
Typeset by Jouve (UK), Milton Keynes
Printed in Great Britain by Clays Ltd, St Ives plc

A CIP catalogue record for this book is available from the British Library

ISBN: 978-1-844-88272-4

www.greenpenguin.co.uk

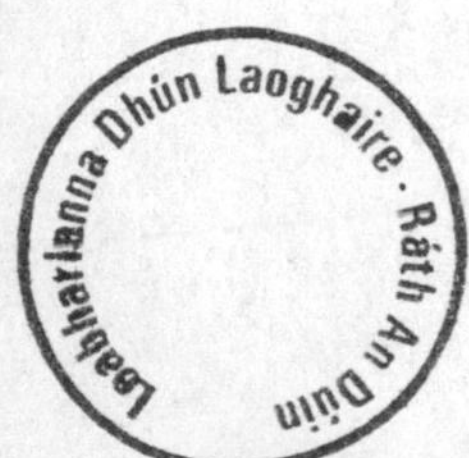

Penguin Books is committed to a sustainable future for our business, our readers and our planet. This book is made from Forest Stewardship Council™ certified paper.

For John, Elly and Jack

# Contents

# Introduction

On my desk as I write are a small bowl of snowdrops and a vase filled with sprigs of daphne, a delicate flowering shrub. Both are bursting with life, the sap flowing freely, straining to fill every bud, stretching every leaf, saturating the air with scent, each its own unique blooming self. They are flourishing. Each of us too has the same instinctive urge to grow and thrive, to feel our life energy stretch and fill every corner of our selves, to reach some high point of self-realization. When we manage to do that, we feel happy. We are able to love more fully, do good work and leave the world a better place than we found it. We are flourishing.

For the last hundred years, psychological science has steadily accumulated a great wealth of insight into the human condition. Over the past decade, much of the focus of psychology has changed in a radical way. Instead of the traditional concentration on disorders and dysfunctions, frailties and weaknesses, psychologists have begun to pay much more attention to what helps us to flourish.

What makes us happy?

What enables us to love and to work in a more successful and fulfilling way?

What helps us to cope with the inevitable problems and frustrations we face, and to bounce back from adversity?

The result has been an outpouring of research on the positive aspects of human functioning, a positivity that is deeply rooted in the science of how the brain works, in how we think and interpret things, in how emotion affects us and how we interact with each other.

While we are beginning to understand what makes us flourish, we are developing a greater understanding of the power of the negative. A sobering body of evidence is showing that negative emotions, and the patterns of thoughts and behaviour they trigger, are far more powerful, contaminating and contagious, and their long-term effects considerably more troublesome, than we once suspected. Of course, we *know* that anger, personal attack, betrayal, contempt and destructive behaviour hurt. But we routinely underestimate their negative impact on ourselves, on relationships and on organizations. We think that these unpleasant effects will disappear.

Sometimes they do.

But not nearly as quickly and completely as we think.

In many ways, our current attitude to negativity is rather like our attitude to pollution before the green revolution. Not so long ago, we thought we could chuck any old rubbish into the air, the ground and the rivers and oceans, and that somehow it would just disappear. Now we know differently. We know that every bit of pollution counts and it comes right back to us. And when the levels become toxic, pollution can destroy whole ecosystems.

So too with negativity.

It counts.

Like pollution, it can undermine or even destroy the delicate psychological ecosystems in our selves, in our relationships, in the organizations we work in and the communities where we live.

That is not to say that we can, or should, eliminate all negativity from our lives. Unless we feel fear, we can't protect ourselves from harm. Unless we feel anger, we won't fight injustice or protect what we value. Without the capacity for sadness and longing, we can't know the power of love. So how do we find the right balance between the positive and negative in our lives? Is there even such a thing as the right balance?

The answer is yes, and that balance is astonishingly precise.

Moreover, the positive–negative ratio in the way we feel, think and behave is what determines whether we flourish or languish in life, and also whether our relationships and the organizations we work in flourish. When we achieve the right ratio, it initiates an upward virtuous spiral. When the ratio is wrong, we are tipped into a downward vicious cycle and we languish, unable to fulfil our potential. This is when we become depressed, when relationships begin to flounder, and when organizations become dysfunctional.

The discovery of this ratio is one of the most important and far-reaching developments in the social sciences for decades. It has implications for how we live our lives, for how we manage our relationships, for how we work in teams and organizations and, indeed, for how we run our society. It means we need to develop a whole new way of thinking about negativity. Far from dismissing it or wishing it away, we have to do the opposite – accord it its full respect. Only then can we see how vital it is to keep our level of positivity so high, in order to balance the much stronger force of negativity. But even when the negative increases exponentially in our lives – when we are faced with great adversity, when we are angry, disappointed, worried and afraid of the future – once we ramp up the positivity so that we maintain the right ratio between the two, we can still flourish.

Learning how to actively build the positive and contain the negative has real and practical results. It can help us flourish while facing the ordinary challenges in life – finding somebody to love, managing our personal relationships, getting on with our career, leading an organization. It can help us deal with adversity – a relationship hitting a bad patch, a new project proving unexpectedly stressful, all the other hidden hurts and disappointments, minor betrayals and secret worries that beset us from time to time. As we try to navigate our way through the fallout of the global financial crisis, it can guide us as we try to deal with the fear – and reality – of losing our jobs, of struggling to shore up troubled organizations, and it can help us cope with the fact that many of us are finding ourselves where we don't want, and never expected, to be.

But that's not all.

When real adversity strikes – if we become ill or disabled, lose our job or our business, suffer the break-up of a relationship, or tragedy strikes somebody we love – it provides a template not just for surviving, or recovering, but for flourishing under fire. As long as we succeed in keeping the right ratio between positive and negative, we can turn the lead of adversity into gold. This capacity to transform a potentially deadly setback into an opportunity to grow, to reach a higher level of functioning than before the crisis, is what we now know as 'post-traumatic growth' or 'transformational coping'.

Out of all this accumulating psychological research comes a central and hopeful message: while we all long for ease and security in our lives, overcoming challenge of one kind or another is at the heart of flourishing. We all have some part of us that is potentially equal to meeting the hard challenges of life, as well as embracing its bright promise. But we also know that this is a potential that we often fail to realize. Learning how better to connect to that potential – to find what the poet Wallace Stevens calls 'our spiritual height and depth' – is what enables us to flourish.

Understanding how the flourishing ratio works, and how we can achieve it in our lives, is the main theme of this book – which aims to serve as a route map through that accumulated store of wisdom.

At our disposal, as we start the journey to flourishing, is that rich body of scientific knowledge and insight – about how our brain and mind work and, in particular, how much of our emotional functioning is automatic and below the radar of the conscious mind. I will show how, without any conscious awareness on your part, you are constantly monitoring threats and potential negatives in your life, as well as clocking up positives. These automatic processes can profoundly affect your moods and feelings and have the potential to prevent you from flourishing and developing your full potential. My aim is to demonstrate not only how you can become *aware* of these processes, but also how you can deliberately *intervene* in their operation and *manage* their impact on your well-being.

Ideally, as you listen to the story unfold, as you dip in and out of different parts of the book, you will gradually begin to reflect in a more personal way on key issues in your own background and psychology. By linking these insights with the psychological information in this book, you should be able to identify the factors that may have prevented you from flourishing emotionally and socially in the past. Armed with this personal analysis, and the specific strategies for flourishing which I outline later, I hope you will be able to develop your own individual agenda for flourishing and renewal.

Part One of the book will tease out the dynamics of flourishing, explaining how we are subject to the push and pull of positivity and negativity and how that plays out at different levels in our selves and in our lives.

Part Two builds on that detailed picture and outlines ten strategies to build the positive and reduce the negative in the way we function.

These ten strategies will help you to:

- build your capacity for happiness
- accomplish important life projects
- take control of one of your most precious resources – your attention
- stay connected to your positive purpose as you go about your life
- learn to manage your mood
- build a life of vital engagement
- live a life that is full of personal meaning
- build your resilience and, if adversity strikes, flourish under fire

- better manage self-defeating behaviour
- face the future with strength and optimism.

This, then, is not a quick-fix book. Instead, its basic premise, and promise, is that a deep understanding of how the human brain and mind work, and an appreciation of the complexity of each individual life, is not just a fascinating enterprise in itself – it pays rich dividends in creating a flourishing life.

# PART ONE
# What is flourishing?

# 1. Your instinct to be your best self

We all have a dream-place, a high place we are journeying towards in our lives. The purpose and direction of travel for each of us, says Aristotle, is to achieve a unique form of excellence distinct to our individual nature, the highest stage of development possible.[1] That is our high place, where we are at our best, where we flourish.

So the goal and goodness of life depend on discovering what the Ancient Greeks called your 'daimon' or true spirit. The good news is that you are not yearning for some abstract 'ideal self'. Your destination is much closer to hand, already present in your inherent capacity to be your 'best self'. You have been to your high-place before – many times. And you can go there again.

When you manage to do that you feel vitally alive because you feel that you are doing what you were put into the world to do. When you feel blocked and frustrated in your efforts, when your spirit is trapped, you are correspondingly unhappy, robbed of your place and purpose in life. That is the anguished cry of the boxer Terry Malloy in Elia Kazan's classic 1954 film *On the Waterfront*: 'You don't understand. I coulda had class. I coulda been a contender. I coulda been somebody.'

Intuitively you always know where you are on your journey to flourishing. Suppose I ask you to tell me about yourself. You will almost certainly start by telling me about the different roles you play in life: in your family, in your work and in the social networks with which you are involved. You will describe your most defining characteristics, your strengths and weaknesses. You will refer to the big events and the major figures in your life to date. Soon, your account will turn into the story of yourself and where you are in your journey. In fact, you will tell me many stories about many 'selves'. But, as you recount your life, three related but quite distinct 'selves' or modes of being in the world will dominate your account.

*The 'good but not great' self*

This is your ordinary, everyday self, the way you are most days: reasonably competent, fairly happy, managing things. A kind of 'getting-on-with-things' mode. You feel you are doing an OK job as a parent, or in your work, or in some bigger project you are involved in, but not in a way that is stretching you. Maybe one important area of your life is blocked. You are working but not loving to full capacity, or vice versa. You know in your heart that you are capable of more. Either way, while your direction of travel is generally right, you wonder: What if I could really get going? If only I could do what I know I could do so well. You sense that you have settled for too long in one place and your destination seems a long way off, sometimes out of sight altogether.

*The 'you at your best' self*
There are times when you manage to break out of that ordinary mode, when you connect to what is great in you. You find the energy to cross some threshold in yourself and your life quickens and picks up pace. You sweep past the 'what ifs' and 'if onlys' and you connect to some elemental capacity within yourself. There are lots of informal ways of describing that experience: coming into your own; being 'in the zone'; finding your 'mojo'; finding your own voice; being at your best. I call it flourishing.

*The 'you at your worst' self*
Finally, there are the times when you feel at your worst, disorganized and shaken by too much stress, or lost and without direction. You feel wounded, all your vulnerabilities on show and your strengths transformed into weaknesses. Your efficiency becomes tyrannical, your conscientiousness becomes obsessive, your capacity to care is wearing you down. Everything you touch seems to go wrong. You make stupid mistakes and mismanage relationships. The harder you try to dig yourself out, the deeper the hole gets.

Most of us are aware of these different selves. Over the past decade, in the course of my work, I have asked hundreds of people to describe themselves in these terms.

*Kate*
Most of the time, I manage my life fairly well. I am regarded as successful at what I do. I always want to get things exactly right,

including trying to please everybody. As a consequence, I often feel over-burdened. And negative feedback really bothers me. There are days when I am very stressed, like I am pushing a big load up a steep hill that keeps slipping back. But, occasionally, I get it right. I stay connected with people but I also stay connected with myself. When I get that connection thing right, it's like I am plugged into an energy source. I just go! I get stuff done, and done really well. That's when I am at my best.

*Joe*

New things really interest me – new ideas, new projects. I love being involved in making something new happen. I am at my happiest then, operating on all four cylinders. That's when I work best myself and work best with other people, when we are all sharing ideas, nobody being territorial. Most of the time, I have to content myself with the more routine aspects but if I don't get enough of the creative side, I just don't feel I am using my strengths. When I am constrained by too many rules and have to deal with too many 'nay-sayers', I just wither. I can't get my energy up. I feel lethargic and irritable. I am very difficult to live with then!

*Patrick*

I am a practical person, a 'do-er'. I like to fix things and solve problems. No big deal but satisfying enough. That's what I do most days. But, sometimes, I get too involved in doing that. I get impatient and I land like a meteor. I make a big impact but I leave a trail of destruction. But other times, I get it just right. I bring all my skills to bear on whatever the problem is – not just my technical skills, but my teaching skills. I get such a kick from showing people what the cause of the problem is and the way to fix it. I really love that. I am not an extrovert, but I really open up then. I am in great humour after a session like that and there is a nice feeling of camaraderie.

*Anne*

Most of the time I would describe myself as OK, but a bit held back. I know I could do more. But I hesitate about committing myself fully to things. I like to tread on safe ground. Yet, at the same time I am envious of people who throw themselves into things.

> As a child I was painfully shy, always hanging around the edge of the group. But there are occasions now and then when I really give things my all. I manage to steady my nerve and I go out on a limb. I get over my ambivalence and go for it. I just step up and do it, but I manage to do it in a way that makes other people feel safe. It's as if I find the perfect balance between risk and opportunity. I wish I could do it more.

Same person, different selves. When we are at our worst, we have not lost any IQ points, nor mislaid any competencies. At our best we haven't become any smarter or suddenly acquired new talents. Our 'worst self' is not some stranger that rises from the depths. It is the mirror image, the shadow of our 'best self'. But, much as we want to be at our best, we are often at a loss to explain why or how we move from one mode to another or what elements need to be in place in our lives so that we can flourish and be at our best.

## *The four elements of flourishing*

Although it is clear from the examples above that being at your best is expressed in unique and individual ways, I have found that in all the accounts I have studied, there are four essential elements.

- *Challenge* – some call or demand to you to do something, to get over an obstacle, to engage with some life task, to make something *happen*.
- *Connectivity* – being attuned to what is happening inside you and outside you. Connectivity orients you to the challenge and gets you ready to deal with it.
- *Autonomy* – feeling free to move and to act in pursuit of the challenge. This gives you the energy to get going and sets the direction of travel.
- *Using your valued competencies* – the experience of using your talents, especially the strengths you most value in yourself, to the full.

When all four work together, they build the upward positive spiral that ends in flourishing. Each is important, but rising to a challenge is the driving element.[2]

### *Challenge*

We mobilize our best self in response to challenge. Sometimes the challenge is positive – an exciting new opportunity, a sudden good turn in our fortunes that opens up new possibilities. But it is remarkable how often our best self is mobilized not in a situation of plenty or ease but in response to a crisis of one kind or another – a health setback, a failed relationship, a family emergency, the loss of a job, or a business crisis. Now, we have to rise to that challenge, to find a way to keep going, to turn things around.

While you have to deal with challenges of one kind or another all the time, you only thrive when you *own* the challenge in a personal way. A crisis may be brewing for a long time or it can come as a bolt from the blue. It may take a while for you to fully appreciate what is happening. But there is always a particular moment when you decide to take it on and to see it through. That is the 'kairos' moment.

The Ancient Greeks had two words for time: 'chronos' and 'kairos'. Chronos is ordinary time – the time of the day, the stage you are at in life, the way you measure how events unfold. Kairos is a deeply personal sense of time, a realization that this is the right time, the opportune moment to respond to something. It is the moment when, as philosopher Viktor Frankl describes it, you stop asking why life has thrown this particular challenge your way, and instead ask yourself: What is life now expecting of me?[3] That is a very profound change of perspective.

Sometimes you take on a challenge because you believe it has a real meaning and purpose. But sometimes, you take on a challenge initially because you have to, but then, once you engage with it, you come to understand that there is something of real substance at stake. You may have started out trying to deal with a family crisis, or trying to turn an ailing organization around – a school that is failing, a business that is in trouble, a junior sports team that is languishing. You may have reluctantly agreed to support some campaign or other. But as you get more involved, what was once just a practical task becomes gradually transformed in your mind into something greater, an expression of a deeper, personal value. Lorna, a young woman who chose to take care of her grandmother with Alzheimer's disease, described such an experience.

> I had always been very close to Granny and when she got Alzheimer's it was awful. She went to live with my mother, and I could

see that was really hard on Mum, though she tried to shield me from what was going on. Initially, I just wanted to help my mum out. She resisted fiercely because she wanted to protect me. But I knew she was exhausted and I insisted.

So I started taking over some of the caring duties. I helped Granny get dressed and undressed and I even changed her 'nappies'. Gradually, I began to feel that this was a lot more than just taking care of my grandmother because I loved her or wanted to help my mother. I had always been a caring person, but now I realized this ran very deep in me. I followed my gut instinct and took more control and I found a new strength in myself. Surprisingly, in this awful situation, I also felt content and positive. Even now, as I recall this, I have tears in my eyes. It's an experience I relive in my memory a few times a year when I am in a bad space, when I am trying to remember that I am a strong person and that I need to be at my best.

And this has helped me in the most unexpected ways. At work, it was totally foreign to me to put myself forward for any leadership position. I dreaded any criticism. But after the experience of caring for my grandmother, I felt different about myself. And obviously it showed. I was able to take on difficult projects and do very difficult things but in a caring way. It was funny. My boss apparently noticed this and he once asked somebody: 'What's happened to Lorna? She is so much more assertive and positive!'

### *Connectivity*

Flourishing requires connectivity, or what is called psychological 'attunement'. Attunement means having a sensitivity to what is going on inside yourself; to being on the same emotional wavelength as other people and accurately sensing how things are unfolding around you. When you are fully attuned in this way, you are like a skilled actor, performing at his or her best, fully in command of the stage. You need that kind of connectivity to flourish because every challenge requires it.

When you feel in tune with yourself, aware of what you are feeling and thinking, and what is motivating you, it is easier to take possession of yourself, to *compose* yourself, so that all the different bits of you are marching to the same beat. Your desire ('I want to do this') is not pulling against your reluctance ('But I don't feel like doing it'), or against anxiety ('I am too afraid to do it'). The psychologist Carl Rogers believed that such un-conflicted energy is the basis of optimum functioning. When you feel this free-flowing energy, like a car at full throttle on an open road, or a runner in full stride, you are flourishing, every part of you working in concert.

When you are internally attuned, it is easier to be attuned to others and you engage with them in a more effective and creative way. You find better solutions to problems. Because you are more attuned to what is changing – in yourself, in others, in your environment – you are readier to work positively with that change. Being correctly attuned to another is at the heart of all flourishing relationships, whether it is establishing a secure attachment between a child and its parent, or between partners in a personal relationship, or establishing effective relationships at work.

You know instinctively when somebody is attuned to you. In psychological terms, you 'feel felt'. When you feel that way, it gives you that fundamental trust that the other person is psychologically available to you and will respond, especially when you feel upset or vulnerable. Equally, you are unconsciously aware when somebody is 'out of tune' with you. Most unhappiness in personal relationships is caused by one (or sometimes both) partner's inability to form that kind of connectivity. Many crises and difficulties in a work environment are also rooted in breakdowns in connectivity – when crucial players can't get attuned to each other.

Teams and organizations also have a 'mental life'. Most leaders work hard to get alignment – getting everybody on the same *thinking* wavelength. But to help organizations and teams to flourish, leaders must also work equally hard on getting attunement – getting people on the same *feeling* wavelength, getting the purpose of the organization and the meaning of the work to resonate with people in a felt way.[4] 'Felt' is the important word here. It is relatively easy to explain the purpose and goals of an organization in a cognitive way. But to function at our best, we have to *feel* the connection between what we are being asked to do and some larger purpose of the group. Leaders of flourishing organizations succeed in making strong feeling connections between the personal goals and values of the people working there and those of the organization, or even the larger society. The tighter the links in the chain, the happier the people and the better the results.

Denis Dempsey, a senior manager in Intel Ireland, describes this process well.*

> I think of the different major start-ups, the introduction of each new wave of technology in Intel Ireland, and each time I felt that I was part of something much bigger, not just in Intel Ireland, but in the sense that we were sitting on the crest of a wave that was getting bigger and moving faster. There was a huge buzz about that and it was coupled with an incredible growth of share price which made us all paper millionaires for a few years. We felt a huge excitement being part of Intel Ireland. We all worked very hard but you could see the clear link between working hard, earning money, learning and mastering the new technology and seeing the success in Intel Ireland and in Ireland as a whole.

A teacher in a school described her experience in similarly 'feeling' terms.

> I think it is vital for a good teacher to be really on top of their subject; to be passionate; to enthuse their students. I am lucky because that is exactly what this school also believes in. Every one of us, individually and collectively, works for these same values: academic excellence; enthusiastic, engaged students. Just a great atmosphere. All pulling together. That is why I am very happy here.

### *Autonomy*

To flourish, you need to have a feeling of autonomy in your life. That means feeling that you can use your free will to set the direction of your life; that you have sufficient elbow room to act; that your opinions count for something. So autonomy is closely connected to feeling that you matter and that what you do matters. Unless you feel like that, there is no real sense of ownership over what you do, no *felt* responsibility for what happens – good or bad. If you don't feel you are autonomous, you won't be happy in your relationships or satisfied in your work.

* I have worked with Intel Ireland for many years, helping them develop and maintain their remarkably positive and flourishing work culture. Because of this, I draw many of my examples of flourishing at work from the senior managers there.

Autonomy does not mean having no constraints, or being totally in control and independent of other people. That is rarely possible and hardly ever desirable. Being rigidly self-sufficient, or exerting untrammelled control, exacts a heavy price on yourself and the people around you. Autonomy means having *sufficient* control and choice over the things that are important to you, and using whatever power you do have to change things in a positive way.

When you take on a challenge, by definition you submit yourself to the demands of that responsibility. But, paradoxically, once you do that you experience a surge of inner freedom. That's because the act of making the choice, of going for something, releases you to direct all your energy towards the target and frees you from ambivalence and anxiety. With the die cast, you feel more in charge of your own destiny, better able to manage yourself and to resist pressures from others, and more likely to judge yourself by your own personal standards.

The result is that you feel you are moving forward in a way that feels right, that you are operating out of your real and true self, that you are living *your* life, not some version of somebody else's life. Hardly surprising, then, that when you experience this kind of autonomy you feel very happy.[5]

### *Using your valued competencies*

Flourishing means feeling that you are using your valued competencies, and so doing what you were put into the world to do. You may be good at lots of things that other people value in you, but there is always a special subset of those competencies that you really value in yourself: an ability to communicate; a facility for resolving conflicts; a knack for fixing difficult problems; an ability to pinpoint the essentials of an issue; a strong capacity to care for others; a way of crafting words; a drive for excellence; a capacity to inspire. Very often, these special competencies are ones that emerged in late childhood or early adolescence, so they are connected in your mind to finding your own personal identity and becoming your own person.

Using your valued competencies is not just about using some aspect of your intelligence or your talents, it also means using the important lessons you have learned in your life, including what you learned from your mistakes, or from your experiences during bad times. In fact, part of the experience of being at your best is the realization that there is as much to be learned – and sometimes more – from the setbacks in your life as from the successes.

When all four elements – challenge, connectivity, autonomy and using your valued competencies – are working together in balance, you will flourish. Together, they initiate a positive upward spiral. You feel more positive about yourself and what you are doing. You have a more open and coherent perspective on things. Because you are performing at your best, it makes it easier for others involved to be at their best, to realize, as Martin Luther King described it, that: 'I can never be what I ought to be until you are what you ought to be, and you can never be what you ought to be until I am what I ought to be.'[6]

When all four elements work together, it is the beginning of wisdom. Cathy is someone who is flourishing in her life and who has developed that kind of wisdom.

> Every time I overcome a challenge well, I feel I have learned something invaluable. And God knows, I have had enough challenges in my life. My mother never had any time for me. I had a serious accident in my twenties. My first marriage broke up. All probably connected in some way. But I eventually managed to pull my life together. I am now, finally, in a very good relationship. I run my own business and I love what I do. I have fantastic friends. I feel very lucky and very loved. But I am my own woman. Every challenge taught me a lesson and I have put those lessons to use in every area of my life. I have learned a lot from my own mistakes, so I understand much better why people act the way they do, and what you need to do to help them be better. I know how hard life can be, but I also know that you can always make it better. I am, I guess, a wiser woman. Sadder? Only sometimes! Wiser, definitely!

Cathy's description chimes almost exactly with how psychologist Paul Baltes at the Max Planck Institute for Human Development in Berlin defines it.[7] Wisdom, he says, is about understanding the 'fundamental pragmatics of life', being able to link the lessons you have learned from very different domains in life; knowing something about the essence of the human condition and the ways to best manage it. It is a rich mix of practical experience; of insight about how people behave; of tolerance of other people and their opinions (mainly as a result of learning from your own mistakes); of recognizing the inherent complexity and uncertainty in life. It is recognizing the limits of your ability to understand and predict things and still being able to positively manage that uncertainty.

## *Remembering your own experiences of flourishing*

All of us have had experiences of being at our best. But, in the rush and pressure of daily life, it is all too easy to forget them – unless you are asked about them. This amnesia is particularly marked if your self-esteem is temporarily battered or you feel disappointed with how your life is turning out. Overwhelmed by your current mood and predicaments, earlier experiences of flourishing can fade from active memory. You become psychologically disconnected from your best self. But these experiences are still there, like buried treasure, waiting to be discovered.

So start your journey to flourishing by setting aside fifteen minutes in which to recall your own experiences of flourishing. Better still, write them down and find somebody with whom to share them. Let your memory roam over experiences in childhood, in adolescence, in your adult life; in your personal relationships and in your work or community life. If you are like most people, you will be able to recall at least five significant experiences of being at your best.

The important thing about this exercise is to try to recall *specific* examples of being at your best because specific incidents are stored in memory in a much richer and more elaborate way. If, for example, you recall a specific event, such as 'Once, when I was sixteen years old, I remember . . .' this will reveal a rich cache of useful information about how being at your best was expressed. Ask yourself:

- What were the circumstances?
- How were you thinking, feeling and reacting?
- What strengths did you discover in yourself?
- How did you manage your usual vulnerabilities or weaknesses?
- What did you learn about yourself from the experience?
- What did you learn about other people?
- What did you learn about life more generally?

On the other hand, if you stick to general descriptions, such as 'I am at my best as a mother' or 'I was at my best when I first qualified', your brain will only generate a list of generalities to explain the experience ('I am at my best as a mother because I always wanted that, and it is the most important job in the world' 'When you are newly qualified you have more energy') that won't give you much insight about the unique nature of your best self.

Also, bear in mind that the experiences of being at your best do not need to have attracted great interest from others or received any formal recognition. On the outside, they may look ordinary and routine: you get a place on a team; you find the courage to declare your love, tell your secret, have a baby, confront a bully or learn to ski. But these moments assume a huge significance if what you are doing is mastering some private fear in yourself, trying out some new talent, or succeeding against some private odds – and the consequences can be surprisingly far-reaching. I recall one such transformative experience in my own life.

When I was at secondary school, I was good at debating. But when I went from my small town school to university, I found myself surrounded by people who were immeasurably more sophisticated than I was, and my confidence suddenly dried up. Week after week, I went to the Philosophy Club, the college debating society. Each week I determined to say something. Each week I baulked. I left university without ever opening my mouth in public, apart from joining in class discussions. I thought then: 'Well, that's the end of that.'

But a year or so after I started my first job, I went to a crowded public meeting in Liberty Hall in Dublin. I don't even recall what the discussion was about, but at one point I just knew that I had to make some point so I sprung to my feet and put my hand up. The person chairing the meeting signalled to me to make my point. Only then did the full horror of the moment strike me. With terror mounting by the millisecond I thought, 'What have I done?' In that split second, I imagined the silence in the room and my own silence stretching endlessly into the future. I tried to say something. All that emerged was a strangled croak. But I persisted and eventually something resembling a full sentence emerged. As I continued I felt my heart thudding violently in my chest, but I kept going. Eventually, my voice got stronger, my heart quietened and I sat down.

The whole episode lasted only a few minutes but it was a transforming experience for me. Most of all, I had re-found my voice. And I never lost it again.

The act of recalling these often half-forgotten experiences provides real and unique data, perfectly tailored to your own self-learning. As you think about them, you can begin to answer important questions.

- What are my most important strengths?
- Where do my strengths come from?
- What kind of people and what kind of situations bring out the best in me?
- Am I happiest around people who are supportive and low key, or intense and competitive?
- Do I thrive in a highly structured or more free-wheeling environment?
- Do I enjoy working closely with others or independently?

You will begin to see patterns, a particular interplay of family influences, personality and social influences on the way you operate. You will begin to get a sense of what made you the person you are – as did these people, when they carried out this exercise.

*Jenny*
I discovered the key thing for me was someone who believes in me. Every single experience of being at my best that I recalled included somebody who singled me out and who saw things in me that I did not see in myself. My history teacher in school, my first boss, and now, one of the more senior women at work who acts like a mentor to me. All very different people, but all had that same attitude towards me. I have been given lots of opportunities in my life but no matter how good the opportunity, I never flourish if I don't feel I have the confidence of the person in charge. I suppose it goes back to my father. I never got the impression he thought much of my talents. Maybe he did, but he never expressed it. But I always wanted him to. When I feel somebody's confidence, it releases something in me. I just take off.

*Alan*
It's funny. I normally like people who are like myself, intensely interested in ideas, always ready to debate issues. But the people who bring out the best in me are the opposite. They are detail people, almost boringly practical. They are only interested in getting things done. I like to have time to develop a concept properly.

But they force me to get my thoughts in order quickly. I resent it at the time. But as I look back on things, I realize these are actually the times I am at my best and do the best work.

*Brian*
What I have learned about myself is that I can't flourish unless I am given a definite and clear task to do. Some people thrive on ambiguity. I don't. It disorganizes me. I like to know exactly what my role is in anything I do. Once I know what is expected of me, I feel I can handle anything. Maybe it's a competitive thing. In our family, there were four boys. I was in the middle and it was a bit of a free-for-all. I didn't like that. I don't like being forced to compete for my position. I like structure. Definite rules and reasonably predictable outcomes. I feel safer, I suppose. What's interesting is that in this kind of environment, I can do my most creative work.

Recalling and analysing your experiences of flourishing helps you to identify the conditions you need to look out for and create – internally and externally – so that you can flourish. But it does more than that. Bringing your actual experiences of flourishing into clear awareness makes them more accessible to your working memory, so you are automatically primed to notice opportunities, to repeat the pattern of flourishing in the present. Recalling those experiences also evokes all of the *feelings* of flourishing again – the surge of energy and vitality, the confidence that you can make things happen. These heightened positive feelings now become available for whatever current challenge you are facing.

Only you have access to that rich seam of information about yourself and only you can mine it. When you do, other people can help you understand and shape it. They can help you fill out the picture by offering their experiences of you at your best. But the journey starts with you.

## *The urge to live your one and only life in a way that counts*

The desire to grow and develop fully as a person is deep within our nature. But that need has been greatly amplified by two powerful and related movements shaping the world we live in.

First, there is pressure like never before to take individual responsibility for our lives, to define for ourselves who we are, and what we want to do with our lives. We don't 'inherit' a life any more: we are expected to make it for ourselves. Second, the growing understanding of the importance of emotional intelligence is redefining what we mean by being at our best at work. This is important because work has assumed a much greater significance in our lives. Correspondingly, in a fast-changing and competitive world, organizations of all kinds are depending more than ever on the quality of the people who work in them.

How are we doing in both respects?

How many of us are flourishing as individuals?

How many of us are at our best at work?

Let's look at each in turn.

### *The desire to purse a personal dream*

The growth of individualism is often presented as a negative development, taken to mean selfish self-interest and an egocentric 'me too' attitude. But individualism is a phenomenon much deeper than that. Ever since the Enlightenment in the eighteenth century, and with increasing intensity, we – in the Western world, at least – have pursued a dream. The dream is best captured in the American Declaration of Independence: that all of us are created equal, endowed with unalienable rights to life, liberty and the pursuit of happiness.

I say 'dream' because despite the intensity of our desire, we have not yet managed to create a society that fully delivers it. But the desire continues to exert a powerful hold on our imaginations and has created a culture, however imperfect, of fostering individual rights, placing value on freedom of choice, self-expression and personal growth.[8] We internalize that culture by increasingly defining our personal worth as taking individual responsibility for our lives. Unlike previous generations, just 'being' in a particular role – a parent, a wife, a husband, a teacher, a manager, a leader – is no longer enough to secure our self-esteem or garner the respect of others. Rather, it is how we personally define and perform that role that counts.

What was previously decided and dealt with by tradition and powerful institutions – family, Church, companies offering lifelong jobs – is now being displaced on to the individual. For the first time in history, says the eminent German sociologist Ulrich Beck, the individual is becoming the basic unit of choice and change, with individuals shaping society as much as society is forming them.[9] The choices we make as individuals about how to live – when, or if, to marry and have children; the decision to stay in a marriage or divorce; when to enter and exit the workforce; the way we define and assert our individual rights – cumulatively make for rapid and often unpredictable social changes, which in turn change individual lives. As Beck observes, neither partner in this endless loop – individuals and the larger society – stays still for long.

While these new freedoms open up opportunities, they also create a new psychological urgency – and a new set of anxieties – about being responsible for doing the best we can with our lives. In traditional societies, we could explain away setbacks and failures as God's will, or fate, or bad luck. Now, there is no hiding place for failure. There is an assumption that if we don't make the most of ourselves and deal with the challenges we face, then it must be because we made the wrong decisions, or failed to make the right ones. That is why we are so ambivalent about tradition. We long for the security it used to bring but also long for a life of our own.

So, for example, when a highly educated woman is considering giving up a successful career and returning to the more traditional role of being a full-time mother, she feels the need to present this as a personal choice, freely made – and a choice that has to be defended against other choices (not least, to herself). Now, any tradition – real or invented – has meaning *only* through being chosen. So there is no escape from choice and responsibility.

The upshot of all this is that the freedom, and burden, of being the author of our own lives is raising in an ever more urgent way the fundamental questions of life:

- Who am I?
- What is really important to me?
- What do I want to do with my one and only life?
- How can I live in a personally authentic way?
- How can I flourish?

Shakespeare's great injunction 'To thine own self be true' is now written deeply in every heart.

### *Nobody comes into work in the morning to do a bad day's work*

Not only do we want to flourish in our individual lives, we need to flourish at work. Over the last fifteen years, the evidence has mounted steadily:

success at work is increasingly less to do with traditional IQ or technical expertise and much more to do with self-development in a more general way, or what we now know as 'emotional intelligence'.[10] The overwhelming evidence from hundreds of studies by Daniel Goleman, the best-known expert on emotional intelligence, and his colleagues, is that self-awareness – the ability to understand and manage your own feelings and to motivate yourself, and the ability to understand and motivate others and to build good relationships – is a key component of success at work. We know this to be true from our own experience. We remember fellow students in school and in university who were top of the class, yet to most people's surprise did not achieve the success in life that was expected of them. We also remember the opposite – those who were average or even struggled academically but who went on to build highly successful careers.

This is not to say that IQ is not important. The ability to understand abstract concepts, to think rationally and to solve problems is more important than ever in this scientific-technological era. Being an effective doctor, a good salesman, a competent teacher, lawyer or manager all require mastery of different bodies of information and the acquisition of technical skill. But increasingly, IQ combined with technical skill is seen as a *threshold competency* needed to get you over the entry-barrier of examinations, qualifying and getting a job. But once you're over the threshold, other factors come into play in making you successful in your career. When IQ is compared with how well people actually perform at work, IQ in combination with technical expertise accounts for only somewhere between a quarter and a third of work success, with emotional intelligence accounting for the rest. For example, in a major study of all the competencies listed by employers as essential for any given job or role in 121 companies, two thirds were emotional and only a third related to IQ and technical expertise.[11]

The more senior the job the more important emotional intelligence is. A study of hundreds of top executives at fifteen global companies found that just one cognitive ability distinguished 'star' performers from average performers – 'big-picture thinking'. This refers to the ability to select the most important trends from the mass of information around them and to think strategically far into the future. Other than that, IQ and technical expertise played no role in leadership success. Instead, close to 90 per cent of the leaders' success was due to emotional competencies: their self-confidence and drive to meet challenges, and their ability to lead a team effectively, to influence people and to understand group dynamics.[12]

Even in highly specialist areas like science, emotional intelligence is critical to life success. For example, Goleman cites one longitudinal study which followed 80 scientists for over 40 years.[13] At the beginning of the study, when the scientists were in their early thirties, they were assessed by psychologists, who measured their IQ and evaluated their personality and emotional competencies in tests and extensive interviews. Forty years later, they followed up the scientists. The success of each scientist was calculated, based on a combination of actual achievements, assessment by fellow experts in their own fields and other forms of professional recognition. The study found that emotional intelligence was about *four* times more important than IQ in determining professional success and prestige in their field.

To be at our best at work, then, we have to get our head and our heart to cooperate and work together as a team.

Every organization, like every individual, wants to thrive. Every business sets out to be profitable. Every hospital sets out to make people better. Every school wants to teach students in the best way possible. All want to be productive, to do high-quality work and to feel that the people who receive their services or buy their products are satisfied.

New research is showing that there is a remarkable similarity between the dynamics of individual and organizational flourishing.[14] I will describe just two such similarities.

First, to flourish, people need to make a connection between the practical things they are doing and some deeper value that motivates them. So too with organizations. Organizational values such as compassion, gratitude, forgiveness, internal trust and optimism may seem remote from profitability, productivity, quality, customer retention. Yet, studies of organizations across a number of sectors have shown that those which score higher on such values perform significantly better than other organizations on precisely those practical things.[15] Having a sense of goodness is just as important for organizations as for individuals.

For example, organizations that pay a lot of attention to being compassionate – particularly in response to the kind of personal and organizational distress that accompanies downsizing and redundancies – are able to repair a lot of the organization-wide problems that can follow such distress. Such compassion builds resilience in the organization and allows it to bounce back faster from downturns. These flourishing organizations practise their values in a systematic way – they don't just talk about them but incorporate them in day-to-day practices and routines.[16] The results are impressive, especially in organizations that are under pressure, resulting in positive spirals of high organizational learning, strong employee commitment and higher productivity.

Second, just as the key to individuals flourishing is having an understanding of what we are like at our best, so it is with organizations. The traditional focus of organizations has always been on rooting out weakness, on identifying the people or the departments that are not performing. That is important, of course. But, to flourish, this must be accompanied, or even preceded, by focusing on the people and parts of the organization that are doing really well, that are 'deviating' in a positive way from the normal way of functioning, and then finding out why they can excel in the same environment and conditions as everybody else.

How are they able to avoid the mistakes and failures that the rest of the organization is prone to?

How do they stay flexible and resilient during crises, when other parts of the organization are floundering?[17]

Just as an individual's personal experiences of being at their best reveals their potential, so the careful study of 'positive deviance' in an organization reveals the highest potential of the whole organization. Excellence always exists – even in the most dysfunctional organization. When an organization taps into that positive core, it releases a surge of positive energy and positive improvement.[18] People become more engaged, more motivated, and more productive.

When organizations focus on building on their strengths, and most especially on the unique strengths of every employee, they achieve significantly better performance than when they focus their efforts on overcoming weaknesses. A survey by Marcus Buckingham and Donald Clifton from the Gallup organization of 80,000 managers, followed up by an in-depth analysis of top-performing managers, found the one quality that sets truly great leaders apart from the rest: their ability and willingness to discover what is unique about each person in the organization and then capitalize on it. Average managers see their employees as workers who fill roles. Exceptional managers see them as individuals around whom they build the roles. As Buckingham puts it: 'Average managers play checkers. Great managers play chess. The difference? In checkers, all the pieces are uniform and move in the same way; they are interchangeable. You need to plan and coordinate their movements, certainly, but they all move at the same pace, on parallel paths. In chess, each type of piece moves in a different way, and you can't play if you don't know how each piece moves.'[19]

We all want to be at our best at work, and the organizations that we work for flourish when we can do that. Yet another study by Buckingham and Clifton of 198,000 employees across nearly 8,000 organizations globally found that only 20 per cent of people felt that they had the opportunity to do what they do best every day. This was despite the fact that people who strongly agreed that they had this opportunity were found to be 50 per cent more likely to work in a business with lower employee turnover, 38 per cent more likely to work in a more productive department or team, and 44 per cent more likely to work in an organization with higher customer satisfaction.

So, many organizations fall short of being the best they can be, of achieving their full potential. This is a source of huge frustration for the people who work and invest in them – the 80 per cent of employees whose jobs do not allow them to use their best talents as often as they could. This is an extraordinary loss of happiness and a waste of human potential, not just for the individuals themselves, but for society at large. Organizations, whether in the realm of business, education, health or other public services, are where the most important goals of a society are met. Finding ways to allow people to flourish in such settings has the potential to deliver a huge boost in human well-being, and in productivity for society at large.

We all want to flourish and be at our best but the reality is that, at any one time, just barely over 20 per cent of us are succeeding. A further 20 per cent are languishing, and the majority of people, nearly 60 per cent, are in between, stuck in 'ordinary mode' – living fairly happy and productive lives but lacking the emotional vitality that comes with flourishing. Psychologist Corey Keyes of Emory University first identified this continuum of well-being.[20] Languishing is a broad category. It includes people who may be holding down good jobs, running a busy family life, and outwardly be living 'the good life'. But, inside, they feel stranded, empty, lost, lacking in purpose. They have a painful awareness of not using their full potential, feeling blocked, frustrated, despondent, 'running on empty'. But it also includes people who are floundering in their lives, who are psychologically distressed and having difficulty managing the ordinary challenges of life.

The fact that so many people are languishing is particularly disturbing. Languishing puts you at risk of depression. While only a small minority (about 5 per cent) of those who are flourishing suffer depressive episodes, well over a quarter (28 per cent) of those who are languishing do. If you are languishing in life, you are five times more likely to have a depressive episode – so, flourishing, apart from its other benefits, is a protection against depression.

The case for learning how to flourish is convincing.

When we are at our best, we are fulfilling a deep human need and in tune with the tenor of the times. We are happier and more productive, we live more satisfying lives, and we help create flourishing organizations. We are more likely to be interested in how our community and society are developing, and to believe that collectively we have the power to change things for the better.

Here, then, is a conundrum: if individuals have such a deep human instinct for fulfilling their potential, if there is such a compelling case for flourishing in organizations and society, if all of us are striving so hard to be at our best, how come so few of us are flourishing?

What prevents us from being at our best?

Unusually for such a complex psychological question, the answer turns out to be stunningly clear.

That is the subject of the next chapter.

# 2. The magic ratio of positive to negative for a flourishing life

We all know flourishing when we see it. We see people around us who are 'at their best' – but in a bewildering variety of ways. Yet, we know intuitively that 'me at my best' is very different from somebody else at their best. So, we may be prompted to ask a fundamental question: Is there some basic underlying dynamic, some 'master recipe', that distinguishes flourishing from 'normal' functioning, and normal functioning from languishing?

The answer is yes. These three states – flourishing, normal and languishing – may take very different forms in different people and in different settings, but the underlying dynamic that drives all three is the same. It is achieving a precise balance between the positive and the negative – in the way you feel, the way you think, and the way you behave.

It turns out that you need a very particular ratio of positive to negative just to function normally. If you ramp up that ratio above a certain threshold, a state of flourishing is established. But there is another invisible threshold that is equally precise. When the ratio of positive to negative falls below that threshold, you are tipped from 'normal mode' into languishing. It is the moment when someone becomes depressed; when a relationship is over or enters a new, dysfunctional state; when a team or an organization is tipped into a downward vicious cycle. I will explain these exact ratios further on in this chapter.

The tipping points at which you are either flourishing or languishing are astonishingly precise and have emerged from many different fields of enquiry. Psychologists who were studying personal relationships, clinical psychologists treating people suffering from depression, researchers studying teams at work have all identified the same positive–negative ratios. However, I will start with the story of marriage because that is where this journey of discovery started (I say 'marriage' because most of these studies involved married people, but the findings apply to any intimate relationship). I will describe this research in some detail because it gives such a clear account of what 'positivity' and 'negativity' – notoriously vague terms – actually mean in the context of human interaction.

## *The magic ratio of positive to negative*

For decades, psychologists have wrestled with fundamental questions about marriage.

- How exactly do some couples manage to build happy and long-lasting marriages?
- Why do other couples languish unhappily or drive each other to distraction and divorce?
- What is the basic dynamic that maintains cycles of flourishing in some relationships or tips others into seemingly irreversible cycles of unhappiness?

Psychologists tried closely observing couples' day-to-day interactions. They asked the couples to explain what they thought was good or bad about their marriage. They studied personality differences. But the key factor that distinguished happy from distressed couples continued to evade them.

A more promising line of enquiry was looking at how couples handled conflict and problem-solving. Unsurprisingly, multiple careful studies showed that unhappy couples, compared to happy couples, were generally more negative in how they dealt with conflict. From these studies, a real understanding about the dynamics of happy and unhappy marriages began to emerge and finally, in the late 1980s, John Gottman of the University of Washington – the world's leading researcher in marriage – cracked the problem.[1] What distinguished couples who were flourishing from those who were not was the precise balance of positive to negative in their interactions with each other. And that magic ratio was 5:1. In other words, for every burst of irritability, every tense exchange, every negative thought and feeling of disappointment, there had to be not double, but *five times* as many positives – an affectionate exchange, a conflict solved, a feeling of being appreciated and understood.

Gottman made this remarkable discovery by recruiting couples for his study who represented the full continuum of marital satisfaction – those who were extremely happy, those who were very unhappy, and everything in between. They were asked about their lives: how they met, how the relationship developed, how they handled the bad times between them and what the good times were like. They were asked about their philosophy of marriage, what their parents' marriages had been like when they were growing up, and how their own marriages compared.

The most ingenious research method Gottman used was what he called the 'talk table'. Each couple sat facing each other at this table and was asked to have three 15-minute conversations. First, they were asked to discuss the events of the day (a neutral topic). Then they were to discuss a problem area of continuing disagreement in their marriage (a negative topic). Finally, they were to select and discuss a pleasant topic.

Unobtrusive sensors were attached to participants' bodies to measure heart rate, blood pressure, sweating and general muscular agitation – all indicators of stress. Two high-resolution cameras (again, placed unobtrusively) recorded their faces and upper bodies as they talked. The images of each partner were shown as a single split-screen image so that speaker and listener could be viewed simultaneously.

The videotapes of the couple were analysed using coding systems that allowed each interaction between the couple – verbal and non-verbal – to be categorized as positive, negative or neutral. So, for example, when a couple described a problem in neutral or positive terms ('We are usually pretty good about compromising with each other but we do have a bit of difficulty agreeing about when my mother can come to stay, don't we?'), when they agreed with each other ('You are right about that'), validated what the other person said ('I think that's a good description of what happened'), expressed affection or love ('Now, my little honey, what have you to say for yourself?' 'I love you. You know that'), expressed empathy ('That was an awful time for you. I know that'), and when they used humour or laughed together or used good-natured teasing – these were coded as 'positive' verbal behaviours.

When they complained ('I think you spend too much money'), disagreed ('You are completely wrong about that'), criticized each other ('You don't pull your weight around the house'), expressed contempt ('You don't know what you're talking about') or disgust ('It makes me sick when I hear you say that'), issued orders ('Drop it!'), stubbornly refused to go along with the other ('No, I'm not going to try that'), put each other down ('The trouble with you is . . .') or expressed sadness ('I just don't know what to do any more') – all these behaviours were coded as negative.

So too were defensive behaviours – making excuses ('Yes, but . . .'), denying responsibility ('No, I did not. It was all your fault'), negative 'mindreading' of the partner ('I don't care what you say. I know what you're thinking'). Withdrawal from interaction was also coded as negative – physical turning away, giving up on the discussion by descending into talk that was incoherent and made no sense ('Blah, blah') or not listening, as evidenced by the absence of little murmurs of interest and disagreement, known as 'back-channelling' ('Mmm' 'Hmm' 'I know').

Each instance of positivity and negativity was not just counted, but rated for its intensity – from minus four (the most negative) to plus four (the most positive) – and the scores totted up at the end. Intensity depended not just on what somebody said but on their non-verbal behaviour – tone of voice, facial expression, gestures and movements.[2] A remark such as, 'Well, if you say so, it must be right!' can be affectionate or bitingly sarcastic – depending on the tone of voice or the facial expression that accompanies it. 'Whining' was also coded as negative – using a high-pitched, sing-song 'poor me' tone, with one or more words or syllables stressed ('I *told* you to remember to come home *early*' 'You never take the kids *any*where'). Gestures of contempt (rolling the eyes, or lifting one corner of the mouth upwards), expressions of disgust (wrinkling the nose and curling the lip upwards) and a cold expression were all coded as negative.

Similarly, non-verbal behaviours such as affectionate touching, smiling, nodding were all coded as positive, as were 'tracking behaviours' such as a steady, interested gaze, or frequent glances at the partner's face (the absence of such behaviours was coded as negative). A tone and rhythm of voice that was relaxed and calm or rapid, animated and excited was coded as positive – what mattered is whether it conveyed an active interest and positive energy in relation to what the other person was saying.

Finally, the researchers matched up all this verbal and non-verbal data with the couples' physiological measures. This proved very revealing. The briefest flashes of contempt and defensiveness by one partner were marked by a spike in stress responses in the other. In the middle of a disagreement, a husband might respond verbally in what seemed like a neutral or positive way ('You know I didn't mean that'), but the physiological measures were showing that his heart rate had risen dramatically, often as high as 100 beats per minute. When the husband 'stonewalled' – psychologically withdrew from the interaction, effectively putting up a stone wall by holding his head and neck in a rigid position, presenting a cold facial expression, arms tightly folded against the chest, looking or leaning away (all expressing 'I am *not* listening to you') – it affected his wife's cardiovascular functioning.[3]

The couples were recalled to the laboratory several days later and were shown the videotapes of their 'talk-table' conversations. Again, they were hooked up to the sensors that measured their physiological reactions as they viewed the videotapes. Remarkably, they showed virtually the same reactions, particularly to negativity, as they had during the original encounter – an indication of the long afterlife of strong emotion.

These couples were followed up four years later. At the follow-up, they provided information on the state of their marriage, whether they had ever considered divorce or actually divorced in the interim, and how their health had been. (Gottman has continued to follow up the couples since then.)

When he put all the data together, Gottman finally uncovered the underlying dynamic of flourishing and failing marriages. He discovered that everything depended not on the *amount* of positivity or negativity but on achieving a precise balance between them. To have a flourishing marriage, that magic ratio had to be 5:1. When it fell below that ratio, the relationship was tipped into a downward cycle that ended in chronic unhappiness or divorce, with the most distressed couples showing a ratio of less than 2:1.

Gottman's central point is that each partner in a marriage has an inbuilt meter that keeps account of the accumulated negativity in interactions with the other. That negativity is reduced or balanced by the flow of positivity between them. Over the course of a single interaction, or a day or even years, this positivity–negativity balance undergoes smooth changes. This rebalancing happens in an effortless and automatic way, largely below the level of consciousness. But there is an invisible threshold in the interaction. Once negativity exceeds this invisible threshold there is what Gottman calls a 'catastrophic change in perception'.[4]

He uses the analogy of perceptual illusions. Most of us are familiar with this phenomenon since childhood. You look at a drawing and see a white vase on a black background, plain and simple. Then, as you keep looking, it flips to an image of two black faces in profile on a white background. Then it flips back again. Another common illusion is the image of a young woman who can flip to an image of an old woman.

In the case of visual illusions, you can flip your perception back and forth. But in an intimate relationship, the 'flip' that occurs when the ratio of positive to negative falls below a certain critical threshold is much more difficult to reverse. In fact, it flips us into a fundamentally different state of mind. The partners now 'see' each other, or their relationship, in a new light. The normal sense of well-being and safety – what Robert Browning described as 'God's in His Heaven / All's right with the world' – is replaced

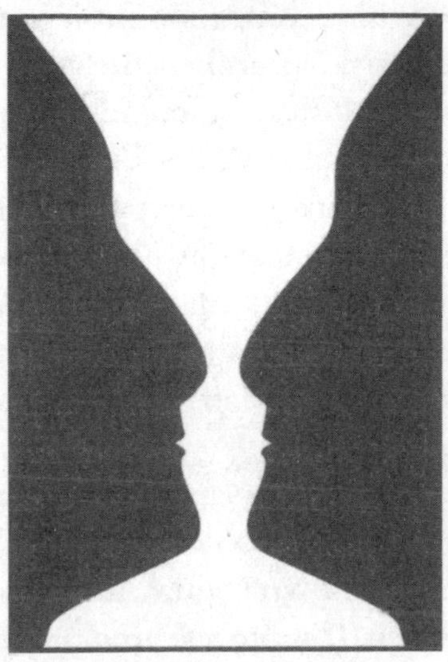

by a sense of deep unease, even danger, which then precipitates a cascade of other changes: in attitude, in thinking, in feelings and in behaviour.

Almost everybody has had this experience, and the easiest way to understand these changes is to recall it for yourself. Think of an important relationship that did not work out. (I give the example of a romantic relationship but it could as easily apply to an important relationship at work.) First, all is rosy. Then, as you get to know the other person a bit better, a few issues arise. But you resolve them. Then a few more, not so easily resolved. Certain things begin to annoy you, or make you feel uneasy. You don't like a mannerism or her views about something. You dislike the way he ignores you when his friends are around. But you remind yourself of the person's good points, the good times you have had together. You balance the negativity with hope and optimism.

You are still thinking it will be OK, still safely in the 'all's right with the world' mode. But then the little negative experiences keep accumulating. Or one big negative event occurs. Suddenly, your sense that 'all is generally OK' is replaced by a deep unease, or even threat. You have 'flipped'. Your belief that the relationship is going through a temporary 'bad patch' is replaced by a more global judgement: 'This is never going to be right.' This moment of truth may occur in the middle of an interaction with the other person, or when you wake in the middle of the night, or while you are sitting on the bus on your way to work.

Of course, you may not be able to face that truth just then and may continue to try to convince yourself that you are wrong, that the relationship is salvageable. But somewhere within you, that flip is never really forgotten. You begin to think differently, especially in the way you explain the other person's negative behaviour. Instead of looking for specific or contextual reasons that would explain what you don't like ('She must be stressed by work. That's why she is being so unhelpful') or dismissing it as temporary ('This irritability is most unlike him and will pass'), the explanation becomes more general and enduring ('He snaps at me like that because he is really bad-tempered' 'That's just typical of the way she behaves'). Statements beginning with the fateful words 'You always . . .' and 'You never . . .' become more likely.

As your explanation becomes more fixed, more personal ('This is happening because he/she is just a bad person') you unconsciously begin to seek out proof that your judgement is correct. Even neutral, ambiguous behaviour is then seen through this new lens. This process becomes self-perpetuating, as any behaviour that fails to confirm your expectations tends to get ignored whereas behaviour that confirms your expectations is immediately noticed, thus further increasing the ratio of negativity in the relationship.

There is a growing chasm between each partner's intent ('I was only trying to help') and its actual impact ('You made the whole thing worse'). You stop giving the other person the benefit of the doubt. Giving each other the benefit of the doubt is the rock on which, imperfect as we all are, we build relationships. It is a precious resource. When it crumbles, it becomes the rock on which the relationship perishes.

This change in your thinking is accompanied by a change in emotional tone. Negative feelings are more easily aroused. Feelings of disappointment, hurt and irritability mount – and a fateful shift in behaviour follows. Complaints turn into biting criticisms. So there is more conflict, more attack and defensiveness, more angry or wounded withdrawal. You begin to feel more worried about the future of the relationship. There is a more enduring sense of hopelessness ('This is a terrible relationship. This is going nowhere'). Even if your partner behaves in a positive way, you find yourself holding back ('OK, he was nice to me this evening. But let's wait and see if it lasts'), being more coolly appraising ('She is all on for a weekend away together. I just wonder why?').

At this stage, each partner's behaviour becomes more highly patterned into rigid, negative sequences from which it is hard to escape. Crucially, the readiness to take a risk with each other – to be flexible, to try something new to make things better – collapses. Once this process progresses, even the past becomes unsafe. The history of the relationship is reconstructed and reordered into a negative chronology ('Looking back on it, this relationship could never have worked. I knew there was something wrong from the beginning'). The good times are forgotten or explained away. Each partner's 'story' of the past begins to differ more and more from the other's. There is a collapse in trust in the whole enterprise. At a particular moment you think: 'This is over.'

## *The three kinds of happy (and unhappy) relationships*

The great power of Gottman's discovery of the magic ratio is that he showed that virtually any combination of personalities and styles of interacting could result in a flourishing relationship – once the couple could achieve that positive ratio of 5:1.

### *Validating couples*

These couples follow the textbook recipe beloved by marriage counsellors – calm partners who frequently 'validate' each other. They have few conflicts but, when they do, they hear each other out, managing to convey, verbally and non-verbally, something like: 'I may not necessarily agree with you on this but I understand and accept that this is the way you feel about it.' That of course is a powerful message of reassurance, acceptance, calm and respect, which more than balances out the negativity of the conflict. In short, each partner accepts as legitimate and valid the feelings of the other.

Some couples did indeed follow this pattern. But others were very different.

### *Volatile couples*

Some couples were volatile. They had frequent and passionate conflicts with each other. They argued and fought with alarming regularity. They interrupted each other. But they were nonetheless very happy. Why?

Because their frequent negative interactions were balanced out by even more frequent positive interactions – at a ratio of 5:1. They laughed and joked a lot together and seemed to enjoy each other's company. The intensity of their irritability and frustration with each other was outweighed five times by the intensity of their continued passionate interest in each other, by their open expressions of physical and verbal affection, by how seriously they took each other as individuals.

Both the validating and volatile couples were very different but had one thing in common – they were prepared to engage in conflict, albeit in very different ways.

### *Conflict-avoidant couples*

Yet another pattern was couples who rarely or never engaged in conflict with each other. In fact, their overall level of interaction was low. Nothing much appeared to be happening in the relationship. When disagreements arose, they moved quickly to shut down the conflict, emphasizing the things they agreed on or minimizing the importance of what they disagreed about ('It's not really a big deal'). When they did argue, each person stated their view in a low-key way and then the 'discussion' was at an end. There was no further exploration of the issues, no attempts to persuade the other to agree, and the 'solutions' tended to be vague ('Let's see how it works out').

In fact, Gottman found it hard to get them to even identify or discuss a problem they had. Yet, that kind of marriage could also remain satisfying and solid because the low negativity did not require much in the way of positivity for the relationship to work. It was enough for these couples to emphasize their general commitment to each other, to accept that some differences could not be solved and to remain calmly philosophical.

Gottman was also able to show how these three types of marriages, using the same styles of interaction, could also result in deeply unhappy and languishing marriages that often ended in divorce. Of course, it is easy to imagine the risks in volatile relationships – volatile partners, by their nature, are highly engaged with each other and so, when in conflict, tend to reciprocate intense negativity in a tit-for-tat pattern. Extremely hurtful things can be said in the heat of the moment that may be very difficult to forget or forgive. In a short time, such negativity overwhelms the positivity and the flourishing ratio collapses dramatically.

The risk for validating couples is quite different. They can simply get bored of each other. All the carefully orchestrated discussions can begin to seem like a business arrangement. Vital interest in each other, excitement and, most of all, sexual passion can begin to drain away. In periods of high stress – for example, when the couple have their first baby – there may not be enough intense positivity to balance out the negatives (the exhaustion, the irritability, the worries, the drudgery). Similarly, at midlife, one partner may feel an urge to *do* something to break out of the routine, but the other may not, or may actively resist, leading to frustration and unease on both sides that can't be accommodated.

Finally, even the meticulously conflict-avoidant couples can get into trouble. They are at risk of a great deal of silent suffering if an issue of importance arises for one of the partners and the other refuses to engage with it at all – a wife who wants more contact with her family, a husband who wants more sex. As the silent stand-off continues, the relationship comes under a lot of strain. Feelings of resignation turn to hopelessness. Interaction narrows to little islands of detail. As the silent negativity mounts, the small amount of positivity bottoms out and the relationship languishes.

That is how the magic ratio works – or does not work – for very different styles of relationships. But that is not all. Achieving or losing the magic ratio is not an additive process. Remember, there is a precise tipping point into languishing, the 'catastrophic' change in state. Similarly, there is a flourishing point – a moment when you enter an upward virtuous cycle. Gottman also provided rich descriptions of those spirals – what he calls 'absorbing states'.

## *Absorbing states and predicting the fate of a relationship*

Some psychologists who studied marriages intensively had noted that as couples interact with each other, they seem to enter what are called 'absorbing states'. An absorbing state is one that is difficult to exit once it is entered. In fact, there is only a 10 per cent chance of spontaneously leaving that state once you are in it. Gottman paid particular attention to negative absorbing states. His observations showed that in unhappy, non-flourishing relationships, when one partner says or does something negative, the other immediately reciprocates in kind – what he called 'fighting on' and 'fighting back'. He found that the reason why unhappy couples can't seem to escape from this cycle is that the usual 'repair' mechanisms that we use to try to resolve a negative interaction fail them.

When we find ourselves becoming absorbed by 'tit-for-tat' negative cycles, we have a number of ways we use to get things back on track. We try what is called 'meta-communication' – we step out of the content of what we are talking about and make an observation on what is happening ('We are getting too angry here. Neither of us is listening to the other'). We try finding out how the other person is feeling about the issue ('Please explain to me why you were so upset about this. I don't understand') or exchange new information ('Let me explain what happened' 'Tell me again what happened'). We try humour. We try to generate some insight by making comparisons with the way we behave normally ('We are normally pretty good at resolving problems') or with others ('We are beginning to behave like . . .). We try to find areas of common ground ('Well, at least we agree about that'). We try appealing to our basic philosophy and expectations about marriage and relationships ('You and I have always really valued . . .' 'We have always agreed to hear each other out. Let's do that now').

The trouble is that most communications – including 'repair' messages – can be interpreted positively or negatively. Much depends not on what is said but on the non-verbal aspect of the communication. Take something as simple as one partner saying to the other in the middle of an argument, 'Stop interrupting me!' Gottman found that happily married couples attend to the positive aspect of that message – the intent to get the conversation back on track ('Sorry. Continue with what you were saying'). But unhappily married couples pick up on the negative aspect – the note of irritation in the person's voice, or the angry look – and respond negatively ('I wouldn't have to interrupt you if I could ever get a word in edgeways'). What follows then is a chain of negative interactions. The couple can't seem to escape or even see that there is an escape. Over time, the negative interaction patterns of distressed couples become very rigid and predictable ('If I say A, then he always says B. So then I do C and he does D').

This pattern of negative reciprocity is accompanied by an absence of positive reciprocity. When one partner says something positive, the other does not respond positively but devalues it in some way, a favourite being: 'Yes, but . . .' In a happy relationship, there is exactly the opposite pattern. One partner will respond immediately to the positive overture of the other and will not respond immediately to the negative.

These 'absorbing states' are probably much more influenced by general feelings about the relationship than what actually happens in any particular situation. If the couple can maintain the right ratio of positives to negatives, this builds a reserve of fondness, admiration and respect that can override specific negative interactions. If the ratio falls below that threshold, this creates a well of disappointment, anger and bitterness that can override any potentially positive interaction. Gradually, all of these experiences get constructed into a narrative about the marriage, a story that each partner tells himself or herself about what is happening and why.

Finally, distressed couples show strong physiological 'linkage'. One partner's physiological stress transfers rapidly to the other. So, for example, as one person's blood pressure goes up so does the other's. These difficulties often arise because one partner (or sometimes both) has difficulty soothing or calming themself once they become stressed. This can happen for many reasons – because of their particular temperament, or because they have endured a lot of stress earlier in their life. If you can't soothe yourself, it is virtually impossible to soothe another person. The more stressed one partner becomes, the more the other finds those reactions unpredictable, overwhelming and disorganizing. As the stress reactions spread across the body (increased heart rate, blood pressure, sweating etc.) each becomes physiologically 'flooded' – an intensely unpleasant feeling in the body that makes it virtually impossible to think straight.

To escape these experiences of 'flooding', the couple begin to distance and isolate themselves from each other. They increasingly see the relationship as having severe problems that are better worked out alone rather than together. They begin to arrange their lives so that they live in parallel to each other rather than together. There is a feeling of intense loneliness in the relationship. Eventually their whole perception of the relationship is affected and each person's 'story' about the relationship diverges more and more from the other's. At the end stage, they express intense disappointment with how the relationship has turned out. They show little fondness for each other and present themselves as separate entities who do not see the path ahead in the same way or share a common philosophy of marriage. They see all the conflict between them as pointless and empty. It is a grim picture.

Once these thinking–emotional–physiological patterns are established, change becomes very difficult.

Contrast that grim picture with the positive spirals built by happy couples.[5] As we saw already, couples in happy relationships are quick to respond positively – not just to positive behaviour from the partner, but also to neutral and negative behaviour. When they argue, they are more open to influence from the other, and are more likely to use and respond to positive persuasion rather than coercion. They are skilled at soothing themselves and each other. As a result of this positivity, they are buffered from the physiological stresses of flooding, and are quicker to recover from negative interactions.

Building up a reservoir of positive behaviour happens primarily in the mundane, everyday interactions of married life, each of which holds the possibility of what Gottman terms 'turning towards' or 'turning away' from your partner.

For example, you say to your partner, 'I'm really worried about . . .'

Your partner responds, 'I don't have time for this now.'

This is an example of 'turning away'. An example of 'turning towards' would be responding, 'Oh, really. What's happened?'

When that verbal 'turning towards' is accompanied by a physical approach – an interested, concerned expression, a sympathetic touch, your partner turning fully towards you – then it is a powerful connection, even if the whole interaction is brief. Similarly, a verbal 'turning away' that is accompanied by physically turning away – looking away, moving away – is experienced as a strong disconnection.

Intimate relationships are full of these bids for connection. When your partner responds to them, you build a mental picture of him or her as a responsive person and this positive perception acts to override specific negative interactions. As a consequence, you have less cause to criticize your partner, who in turn has less need to get defensive. This positive override also means that your efforts to 'repair' an argument work more effectively because each partner will be inclined to believe that the other is positively motivated. So, the couple becomes skilled at escaping long, destructive interactions. They become skilled too at 'editing' – not expressing every negative thought, every disappointment, every irritation that comes into their mind. Editing leads to fewer negative 'start-ups', with less chance of a neutral state becoming a negative state.

Happy couples are also characterized by their use of respectful influence. Some couples try to influence each other a lot. Others are content to make a more modest number of attempts. Still others make very few. But whatever the number of attempts, each partner must be able to feel that influence is *possible* without a huge fight. The core of respectful influence means that each partner gets the opportunity to present their 'case' – their views and feelings about the issue at hand. That sets the right agenda for the next phase – arguing their case. When happy couples argue their case, they punctuate long sequences of disagreement with frequent attempts at repair. Finally, as they move into the final phase, they strive for compromise – easier because they have moved through the argument in this way.

In unhappy couples, on the other hand, one or both partners try to prevent the other from stating their case so the agenda is only partially set and the argument that follows then goes off course and leaves one partner feeling very frustrated. They are less successful at repairing the negativity, and so end up unable to compromise. Each makes proposals that are shot down by the other, who makes a counter-proposal ('I think we should buy the car' 'No. I want to save the money').

Happy couples also allocate enough mental room for the relationship and for each other. They make time and effort to understand what matters to the other. They frequently express affection and admiration for each other – the best antidote to the carelessness and over-familiarity that can creep into intimate relationships. They learn how to soothe each other, physically and psychologically – they learn the mix of empathy, listening, validating the other's experience, touching, humour and reassurance that works the best when the other is worked up about something. Like a good parent, they make it their business to keep updating this intimate knowledge. Gottman calls this the 'love map'.[6]

One man once told me:

> When Mags gets stressed about something, I've learned there's no point trying to put my arms around her or telling her not to worry. That seems to get her even more agitated. I used to go into overdrive trying to be helpful, offering to help her or making suggestions. But I discovered that all she wants is for me to listen and say nothing – not a word – until she's finished. Then, as often as not, she has straightened out her thinking and calms down. Then she says, 'That was really, really helpful!'

Whereas another women reported:

> I know immediately when Tom is stressed. He completely withdraws and clams up. The only way to reach him is to go over, sit down next to him and rub his neck. Works wonders every time.

Having studied over 700 couples during a 10-year period, Gottman and his colleagues have developed a formula that can predict with almost perfect accuracy (94 per cent) whether a couple will stay together happily married, or will develop problems and ultimately divorce. The formula includes each partner's positive and negative scores, combined with other crucial measures, such as the extent to which each partner feels they can *influence* the other (the harder it is to influence a partner, the more likely the marriage will fail) and the level of linkage between partners' moods (the more powerfully one partner's negative mood affects the other's mood, the worse the outcome for the marriage).

## *The magic ratio in the workplace*

In 2005, the first hard evidence emerged that the same principles that emerged from the intimate world of love, marriage and domestic conflict also applied to the very different world of work. A collaboration between Barbara Fredrickson, the foremost researcher on positive emotions, and Marcial Losada, a business consultant with a passion for mathematical modelling of group behaviour, showed that successful business teams also exhibited the magic 5:1 ratio.[7]

A few years earlier, Losada had studied the interpersonal dynamics of sixty business teams as they engaged in day-long annual strategy meetings.[8] The teams were observed from behind a one-way mirror, and every interaction was videotaped and analysed. Losada wanted to know whether his measures of team dynamics could predict which teams were flourishing in objective business terms. From those 60 teams, 15 were independently identified as showing consistently high performance in three domains crucial for business success: profitability, customer satisfaction and how members rated each other and the team. Of the remaining teams, 26 showed mixed performance on those three indicators, and 19 showed uniformly low performance.

When Losada matched up these measures of business success with the observations, he found that the highest performing teams also had the highest positivity ratio – nearly 6:1. They showed this positivity ratio from the beginning of their meeting and succeeded in maintaining it throughout their day-long discussions. These teams also showed the highest 'connectivity' – the team members were highly 'attuned' and responsive to each other.[9] They showed the best balance between talking and listening – asking more open-ended questions to explore issues – and were open to the broadest range of viewpoints and spoke up for them. While individual team members argued vigorously for their own positions, they also strongly supported others' viewpoints and argued for the position of those who were not present at the meeting who might have a different view, such as the customers and the suppliers.

Importantly, they were open to positive influence from others. These top-performing teams, then, were not just highly connected and attuned to each other but were also focused outwards, not exclusively on their own individual concerns. It is a portrait of flourishing that is remarkably similar to flourishing in the more intimate domain of marriage.

In contrast, when Losada matched the medium-performance teams with his data he found that these teams started with a lower positivity ratio – almost 2:1. But, impressive as it might appear, twice as much positivity as negativity was not enough to withstand the inevitable conflicts and stress that arose during the day-long discussions. When they experienced what he called a 'moment of extreme adversity' their positivity levels dipped precipitously. In that moment, the team dynamics changed dramatically and they lost their ability to ask exploratory questions and to act flexibly, both of which are crucial for problem-solving. Instead, the teams stayed stuck in an endless closed loop where each team member simply defended their own position and criticized all other points of view.

The most poorly performing teams, those whose work was consistently unproductive and unprofitable, rated as unsatisfactory by team members themselves, showed the lowest positivity ratio – less than 1:1. Such teams never got off the ground at all, and stayed stuck from the start. There was no real enquiry or engagement with other people's positions. Each member remained preoccupied by defending their own position. There was no connectivity, no openness to influence. Hardly surprisingly, these teams lost all behavioural flexibility.

Losada set out to discover which exact aspects of team behaviour predicted what happened as the meeting unfolded. His findings mirrored the discovery of Edward Lorenz, the meteorologist, about the complex dynamics of weather forecasting – that very important things happen in a dynamic, non-linear way.[10] A small event can change a whole system. Intuitively, we think that if you do something big, it will cause big things to happen and if you do something small the effects will be correspondingly small. Not so. Essentially, Lorenz showed how systems of weather are extremely sensitive to small changes in one part of the world that can then balloon into major events in another. When he mapped these small changes graphically, he produced the now famous 'butterfly shape', showing how something small – the metaphorical flapping of a butterfly's wings – in one part of the world can trigger major weather conditions in another. When Losada mapped what happened minute-by-minute in business teams, he found the same effect.

That initial positivity – especially the connectivity and attunement to each other, combined with an openness of attitude – allowed the team to be more flexible, more creative, more resilient in the face of setbacks and stress.

As the team went about its work and tried to deal with the challenges it faced, this positivity ensured that it did not get stuck in behavioural ruts. It enabled members to bounce back with new ideas when they confronted problems, which in turn generated more confidence – a collective synergy that served as an entirely new kind of resource for the group. The more the positivity rose in the team, the more attuned team members became to each other, and the more open and outward-looking their behaviour became. And so, onwards and upwards – the classic virtuous cycle.

This discovery has real and practical implications. If you are in charge of a team, and know only the initial ratio of positivity to negativity – something that may appear trivial in big projects – you could predict really important things, such as how effective and productive the team will be, how successful the outcome of their work will be, and how satisfied the customer or client will be at the end.

But that was not all that Losada discovered.

He found the precise tipping point that separated the upward dynamics of flourishing from the downward spirals of languishing: a positivity ratio of 3:1. He calls this the 'Losada line'. He also discovered another tipping point. The complex dynamics of flourishing disintegrate when the ratio of positive to negative goes above 11:1. Too much positivity is problematic. Imagine an important relationship in your life – with your partner, your adolescent child, with an important staff member – and suddenly there is no negativity at all: no complaints, no problems, no conflicts of any kind. You might get suspicious, and you probably should be. Because the likelihood is that something negative is happening under the surface – the other person has become disengaged or is trying to avoid a problem or hide it from you. Remember the ratio for flourishing is not 5:0. It is 5:1. Problems arise and things go wrong – that is the nature of life. Appropriate negativity has an important role to play in flourishing – most particularly the constructive confrontation of problems and bad behaviour.

As a result of Losada's work, we can now define the zone of flourishing. It is when the ratio of positivity to negativity is between 3:1 and 11:1, with the typical flourishing point at 5:1. Or to put it another way, you need a minimum ratio of above 3:1 to function normally. If you go above that and achieve a ratio of 5:1, you flourish. If you fall below the critical threshold of 3:1, you enter a cycle of languishing.

## *The magic ratio in individual lives*

Barbara Fredrickson was so intrigued by the findings of the positivity ratio of 3:1 in business teams that she set out to discover if the same dynamic applied to individuals.[11] As it happened, she had already recruited two large samples of people on whom she had gathered a great deal of information. Just 20 per cent of the people in her study were found to be flourishing. She now asked everybody in the study to record each evening for 28 consecutive days what positive and negative emotions they had experienced during the day, and how intensely. Positive emotions included contentment, gratitude, hope, interest, love, pride, amusement, compassion and sexual desire. Negative emotions included anger, fear, guilt, sadness, shame, embarrassment, contempt and disgust. Since we can all have exceptionally good or bad days, the positivity ratio was calculated on the basis of all the negative and positive emotions experienced by the person over the full month.

She found that the ratio for flourishing individuals was always above 3:1, whereas the ratio for those who were languishing was below that critical threshold, hovering around 2:1. So, even if we experience double the number of positive to negative emotions in the average day, we muddle along, doing OK but without enough positive credit on our balance sheet to withstand the inevitable stresses of life. Just like the medium-performing teams, we can't be at our best.

In an entirely independent field of enquiry the same magic ratio was appearing. In 2002, clinical psychologist Robert Schwartz and his colleagues tracked the outcomes of 66 men receiving treatment for depression.[12] Before the treatment started, the men recorded their day-to-day experience of positive and negative emotions. Their positivity ratios were very low – less than 1:1. The men were then assigned to cognitive behavioural therapy or were treated with drugs – both powerful treatments for depression. Their progress during treatment was evaluated every two weeks by clinicians who were not treating them.

During and after the treatment, the men were asked to complete surveys of their feelings. The results almost exactly echoed those of the languishing, medium-performance and flourishing teams. For some of the men, the treatment slightly increased their positive feelings or slightly reduced their negative feelings, but the ratio stayed below 1:1. These men continued to be depressed and to languish. Others showed an increase in their positivity ratio to nearly 3:1 – the crucial tipping point for 'average' functioning. These men went into remission – showing relief from the symptoms of their depression for at least four weeks in a row. But the men who managed to increase their positivity ratios to just over 4:1 showed the most dramatic improvement. Not only did they show virtually no symptoms, but they also showed clear signs that they were functioning well in their lives.

All of this research into different worlds – intimate relationships, business teams, the day-to-day lives of individuals, and those with clinical depression – answers the fundamental question posed at the beginning of this chapter: Is there some basic underlying dynamic, some 'master recipe', that distinguishes flourishing from 'normal' functioning, and normal functioning from languishing?

The answer is a definite yes. We have to experience at least three positives to every negative in order to function normally in our personal and working lives. That is the minimum platform. If we want to flourish, to be at our best, the positivity ratio has to be ramped up to reach 5:1. If we fall below the 3:1 threshold, we will be trapped in a downward spiral of languishing and failure.

That is the economy of the heart.

But we now have some more questions to answer.

- Why do we need so much positivity?
- Why is *double* the amount of positivity to negativity not enough?
- Why do we need five times as much positivity as negativity in order to flourish?

In short, we need to find out why the negative is more powerful than the positive.

That answer lies in the way the brain and mind are organized, and is the subject of the next two chapters.

# 3. Understanding how emotions work

The fundamental drivers of positivity and negativity in your life are emotions – how your brain reacts emotionally to the things that happen to you. Emotions are your instant decisions about what is important, so they affect every aspect of your existence. They determine what you pay attention to; how you think; the meaning you put on events; and even what you remember. They affect how you make judgements of right and wrong; how you make decisions, particularly in complex situations; what you consider important and valuable; and how you judge risk. Emotions shape your intimate life, your relationships, the networks and organizations you work in. They mould your identity; galvanize you into action; determine which goals you work for, and what kind of life you have.

Emotions are nature's way of equipping us for the most fundamental task that faces us as human beings – survival. Negative emotions are designed to alert us to and help us deal with threat – the first task of survival. Positive emotions are designed to alert us to opportunities and help us to avail ourselves of them quickly. However, negative and positive emotions are not equal in terms of their impact on us. That is because if we miss an opportunity, we will likely get another. If we miss a threat, we may no longer be around to take advantage of any other opportunities. To flourish in life, we need an optimum balance between the negative 'threat alert' and the positive 'opportunity alert' systems – and the only way we can do that is by countering the power of the negative by building up the positive to a ratio of 5:1.

To get the right ratio between positive and negative, we need to first understand how emotions work, how we are affected by them in our everyday life. And in order to understand the complex relationship between emotions, thinking and behaviour, we need to look at the workings of the brain.[1]

That is what this chapter is about.

## *Our twin pillars of survival*

Over the past thirty years, all areas of psychology have made massive strides in understanding how the mind works, how children develop, and how we behave in relationships and in social groups.[2] Over the same period developments in neuroscience have revolutionized our understanding of the brain.[3] Together, these dramatic new insights have changed the way we think about human nature. In particular, they have revealed just how crucial a role positive and negative emotions play in virtually every aspect of our functioning, and that crucially – and contrary to what we once thought – negative and positive emotions are not 'opposites'; rather, positive and negative emotions are organized as relatively independent systems in the brain. These positive and negative systems are our twin pillars of survival.

Imagine your ancestors wandering around the savannah at the dawn of time. They are surrounded by threats – predators, rivals, natural dangers. But they are also surrounded by opportunity – better hunting grounds, more fertile land, safer habitats, fertile mates. But managing threats and opportunities requires a lot of decision-making. For example, what were they to do when they came across an unfamiliar bush covered with red berries? They did not *know* if these berries were edible or not. This is where emotions come into play. Whether your ancestors decided to approach the bush and try the berries depended on their feelings about the berries. Did they *like* the look, the smell and taste – the first little bursts of sensory pleasure. Their willingness to try them out is a reflection of their 'positivity bias' – their faith that the berries will be good.

But now, imagine them coming upon an unfamiliar river. The water looks dark and murky and they see shadows moving beneath the surface. They don't *know* for sure what is there, but they experience a stab of fear – so they decide to withdraw and avoid crossing that river. That tendency – to immediately go on high alert, to stop what they were doing and pay full attention to the possible threat – is their 'negativity bias' at work.

The negativity bias is offset by a positivity bias – the mild tendency, in the absence of any obvious danger, to keep approaching things we like. This positivity bias is signalled and fuelled by positive 'liking' emotions such as interest, love, lust, contentment, hope. We need it because it is clearly adaptive for us to be open to possible opportunities, to keep venturing where no man (or woman) has gone before. On the other hand, the negativity bias – the tendency to pull back from the unknown for fear of putting ourselves in harm's way – is signalled and fuelled by negative 'disliking' emotions such as fear, anger, loss. The negativity bias is vastly more powerful than the positivity bias since, in primitive terms, missing an opportunity may be disappointing but there will always be another; however, if we miss a threat, we may not survive.

In the far more complex modern world, our positivity and negativity biases continue to play similarly crucial roles in how we manage our lives. Both the positive and negative emotional systems have evolved together and continue to work together in a world where threat and opportunity still go hand in hand.

Most of the time, happily, we are not in mortal danger, so the 'normal' state is to be mildly positive, mildly motivated to keep going and to keep trying out new things. Nature has even made it easy for us by ensuring that we generally tend to like the things that are important for our survival – food, sex, company, adventure, even the best places to live. For example, what is generally considered a beautiful and pleasing landscape will also have definite survival advantages. We instinctively like places that are neither completely exposed (which leave us vulnerable) nor overgrown (which impede vision and movement). We like good views to the horizon (to spot enemies coming). We like big trees, rivers and lakes – not just because they provide shelter or food, but because they help us identify where we are. We like places with plenty of wildlife and flowers. In this kind of place we can get shelter, food and refuge, yet keep alert to what is happening in the wider environment. But we also like a bit of mystery – winding paths, hills and mountains – because they excite our interest, urging us to explore and conquer.[4] In the same way, we tend to dislike things that are bad for us – snakes, rats, large toothy animals, the dark, anything that tastes bitter, the smell of rotting, being confined in very small spaces, the sight of blood.

We have to constantly manage our positivity and negativity biases in such a way that we can keep availing ourselves of opportunities and warding off threats. Though most of us don't routinely have to deal with life-threatening emergencies, we do have to deal with threats to our self-esteem and our place in important relationships and groups. If we are experiencing a lot of conflict or stress in our lives, or because of our temperament, and our negativity bias is too reactive, this can overwhelm the weaker positivity bias and plunge us into cycles of languishing – like Gottman's volatile couples (see Chapter 2) who did not ramp up the positive to counter the negative effects of conflict. Our natural 'liking' and 'disliking' systems can also be distorted by very unhappy experiences – particularly in early life. We can be fatally attracted to people who are bad for us, and be put off by things that are good for us, such as learning and challenge.

The relative independence of the positive and negative emotional systems means that *even* when you are feeling negative, you are capable of experiencing positive feelings at the same time. This means that to maintain the right ratio, you have to learn to manage both emotional systems independently – to actively build up the positive and to contain and reduce the negative. You can help yourself to do that by understanding how both systems are wired in the brain.

## *The 'heart' of the brain*

Neuroscientist Daniel Siegel suggests a useful way to visualize the structure of the brain.[5] Make a fist with your hand, with your four fingers curling over your thumb in the middle. Your wrist represents the spinal cord. Below your fingernails is the face; and the fist is the brain. The palm of your hand is the brainstem, located at the top of the spinal cord. This is the earliest, most primitive part of the brain, the so-called 'reptilian brain' that we share with most other species. This part of the brain does not think or learn. Its function is concerned with basic physical survival and it does this by regulating basic body functions, such as breathing and metabolism, but also, crucially, by providing us with a set of preprogrammed reactions. These include the four great hard-wired programmes that cognitive scientist Steven Pinker refers to, tongue-in-cheek, as the 'Four Fs': feeding, fighting, fleeing and sexual behaviour – with all of their accompanying primitive impulses.[6]

Millions of years later – as our immediate ancestors, the mammals, appeared – a new layer was added to the brain. This is the limbic system, the 'primitive mammalian brain', which encircles the brainstem (taking its name from the Latin word 'limbus', meaning 'ring or border'). This added the capacity for a new set of emotions: passion, love, rage, dread, pleasure and forming attachment to offspring. The limbic centre also created new vital structures that added a further capacity to the brain – the ability to learn from experience and to store that learning in memory, freeing us from being slaves to instinctive and automatic responding. This means, for example, that human beings now had the capacity to master primitive urges – such as the urge to simply grab what attracts us (somebody else's dinner or a sexually attractive passer-by) or to physically attack what threatens us (hit the person giving us negative feedback)–because we are able to *learn* from our experience, and can *remember* that such behaviour can create a lot of trouble.

The most important of these new brain structures were the hippocampus and the amygdala. The hippocampus is what enables us to remember the *facts* of our experiences: their context and the where, when and how. For example, it is the hippocampus that enables us to remember the physical details of a particular room, and to recognize the room when we see it again. It also stores the context of that memory ('This is the room where I had a crucial meeting with my boss' 'This is where I first kissed my beloved'), which is crucial for the meaning we put on the memory.

But it is the amygdala, a small almond-shaped organ – one on each side of the brain, towards the bottom of the limbic ring – that stores the emotional reactions experienced at the meeting. The amygdala is where any incoming information to the brain – each of our experiences – is assigned an emotional meaning, and where the memory of those emotional experiences is stored. The amygdala is the heart of what is now called the emotional brain.

Finally, with the advent of *Homo sapiens* came the neocortex (Latin for 'new covering'), the so-called 'modern mammalian brain'. Imagine it located at the front of your curled fingers. The human neocortex is bigger than its equivalent in any other species and is what makes us distinctly human. It is what makes thinking and language possible, allowing us to make sense of experience; to imagine and plan for the future; to engage in abstract thought; to use symbols; to make art; to create complex cultures and civilizations. The neocortex also added a whole new range of more subtle emotions: empathy, sympathy, sensitivity, cunning and self-control. Crucially, it allowed us to *think* about our feelings.

You might think that once humans achieved that capacity to reason, our troubles were over – or that they would be over if, as it were, we managed to keep out of the bad side of town (the primitive brain) and tried to stay uptown in the more sophisticated neocortex. Then, we would be freed from our animal urges and unruly feelings. We would be able to devote our intelligence to coolly planning great strategies, executing well-crafted plans and making rational decisions.

Alas, no. For all its incredible complexity, the rational neocortex is not in charge of the brain. Each evolution of the brain did not just sit on top of the older part, but changed and modified what came earlier. Thus, all the systems of the brain are deeply interconnected. The neocortex grew and evolved from the emotional areas of the brain, and the two systems remain connected in myriad ways. As Daniel Goleman puts it, there was an emotional brain long before there was a rational one, and in crucial matters of survival, what he calls 'emotional emergencies', the neocortex defers to the limbic system.[7] So, while thinking and emotion are separate functions, they are closely joined by separate but interacting systems in the brain. When emotion is intense enough, it can shut down the thinking brain completely – and because negative emotions are so much stronger than positive emotions, our experience of negative emotion can fundamentally affect us in life-altering ways.

## *Why negative emotions can be good for you*

In one of the most famous opening lines in literature, Tolstoy wrote that all happy families are alike, but each unhappy family is unhappy in its own way. A romantic idea – but the opposite is far more likely, as negative emotions and the responses they provoke are actually more rigid and stereotyped in how they are expressed than positive emotions.

Negative emotions can be your best friends – they will always come to your aid if you are in real trouble – but they are friends not to be trifled with. When aroused, they are overpowering and can turn nasty. This is because, as said earlier, negative emotions are designed to grab your attention and to keep it focused on whatever threat you are facing until you have dealt with it satisfactorily. The immediate effect of a negative emotion is instantly to narrow your focus. Of course, this is highly adaptive in life-threatening or emergency situations. If a rogue elephant is galloping straight towards you, or your child is about to put her hand into the fire, this is not the time to be thinking of anything else, such as the plight of wild animals in disappearing habitats, or whether the child needs a haircut.

This contraction of your attention allows you to react instantly. To make this even more efficient, negative reactions carry with them a preprogrammed automatic 'action tendency'. And just as well: in an emergency, you don't want to be in any way unsure of what to do next. There is no time for a 'compare and contrast' approach. You rely on an instinctive, tightly connected pattern of emotion–thought–action – so, you run to safety; you grab your child.

Fear, anger, sadness, disgust, contempt, shame, jealousy and envy are the *big* negative emotions. They alert you to what you perceive to be threats to your welfare and mobilize you to act to protect your interests.

Each emotion prompts a compelling urge to act in a specific way. When you are afraid, you experience a strong urge to escape or avoid the threat. When you feel angry, you feel the urge to fight on or fight back. When you feel contempt, you feel the urge to put down the other person, thereby 'lessening' the threat they pose to you. When you feel disgust, you feel the urge to get rid of the object of your disgust, to spit it out and move rapidly away from it. When you feel sad about some loss, you instinctively want to shore up or conserve your energy following the loss, so you feel an urge to withdraw, become inactive and passive. In our complicated 21st-century world, we express these action tendencies in complex and subtle ways. We try to disguise them. But, at heart, our responses are highly stereotyped and patterned.

You experience these emotions in a very pure sense and at intense levels when the threat to you is great, or perceived to be great. When the threat is milder, you experience less intense variations. Thus fear can take the form of worry, concern, anxiety or apprehension, and can escalate all the way up to fright, dread, panic or terror. Anger can start as indignation or mild irritability but work its way up to outright hostility, hatred and violence. Sadness may be experienced as no more than feeling vaguely down or disappointed, but grow into acute disappointment, dejection, grief and despair. Your feeling of disgust may be no more than a slight aversion to someone or something but can escalate to complete revulsion. Shame can escalate from embarrassment to complete humiliation; guilt from mild regret to crippling remorse. Contempt can range from scorn to outright disdain.

While these emotions were designed to help us survive, we are all too painfully aware that they also surface when there is no survival advantage. They can sometimes bypass the thinking system entirely and create consequences that make us very unhappy and do a lot of damage to ourselves and to others. And, we also know that once a strong emotion is turned on, even the smart sophisticated thinking brain has trouble turning it off.

So why do negative emotions have such a grip on us?

To understand that, we need to see how negative emotions are organized in the brain.

## *The brain's instant messaging system*

Remember the amygdala? That's the little almond-shaped organ that evolved in the brain to help you understand the emotional significance of things, and where you store the memory of those emotional experiences. Over the past twenty years, neuroscientist Joseph LeDoux of New York University has revolutionized how we understand the brain.[8] He has shown that the amygdala plays a key role in its emotional circuitry.

Prior to LeDoux's discoveries, the traditional view was that when you register any information coming from your five senses, this information is sent to a relay station of the brain (the thalamus) which then directs it to the relevant specialist areas of the higher thinking brain, the 'grey matter' comprising the surface of the brain. The thinking brain then coolly analyses the information, assigns it a meaning and organizes an appropriate response. If the neocortex 'decides' that what you have seen or heard requires an emotional response, it sends messages to the amygdala in the limbic brain, and the limbic brain springs into action.

However, LeDoux's revolutionary discovery was that the amygdala plays a much more powerful and independent role in organizing your emotional responses – and, in fact, can organize those responses without involving the thinking brain at all. Using tracer chemicals, LeDoux mapped the route emotions take in the brain by tracking what happens when information from the senses travels along the neurons (or wiring) in the brain. He found that the information taken in by the eye or the ear does indeed go to the relay station in the brain (the thalamus) which then forwards *most* of the message to the thinking brain for analysis. But he discovered a bundle of neurons that formed a direct pathway between the thalamus and the amygdala, which allowed the amygdala to receive part of the messages coming in from the senses – even *before* they reach the thinking brain. The amygdala then sets off an emotional response before the thinking brain has fully understood what the signal is all about.

This is why you find yourself jumping out of bed when you hear a loud bang, or letting out an involuntary scream when you see something alarming in a film. It is why you have already started reacting emotionally when your teenager phones you late at night, audibly upset – even *before* your thinking brain has consciously registered what she is saying. Your amygdala has reacted in a thousandth of a second, interpreting this call as a potential threat, and has organized an immediate response by sending signals all around your body – to your hormonal glands, your muscles, your cardiovascular system, as well as to different organs in your body – mobilizing some version of your fight-or-flight reaction. Your heart starts beating faster, your blood pressure goes up, your gut contracts and your hands may clench or get sweaty. Your senses go on high alert.

But it is also an exquisitely differentiated response. For example, when you are angry, the temperature in your fingers increases because there is increased blood flow to your hands to help you physically fight. When you are afraid, your blood remains near your chest to help you mobilize for flight – so you may become pale. And this may all have happened before you even become *conscious* of your feelings of fear or anger.

Even as the amygdala is gearing you up for an emergency, your thinking brain is simultaneously analysing the much bigger set of available data, such as what your child is actually saying ('I lost my bag, which I borrowed from Kate. She'll *kill* me. And all my money and best make-up!'). It is also busy accessing information stored in your memory – your daughter is given to dramatics. Your thinking brain weighs all this information in a considered way; you realize there is no need for alarm. You feel a flood of relief. Yet (as you drive into town to collect her), your body is still processing the stress reaction triggered by your amygdala. When your initial stress reaction to a situation is strong, even if it proves to be misplaced, you may remain in a mildly stressed state for some time afterwards – your neck muscles remain tight, your stomach is slightly upset, your body is restless. That is why living with a very tense or unpredictable person is so wearing. You are on high alert to their reactions – and even when they don't react negatively, you spend a lot of time processing your initial stress response to the possibility that they might.

This combination of feeling and thinking is how the brain operates most of the time. The thinking brain damps down your stress response and allows you to work out a strategy and to choose the best from a wide range of emotional responses, including, as Daniel Goleman puts it: 'When to attack, when to run – and also, when to placate, persuade, seek sympathy, stonewall, provoke guilt, whine, put on a facade of bravado, be contemptuous – and so on, through the whole repertoire of emotional wiles.'[9]

## *The amygdala never forgets*

There is a significant downside to the automatic reactions set off by the amygdala – the risk of emotional overreaction. The system is designed to be fail-safe in real emergencies – and, indeed, the amygdala's immediate response may save your life or somebody else's. But to be that powerful it has to be super-reactive and trigger-happy. Like a particularly sensitive house alarm, it will stop the burglars getting in all right, but it may also be set off by the cat scratching at the front door. As LeDoux points out, the double-wiring of the brain (the wiring connecting the amygdala to the thinking brain and vice versa) creates particular problems because the neural connections from the thinking brain back down to the amygdala ('Stop worrying, this is not important') are less well developed than the connections from the amygdala back up to the cortex ('Oh God, now I'm in trouble'). Thus, the amygdala exerts a greater influence on the cortex than vice versa. Once an emotion is turned on, it is difficult for the cortex to turn it off. 'This is why we have trouble controlling our emotions,' LeDoux says. 'They can really trip us up.'[10]

The amygdala works this fast because it is never off duty. Like a sentry at a gate or a doorman at a club, the amygdala scans every entrant and passes instant judgement.

Is there something about this person that I like or I don't like?

Is this likely to create trouble for me?

In making these instantaneous, unconscious judgements, it relies heavily on first impressions, paying attention only to the most vivid aspects of an experience. More importantly, it works by association, rapidly comparing the new experience to other emotional experiences stored in its archive.

Just to make sure that you learn from your emotional experiences, emotional memories are stored in a particularly powerful way, using the same neurochemicals involved in the 'fight-or-flight' response. The more emotionally aroused you are during any experience, the more vividly the memory is stored. This is nature's way of ensuring that your experiences of great danger and of great opportunity, and how you responded to those threats and opportunities, are not lost and remain available to help you survive. In fact, LeDoux's work shows that this is such a powerful mechanism that you can store emotional memories without even being aware of doing so. It is this database of emotional memories that the amygdala scans to get a fix on a new emotional experience.

Did something like this ever happen to me before?

How did it work out?

Was it dangerous or safe?

Good for me or bad for me?

This comparison is done by way of association, not in a logical way. This means that if an aspect of the new situation you find yourself in matches an old memory in any way, the two experiences become associated and the amygdala reacts as if they are the same, mobilizing you to react to the experience now as you did in the past – even though you may have no conscious memory of the previous situation, let alone how you reacted then.

The way the amygdala works – laying down emotional memories consciously *and* unconsciously; working by loose association with stored memories; and reacting as if the present were the same as the past – helps explain why childhood experiences, even forgotten ones, can continue to affect you well into adult life. A young child is vulnerable and dependent for its survival on its relationship with its parents and caretakers. Thus, experiences with your parents that aroused a lot of emotion – positive, but especially negative – are laid down in a particularly vivid way, as are the reaction patterns you had to those experiences. That is also why in adult life when you are confronted by people or situations that, consciously or unconsciously, remind you of one of your parents, or of significant childhood experiences, you may automatically react in the same way you did as a child.

Now, let's look at how positive emotions work.

## *Positivity breeds positivity*

Barbara Fredrickson of the University of South Carolina, the leading researcher on positive emotions, identifies ten major positive emotions.[11] Listed in the order in which we most frequently experience them, these are:

1. love
2. joy
3. gratitude
4. contentment
5. interest
6. hope
7. pride
8. amusement
9. inspiration
10. awe.

While each of these emotions operates differently, what they share is this: they trigger the urge to engage with life, to become pleasurably absorbed in experience, to be open, receptive and alert to possibilities. At the most basic level, the function of positive emotions is to encourage us to approach things, to engage with new things, new people, new situations, to rise to challenge and to keep going in the face of setbacks – key components of flourishing.

The positive emotional system originates deep in the midbrain.[12] When this part of the brain is activated, there is a release of dopamine (a neurotransmitter or brain chemical) that stimulates the brain's reward and pleasure centres, which delivers an immediate dose of pleasure. From the midbrain, the dopamine system branches out. As it reaches specific areas, it stimulates and increases cognitive flexibility, problem-solving, working memory, the capacity to switch perspectives and social interaction. The area of the brain that processes positive emotions, the front left hemisphere, is particularly rich in dopamine receptors.

When we are experiencing positive emotions, another part of our central nervous system is also being activated, a part controlled by the vagus nerve. This nerve is found only in mammals, suggesting that as our autonomic nervous system evolved, our capacity for a wider range of more subtle positive emotions grew with it. It is this bundle of vagus neurons that affects the functioning of the heart in such a way as to enable us to adapt rapidly to changing social conditions, and to manage complex social relationships. Our heartbeat speeds up when we are meeting a challenge or involved in a heated discussion, and slows down when we are doing routine work or sitting companionably together.

Just as the brain mobilizes the release of a cocktail of stress hormones to help us mount our 'fight-or-flight' response to danger, it also mobilizes the release of another hormone – oxytocin – to get us ready to feel love and compassion, and to form attachments. This is the so-called 'tend-and-befriend' response.[13] Oxytocin causes the womb to contract, and the breasts of new mothers to fill with milk. It helps a mother to bond with her infant. It makes us desirous of sexual activity. Oxytocin is increased by soothing, by touch, by fondling. When primates are injected with oxytocin, their attachment behaviour increases. When humans are given oxytocin in a nasal spray, they become twice as likely to trust strangers as those who did not receive oxytocin.

As we have seen, the basic function of positive emotions is to encourage us to approach things, to explore and engage with new things, new people, new situations. Beginning with the work of psychologist Alice Isen[14] at Cornell University and of Barbara Fredrickson,[15] we now know that positive emotions do much more than that. While the role of negative emotions is to narrow our reactions to tightly patterned instinctive responses – 'contract and react' – Fredrickson showed that positive emotions do the opposite: they 'broaden and build' our menu of possible responses.

This process of broadening and building our relationship with the world begins in infancy. Children become securely attached when they receive sensitive and loving care from their parents. They feel psychologically safe in the world because they know they can always turn to their parents when they feel vulnerable and will be assured of a caring and helpful response. They respond with happiness, joy and playfulness. Evolutionary psychologists have pointed out that the young in every species spend a huge amount of time playing – a typically joyful activity. Every parent knows that when children are unhappy or afraid, they stop playing or play less creatively. In contrast, when they feel safe and secure, they play with great energy. The happier and safer they feel, the more they play. The more they play – and the more curious and interested they are in exploring the world through play – the faster they learn and the more creative and resourceful they become at solving problems.

The universal patterns of play – games of chasing and escaping, killing monsters, minding dolls, setting up playhouses, 'doctors and nurses' – allow the young to safely experiment and practise patterns of activities that will form the building blocks of important adult behaviour, such as dealing with threat and taking advantage of opportunity, caring for other people, organizing complex activities, forming coalitions and alliances, managing conflict. These games allow children to build up not just physical, intellectual and creative resources but also emotional and social ones. This build-up of personal resources transforms them in an enduring way, so they become more creative, more resilient and better integrated into their peer group. These traits in turn create positive upward spirals, making it more likely they will experience even more positive emotions.

So, positive emotions broaden, build and transform us.

Right throughout life, an approach to new challenges that is characterized by interest and curiosity and positive engagement, as opposed to an approach that is cynical or bored, will result in accumulating better, more accurate knowledge of the situation and so enable a more effective response.

Look at how an eight-year-old approaches a new video game or a piece of technology, engaging with it so eagerly that by the end of their explorations there is little they don't know about it. Or how a young teenage boy gets up the nerve to approach a girl for the first time. Initially prompted by feelings of interest, excitement (and hormones), he is urged to find out more about girls, and every encounter gives him a chance to test out his theories about what makes girls tick. A bare few years later, he has broadened and built enough real-life knowledge about girls to make him an expert. Contrast that to the young teenager who is prey to negativity, who is nervous and unsure about girls and reacts by avoidance and self-protection, a strategy that allows no opportunities to correct false impressions.

When you experience a positive emotion, it opens your mind and your heart. It puts you in a more receptive frame of mind. It triggers patterns of thought that are more broad-ranging, flexible, unusual, creative and inclusive. When you feel positive, you can immediately think of many more things that you would like to do in comparison to when you feel negative. You can express feeling happy in many ways. In contrast, when you feel sad or unhappy, it is hard to motivate yourself to do anything except think about your troubles.

> For many years I was a member of a network of eight women who met once a month to support and advise each other on any issues that we were currently grappling with. We had a rule that was sacrosanct: no matter what was going on in our lives, we each had to start by describing briefly something that had gone right for us since the last meeting.[16] This was surprisingly hard to do sometimes. I occasionally drove to meetings so preoccupied by some stress or problem that I had real difficulty recalling anything good. But because the rule was always observed, I found I eventually could come up with something. Even if I was stuck, just listening to the other women recount their positive experiences would trigger a positive memory in me.
>
> The effect of this simple rule was quite marked: the mood of the group became more positive, so we were better able to come up with solutions to the problems we were each grappling with.

As you will see later in this chapter, a positive mood helps thinking become broader and more flexible – when feeling positive, we think more efficiently and effortlessly. But our thinking is also more thorough in the sense that we are more inclined to consider many aspects of a situation simultaneously, and make better judgements and decisions that respond to the demands of the task. In contrast, when we feel sad, our thinking is more effortful and we deliberate about details and are preoccupied by risk. In situations of high risk, this is highly adaptive. But, outside of these real emergencies, feeling positive helps decision-making.

Contrary to what you might think, this does not lead to high risk-taking. Indeed, the opposite is the case – judgements are more considered and people are especially mindful of dangerous risks. This is because while feeling positive makes people more optimistic, it also alerts people to how badly they would feel if things did not work out, so they are more motivated to avoid taking a dangerous risk.[17]

The influence of positive emotions on the ability to think well has been intriguingly demonstrated in studies showing that doctors are better at diagnosis if they are feeling positive. For example, in one study on medical decision-making among third-year medical students, they were asked to decide which one of six (hypothetical) patients with particular symptoms was most likely to have lung cancer.[18] They also had to describe their clinical reasoning as they solved the problem. Those who were in a positive mood did not differ in the ultimate correct choice they made, compared to those who were less happy, but the more positive students were significantly faster in doing so. They were better able to integrate all of the information about the case – the patient's symptoms, clinical signs during the physical examination, and lab findings – and they showed less confusion and disorganization in their protocols. In other words, they were faster, more effective clinical problem-solvers. They were also much more likely to go beyond the assigned task, expressing interest in the cases of the other patients and suggesting treatments.

It does not even take much to make doctors (or, indeed, any of us) feel more positive, particularly when we feel appreciated. In another study, qualified practising doctors were asked to make a diagnosis.[19] They were presented with the clinical material in a large envelope. Included in some envelopes was a small bag of sweets, described as a token of appreciation for their participation in the study. Other envelopes contained exactly the same clinical material, but no sweets. The doctors who received the small gift did better in a test of creativity than those who had not. Creativity was defined as the ability to see potentially useful relationships among different things – which, as we can see from the previous study, is crucial for good diagnosis. These doctors were also found to derive significantly more satisfaction from helping their patients in a compassionate, caring way and forming a good rapport with them, rather than from other external sources of satisfaction such as high income and status.

## *Why positive emotions are good for you*

Positive emotions not only enable you to feel good, but also to do good and to recover from stress faster. When you are feeling positive, you behave in a more generous, helpful and altruistic way. You are more inclined to be sociable and friendly and more socially responsible. You are less inclined to get involved in interpersonal conflict and, if you do, you are better at managing it. When negotiating with another person, you are more effective at reaching agreement and at crafting solutions that provide optimal outcomes for each party. Part of the reason is that positive emotions do not just create more harmonious and enjoyable interactions, but they also make it easier for you to see the other person's perspective during the negotiations.[20]

Positive emotions help you to develop better coping strategies. Because feeling positive makes you more cognitively and socially flexible, you are more likely to be open-minded and less defensive when you have to deal with problems, and therefore less likely to ignore or distort information that you do not like or that does not fit in with your preconceptions. Feeling positive helps you persist in trying to solve the problem, but at the same time leads you to disengage faster from things that can't be solved and turn your attention to things that can.

When you are stressed, positive emotions help you recover rapidly. Stress creates immediate and negative changes in your body. It raises your blood pressure, and prolonged cardiovascular reactivity is a precursor to heart disease. However, if you experience even a mildly positive emotion immediately after a stressful situation, it will undo these effects. It will bring your blood pressure back to normal and calm your heart rate.[21] It will also damp down the inflammatory response, reduce the levels of stress hormones and increase the levels of hormones that promote bonding and strengthen immune functioning.

This is a crucial point – and a useful summary of why we need the right ratio of positive to negative. Positive emotions seem to work by breaking the powerful hold negative emotions have on us – on our bodies, our thinking and our behaviour – by interrupting the normal cascade of changes that are triggered by negative emotions. That is why the merest touch from somebody who loves you can calm you instantly and why giving yourself a little treat – something nice to eat, a five-minute break in the fresh air, a glance at a photograph of your children, a quick phone call to a friend – can literally undo the most complex and hidden stress reactions happening in your body. It explains why having somebody who cares about you present when you are undergoing a painful or stressful medical procedure makes not just a psychological difference, but a difference in how your body reacts. It helps control your blood pressure, and you feel less pain and sleep better afterwards. It explains why an affectionate hug or a kind word can stop a conflict escalating and can undo its effects.

Over time, the patterns of response that positive emotions create in us confer great benefits. Even transient positive emotions make a real difference to how we perform complex tasks, and a steady build-up of positive emotions creates a powerful reserve of personal resources. We build substantial knowledge of the world; we find out how people and things work; we learn how to cope better with setbacks by developing a variety of coping strategies; we build up a network of social connections. We construct an accurate set of what Fredrickson calls 'cognitive maps', a fund of knowledge and confidence that guides us safely through life.

Far from being just a signal that we are well and happy, positive emotions actually *produce* well-being and flourishing by making us more competent, more knowledgeable, more effective, more socially connected and more resilient.

That is why you need to look again at Barbara Fredrickson's list of positive emotions – love, joy, gratitude, contentment, interest, hope, pride, amusement, inspiration and awe – and ask yourself some crucial questions.

- How often in the past month have I experienced each of these emotions in my life?
- In my closest relationships?
- In my work?
- In the organization I belong to or lead?

While we can't realistically expect to feel all of these emotions all the time, we do need to cycle through them regularly in every important domain in our lives. If you find that one or more of these positive emotions is notably absent in your life, a first step to flourishing is to find out why and address that.

We will be looking at ways you can do that further on in this book.

The benefits of positive emotions only happen if the emotions are genuine. Human beings are adept at detecting insincere emotions. The humour of the TV series *The Office* is based on how brilliantly it depicts the fake positivity of the anti-hero, David Brent. As he spouts motivational 'corporate-speak', his underlying negativity – his insecurity, his lack of real connection with his team – is on full view. But, even as we laugh, we are reacting emotionally and instinctively to the attempted deception. That is why we cringe and feel a slight sense of unease.

In real life, trying to be positive when it is not genuine not only does not work, it is bad for your heart. In a study of 114 men with coronary artery disease, their facial expressions (a strong indicator of underlying emotions) were recorded on videotape as they took part in an interview. Meanwhile, their heart functioning was also monitored. During the interview, the men's faces expressed an emotion every few seconds. The researchers matched these fleeting expressions of emotion to the men's heart functioning – particularly to any incidents of myocardial ischemia – abnormal contractions in the left wall of the heart and reduced blood supply to the heart. These ischemic incidents were 'silent' – the men felt no pain – but they were potentially deadly as they could precipitate another heart attack.[22]

The ischemic incidents were found to be associated with two facial expressions. One was anger – no surprise there, as anger and hostility are well-known factors in coronary heart disease. But, surprisingly, the other was what the researchers called a 'non-enjoyment' smile – the kind of tight smile that raises the corners of your mouth but does not spread to the rest of your face. We know from our own experiences that such tight 'smiles' are not associated with any real feeling of happiness. Rather, they are our way of trying to disguise and manage our negative feelings that we believe, for one reason or another, we have to hide.

The lesson is clear. To keep your heart healthy, you need to find a way to deal with your underlying negative feelings, and find a constructive and positive set of solutions. Continuing to be angry, or trying to fake positivity, will damage your heart. But you cannot manage your negative feelings if you don't understand and accept the strength of your inbuilt negativity bias.

In the next chapter you're going to see just how extraordinarily dominant the negativity bias can be. When you get to grips with how it operates, you will be in a position to consider the root causes of your own negative emotions and to adopt whatever strategies you need to manage them.

And you will be well on the road to flourishing.

# 4. Why negative trumps positive

The powerful negativity bias in our brain operates automatically, so we are often unaware of the range and scale of its influence. It is only when we look at specific examples of how it operates in our lives that we can fully understand its power and realize how important it is to circumscribe these effects if we are not to be psychologically paralysed and our capacity to flourish diminished or crushed. This is the main purpose of this chapter.

Take an ordinary day. Things happen. On the average day for the average person, most experiences are mildly positive. The car starts; the kids are settled in school and in good form. You complete some tasks on your never-ending to-do list. Your thoughts run to mainly positive or neutral things. You make a plan with a colleague. You enjoy your lunch. You chat to a friend. You solve a problem. You watch a good programme on TV. Nothing too important. These mildly positive events put you in a mildly positive mood. When something really positive happens, you cheer up even more.

But inevitably, some negative things also happen. One of your children seems in a bad mood. You have a tense exchange with someone at work. You sit through a boring meeting that seems to be going nowhere. You put the laundry on the wrong cycle and shrink your silk blouse. You get a parking ticket. You try to fix a problem but it does not work. You find yourself ruminating about something that bothered you at work. Again, nothing too important – the negative equivalent of the mildly pleasant events described above. But not really. While these negative experiences may be 'equivalent' in some 'objective' way to their positive counterparts (spending two hours solving a problem versus spending the same time and failing to solve it), they are not equivalent in their *impact* on you. Having a pleasant conversation with a colleague, or finding a parking space does not deliver a positive impact equivalent to the negative impact of having an argument with somebody or getting a parking ticket.

Once anything negative appears, your brain is on high alert, concentrating on assessing just *how* negative it is. For instance, you know instantly, without anybody telling you, if you have made a mistake in something you are doing. Within 80–100 milliseconds (that is, thousandths of a second), there is a change in brain response. There is no similar neurological reaction that takes place when you do something right.[1] Feelings of anxiety, distress, anger or disappointment last much longer than positive reactions to a pleasant experience. And negative events have a stronger and more pervasive effect on your subsequent mood than positive events. Having a good day generally has no noticeable effect on your sense of well-being the following day, whereas having a bad day tends to carry over and influences the next day in a negative way. That's the negativity bias at work.

In the last chapter we saw how, because negative emotions were designed to help you survive, the way they are wired in your brain makes them very powerful – designed not to fail when you need them. So, far from being an equal counterpart to your positivity bias, the negativity bias hard-wires you to pay more attention to and be more influenced by the negative than by the positive.[2]

Most of the time, you are not fighting for your physical survival. But you are almost always striving for what you see as your emotional survival.* Threats to it are more subtle, more psychological – and much more common. Your emotional survival agenda is:

1. to feel psychologically safe
2. to feel good about yourself, and
3. to feel close and respected in relationships and groups that are important to you.

You are constantly monitoring, consciously and unconsciously, how you are doing in these three respects. When the signals are positive and reassuring, you feel happy. When you are picking up signals that all is not well, you feel stressed. Coldness in your partner, conflict with your child, disapproval by your boss, being dropped from a team – all of these can

* Of course, sometimes the fight for emotional survival is the equivalent of fighting for your life. In the case of a traumatic life event, the power of the negative can be overwhelming. For instance, a single episode of childhood sexual abuse can produce severe and enduring effects on behaviour and have serious long-term consequences right into adulthood, and it is hard to conceive of a corresponding single positive event that could undo the harm caused by such an event. People do recover from trauma, of course, but only after they have experienced a lot of positivity, such as regular and consistent support and encouragement over a long period.

assume huge negative significance and be experienced as the equivalent to an actual physical threat. That is why we talk about such experiences as being 'a blow' to our self-esteem or an 'assault' on our sense of security.

The reason is that your amygdala treats the signals about possible threats to your psychological safety, your self-esteem or your status *as if* they were the same as actual threats to your physical survival. In early childhood, when we are at our most vulnerable, this makes sense – if a parent rejects an infant, and is cruel and neglectful, this is a serious threat to the child's survival. As an adult, rejection and emotional neglect are very hurtful – but they are not a threat to your physical survival. But because of the way the amygdala works, you continue to react as if they were.

The seeds of this can lie in infancy, when you first started laying down vivid emotional memories. If, as a young child, you were repeatedly exposed to criticism that made you feel anxious, rejected and unworthy, you are likely to develop an acute sensitivity to any signs (real or imagined) that you are being criticized. You will also tend to react in the same way as you did as a child, for example, by withdrawing, or trying to please or placate, or by becoming enraged. According to neuroscientist Joseph LeDoux, such memories are stored in the amygdala as 'rough, wordless blueprints for emotional life',[3] or what the pioneering child psychiatrist John Bowlby called 'internal working models' about yourself, about other people and about how you think the world works.[4]

The price of having such a highly reactive amygdala is that negative emotions are easily aroused and given to overreaction. Sometimes, the results are highly stressful or just plain embarrassing. You suffer a setback at work and you react as if you have been given a diagnosis of terminal illness. You miss the plane, and you act like it is a life-threatening emergency. You get riled up over a slight and feel foolish or ashamed afterwards.

But sometimes this trigger-happy response results in real tragedy. A man interprets someone jumping him in a queue as such a serious threat to his self-esteem and place in the world that he treats it as life-threatening – and acts accordingly. An adolescent reacts to a relationship break-up as a sign that they are worthless and that life is not worth living any more. A woman interprets her husband's threat to leave as a sign that she (and sometimes her children too) may as well be dead.

The evidence for the overwhelming power of the negativity bias has been accumulating for twenty years. But it was not until 2001, when Roy

Baumeister of Case Western Reserve University and his colleagues summarized this evidence and published it in an article with a rather startling title – 'Bad is stronger than good' – that this phenomenon first really registered.[5] In the same year, Paul Rozin and Edward Royzman of the University of Pennsylvania published an equally important research paper that came to the same conclusion.[6] Hundreds of studies in many different areas of the social sciences all point in the same direction – confirming the greater power of negative over positive in virtually every arena of human functioning.[7]

## *The negativity bias in your daily life*

At the most basic level, your attention is grabbed more quickly and decisively by anything negative. When people are asked if they want the good news or the bad news first, most choose to hear the bad news first because their attention is immediately grabbed by the information that there *is* bad news coming so they know that they can't properly concentrate on listening to the good news.

You pay more attention to negative facial expressions, especially anger, than to pleasant expressions. When you scan a group or a crowd, you are much faster at identifying an angry face than a happy one. When you encounter somebody with a sad expression, you spend more time trying to figure out their state of mind than you do when someone seems happy.

### *How you think*

You don't just pay more attention to negative events, you devote more time and thought to what is going wrong than to what is going right in your life. Suppose I asked you to make two lists.

- First, list the things that you think about a lot.
- Second, list the things that you think about very little.

If you are like most people, the first list typically includes more negative than positive things – worries, problems in a relationship, anxiety about some forthcoming event, frustration about some personal goal that is being blocked, unexpected difficulties in a project.[8]

When something negative happens, you spend a lot of time trying to understand why it happened and what it means. You don't generally go around wondering about why something went right. But when something goes wrong, even something small, you try to make sense of it by constructing elaborate interpretations of what caused it and whose fault it might have been.

Not only do you spend a lot of energy processing negative things that have happened, you start worrying about future negative events well in advance. And even when you anticipate a pleasurable event – say, a family get-together where you will connect with people you really like – if this also entails meeting someone you don't like, that's what will dominate your thinking as the event approaches. Expectation of negative events is actually the strongest determinant of negative mood.[9]

### *How you feel*

Negative feelings and mood affect you in a much stronger way than positive feelings and mood. When you are in a bad mood, you will use up a lot of your brain energy trying to understand and deal with it. And you will expend far more energy trying to avoid or escape a bad mood than trying to create or prolong a good mood. Most people have no trouble listing a few tried-and-tested techniques that they have developed to get them out of a bad mood. But we devote much less time (apart from sex) to thinking about how to prolong or intensify our good moods.

This universal experience is reflected in language. There are more words for negative than for positive emotions, for negative personal characteristics than for positive ones. When you are happy, it's enough to say just that. But when you are annoyed, or disappointed, worried or grief-stricken, you feel the need to explain in a more elaborate way how you are feeling and why.

Ask somebody how they are and, if they are happy, they will simply say: 'Fine, great, thank you.'

If, on the other hand, they are in bad form, be prepared for a longer, more considered answer: 'Well . . . all right, I suppose, but you know that my relationship just broke up/things are pretty rough financially/I am just getting over a bad bout of flu . . .'

When people in different countries were asked to write down as many emotions as they could think of in five minutes, joy, sadness, anger and fear appeared in the top twelve words in all countries. Three of those four emotions are negative – suggesting that negative emotions hover near the top of our consciousness.[10]

### *How you look back and look forward*

Recent negative events also stay lodged in your memory longer – at least, in the short term. When people are asked to recall a recent important emotional event that they either shared with other people or experienced in private, both positive and negative emotional events are recalled. But people typically report four times as many bad events as good events, suggesting not so much that we experience more negative than positive events (we don't), but rather that negative emotional events remain more vivid in our minds.[11]

This sensitivity to the negative also extends into the future. When we are asked to forecast how positive and negative events in our lives will affect us, we generally overestimate the effect of such events, but we do this to a much greater extent in the case of negative events.

## *The negativity bias is with us from infancy*

In infancy and childhood we are most primed to learn, so that we can understand this strange new world in which we find ourselves. Amrisha Vaish and colleagues from the renowned Max Planck Institute reviewed hundreds of studies on child development.[12] They found that, from early in life, babies pay more attention to and are more influenced by the negative rather than the positive aspects of their environment. Thus, from the very beginning of our lives – and at every level of our functioning – bad and good, positive and negative, are not equal in their impact.

One of the most important ways in which babies learn about the environment is by using the emotional information they receive from their parents and caregivers. In this process they show a strong negativity bias: a negative reaction from an adult has a much more significant effect on their behaviour than a positive or neutral reaction, and they are exquisitely sensitive to the slightest negative cue from their mothers. In one experiment mothers who were holding their babies on their laps were asked to convey by touch alone their own feelings about novel toys that were presented one at a time to the baby.[13] The mothers did that in instinctive ways. When the mother wanted to convey a positive feeling, she slightly relaxed her grip and her posture. When the reaction was negative, she tensed her fingers slightly around the baby's abdomen and inhaled sharply. When her reaction was neutral her grip remained unchanged.

You might imagine that a baby being presented with all these new toys would not notice subtle changes in its mother's touch. Not so. The mother's negative reaction was picked up instantly by the baby, who then reacted negatively to the toy. Whether the mother reacted in a positive or neutral way did not affect the baby's response.

In another study babies were placed on the 'shallow end' of a visual cliff (a visual illusion used by psychologists to investigate how infants perceive the world).[14] A sheet of clear plexiglas was placed over a cloth that had a black and white chequerboard pattern. On the side where the baby started to crawl, the cloth was placed immediately beneath the plexiglas, so it looked as if the infant was crawling on a shiny tiled floor. But, further on, the cloth was placed about four feet below the plexiglas, so it appeared to the infant that there was a steep drop.

In this experiment, the babies' mothers were positioned at the 'deep end' of the plexiglas while their babies crawled towards them. Some were told to adopt a fearful facial expression. Others were told to look angry, or happy, or interested. Not one of the babies whose mothers adopted a fearful expression took the risk of crossing the 'cliff'. When mothers looked angry, only 11 per cent of their babies took the risk and crossed to get to her. But when mothers adopted a happy or interested expression, three-quarters of the babies went ahead.

So, fear was the most powerful negative signal. It had a much more significant effect on the baby's decision to take a risk than any positive cues.

Of course, babies are temperamentally different (and we will talk about temperament in Chapter 5). Some like to take risks and some don't. But the implication of this research is that no matter how inclined they are to take risks, a negative reaction from their mothers will override that tendency.

Children's language development also shows a negativity bias. Children first begin to use words for positive and negative emotions somewhere between 20 and 24 months of age – words such as 'happy', 'sad', 'mad' (angry) and 'scared'. Up to the age of about three they know roughly the same number of positive and negative words. However, after that age, the proportion of negative to positive words almost doubles. Toddlers talk to their mothers most frequently about negative things – about being tired, or distressed, or having a pain or hurting somewhere.

Not only do children discuss and remember negative emotions and events more, they also show more sophisticated thinking and social understanding when doing so. They give more elaborate, detailed descriptions of what happened and focus particularly on internal feelings. Just like adults, they justify themselves more when discussing what went wrong than when discussing positive or neutral events.

Even very young children show a surprisingly sophisticated understanding of negative emotions, frequently explaining why they or other people are feeling sad or angry about events that happened, including events that happened some time ago ('Granny is feeling sad now because Christmas is coming, and Granddad won't be here because he died after my birthday'), whereas they don't try to find such links when somebody is feeling happy. In some respects, of course, this is mirroring what their mothers do. Mothers are much more likely to discuss and explain the causes and consequences of negative emotions ('You are upset now because your friend won't play with you. This is what happens when you won't share your toys') than positive emotions. When children are happy, mothers are unlikely to comment on it except in a very casual way ('You look like you are having a good time playing').[15]

Developmentally, children acquire an understanding of 'bad' actions and their consequences earlier than a conception of 'good' acts and their consequences. As a result, they become more punishment-oriented, learning the rules that govern bad behaviour before learning those that govern positive behaviour.

Given that children are primed and ready to learn quickly from even the most subtle negative pressure – facial expression, tone of voice, even the lightest touch – this suggests that we need to punish children less, not more, in these early years. It's relatively easy to teach children *what not to do* because you are being helped by their predisposition to be influenced by the negative. But if you want to teach them *what to do* – to help them become happy, resourceful, achieving, to have a strong sense of values and to flourish – you have to make the effort to pay far more attention to the positive.

## *The negativity bias up close and personal*

If you ask people whether their life satisfaction depends on becoming more like their ideal self or becoming less like their undesired self, nearly 90 per cent will say that their desire to be like their ideal self is stronger. However, the evidence is otherwise.[16] You might think that if you judge yourself to be close to your ideal self ('Ideally, I would like to be successful at what I do and be active and fit, and I think I have achieved that'), this would predict how satisfied you are with your life. It does – but not nearly as strongly as how uncomfortably close you feel you are to your undesired self ('I would hate to be a failure and to become a slob – and I am heading that way').

In a similar vein, most of us love to get positive feedback about ourselves. But we are more motivated to avoid negative feedback than to maximize positive feedback, suggesting that negative feedback has a more powerful impact.[17] In the course of my work, I routinely ask people for examples of the worst and best feedback they have ever received. Generally, negative feedback is recalled quickly and vividly, even if it happened many years earlier. One senior (and very successful) manager was so wounded by written feedback he had received two years earlier that he was able to produce the offending feedback report from his pocket.

The effect of negative feedback is even stronger when it is embedded in generally good feedback – the most common way feedback is given in a work situation ('Well, you have many strengths and have done well in a lot of areas. But there is an area of weakness that needs more attention'). Why? Because in the context of getting generally good feedback, you are lulled into a false sense of security. You let your defences down, so the criticism, when it comes, catches you unawares and unguarded, and thus lands a powerful blow to your self-esteem.

When it comes to our close relationships with partners, family and friends, negative interactions have a much stronger effect than positive interactions, and their extent has a more decisive influence on how the relationship will turn out in the long term. In the early years of marriage, the level and intensity of the negative interactions are more predictive of trouble down the line than the level and intensity of pleasant interactions. In most young marriages, positive interactions – sexual interest, showing affection, having a good time together, constructive problem-solving – are common. But their presence does not predict which couples will stay together and which will end up divorcing.[18]

However, the presence of specific negative behaviour patterns, such as destructive problem-solving, can predict the relationship failing in the long term. And we saw the reason why when looking at John Gottman's work in Chapter 2: negative relationship patterns – criticizing, threatening, rejecting or being contemptuous – have a more profound effect on the long-term health of the relationship because it is so difficult to balance them by equally intense positive interactions, especially *five times* as many.

Partners in a marriage spend more time thinking about the other's negative behaviour than their positive behaviour. They do this even when such negative behaviour is a frequent occurrence.[19] The fact that your husband frequently loses his temper with you, or your wife usually sulks when she doesn't get her own way, will not stop you devoting a lot of your cognitive energy to trying to understand why this has happened yet again. So the next time your beloved says, 'You're on my case about everything I do wrong, but you never remember what I do right,' you know why.

Roy Baumeister summed up all the evidence starkly: 'The long-term success of a relationship depends more on not doing bad things than on doing good things.'[20] One of the cardinal principles of medical ethics that all medical students are taught is *Primum non nocere* – the Latin phrase meaning 'First, do no harm'. It might also be the first rule of relationships.

The same general pattern of bad being stronger than good applies to other close relationships. For example, we all know that social support – receiving emotional and practical help from a network of friends and family – has an enormously positive impact on our health and well-being. What is not so well known is that if that support is accompanied by a lot of upsetting conflict and undermining behaviour, this outweighs any positive effects and has a very negative effect on our well-being, leading to depression, dissatisfaction and distress.[21]

## *The negativity bias and work*

In the world of work, negative events have a powerful impact. As organizational psychologist Kim Cameron says, 'A single traumatic episode, a single incident of negative feedback, or a single loss, for example, has stronger effects on people than a single happy episode, or a single incident of positive feedback, or a single win. Multiple positive events are required to overcome the effects of a single negative event, and a single negative event can undo the effects of multiple positive events.'[22]

Trust in an organization – between employers and employee; between colleagues; and between the organization and its customers – is the fundamental basis not just for high levels of work satisfaction and low levels of conflict, but also for high levels of productivity and innovation. But because of the stronger effect of negative events, trust in an organization is easier to destroy than to create.[23]

Compared to equivalent trust-building events, trust-destroying events capture more attention. They are talked about more and are judged as more important and credible. They are remembered for longer, and more vividly. People ruminate about them more, and thus become more vigilant in a general way. After big negative events like cutbacks and redundancy, it can be remarkably difficult to rebuild trust. Once people no longer trust a manager, or the organization, they become reluctant to take any further risks. They retain their distrust and negative views and *presume* that there are still good reasons to feel like that.

Sometimes we are right. But even when we are wrong, and there is a reasonable basis for trusting again, we often won't take the risk to trust again – making it impossible to correct our negative assumptions. As Robert Kramer of the Stanford University Business School concludes, 'presumptive distrust tends to become perpetual distrust'.[24]

## *The negativity bias and how we judge other people*

Suppose you are on an interview board. The person being interviewed has impressed you. He seems intelligent, charming and experienced. You are disposed to offer him the job so you telephone his former employer for a reference. Yes, says his former boss, he is very intelligent and has a lot of experience. But, she adds, he can be a bit unreliable on occasions.

Clunk.

Immediately, you start to ply her with questions.

What does she mean by 'unreliable'?

How often does that happen?

What does she think is the reason for this unreliability?

In the light of this, would she recommend you to offer him the job?

That one 'but' has put you on high alert. You are now wary, uncertain about this person, and you want to be very sure you have a clear picture about this reported negative characteristic before you offer him the job.

In decisions about hiring or promotion, negative information exerts a more powerful effect than positive information. We can even quantify this effect precisely. If you have formed an initially favourable impression of somebody, fewer than four new 'bits' of negative information are enough to reverse your original impression. If, however, you have formed an initially unfavourable impression, it will take nearly nine bits of positive information to reverse that view.[25]

We consider negative information more 'diagnostic' and useful than positive information. And because we feel much more confident that we are making the right judgement when we are basing it on negative rather than positive grounds, we make decisions very quickly on the basis of even limited negative information. This is particularly the case when it comes to finding another person socially or sexually attractive. (Speed dating operates on this rather brutal principle!)

The first impression you form of somebody exerts a very powerful influence and sets the tone for what you expect from them. Sometimes you change your mind when you get to know somebody better. But here's what's interesting. You will react in a much stronger way emotionally if your initial positive impression is violated by somebody letting you down than you will when your initial negative impression changes in a positive direction. It's the difference between feeling outraged and hurt rather than pleasantly surprised.

How you judge somebody's character – whether you judge them to be good, honest and trustworthy – will determine whether you trust them, and trust determines virtually everything about the subsequent interaction (or absence of interaction) between you. It takes quite a while to judge somebody to be of good character because to be seen as honest or trustworthy someone has to be honest all the time in all their dealings with you. So, to judge character you have to know somebody rather well and to have a lot of information about them. On the other hand, to decide someone is dishonest or untrustworthy, only a limited amount of information is needed. If you catch somebody out in a lie, or somebody cheats on you, it seriously undermines your trust in that person. It is a salutary thought: we are judged on the basis of one moral lapse rather than on all the good things we have done. That is also why slander and defamation are such serious offences.

This is an illustration of the contagion of the negative: how a single vice – dishonesty, greed, cowardice – in someone who might otherwise be good tends to contaminate our view of their character. Yet, a single virtue in an otherwise bad person will not redeem them in most people's eyes. And once a person has done a morally bad thing, almost no amount of good deeds they might do subsequently will reverse our negative impression.

This contagion effect even extends to everyday experiences. Disliking somebody produces a larger contagion effect than liking somebody. If you dislike somebody, you typically come to dislike virtually everything about them: their views, their mannerisms, their tone of voice, even their clothes. If you like somebody, there is much less 'positive contagion'. You may like their views, or admire their skill, or enjoy their company – but you don't necessarily come to like everything about them. You can still be coolly objective (as you like to think) about their dress sense or their wrong-headed opinion on politics. The only exception to this is the first dizzy flush of lust and love ('She is just unbelievable in every way') and, of course, your own young children – who are, naturally, just perfect.

## *The negativity bias and our decision-making*

Just as the power of the negative hugely influences our judgements of people, it also influences all of our choices and decisions. When we are considering a course of action, we will generally pay significantly more attention to the potential risks or costs associated with it than to the potential benefits (although different personalities vary as to how much attention they give to risk). We are attuned to risk to a much greater degree than we know. Nobel laureate Daniel Kahneman of Harvard University was the first to show just how much more strongly motivated and influenced we are by the negative possibility of loss than by the positive possibility of gain.[26]

Your brain is highly sensitized to loss of any kind. You will be more distressed by the loss of €50 than made happy by the gain of €50. You are generally not willing to take a bet on losing €10 unless you have the chance to win a minimum of €25. In other words, the possible gain needs to be two and a half times greater than the risk – another example that the positive has to be near 3:1 for ordinary risk-taking. If the stakes are higher, the possible gains may not tempt you at all. When offered the opportunity to take a gamble on something that would give them a very high probability of doubling their life savings and a very small chance of losing them, most people refuse to consider it.[27]

You are even more sensitized to loss when you face the possibility of losing something that you currently own. John is looking to buy a car and Mary is selling the exact model he wants. The trouble is, if Mary is like most people in Kahneman's experiments, she will value what she owns (and may be about to lose) by up to *twice* as much as John. This is because she is paying way more attention to the negatives ('Look at how long it took me to find that car, and all the care I lavished on it, how often I got it serviced. Not a scratch on it. And look at all the extras!').

You might think our aversion to risk and loss is a rational response. On the contrary, it's powerful enough to *overcome* our rationality. Suppose I ask you which you would prefer:

- Job A: with a salary of €30,000 the first year, rising to €40,000 the next year and €50,000 the year after, or
- Job B: with a salary of €60,000 the first year, falling to €50,000 and then €40,000.

If you are like most people, you will choose Job A – in spite of the fact that the net income is less – because you instantly react against the prospect of your income falling every year.[28] Even if, after doing the arithmetic, you decide to make the rational choice, you still have to fight against your instinctive aversion to loss by continually reminding yourself of the long-term gain.

This irrationality can affect life-and-death decisions. A member of your family is seriously ill. Her doctor tells you of an experimental but risky treatment that may save her life. Should you take the risk? Well, you might say, that depends on the risk. In fact, it actually depends quite a lot on how the doctor 'frames' the risk. If the doctor says that, without this treatment, two out of three people die of this disease, you are more likely to authorize it. If, however, he says that only a third of patients have been saved by the treatment, you are more likely to refuse. You are more inclined to authorize the treatment if it is framed as avoiding a loss – the death of your relative – than you are to take the same risk if it is framed as a possible gain – that is, your relative's recovery.

Aversion to the negative becomes even greater as a perceived risk gets nearer. For example, an adventurous friend persuades you to join her on a trip to somewhere exotic but potentially dangerous. You agree, focusing on the positive (the possibility of a glorious adventure) and minimizing the negative (the risk to life and limb). But, the closer you come to the moment of decision – when you have to actually buy your plane ticket – the (remote) possibility of getting dengue fever, or being kidnapped by bandits, becomes the focus of your sustained attention whereas the (very likely) prospect of exotic experiences fades.

So you decide to stick with Spain instead.

You might be a little ashamed of your timidity, but you can console yourself with the fact that you are reacting to forces in your brain that are very powerful indeed.

## *Balancing negative with positive*

All of the studies described here point to the power of the negative – to dominate, to overwhelm, to 'stick', to become contagious. At the most fundamental neural level, your brain shows greater reactivity when you see, hear, feel or experience something negative as compared to something positive.[29] At a physiological level, any negative bodily sensations – extreme heat or cold, hunger, thirst or, most of all, pain – signal that something is wrong and needs to be dealt with immediately. Pain always grabs your attention and is extremely difficult to ignore. Your body is designed to prioritize pain. That is why pain can be produced *anywhere* in the body, and at excruciating levels, whereas intense pleasure is located in fewer bodily locations. This is crucial to basic survival.

Negative emotions are the psychological equivalent of pain. In the middle of a crisis they can save your life and protect your vital interests. But, as soon as the crisis is over, you need positive emotions to help you get back on your feet and back on course with your life. Fortunately, nature has provided us with the positivity bias to help us do just that. In the absence of information to the contrary, we have a tendency to hold a mildly positive view of the word, to believe that things will work out, that new things are worth exploring – a kind of Pollyanna principle.[30] This is a generally adaptive stance as it encourages us to engage with the world and learn about it – and, for most of us, the majority of our day-to-day experiences are indeed safe and mildly positive. As long as we keep feeling mildly positive, we carry on.

But suppose you are the kind of person whose negativity bias is set too high or whose positivity bias is set too low, leaving you susceptible to experiencing frequent or intense negative emotions, or infrequent and weak positive emotions.

Can you change that?

The answer is encouraging.

Evidence is mounting steadily that the brain is 'plastic' and malleable – capable of responding to new experiences, and changing. As you will learn in a later chapter, emotional experiences can rewire and alter the way the brain works, changing the actual number of neurons in the brain and how they connect. For example, if you have experienced chronic rejection, hurt or anxiety in a significant relationship in early life, these experiences establish a pattern of neural connection in your brain that in turn results in a pattern of negative responding that becomes your default option, a well-trodden road in the brain. Meanwhile, your positive response pathway is so infrequently used it becomes like a disused and overgrown lane. But if you begin to have different, more loving, affirming and encouraging experiences, in time this can change the wiring in your brain. Gradually, the negative route gets less traffic. And, by constantly building your capacity to experience positive emotion, you can clear and extend that laneway, see its beauty and pleasures and come to use it as your route of choice through life.

So the only way to balance the positive and the negative is actively and consciously. With deliberate effort we can build the positive so that we have five times more positives than negatives in our lives. That's the first and over-arching principle of flourishing. The second is to reduce the frequency and intensity of the negative whenever possible – and particularly to avoid gratuitous, destructive negativity at all costs.

But before we adopt these principles and start exploring strategies to help us live with greater awareness, each of us needs to understand our individual make-up.

That is the subject of the next chapter.

# 5. Knowing who you really are

Who are you? To flourish and find your best self, you have to be able to answer that fundamental question. But understanding the self is no easy business. The great psychologist William James said that we have as many different 'selves' as we have significant people in our lives whose opinion we care about.[1] In other words, our different 'selves' are shaped by the expectations of important people in the past, in the present and in our imagined future. We also know intuitively that we are formed by early experiences and that we are constantly changing in response to what happens to us. We know that we operate at different levels – consciously, unconsciously and imaginatively. The seeds of flourishing or languishing are contained in all these different parts of the self, so becoming aware of that complex landscape and how it works is crucial to flourishing.

In an effort to describe the complex landscape of the self, I take as a useful starting point the model by the Italian psychologist Roberto Assagioli.[2] He described the Self* as being like a large oval with the bottom part of the oval representing the 'unconscious', the middle part representing the 'conscious' part, and the upper part representing what he called 'higher unconsciousness'.

The outer boundary of the Self is like the membrane of a cell in the body – engaged in a constant interchange of nutrients and toxins with the whole body. In the same way, you are constantly being influenced by physical and social forces in your environment – and, in turn, you are influencing them. Every time you change the world around you, it changes you. So, the Self is in a constant state of flux. And the better you understand those dynamic processes, the more effectively you can shape them into a pattern of flourishing.

* In this context, I capitalize the Self for clarity – to distinguish the whole Self from the many parts of self I am describing.

## *The unconscious self: the raw ingredients of the Self*

Your unconscious is where the raw material of your Self is located – your instincts and drives, your basic temperament (which I will explain shortly) and other inherited or hard-wired aspects of the Self. Based on scientific findings from evolutionary biology and insights about human behaviour in social science, Paul Lawrence and Nitin Nohria of Harvard University propose four innate drives.[3]

- The drive to **defend** ourselves, those we love, what we own, what we believe in and what we value.
- The drive to **acquire** objects and experiences that improve our status relative to other people, what we might loosely call a drive to achieve or compete.
- The drive to **bond** in long-term relationships of mutual care and commitment, in social groups for pleasure and company, in networks of cooperation to secure resources and get things done.
- The drive to **learn** and make sense of the world and of ourselves, to master things, to experiment, to innovate and create.

Neurologist Antonio Demasio shows how everything we experience in our everyday lives is 'coded' as to how relevant and important it is to these drives ('Is this going to help me bond with someone, or acquire something, or learn something?' 'Is it going to threaten my interests in some way?'). As we now know, this coding process is not about coldly weighing things up; emotions play a vital role. The drive to defend against threats is wired into our negative emotional system – our negativity bias. In the absence of threats, the other three drives are stimulated by our positivity bias.

We are all born with these four drives, but the strength of any one drive varies among individuals. Some people have an exceptionally strong drive to achieve, others to learn or to bond with others. Individual variations are profoundly affected by basic temperament and by early learning experiences, especially in the first five years of life. If our early drive to bond is frustrated, we can react by unconsciously switching off the cues to bond, with long-term consequences for our intimate relationships. If our early drive to learn is encouraged by parents or teachers, it grows into a powerful capacity that influences not just our formal learning but also our capacity for happiness, because it allows us to transform any setback into a learning experience.

If one of these drives is overdeveloped or underdeveloped, it can seriously unbalance our lives.

When the four drives work together and in harmony, we flourish.

### *Temperament*

Every individual is born with a unique temperament, determined by genetic and other prenatal influences. Temperamental differences are a major factor – although not the only one – in accounting for the differences amongst babies, even those from the same family. Temperament is the predisposition to react in a particular way in nine main areas:[4]

1. activity levels
2. regularity (for example, how predictable a baby's eating, sleeping and bowel movements are)
3. approach-avoid attitude
4. adaptability
5. intensity of reaction
6. level of responsiveness
7. mood
8. distractibility
9. attention span.

These differences can be detected in the early months of life. On the basis of these nine aspects, about two-thirds of babies can be categorized into three distinct types of temperament (the remaining third of babies have more mixed temperaments):

- easy – about 40 per cent
- slow to warm up, more fearful and shy – about 15 per cent
- difficult, cranky and highly reactive, with poor concentration – about 10 per cent.

These types remain relatively stable throughout adolescence and adulthood. Being temperamentally active, sociable, shy or fearful remains much the same throughout life. But some aspects of temperament do change – cranky and 'difficult' infants often settle down later.

Temperament, in turn, strongly shapes the type of personality you develop – how sociable you are; how open to exploring new things; how actively you pursue your goals; how prone you are to negativity and positive feelings – particularly how fearful or confident you are, and how easy or difficult you find it to calm yourself when distressed.

Learning to manage your temperament and personality is a key component of flourishing.

### *Experiences in the early years of life*

As we saw in Chapters 3 and 4, your brain stores emotional memories in a different way than it stores ordinary facts.[5] These emotional memories can be laid down outside the sphere of consciousness yet continue to significantly affect how you perceive and react to the world. This is especially true in the case of emotional memories laid down in early childhood. LeDoux's description bears repeating: they become the 'rough, wordless blueprints for emotional life'.[6]

How a baby's temperament plays out is affected by the quality of parenting they receive – which, in turn, affects the quality of the attachment bond they form with their parents. John Bowlby, Mary Ainsworth and other psychologists first revealed the crucial role attachment plays in infancy.[7] Whether a baby forms a secure or an insecure attachment with its parents – particularly its mother – affects its emotional, cognitive and social development throughout childhood, into adolescence and adult life, and right through to the parenting of the next generation.

Secure attachment depends particularly on a parent's ability to correctly 'attune', and to respond to a baby's signals – especially in the first years of life. But a baby's temperament can also influence the quality of care they receive. Babies who are more adaptable, sociable and easy to soothe are more likely to receive warm and responsive parenting. Babies who are more irritable, demanding or fearful, who are prone to respond to stress with high-intensity negative reactions and negative mood, are more likely to stress their parents and are therefore more likely to be at risk of receiving poor-quality parenting. A baby's temperament can set in motion a chain of reactions from parents and other people that will protect babies from developing behavioural and psychological problems, or it can put them at risk.[8]

But temperament is not destiny. Even the most temperamentally difficult babies can, and do, thrive – if they are lucky enough to have the right kind of parents. Parents who are warm, calm and responsive, who are positive (about the baby and about being a parent generally), who enjoy a high level of social support (and generally more favourable life circumstances) are able to respond to a baby with a difficult temperament in a better way. They manage to find a way to soothe the baby's distress, to ease the difficult passage through the first few years of life, to foster confidence and bring out the best in the infant.

The quality of our early attachment experiences profoundly shapes those 'internal working models' John Bowlby identified – how positively or negatively we feel and think about ourselves, about other people and about the world in general. These assumptions form the basic emotional architecture of self-esteem and trust and, in turn, influence our expectations of ourselves and others. They colour new situations we encounter, shaping what we perceive and how we react.

Together, then, the combination of your genetic temperament (which later finds expression in your personality) and your early learning experiences (particularly the quality of your attachment bonds) significantly influences the emotional tone of your life – and your 'default' positivity–negativity ratio. If you have been fortunate in life, that default ratio is set above 3:1. If you have been less fortunate, your proneness to worry and distress can tilt the ratio downwards.

But, either way, that ratio remains dynamic and changeable throughout life.

## *The conscious self: the 'executive manager' within*

Your consciousness is the part of the Self that is most familiar to you. This is where the 'executive self' resides, the part of yourself that tries to manage your life by striving to exert control, over yourself and over the environment, so that you can achieve your goals in life and flourish. The conscious self also manages how you achieve your individual goals, and how you express your unique talents and interests. It is where your personality and basic needs are 'housed'. All of these elements, and how you manage them, are crucial components of flourishing.

### *Goals and values*

Psychologist Steven Pinker argues that having goals explains why we act *at all*.

A large part of your happiness (and unhappiness) is tied to how successful or unsuccessful you are (or feel you are) in pursuing your goals. When you feel you are making progress towards a goal that you value (finding someone to love, finishing a project at work, communicating well with a teenage child, buying tickets for a big match), you feel happy and satisfied. When you are blocked or stuck, you feel frustrated and unhappy.

Your goals are intimately tied into your values because, at the most fundamental level, without a hierarchy of values you would be unable to choose or to prioritize which goal to pursue. You may be conscious of only some of the values that are motivating you. Other values may be pushed out of your awareness, yet still be exerting a lot of influence on your behaviour. They may even be in conflict with the goals you are consciously pursuing. In later chapters we will explore just how important goals are for flourishing, and how best to pursue them.

### *Talents, interests and accomplishments*

Each of us has a unique portfolio of talents, personal interests and accomplishments.[9] Expressing and developing that portfolio is an important part of flourishing and a reliable source of everyday pleasures and enjoyment. Psychologist Howard Gardner has identified seven basic areas of talent or ability:[10]

1. linguistic/verbal
2. logical-mathematical
3. spatial
4. musical
5. physical
6. personal
7. social.

These could also be described as the different components of your emotional intelligence. In addition to your innate talents, there are the special passions you are drawn to – hobbies, social or work interests, sports. It cannot be emphasized enough that, providing you keep your life generally in balance, investing in your particular interest pays huge dividends in terms of your happiness and is a substantial building block for a flourishing life.

At the heart of accomplishing anything in life is the ability to master something. Even though it requires hard work and effort, when you master a skill of any kind – playing a musical instrument, making a cake, painting a room, solving a software problem, writing a clear report or running a successful political campaign – you feel immensely satisfied. However, the relationship between your actual abilities and how well or badly you *perform* is not straightforward. Rather, whether you can translate your abilities into performing well depends very much on how you *judge* your capabilities – and that judgement, in turn, affects your motivation and behaviour. This is what psychologist Albert Bandura calls your 'self-efficacy'.

Self-efficacy has three components:

- having a positive view of your capabilities
- having the ability to marshal your feelings, your thoughts and your actions into an effective course of action, and
- believing you can do this effectively.

Your sense of self-efficacy is shaped by your internal working models. No matter how intelligent and skilled you are, if you entertain serious doubt about your efficacy, it undermines your ability to accomplish anything. When you undertake a task, you are more likely to become beset by worries about your personal deficiencies and exaggerate the potential difficulties. This self-doubt impairs your performance by diverting your attention away from how best to approach the job. As a consequence, you will tend to avoid taking on challenges, and give up more easily. As Bandura, who spent a lifetime studying self-efficacy, ruefully remarked: 'Indeed, there are many competent people who are plagued by a sense of inefficacy, and many less competent ones who remain unperturbed by impending threats because they are self-assured of their coping capabilities.'[11]

### *Personality*

Your genetically based temperament finds conscious expression in your personality, mainly through what psychologists identify as the 'Big Five' personality traits.

- Extroversion (being sociable, talkative, energetic, assertive, adventurous)
- Agreeableness (the ability to get on well with people, to have harmonious relationships)

- Neuroticism (the tendency to self-doubt, to worry, to pay a lot of attention to negative feelings and to express them frequently)
- Conscientiousness
- Openness to experience

We all have a unique combination of these five characteristics – that's what we refer to as our personality. (You will learn more about how these personality traits influence our happiness in Chapter 7.) Personality exerts a strong influence over everything we do and, like temperament, can tilt the default ratio of positive and negative in our lives. If you are born extroverted, you are predisposed to experience things positively. If neuroticism is high in your personality, you are predisposed to negative feelings.

### *Awareness*

In this survey of the conscious self there are many hints that other forces are operating at the edge of consciousness, or even outside of it. You do, indeed, have an 'executive self' that is managing your life, but this occupies a fairly small island or zone of pure awareness – and this island is surrounded by a sea of semi-consciousness full of forces that are constantly interfering with its grand plans.

The very epicentre of your conscious self is the point of pure self-awareness. When you sit still for a minute, particularly if you close your eyes, you become immediately aware of this zone of awareness – and the stream of consciousness that flows through it. This is the constant, and often highly repetitive, stream of sensations, thoughts and feelings that is coursing through your mind. At any one moment, you are (to some extent) conscious of what thoughts are preoccupying you – thoughts about what is happening now, what has just happened and what is going to happen next. You are also somewhat aware of how you are feeling – the physical sensations that are coming from your body, the emotions you are experiencing. You are (again, to some extent only) aware of what you are doing, and of the impressions you are forming of your immediate environment.

This little zone of awareness is expanded or constricted depending on your level of self-awareness and your mood. Feeling negative constricts your awareness, focusing it on immediate threats, on the unpleasant sensations created by stress in your body, and on the negative thoughts and emotions aroused. Feeling positive has the opposite effect, expanding your zone of awareness so that you become more aware of opportunities in the environment. Positive emotions stretch your immediate mental space to include your longer-term goals so that you are less enslaved to the moment and more strategic about the future, less likely to be swept up by immediate emotions and perceptions, and readier to keep a more balanced perspective on how to react.

This brings us to one of the central themes of this book: the importance of attention. Everything that your conscious self is trying to achieve depends on this most precious commodity. If you can focus and marshal your attention, you can better control your thoughts and feelings and, as a consequence, be much happier. You can pursue your goals more effectively and develop your talents and interests more fully.

However, attention turns out to be remarkably elusive and difficult to control. We all work under the assumption that we go through our day consciously choosing and shaping by our own will what we attend to and how we act. In short, we believe that we possess a free will. We do – but we use that free will not nearly as much as we like to believe. In fact, a large part of our everyday life is determined by powerful automatic mental processes that operate outside of our awareness. This is largely why our many and well-intentioned efforts to achieve our goals and change ourselves – for example, deciding to be less negative and more positive – can fail.

If you want to live a flourishing life, understanding how these automatic processes work and learning how to control your attention are crucial. That is the subject of Chapters 9 and 10.

## *The higher self: the realm of the possible*

This realm of Self is the hardest to describe. It is unconscious to the extent that we are normally very preoccupied by the demands of surviving and managing our daily lives, so we lose sight of this higher part of our consciousness. Yet, intuitively we know it is there. It is where our capacity for imagination, creativity and spirituality resides, where we feel connected to some bigger force outside ourselves and know that we are more than just how our past and present circumstances define us.

For some people, this part of themselves finds expression in religious belief. For others, this kind of spiritual intuition may be expressed no more definitively than as a sense that 'out there, somewhere, is a force that gives meaning to all this'.[12] Poets, writers and artists of all kinds are usually very connected to their higher self because they draw their creative energy from there.

This is also where your highest values and character strengths reside: your capacity for wisdom; for courage; for love; for justice and leadership; for forgiveness and integrity; for faith, hope and purpose. These are the character strengths that most of us would like to be described as possessing, and would like to instil in our children. They constitute a vital part of flourishing – not just in our individual lives, but in organizations, communities and society.[13]

This higher realm of yourself is where you bring unity and coherence into your sense of self. Hovering half within and half outside consciousness is your need for identity, for purpose and meaning in your life. You need to feel you are somebody and that your life matters. Much of this psychological work is done through creating a life narrative. Your overall narrative of 'who I am' is a combination of the story you tell yourself about yourself, the stories that important others tell you about you, and the stories you act out in your life.

Many of these stories about your identity are constructed around significant people and roles in your life – your parents, your siblings, your partner in life, your children, your friends and your colleagues. You create a particular 'self' in relation to each. These are the many 'selves' to which William James referred, and you may experience yourself quite differently in each.

All of these different stories and selves have been shaped by repeated interactions with others and most of the time a particular self is activated automatically. So, for example, in the presence of an authority figure, you may automatically activate the 'me as daughter' self. When faced with a challenge, you may activate the 'me as high achiever' self. The more often you activate a particular self, the more dominant it becomes, becoming your 'typical self'. That is how your experiences of being loved or rejected, encouraged or criticized, get played out automatically again and again in your life – either helping you to flourish, or keeping you in a cycle of languishing.[14] This life narrative can be profoundly shaken by major setbacks, and by loss. But, most importantly, it can also be rewritten in a way that helps you flourish under fire.

One of the most powerful ways that narrative can be reshaped is through your capacity to reflect and to imagine – which happens at the higher level of self.

This is the subject of Chapter 19.

### *The routes to our higher self*

What moves us into this realm of self, this different level of awareness? Sometimes it is when we find ourselves deeply engaged in some activity that we love – the experience of what psychologists call 'flow', when the boundaries between ourselves and what we are doing disappear and we have a near euphoric sense of being part of something much bigger. These experiences are described in Chapter 15.

Sometimes it is when we meditate – the subject of Chapter 10.

The experience of intense emotion – what the influential psychologist Abraham Maslow called 'peak experiences' – also connects us to our higher self.[15] These can be moments of great joy, intimacy and unity with other people – falling in love, the birth of a baby, when your team wins the World Cup. Or they can be moments of great suffering or sadness – the death of somebody you love. Whether these are points of intense connection or disconnection, they can be transformative and set you on the path to flourishing.

But it is not the experiences themselves – positive or negative – that transform you. It is the process of finding meaning in them.

This is the subject of Chapter 16.

## *Starting the journey to flourishing*

As we can see, there are many competing forces within the Self, resulting in many and competing 'selves'. Hardly surprising, then, that managing ourselves turns out to be no easy job.

To flourish requires a good understanding of how all the different parts of yourself work, separately and together, and how to manage them most effectively. Remember, you have an inherent ability to know what your best direction in life is.

Flourishing requires engaging with all aspects of yourself, but you can start the journey by working on just one. You can concentrate on learning to be happier and to be more vitally engaged with life. Or you can focus on changing your patterns of negative thinking, on becoming more optimistic or more resilient. Or you can try to become more effective at setting and achieving your goals.

Achieving goals – even small ones – is marked by an immediate burst of pleasure and a steady build-up of positive feelings. This, in turn, increases your motivation and confidence. If you mange to marry your personal interests and natural talents to your goals, you have not just the formula for accomplishment and success in your life, but a critical component of flourishing. Pursuing what interests you – and suits your personality – also increases positive feelings. So, how vitally engaged you are in your interests is a very strong predictor of a high level of life satisfaction. A well-developed interest or hobby can provide you with a valued identity and an opportunity to be at your personal best – an identity that is not dependent on family or on work. You can be a different person, and sometimes that is a vast relief from those other workaday 'selves'. When you get the formula right, you will experience a sense of 'flow' – an experience of pure happiness.

You can also choose to start the journey to flourishing by developing a better understanding of the forces that made you the person you are, enabling you to redraw the blueprints from childhood that no longer work for you. In particular, if you learn to control your attention, you can achieve a glimpse of the patterns of automatic thoughts and reactions that are keeping you trapped. You can start building your resilience and break free of the absorbing negative states that keep you stuck.

Or you can choose to develop your higher self, your capacity for creativity and imagination and service to others. You can do this by rewriting your narrative – constructing a different framework of meaning in your life, a better story of yourself, of your rightful place in the world and your capacity to make it a better place.

That capacity to re-imagine ourselves is an important step to flourishing. Nobel laureate Seamus Heaney cautions us to keep the lines of connection open between the different levels of ourselves, between what he calls our 'earthy origin and angelic potential'.[16] He uses a beguiling image from a story contained in the medieval annals of the Irish monastery of Clonmacnoise to describe how we are placed between the givens of our life and immediate environment, and our imaginable future.

> One day the monks of Clonmacnoise were holding a meeting in the church, and as they were deliberating they saw a ship sailing over them in the air, going as if it were on the sea. When the crew of the ship saw the meeting and the inhabited place below them, they dropped anchor and the anchor came right down to the floor of the church and the priests seized it. A man came down out of the ship after the anchor and he was swimming as if he were in water, till he reached the anchor; and they were

> dragging him down then. 'For God's sake, let me go,' said he, 'for you are drowning me.' Then he left them, swimming in the air as before, taking his anchor with him.
>
> I have been entranced with this story ever since I first read it, and I take it to be a kind of dream instruction, a parable about the necessity of keeping the lines open between the two levels of our being, the level where we proceed with the usual life of the meeting and the decision, and the other level where the visionary and the marvellous present themselves suddenly and bewilderingly. We must, in other words, be ready for both the routine and the revelation. Never be so canny as to ignore the uncanny.

Like the monks, we too have to stay securely based in our day-to-day lives and responsibilities. We have to engage with challenges, build secure connections and act with autonomy. We have to deal with stress and bounce back from setbacks. But we are also like the sailors – unless we stay connected to the 'visionary and the marvellous' we will drown.[17]

You can start the journey to flourishing from any part of yourself – and the more of yourself you involve, the richer the learning.

Where you start does not matter.

All that matters is succeeding in changing just one step in the dance, and you will eventually transform the whole choreography of your life.

PART TWO

# Ten strategies to nurture a flourishing life

# The ten strategies

**Strategy one: Build your capacity for happiness**

Chapters 6 and 7

**Strategy two: Set yourself goals**

Chapter 8

**Strategy three: Control your attention**

Chapters 9 and 10

**Strategy four: Always know your positive purpose**

Chapters 11 and 12

**Strategy five: Take charge of your mood**

Chapters 13 and 14

**Strategy six: Master the art of vital engagement**

Chapter 15

**Strategy seven: Know the meaning of things**

Chapter 16

**Strategy eight: Build your resilience**

Chapters 17, 18, 19 and 20

**Strategy nine: Stop sabotaging yourself**

Chapter 21

**Strategy ten: Embrace the future**

Chapters 22 and 23

STRATEGY ONE

# *Build your capacity for happiness*

'Happiness is the meaning and purpose of life,
the whole aim and end of human existence.'

Aristotle

# 6. How happiness helps you flourish

During periods of great affluence, prompted by the general air of security, prosperity and what has been called 'a culture of surplus', we instinctively put an emphasis on happiness.[1] Witness the explosion of books on the subject during the years of the boom – from the excitement of the new millennium in 2000 to the crash in 2008. Correspondingly, in times of economic adversity and crisis, there is a temptation to retreat into survival mode, to let the negativity bias run riot, and a corresponding tendency to treat happiness as a luxury, something that has to be deferred. 'I haven't time to be thinking of happiness,' you might say.

But working on increasing your day-to-day happiness is a critical factor in surviving and ultimately flourishing. It can help compensate for losses you have suffered, and build your resilience to withstand stress, so that you are ready to avail yourself of opportunities when they arise. Far from being an accessory, happiness is a precursor to success, a strong staff to lean on in the journey back to where you want to be, and as well as making the journey more enjoyable.

It seems intuitive that when you are flourishing you are happy. After all, most of the things you devote your time and energy to – your relationships, your children, your work, projects or hobbies – you choose to prioritize because you think that ultimately, if you succeed with them, you will feel happier. This natural assumption that success in life brings happiness is generally (though not always) true. But now – and much to the consternation of the puritans amongst us – evidence is emerging that the relationship between flourishing and happiness can also work the other way round: happiness makes you flourish. Happiness is not just *associated* with success but *engenders* it.

Consider the four ingredients of flourishing:

- rising successfully to life's challenges
- being in tune with yourself and with other people
- feeling free to act, and
- using your valued competencies.

When all four are present and working in harmony, you feel buoyant and happy. But flourishing necessarily means having the capacity to rise to the challenges of life – expected and unexpected – while *at the same time* being able to maintain a high level of positive feelings. If the effort of meeting the challenges of everyday life depletes you, you are surviving, not flourishing. You might seem outwardly successful, but you may not be happy. Flourishing is not just about being good or doing well, it is also about feeling good and happy.

We are now all too familiar with the need to 'stress test' the banks – to ensure that they have enough reserves to cover the demands that may be made on them. So too with yourself: to flourish you need to stress test your reserves. The steady build-up of happiness – in the sense of frequently experiencing the Positive Big Ten emotions (love, joy, gratitude, contentment, interest, hope, pride, amusement, inspiration, awe), and being able to limit the frequency and intensity of the Negative Big Eight (fear, anger, sadness, disgust, contempt, shame, jealousy and envy) – can precede flourishing. This is because in the face of inevitable stresses, setbacks and failures, you need a substantial reserve of well-being to keep you going. Your reserves of positive feelings need to reach the magic 5:1 ratio – and never dip below the critical 3:1 threshold.

The important point to note here is that happiness is defined as having frequent positive feelings *as well as* having infrequent and less intense negative feelings. Because the positive and negative emotional systems operate somewhat independently of each other, in order to flourish it is not enough just to have frequent positive feelings – as they can be overwhelmed by frequent negative feelings, and vice versa. Concentrating on reducing negative feelings will not get you to the flourishing ratio unless you simultaneously build up positive feelings.

Positive feelings build up the necessary resources – confidence, energy, courage, nerve – required to take on life's challenges successfully. It turns out that how happy you are can determine:

- your physical and emotional health
- how long and how well you live
- the quality of your personal, economic and career success, and
- your ability to withstand stress, setbacks and failure.

And these benefits are not confined to the happy individuals themselves. Happy people make for flourishing families, thriving communities and successful societies. (Of course, it is important to bear in mind that the benefits of happiness for a society only apply if the happy person is not acting destructively; nobody benefits from a happy, charming psychopath – except the psychopath himself.)

Sonja Lyubomirsky of the University of California, Ed Diener of the University of Illinois at Urbana and Laura King of the University of Missouri – three of the world's leading researchers on happiness – recently analysed nearly 300 studies of happiness involving over 275,000 participants.[2] The results from all the studies were consistent. Compared to their unhappier counterparts, happy people are more successful in virtually every domain of life.[3]

Let me count the ways.

## *Happy people have better health and live longer*

That happiness is good for mental health is hardly surprising. Happy people have higher self-esteem, and a greater sense of personal competence, mastery and control – all crucial for effective functioning in every domain of life. What is more striking is the effect of being happy on physical health. Happier people consistently report fewer symptoms, have fewer allergic reactions, and report less pain than their less happy counterparts. They are less likely to suffer colds, respiratory illness, sports injuries, heart attacks or strokes. If you expose healthy volunteers to the common cold virus, those who are happier are less likely to develop a cold.[4] If volunteers suffer from chronic stress, 69 per cent develop a cold when exposed to the virus, compared to only 27 per cent who are not stressed.[5]

Chronic negative feelings compromise your immune functioning. In what can only be described as a heroic contribution to our knowledge of how stress can affect the immune functioning, eleven dental students volunteered for an experiment in which they endured cuts to their palates made by keen researchers (admittedly the cuts were small, exceedingly precise and made with sterile scalpels). These wounds were made twice – first during their summer holidays (when they were relaxing) and then again during their first major examination (when they were presumably under a lot of pressure and stress). Researchers measured the size of the wounds from the time they were inflicted to final healing. The rate of healing was a full 40 per cent slower during the high-stress examination period than during the more relaxing holiday period. This slow rate of healing was accounted for by a 71 per cent decline in immune cells from the time they were on holiday to the time of their examinations.[6]

When happy people get sick, they pay fewer visits to the doctor or to the hospital A & E department, and they take less medication. They enjoy a better quality of life when diagnosed with cancer and show much better recovery after cardiac surgery. Even more dramatically perhaps, happier people survive longer after a recurrence of breast cancer (seven years), in end-stage renal disease (four years), and following spinal injuries (eleven years).[7] They also miss less work due to illness.

After all that, you won't be surprised to learn that happier people live longer. In a classic study, researchers at the University of Kentucky came across personal essays that were written by young Catholic nuns in the 1930s.[8] The nuns wrote about their early lives, their religious experiences and their vocation to enter the religious life. The researchers analysed each essay and rated the frequency and intensity of positive emotions expressed in it. The nuns were perfect subjects for such a study as their lives – their diet and their daily routines – were similar in every way. What distinguished them was their outlook at the age of twenty-two. Astonishingly, the researchers found that the nuns who had expressed the most positive emotions at that stage lived up to ten years longer than those who expressed the fewest positive emotions. To put that in context, this is a greater increase in life expectancy than would be expected if someone gave up smoking.

Other studies have pointed in the same direction. Older people with high levels of positive feelings live, on average, seven and a half years longer than unhappy people – irrespective of gender, socio-economic status, levels of loneliness and actual health status. In terms of living longer and healthier, positive feelings are more important than body mass, smoking or exercise.[9] That is not to say that giving up smoking, or losing excess weight, or exercising are not important. It's just that learning to be happy is also good for you. Needless to say, doing all four is best of all.

## *Happy people have more friends and better relationships*

Compared to unhappy people, happier people have more friends – and other people – in their lives, who they feel they can rely on. They are less likely to experience loneliness because both the quantity and the quality of their relationships are higher. They report higher satisfaction with friends, and are less envious of others. They get more support from colleagues and supervisors at work. Before marriage, happier people are more likely to describe their current romantic relationship as being of a high quality. They are more likely to marry, to have more fulfilling marriages and to describe their partner as being their 'great love'. Not surprisingly, they tend to have partners who are also more satisfied with the marriage.

Obviously, being stuck in a deeply unhappy romantic relationship or marriage diminishes the happiness of even the most positive people. But if you are a generally happy person, you are more likely to deal with it effectively – either going about resolving the issues or, if they're insoluble, leaving the relationship. Either of these approaches may temporarily increase feelings of anxiety, loneliness, disappointment or desolation. But in the long term, they safeguard eventual happiness. Even when they separate or divorce, happier people are more likely to find another love and remarry.

People who are happy are judged as more likeable, friendlier and warmer in their relationships. More unexpectedly, they are also judged as more physically attractive, more intelligent, more competent and assertive, less selfish, more moral, and even more likely to go to heaven.

A study of American women conducted over three decades demonstrates how happiness can deliver such impressive results.[10] The study started when the women were twenty-one and had their photographs taken for the college yearbook. Psychologists LeeAnne Harker and Dacher Keltner of the University of California set out to discover if positive feelings expressed in these photographs could predict the personality and life outcomes of the women as they grew older. The pictures were scored out of ten for the genuineness of the smile (did it reach the eyes and make the cheeks lift) – the best indicator of sincere positive feelings and happiness – and for physical attractiveness. The women were followed up at ages twenty-seven, forty-three and fifty-two and their personalities, attitudes and circumstances were studied and recorded.

Over thirty years later, it was those girls with the happiest smiles – not those who were rated most physically attractive – who were found to be most satisfied with their marriages. They were also judged to be more nurturing, more caring and more sociable. Over time, they were found to have become more organized in their lives, more focused and achievement-oriented and less susceptible to repeated and prolonged experiences of negative feelings.

In this study, we get an extraordinary glimpse of how being happy at twenty-one (at least, as evidenced by the genuineness of a smile) may have a significant shaping effect on personality and life outcomes throughout adulthood. Of course, it's possible that the influence runs in the other direction – that the young women who were smiling so intensely were reflecting the fact that they were already successful. But it is equally or even more likely that their positive feelings preceded and predicted their success.

The researchers also asked people who knew nothing about the women to look at the yearbook pictures and, just on that basis, form a view on their likely personal qualities and attributes. The judgements were remarkably favourable on the young women with the genuine smiles – a signal that we have an intuitive sense that happy people are more likely to be easy to get on with, competent and dependable. Because we judge them to be better bets in relationships and at work, we are more inclined to offer them opportunities and also to expect the best of them – which, in turn, makes success more likely.

In other words, positive feelings create upward spirals of flourishing.

## *Happy people do better in work and earn more money*

There is increasing evidence, from longitudinal studies in particular, that happiness is a significant factor in career success. The studies show that if you compare students Jack and Joe, or Jill and Jeanie at age eighteen, if Jack and Jill are happier than Joe and Jeanie, when you follow them up in their mid-twenties the happier pair are more likely to have graduated from college. They are more likely to secure job interviews, and to be offered higher quality jobs – jobs with more autonomy, meaning and variety.

When they start work, they are likely to be evaluated more favourably by supervisors in terms of the quality of their work, their dependability, their creativity and their teamwork. They are more likely to handle managerial jobs more effectively and to have better leadership skills. In turn, they are happier and more satisfied at work. These positive experiences at work are likely to increase their initial positive feelings even more, creating a virtuous flourishing cycle. They are less likely to lose their jobs, but even if they do, they are re-employed more quickly and are much less likely to suffer long-term unemployment. Happier young people are also more likely to earn more money, to receive more pay increases and to be more financially independent.

Ah, you might say, not so fast. Maybe the happier students earned more money because they came from well-off families? But Ed Diener and his colleagues asked just that question in one of their studies.[11] They measured how cheerful students were at age eighteen, but they also found out how much their parents earned. Unsurprisingly, the combination of being happier and having parents with higher incomes had the biggest effect on subsequent earning power. But when the students were followed up in their thirties – more than sixteen years later – the more cheerful students were found to be earning more, irrespective of their parents' income.

So, even if your parents are not well off, feeling positive counts in terms of your future income.

## *Happy people are better bosses and lead more successful organizations*

Sigal Barsade and a team from the Wharton Business School studied the chief executive officers of 62 organizations and 239 of their top management teams.[12] They included those from Fortune 500 and leading private companies, as well as from government, education, advertising, consulting, professional, accounting and non-governmental organizations. Compared to their more negative counterparts, chief executives and senior managers who were emotionally positive – enthusiastic, energetic, mentally alert, engaged and determined, and who often felt happy and satisfied and enjoyed moments of real joy and fun at work – were found to work in teams that had high levels of cooperative working.

They genuinely thought of themselves as a real team and showed a strong sense of solidarity, expressed in such opinions as: 'When our team has done well, I have done well,' and, 'Members of this group care a lot about it and work together to make it one of the best.' They had significantly fewer disagreements on work issues, and also experienced the fewest interpersonal conflict and personality clashes. As we all know, this kind of internal friction and bad feeling is precisely what drains vital energy in a team and gets in the way of good work being done. Moreover, when the team was composed of similarly positively disposed people, the more satisfied the team members were with the interpersonal relationships in the team – and the more effectively they worked together.

In contrast, teams where the chief executive and the senior managers were unhappy – feeling dull and sluggish, downhearted, easily irritated, tense, miserable – showed the opposite pattern. Interestingly, mixed teams – where there were both positive and negative people – showed the greatest amount of work disagreements, interpersonal conflict and the least cooperation. It's not hard to guess why.

Many other studies show that when organizations are led by emotionally positive chief executives, their employees report themselves to be happier and healthier, and they rate the work culture as upbeat, warm and conducive to high performance. Such organizations are more likely to be highly rated by their customers, to be more productive and more profitable. There is less absenteeism, less staff turnover, less job burnout, less conflict and less destructive behaviour. The people who work in such organizations are more likely to be good organizational citizens (that is, to go beyond the requirements of the job), to be helpful to co-workers, to make constructive suggestions, to develop their own work skills, and to be motivated to protect and help the organization grow and prosper.

## *What do happy people do that produces such good outcomes?*

### *Happy people seek out other people*

One of the most robust findings about happy people is that they have a high level of engagement with other people.[13] Happy people actively seek out other people. They have positive attitudes to others, liking and trusting them more. They are open and friendly to people they don't know. They enjoy social activities and, in social situations, they are more outgoing, warm, gregarious, sociable, lively and energetic. After a conversation with somebody, happy people tend to like the person they were talking to, and to have found the conversation enjoyable, pleasant and relaxed.

In a general way, happy people are more active, attend club meetings more frequently, and join more organizations. They are rated as energetic and active by their families and friends. Among older people, those who are happier are more likely to keep learning new skills or take a class. They are interested in a larger number of cultural and educational activities in their communities and are better informed about politics. People with an extrovert temperament actually like interacting with others, seek out opportunities to do so, and are generally more socially active, so they have a head start on happiness in this respect.

### *Happy people are helpful*

Happier people are more likely to want to help, and to actually enjoy helping, other people. They volunteer more and invest more hours in the effort. They are more likely to donate blood and give to charity. They express a stronger desire to contribute to society.

So, if you feel good, you are more likely to do good.

Why?

Because when you are in a positive mood, you are more predisposed to like other people. This is true all the way from happy preschoolers to contented senior citizens. These findings undermine a commonly held view that happy people are self-satisfied and not motivated to work for a change in the world. People who are happy with their lives are not inevitably happy with the way society is run. In fact, satisfaction with their own lives and satisfaction with society and government are quite distinct.[14]

### *Happy people set goals for themselves*

Happy people engage in a lot of day-to-day projects. They have the knack of seeing any activity – even a routine day-to-day activity – as intrinsically motivating and worth doing. They have mastered the art of transforming a duty into a meaningful project. They like to set goals for themselves, and more often feel they are achieving their goals. They are optimistic. They like finding new ways to solve problems and to approach issues in their daily lives, and they keep performing well even when they encounter setbacks. As a result, they are more likely to experience themselves as personally competent –and that, in turn, boosts their self-esteem and gives them a sense of mastery and control over their lives.

### *Happy people look on the bright side of life*

When happy people encounter setbacks, they react in a very characteristic fashion: they immediately try to build up positive feelings in the face of the negativity. They actively try to see a positive side – either seeing the stress or setback as a valuable learning experience, or actively focusing on the positive aspects of their lives. This is really important because, as we saw earlier, positive emotions – even fairly mild ones – if experienced immediately after a stressful event can help to restore heart rate and blood pressure to normal.

Positive emotions experienced during chronic stress help people to cope better and to attend to important information – even if it is negative. For example, compared to pessimists, optimists pay *more* attention to medical diagnoses and to treatment details, thereby maximizing their chances of recovery.[15]

Faced with a stressful challenge, happy people don't engage in denial but try to reinterpret the situation in a positive way and to maintain their sense of humour.[16] Indeed, in stressful situations, they actively build up their sense of control, competence and optimism. This serves them well and keeps them motivated as they deal with the problem in hand.

When happy people get negative feedback about themselves and their performance, like everybody else, they don't like it. But they are not thrown off balance. Even when they feel deflated, they try to maintain their optimism, expecting things to get better in the future. Crucially, they tend not to compare themselves to others – especially unfavourably – and work at being more satisfied with what they have, even if it is not their first choice. Unhappy people do the exact opposite. They constantly compare themselves negatively to more successful people – or people they *believe* to be more successful – and fall prey to envy, making them feel even worse.

In a competitive situation, when they do better than their peers, both happy and unhappy people get a boost in self-esteem – unworthy, maybe, but very human. But when peers do *better* than them, happy people are not negatively affected by their peers' success. Unhappy people are. In Gore Vidal's immortal phrase, every time they hear of a colleague's success a little something in them dies. Maybe we all feel like this, now and then. But people who are very unhappy routinely react this way. In contrast, happy people remain focused on their own goals.

The important point about all this is that happy people are not just simply passively happier with their lot in life. Rather, they *actively* work to find the positive in a negative or uncertain situation.

## *What we can learn from happy people*

The scientific evidence linking happiness to success is impressive. Having said that, it is important to keep a perspective on all this: just being happy does not guarantee success in life. There are many other factors involved in success – intelligence, perseverance, conscientiousness, a social and economically privileged background – and, of course, luck (being in the right place at the right time). However, happiness is an important part of the mix and, crucially, something you have control over yourself.

Even people who are born with a predisposition to be happier find that prolonged stress and setbacks and failures can depress their capacity for happiness and for success.

But what about those who are not disposed to happiness, people who are born with a high level of temperamental neuroticism – a tendency to self-doubt, rumination and worry? Well, the good news is that there is now a growing body of evidence on the most effective strategies to increase happiness that actually work effectively.[17] I will be describing some of them in later chapters. But, we can also all *learn* to become happier simply by practising the attitudes and the behaviour of happy people.

One study provides a serviceable and immediate formula for happiness: what you might crudely call 'fake it till you make it'. In this study, introverts (normally more reserved in social situations) were instructed to imitate the behaviour of extroverted colleagues, irrespective of how they were feeling. As we know, extroverts tend to be happier than introverts – mainly because they have a natural inclination to seek out the company of other people, and that is a sure-fire recipe for increasing happiness.

So, guess what?

When the introverts mimicked the behaviour of extroverts, often reluctantly, they actually felt happier.

Read again the descriptions above of how happy people characteristically think, feel, behave and react to stress. Select just one of those characteristics and try it out.

- Spend more time with your friends.
- Practise trying to see the bright side of things.
- Stop comparing yourself to other people.
- Work on developing better coping strategies.

Even if it doesn't make you happier the first time you try it, it will begin to feel more natural as you keep practising. And you will begin to feel genuinely happier. All these strategies reliably increase happiness – even if initially it does not feel right.[18]

As Hitchcock famously said to Grace Kelly, who complained that she could not *feel* the part she was playing in the film: 'Then fake it, my dear.'

I don't mean fake it in the sense of attempting to fool yourself or other people. As we saw previously, the positive effects of positive feelings only happen if the feelings are genuine. But fake it in the sense of making a genuine effort to change the way you are behaving – even if the way you are acting is not quite in tune with your feelings. This is a crucial point: at any given moment – no matter what your emotional state – your feelings, thoughts and behaviour are organized into tightly patterned interrelated responses. For instance, when you feel down, you feel unmotivated to do anything except ruminate on your disappointments and losses. You feel powerless, and your thoughts are pessimistic. Your facial expression is sad, your mouth set in the characteristic downward arc. Your body seems pulled down into heaviness and inertia, your shoulders drooping and your breathing heavy and slow. Each element – emotion, thoughts, physical responses, behaviour – feeds on the other in an ever-tightening knot.

However, if you change just one aspect of this set of responses, it breaks up the dismal choreography. The physical expression of sadness is often the easiest to change. If you get your body to move vigorously, for example, it changes your breathing. If you put your shoulders back and strand up as straight as you can, you feel less heavy and weighed down. By doing this, your brain gets confused – these are not the body's signals of sadness and powerlessness; these are the signals of vigour and confidence – and the patterning of sadness is loosened. You can sense a slight shift in your feelings – you feel more in control, more energetic. Your thoughts take a positive turn. All these changes may be small and subtle, but if you pay attention to them and build on them, your sadness lifts.

You will learn more about this in Chapter 11.

To flourish in your life, to build flourishing relationships, teams – and, indeed, a flourishing society – it pays to take happiness seriously.

Never more so than now.

The severity of the economic downturn may have affected your own life and the lives of other people you care about. As a result, your happiness may be compromised. You may be feeling more worried and despondent. Your sense of personal purpose and autonomy may be temporarily blocked because of lack of opportunities or resources.

Or, at the other end of the scale, you may be working harder – and for less reward – than ever before. In such a situation, you might understandably consider that being happy is the least of your priorities. However, building your capacity for happiness can be a crucial step in finding a new path in life.

In the next chapter we will look at what makes us happy and, crucially, just how much control we have over our own happiness.

# 7. Discover what *really* makes you happy

Let me ask you a question: 'Taken all together, how happy would you say you are?'

Very happy?

Quite happy?

Not very happy?

Not at all happy?'

This is a big question. Yet, if you are like most people, you will have no difficulty coming up with an answer in moments. In those few moments, you will perform a complex internal audit, registering your current mood, scanning any positive and negative experiences you have had recently, judging the state of your relationships, your work, maybe your finances and even the country, reviewing where you are in your life narrative and comparing that to where you expected to be or feel you should be. Having amassed all this information, you come out with a remarkably accurate assessment of precisely how happy you are.[1]

Reflecting on how you answer that question also provides a very good introduction to the complex experience of happiness. Recall the map of the Self in Chapter 5 – comprising the conscious, unconscious and higher selves. Well, happiness can originate, and be experienced, at *all* levels of the Self.

## *Happiness and the conscious self*

At a conscious level, we are happy if we feel we are getting on with our lives and overcoming whatever challenges we are dealing with. At the simplest level, we are happy if we are experiencing little bursts of pleasure throughout the day – tasting something delicious, laughing at a cartoon, hearing the hum of the car as it starts, catching a glimpse of the sky, getting a smile from our child, having a really good conversation, finishing a job well. And, we are correspondingly unhappy if we are experiencing too many hassles – an ache in our shoulders, being stuck in traffic, being treated rudely by somebody, doing a very boring task, ruminating over a mistake we have made. If these experiences are intense enough, they can trigger a positive or negative mood lasting for hours, or even days.

Again, it is the balance between the positive and negative experiences that counts in our judgement of our happiness.[2]

## *Happiness and the unconscious self*

Our more persistent temperamental and personality characteristics affect our happiness.

- Are we optimistic or pessimistic?
- Trusting or cynical?
- Hopeful or sceptical?
- Sociable or reserved?
- Are we interested and engaged in lots of things or easily bored?
- Do we like challenges or avoid them?
- Do we persist with things or give up easily?
- Are we forgiving or do we hold grudges?
- Are we highly reactive to what is happening around us and to us, or are we calmer and imperturbable?

These determine patterns in the way we think and make judgements about ourselves and our lives and whether we are happy and satisfied.

## *Happiness and the higher self*

At our higher level of consciousness, we are making judgements about the overall quality of our lives.

- Do our lives have purpose and meaning?
- Do we feel that we are good people – having what most other people around us define as a good life, and contributing to a good life for other people?
- Are we using our unique talents and strengths and doing what we were put into the world to do?
- Are we living in a society that enables us, and the people we care about, to meet our basic needs and fulfil our potential?

★

Happiness or unhappiness, satisfaction or dissatisfaction, emerges from the interaction of all these different levels, and there are very complex feedback loops between them. At the most basic level, our emotions, physical responses and thoughts are all tightly linked and all loop back on each other.

Take one example – how our facial expressions affect our feelings and thoughts. In a remarkable study, women who had been clinically depressed for long periods, and whose depression had not responded to a variety of treatments, were injected with Botox. This had the effect of smoothing out the frown lines on their faces. As a result of this treatment, the women were physically unable to adopt the characteristic facial expressions of distress. Two months later, 90 per cent were no longer depressed and the remaining 10 per cent had significantly improved.[3]

This is not an argument to have Botox injections if you are depressed. But it *is* an argument to take seriously the power of simple actions such as changing your facial expression or posture. In the same way, both temperament and the state of society can exert a 'downward' effect on how the events of the day are interpreted.

So, if happiness can be experienced and influenced by all these different aspects of our selves and our lives, it also follows that learning to be happier can start anywhere.

Now, let's take a more detailed look at each of the ingredients of happiness.

## *Genes*

Each of us is born with a particular biological predisposition to happiness. This has been described as a 'set point' to which we keep returning, similar to many other biological 'set points' that we inherit, such as the tendency to be fat or thin.[4] For example, some of us inherit a susceptibility to depression – if somebody closely related to us suffers from depression, we have a higher *probability* than the average person of becoming depressed.[5]

At the very deepest level of self, our genes influence our brain function and psychological make-up in ways that affect our happiness. In particular, they influence how the brain processes the hormones that govern mood. Scientists are getting closer to identifying precisely how this works. For example, people with a particular variation of one specific gene react more strongly in the parts of the brain that regulate emotion, including the amygdala. When they are exposed to minor stress, they ruminate and worry more in response.

This gene also influences the levels of serotonin – the 'antidepressant' hormone – in the brain.[6] But this is a two-way street. When we take vigorous exercise serotonin levels are raised and we feel happier. We can even experience a rush of endorphins and feel a 'high'. Pumped up by adrenaline when facing a big challenge, we are capable of suppressing pain and discomfort.

A lot of what we know about the effects of genes on happiness and personality comes from twin studies, particularly what are known as the Minnesota Twin Studies – studies of identical and non-identical twins, some reared together and some apart. These studies were an ingenious way of examining the different effects of nature and nurture. If happiness levels were completely influenced by genes, we could expect that the identical twins would show equal levels of happiness whether they were reared together or apart. If happiness levels were totally determined by the environment, we would expect that twins reared together, whether identical or non-identical, would show similar happiness levels.

What the Minnesota studies showed was that while there were different levels of happiness among the four sets of twins, about half of those differences were due to genes. Identical twins, even though they were reared apart, were more alike in terms of their happiness levels than non-identical twins who had been reared together. In other words:

- genes significantly influence our characteristic emotional responses to life, and
- we have reasonably stable patterns of happiness.[7]

While we may experience boosts in our happiness levels after major achievements – and dips after experiencing setbacks – these are short-term reactions, and we revert to our characteristic genetically determined level.

More recently, happiness researchers are beginning to describe our predisposition to happiness not so much as a set point, but rather as a potential *range* for happiness.[8] So, suppose the absolute capacity for happiness ranges from 1–10, some people have the potential to experience happiness in the high range of 6–10. When they are very happy, they are ecstatic. Others have a somewhat lower potential range – maybe 3–5. For them, being very happy is experienced in a lower register – say, being quietly satisfied.

What *is* under our control is where precisely we are in our range day to day, and whether we practise trying to reach the top of our particular range as frequently as possible.

Remember, the effect of genes on happiness is not direct. Rather, genes predispose you to respond in a particular way emotionally, to seek out particular experiences, or to act in a particular way. Most particularly, they predispose you to pay attention to certain things and not to others.

This means that if you manage to change how you direct and use your attention, you can significantly increase your happiness levels. That is why I have devoted Chapters 9 and 10 to managing your attention.

## *Temperament and personality*

Your genetic tendency to happiness is mediated through the basic temperament you inherit. That temperament, in turn, shapes your personality, including your predisposition to experience negative or positive emotions frequently and intensely – to be moody and cranky, or to be cheerful. One of the best-researched and most influential theories of personality has identified the so-called Big Five personality traits (introduced briefly in Chapter 5):

- extroversion
- neuroticism
- openness
- conscientiousness
- agreeableness.

Of the Big Five, extroversion and neuroticism have the most influence on your level of happiness.[9] In fact, both these aspects of personality are *more* important in determining happiness and life satisfaction than the things that happen to you in life – good or bad.[10] If you are lucky enough to be born extroverted and also with a low tendency to neuroticism then, to some extent, you have won the happiness lottery – although, of course, life circumstances do matter as well.

Being extroverted strongly relates to happiness because extroverts are naturally sociable, enthusiastic and self-confident – and engaging actively with a variety of people is one sure route to happiness. This does not mean that introverts are unhappy. Rather, they tend to experience fewer positive emotions on a day-to-day basis, and they feel them less intensely than extroverts. But, as you saw in Chapter 6, introverts who were prevailed upon to do what extroverts do naturally actually became happier.

The unfortunately named 'neuroticism' (which erroneously suggests a psychological disorder) is the predisposition to self-doubt, guilt, worry and rumination – all of which decrease happiness.

Does that mean that those with this predisposition are inevitably going to be unhappy?

No.

What is important to remember is that a tendency to be negative is a *predisposition,* not a life sentence. All of us have inherited some less than perfect characteristics – a tendency to be clumsy, or stammer, or write illegibly, or put on weight easily, or be shortsighted. We take it for granted that to perform well or look good, we have to learn to manage these 'imperfections' or compensate for them in other ways. The same is true if we are inclined to dwell on the negative. The trick is to learn to manage rather than be overwhelmed by this natural predisposition. Someone with a tendency to neuroticism needs to become attuned to their own nature. They can learn how to manage it better – and, in particular, how to tackle their tendency to rumination.

We can also cheer ourselves up by considering that this predisposition to worry and guilt is unlikely to have survived throughout evolution unless it served an adaptive purpose. People with this characteristic almost certainly serve a vital function in human society by possessing an exceptional sensitivity to threat – alerting the rest of us to possible danger – and an exceptional sensitivity to the bad consequences of negative behaviour. It may be a hard road for them, but they also sensitize the rest of us and humanize society at large. Perhaps their most precious gift is to human culture. Among the ranks of artists, poets and highly creative people are many individuals who are exquisitely sensitive to human suffering and can transform that sensitivity into great art.

Even though the Big Five personality traits are generally 'set' by about the age of thirty, their intensity is also influenced by changing life experiences. For example, conscientiousness and agreeableness tend to increase throughout early and middle adulthood, as life responsibilities at home and at work increase, particularly caring for young children. And – good news for women – neuroticism declines in adulthood. The self-doubt and agonizing that characterizes adolescent girls and young women – most probably as they struggle to understand and deal with romantic relationships – gives way to a sense of personal competence in their thirties and forties, and they become markedly less emotionally dependent.[11]

In a more general way, when the Big Five work together in harmonious balance, you are more likely to be happy. If one trait is overdeveloped, it can create problems. The best way to manage this is by strengthening another trait. For example, if you have a tendency to perfectionism, you can work on toning down your conscientiousness by strengthening your capacity for openness. If you are so intensely engaged with people that you are disposed to get into frequent conflicts with other people, you can work on developing your disposition to agreeableness.

It's not just who we *are* that matters for our happiness. The way we characteristically *think* about the world is also highly significant – and easier to change.[12] Thus a thinking style that is open and mindful will significantly reduce stress and increase happiness. An expectation that you can control events in your life and be energetic about pursuing your goals has a big impact on happiness, as does a disposition to be optimistic.

These issues will be dealt with in more detail in later chapters.

## *Life circumstances*

What about your life circumstances? For example:

- age
- gender
- education
- appearance
- ethnicity
- socio-economic status
- marital status
- having children
- health
- religious beliefs.

How do they effect your levels of happiness?

Considering the amount of time, effort and attention we give to bettering and managing our circumstances, the answers to these questions contradict many of our cherished beliefs about what will make us happy. Study after study has shown that many of these life circumstances have a small-to-zero correlation with happiness.

### *Age*

Let's start with the good news.

In a society obsessed with youth and the fear of ageing, age has only a small effect on happiness – and that effect is not what you might think. Happiness *increases* with age, with older people more likely to be happy and satisfied.

Now for the bad news.

You may have to go through a few less happy years before you get there. A recent major study shows that in middle age, from mid to late forties, levels of happiness and life satisfaction dip to their lowest, and depression and psychological distress are at their highest.[13]

This happiness dip happens to men and women, whether they are married or single, rich or poor, have children or not. From Boston to Berlin, Brazil to China, Azerbaijan to Zimbabwe. This unhappiness does not happen all at once but seems to come on slowly, and you only emerge from it in your early fifties. But, as this study reveals, your happiness starts to increase from then and by the time you are seventy, providing you are physically well, you are as happy and psychologically healthy as a twenty-year-old.

This dip in happiness is not very big in absolute terms, and there is lots of individual variation, but the average dip is still significant – about a third as distressing as losing your job. Other independent studies have shown that there is also an increase in depression and psychological distress in middle age, manifested in symptoms such as losing sleep from worry, feeling constantly under strain, believing that you can't overcome difficulties, feeling unhappy, and losing confidence in yourself.

People in middle age may experience this low period because of the nature of stresses in their lives – the 'midlife squeeze'. Many people, particularly women, are carrying a heavy load of responsibilities: trying to juggle simultaneous and competing demands from work, teenage children and their own ageing parents. They begin to feel that they are writing the chapters in other people's lives and have lost the plot of their own story.

But middle age also presents the natural moment to do some stocktaking on your life – an opportunity to think about where your life is going, and where you want it to go. Middle age is also the time when you have accumulated a lot of valuable life experiences and have learned to trust your own judgement. You are now able to reflect in a new way on your patterns of feeling, thinking and behaving and how they are affecting your capacity for happiness or standing in the way of flourishing.

### *Gender*

The evidence on whether women or men are happier is mixed.[14] However, there is consistent evidence that women experience emotions more intensely and express positive feelings more openly than men. They laugh and smile more, but they are also more susceptible to negative moods – to feeling anxious, sad and guilty. They are more vulnerable to episodes of depression and anxiety. Males tend to 'act out' their distress by excessive drinking, drug use or antisocial behaviour, or by withdrawing from intimate relationships – strategies that put them at risk of many adverse health outcomes.

These gender differences emerge in early adolescence, with girls showing a dramatic escalation in the risk of depression and anxiety between the ages of eleven and fifteen. These difficulties mainly arise as adolescent girls struggle to understand and manage their relationships – particularly with their mothers – and, above all, their relationship with teenage boys.[15] They feel *responsible* for managing the quality of those relationships. When difficulties arise, women and girls characteristically respond by what is called 'silencing the self' – that is, silencing their own desires and needs in the relationship in favour of maintaining closeness. They are highly attuned to the needs of others, but not to their own.

The secret for increasing happiness for women and men is twofold.

Women need to learn how to achieve a better balance between their own needs and the needs of others in relationships. They also need to find ways of managing the intensity of their negative emotions while making the best of their positive feelings.

Men can substantially increase their happiness by lifting their self-imposed restriction on where and how they feel they can express their positive feelings of love, joy, appreciation – particularly in close relationships. They also need to find ways to manage their impulse to 'act out' strong negative feelings in destructive ways, and they should resist the temptation to withdraw from intimacy when stressed.

### *Beauty and physical attractiveness*

Being tall makes men slightly happier, and being very attractive makes young women more popular. That's about it. Attractive people may be happy with the way they look but this does not translate into feeling happy more generally. Indeed, how you *actually* look has little to do with how happy you are – it's how you *think* you look that counts. In experiments where people's attractiveness is rated by objective observers, those who perceive themselves to be attractive and are satisfied with their appearance are found to be happier – despite the fact that they are not regarded by other people as being particularly attractive.[16]

Worrying about how they look frequently causes women a great deal of personal distress. They are convinced that if only they could lose weight, fix their nose or change the size of their breasts, they would be significantly happier. This conviction has given rise to an exponential growth in eating disorders and cosmetic surgery. While many women report an immediate boost in happiness after cosmetic surgery, this is likely to be temporary and can become addictive.[17]

Needless to say, it is very important for your general appearance (and self-esteem) to live healthily, keep fit, and look well cared for. But the evidence is clear for women: you could spare yourself an enormous amount of time, effort, money and angst trying to beautify yourself – *and* feel significantly more attractive – if you invested the same time and effort in learning to be happier.

### *Health*

When people are asked to judge the importance of various domains in their lives, 'good health' gets the highest rating. While it is true that people who report themselves to be healthy are also happy, the important word here is 'report'. This is because when people's health is objectively assessed, the correlation between people's *perception* of their health and their actual health is often quite low. In other words, people who are objectively suffering from health problems can also be very happy – if they *perceive* their health to be good. Perhaps this is because happy people are more inclined to take a positive view of things, even when they are sick – and, as we saw in Chapter 6, they cope more effectively with any health problems so as not to allow them to interfere with their levels of happiness.

This is not to say that chronic and severe health problems don't depress people's levels of happiness – particularly among the elderly, when increasing health problems may interfere with mobility, independence and opportunities to socialize. But, having said that, it is remarkable how well most people cope with even the most serious health problems. For example, in one study of patients who suffered from very disabling conditions, an impressive 88 per cent said that they were 'somewhat satisfied' or 'very satisfied' with their lives, compared to 90 per cent of the healthy comparison group.[18]

The lesson to be learned from these studies is that we should not assume that unhappiness will inevitably follow if we are unfortunate enough to suffer health problems. Rather, we should remind ourselves that how we think about health and illness is more important for happiness than our objective condition.

### *Marriage*

Well, this is one area where the evidence, at first glance, seems pretty unambiguous. The association between marriage and happiness has been replicated over and over again.[19] Married people report greater happiness compared to those who have never married, and those who are divorced, separated or widowed. Married people also report less depression, less anxiety and lower levels of psychological distress. Studies that follow couples over a number of years show that when people marry, their mental health improves substantially – especially for men. When they separate or divorce, they suffer substantial deterioration in their emotional well-being and show increased levels of depression.

What about non-married couples who live together?

Many studies have found that couples who cohabit are usually somewhat less happy and more likely to break up than their married counterparts.[20] This pattern holds true in the USA, but in some European countries – for example, in northern Europe – this is not the case.

However, before we get too carried away with the benefits of marriage for happiness, a few caveats must be entered. Just *being* married will not guarantee happiness, even though it will make it more likely.

First, the happiness boost of finding someone to love and getting married wears off. A large-scale study which tracked the life satisfaction over fifteen years of 25,000 people in Germany found that happiness levels did indeed increase around the time of the wedding. But, over time, people went back to the level of happiness they had enjoyed before they married.[21]

Second, people in unhappy marriages show more psychological distress than single people. There is some evidence that this is particularly true for women.[22] Feeling lonely and unloved in a marriage is a sure-fire route to unhappiness.

The importance of being married versus being single for your happiness probably depends on a lot of factors, such as the stage of life you are at, how society views being single and, crucially, the number of close friends you have. For example, there is very good evidence that people who never marry – particularly women – fare very well psychologically because they generally have positive, enduring and important relationships with their friends.[23]

We can conclude, then, that while being married makes it more likely that you will be happy, and contributes to your happiness, it is no guarantee of happiness.

Many other factors will determine your overall level of happiness.

### *Having children*

Most people believe that having children is the greatest source of happiness in their lives. But while children provide a deep sense of purpose and meaning in our lives, they do not make us happy in a day-to-day way. Many studies have now confirmed that marital happiness declines dramatically after the birth of the first child, dipping to its lowest point when the children reach the teenage years, rising again to relatively high levels (in some studies near honeymoon levels) in the empty nest stage.

But, you might argue, the parents may be pretty dissatisfied with each other and the general state of marriage, but they are probably very happy when they are actually taking care of their children. Well, no again. Studies that tapped into mothers' 'real-time' feelings (which are much more accurate than retrospective accounts) as they carry out the ordinary routines of the day show that they experience fewer moments of happiness when looking after their children than while preparing meals or even doing the shopping.[24]

### *Friendship*

The number of close friends you have and how often you socialize with them is strongly associated with being happy and satisfied with your life. The word to pay attention to here is 'close' – meaning supportive. Friends who consistently drain and undermine you reduce rather than increase your happiness. People experience a more positive mood when with their friends than with their family, or when alone.

Why are they more positive when spending time with their friends, rather than their family?

Because being with family often involves being responsible – doing household tasks, taking care of children, tending to elderly parents, feeling obligated to attend extended family gatherings – whereas time spent with friends is usually freely chosen and frequently involves leisure and relaxation.

Ease at making new acquaintances, involvement in social organizations such as clubs and sports teams, and generally being socially active also increase your happiness substantially – and all these positive effects are even stronger if you are extroverted.[25]

How happy or depressed your friends are also counts for your happiness. You can 'catch' the mood of your friends, a phenomenon called 'emotional contagion'. If one of your close friends is happy, this boosts your happiness by 15 per cent. Even if a friend of a friend is happy, it still gives you a 10 per cent boost. Amazingly, the happiness of someone at three degrees' remove from you – a friend of a friend of a friend (who you may not know directly) – will give you a 6 per cent boost in your happiness. This may not look like much, but bear in mind that a substantial income increase of about €8,000 will only deliver a 2 per cent boost to your happiness.[26]

The emotional contagion can also work negatively, most seriously in the case of epidemics of suicide among adolescents. Boys who have a friend who committed suicide in the previous year are at triple the risk of considering suicide themselves, and are twice as likely to actually make a suicide attempt. For girls, the risk of considering suicide is slightly lower but the risk of attempting it is the same.[27]

Investing in personal relationships pays big happiness dividends. But the word to watch here is 'investing'. Just 'being' married or 'having' friends will not make you appreciably happier. But investing time and effort in improving the quality of your relationships certainly will.

### *Intelligence and education*

Like having children, being intelligent and well educated confers many benefits in life. But, unfortunately, happiness is not one of them – at least, not directly.

However, those fortunate enough to have a good education can generally command more resources, which helps them cope with the challenges of life. It also makes it more likely that they will have more interesting and satisfying jobs.

### *Work*

Having a job or career that you like and find satisfying significantly increases your happiness. Stimulating work is enjoyable in itself, and being at work brings with it a whole new set of colleagues, friends and opportunities for social interaction – and regular opportunities to achieve and rise to challenges. It is also true that people who are generally happy with their lives are also more likely to be happier with their jobs.

But much more important than your job satisfaction is whether you have a job at all. Being unemployed has a devastating effect on happiness. Loss of a job is not just loss of income, but loss of status, identity and social interaction. People who are unemployed – particularly for long periods – experience greater distress, lower life satisfaction and higher rates of suicide than those who are employed. The more committed someone is to work, and the more their identity is bound up with their job, the greater the personal distress brought on by unemployment.[28] This is a particularly strong argument not just to create jobs but also to provide strong and sophisticated support services to the unemployed to help them maintain their psychological well-being.

### *Leisure*

What people enjoy as leisure has almost no bounds. Being actively involved in leisure activities that you enjoy has a very positive effect on your happiness levels.[29] Listening to music, especially for music lovers, reliably raises your spirits. Sports and exercise are particularly effective for boosting happiness levels. The case for regular aerobic exercise in terms of increasing happiness and well-being and reducing clinical depression and anxiety is particularly strong. The fact that many leisure activities involve interacting with other people also adds to their happiness potential. And for some people who become deeply engaged in their interest or hobby, it provides them with an alternative identity.

Many people enjoy watching television as a way of relaxing. But heavy television viewing is not psychologically rewarding: Afterwards, people feel lethargic, passive and less alert. However, the most serious negative effect of watching a lot of television is that it interferes with active social engagement with other people – which is one of the strongest predictors of happiness.[30]

### *Religion*

Being religious is associated with being happier, especially when this is expressed in actual religious behaviour, such as attending church services. But this effect is less marked in European countries than in the USA. In a survey of 163,000 people in 14 European countries, 84 per cent of those who attended church once a week were 'very satisfied' with their lives, compared to 77 per cent of those who never went.[31] Being religious makes people happier for many reasons. It provides a framework of meaning for people in their daily lives, as well as during major life crises. It also offers a collective identity and a reliable social network of like-minded people who share similar attitudes and values.

If you have religious or spiritual beliefs, your level of personal commitment to those beliefs, the nature of your relationship (formulaic or deeply felt) with God – or with a higher power, however you conceive that higher power to be – all affect the amount of happiness you will derive from those beliefs. But, from a scientific point of view, the consensus seems to be that it is the strong social support the churches give to their members that mainly accounts for the positive effect of religion on happiness.

However, there are downsides. Being highly religious, particularly in a small community of believers, can exert a lot of pressure on individuals to conform, lessening people's capacity for self-expression and personal autonomy. So, for example, the negative effects of highly stressful events such as a marriage break-up or the discovery of sexual abuse can be exacerbated by social disapproval or exclusion from the faith group.

### *Income*

People with higher incomes are a little bit more satisfied with their lives than those on lower incomes. However, studies of how high earners actually live their lives reveal that their day-to-day happiness levels are no higher, and their negative mood somewhat higher than those who are less wealthy.[32] At an individual level, a study that followed people over a ten-year period found that people's happiness stayed much the same irrespective of whether their income went up, went down or stayed the same over the ten years.[33]

Since increased income can buy so many advantages in life – nicer houses, a higher standard of living, easier access to good schools and medical care – how come it does not deliver a lot more happiness?

And how come most of us persist in believing that if we were given a 25 per cent pay increase, we would be much more satisfied with our lives – even though people with incomes which are now at that higher level are not, in fact, any happier or more satisfied with their lives?

One reason is that it is *relative* income – how much we earn compared to our peers – rather than *absolute* income that affects our happiness. If we feel that we should be earning more, or we expected to earn more than our colleagues and friends, we will feel unhappy – irrespective of how much we are earning. Similarly, if we are earning much less than we expected to earn, or earned in the past, this also negatively affects our happiness.

It is the human tendency to constantly compare ourselves to others, and jockey for position, that drives our desire for more money and the status that goes with it. We are even prepared to take a hit in our actual income if doing so would allow us to earn more than our peer group – and, even more so, a rival group.[34]

So, the lesson is clear.

From the point of view of increasing your happiness and life satisfaction, it is better – once your income can meet your basic needs – to devote your energy to reducing your status anxiety and your urge to compare yourself to others. When you have money to spend on luxuries, consider spending it on things that will reduce frequent sources of stress and friction in your life. For example, pay for extra help in the house. Or move house, so that you reduce long commutes to work – a significant source of chronic day-to-day stress. But also consider donating some of that money to a charity or cause that concerns you. This act of kindness and social solidarity will bring with it a guaranteed burst of happiness – and help make a happier society.

### *Social class and ethnic group*

In general, social class has only a small effect on happiness levels.[35] However in countries where there is greater class distinction and more inequality, social class has a more marked effect. Those who think of themselves as belonging to a high social class have higher levels of happiness and satisfaction than those in the lowest rungs of society.

In so far as social class has an effect on happiness, part of the explanation, of course, is that those from a higher social class generally have better jobs, better housing, better marriages (less separation and divorce) and, significantly, more leisure. Middle-class people have more friends. Working-class people socialize more with their extended families. This has implications for happiness, as friends are a much bigger source of happiness than relatives.

Being a member of a minority ethnic group in society has a small but negative effect on happiness, usually because members of ethnic minorities have lower incomes, a poorer standard of education and less-skilled jobs. Much depends on the type of society. Living in a racist and intolerant community can destroy the happiness of minorities. Living in a tolerant, welcoming society negates the unhappiness effect of being in the minority.

### *The kind of society we live in – what we value*

In general, living in an economically prosperous, politically democratic society, with access to a free media, to education, and to other health and social services is associated with higher levels of national happiness. Freedom for women is particularly important, seeming to operate as a proxy for individual freedoms. In other words, societies that enable women to enjoy more personal freedoms are generally also free in other important respects – for example, in terms of civil rights and the freedom of the press.

People who strongly desire money or material goods tend to be unhappier than those who are less materialistic. Ironically, in a celebrity-obsessed age, the pursuit of fame or image is not associated with increased happiness. The least materialistic and image-obsessed people report the most satisfaction with life, perhaps because an acquisitive lifestyle interferes with other life goals. It uses up energy that could be put into family, friends and community, which are very strongly related to happiness.[36]

Living in a hyper-consumer culture also creates its own stresses. Much as we value choice, too much choice actually diminishes well-being. The ethic of individual choice and control is one of the most powerful currents in modern society, and we are increasingly judged by the quality of the choices we make. With so much choice, there is less tolerance or forgiveness for failure, and no hiding place (in particular for personal failure) – 'only yourself to blame' is the unwritten price for personal choice.

We are under pressure to put increasing time and effort into decisions, even about trivial things. This creates worry – in case we make the wrong choice. Being a 'maximizer' – trying to make the very best possible choice about work, relationships, holidays, clothes, leisure, home decorating – can create an exhilarating sense of excitement and control, but if overused it can tip us into feeling more tired, more anxious, more worried, more overwhelmed, more regretful, more disappointed, more frustrated and more depressed. And less satisfied with the outcomes.

As one researcher put it, we end up doing better but feeling worse.[37]

The solution is to aim to be a maximizer only in areas where the quality of your choice is really important. As for the rest, learn to be a 'satisfier' and aim to make a good choice that you can live with – rather than the perfect choice – and get on with more important things in life.

## *The happiness treadmill*

How can we account for the fact that so many of the things in which we invest so much time, effort and psychological effort deliver so little by way of happiness?

The explanation is what happiness researchers call the 'hedonic treadmill' – or what ordinary mortals might prefer to call the 'happiness treadmill'. This refers to the phenomenon that major boosts or dips in our happiness due to changes in life circumstances tend to be short-lived. We adapt to our circumstances.[38] And that is why, alas, as soon as we have achieved an improvement in our income – or in our work, or in anything else – we soon get used to it and begin the search for something else, something more.

Our capacity to adapt is undoubtedly good news when it comes to dealing with adverse circumstances. But it is bad news when it comes to hoping for happiness by improving our life circumstances.

This raises a fundamental question: Why do we persist in trying to improve our life circumstances in the hope that this will make us happy?

Part of the answer is that, while we long for happiness as the 'whole aim and end of human existence',[39] we also have our other basic drives to contend with. We are instinctively motivated by our drive to achieve, to accumulate material wealth and improve our status and the status of our family. And short of a general retreat from life, we are going to continue doing that. We are also going to continue believing that having children will bring happiness and that, whatever we may think about any other couple exchanging wedding vows, our love will last for ever.

As psychologist Daniel Gilbert of Harvard University explains, these drives produce results that are good for families and whole societies – so everybody conspires (including ourselves) to make us believe that we will be happy if we do all these things.[40] These intuitive beliefs – although based on shaky evidence, to say the least – lead to good economic and social outcomes for society at a general level. They keep us working hard to change and improve not just our own economic and social circumstances, but the lot of society in general.

However, beyond a modest level, it is clear that investing huge time and effort in trying to increase our incomes and improve the material conditions of our lives will not deliver greater levels of happiness.

So, are we doomed to run endlessly on the happiness treadmill? Doing ever more, only to go right back to our set point?

The good news is that we are not.

In 2005, Sonja Lyubomirsky of the University of California, Riverside, along with colleagues Ken Sheldon and David Schkade, asked the question: Are we doomed to march endlessly on the happiness treadmill?[41]

Drawing on the extensive research literature, they attempted to quantify the effects of the three major factors that determine happiness:

- our genetic inheritance
- our life circumstances, and
- our 'intentional activity' – things we choose to pursue in life (including the way we choose to think and behave).

As expected, they concluded that about 50 per cent of happiness is heritable. Some life circumstances – being married, having a good job and an adequate income, being healthy, being religious – each matter to happiness but, added all together, they account for just 10 per cent of overall happiness. The remainder, a full 40 per cent of happiness, derives from our intentional activities – things we consciously and freely set out to do.

What these percentages mean is that, if I picked a random sample of people, all with very different life circumstances, and could magically arrange for everybody to be given the same set of life circumstances – the same age, marital and social status, the same quality lifestyle, the same state of health etc. – you might expect that, depending on their starting position, the differences in people's levels of happiness would be substantially reduced or increased.

In fact, they would be reduced or increased by no more than a mere 10 per cent.

You can do nothing to change your genetic make-up – at least, not yet – although you can make changes to the way in which you manage your temperament and personality. Trying to achieve happiness by improving your life circumstances will contribute only modestly to your happiness, and putting all your eggs into that particular basket will condemn you to be on the happiness treadmill for ever. But a full 40 per cent of your potential for happiness lies in your own hands:

- what you choose to attend to in your life
- the way that you choose to think
- the activities that you choose to engage in day-to-day
- the goals that you set for yourself and pursue.

As the researchers put it: 'Circumstances *happen* to people, and activities are ways that people *act* on their circumstances.'

These intentional activities can be major 'life projects', or they can be small projects that focus on changing a particular way of thinking or behaving. Lyubomirsky calls it 'the 40 per cent solution' to achieving happiness.[42]

So, the key to increasing your happiness and to flourishing in a sustainable way is to take hold of that extraordinary and heartening finding.

Shape your own personal 40 per cent solution through the projects you engage in.

Over the next chapters, I will be suggesting what these might be.

## STRATEGY TWO

# *Set yourself goals*

'The best prize that life has to offer is the chance to work hard at work worth doing.'

Theodore Roosevelt

# 8. Take on three life projects

A key element of flourishing is the ability to rise to a challenge. Turning a challenge into a personal project is an example of flourishing in practice. Having life projects will significantly increase your feelings of happiness and satisfaction, providing you with structure and meaning in your life, giving you a sense of direction and personal control – all key factors in enabling you to achieve and maintain the magic positivity ratio for flourishing.

The exact nature of the life projects does not matter greatly. They can be big or small: turning a whole business around or starting an initiative in your own area of work; planning to relocate your whole family abroad or helping one child in a very specific way; raising money to start a local theatre or trying your hand at acting in the local drama group; getting fit or working to help your favourite political party get back into (or stay in) government; reducing your golf handicap or trying to save the planet from global warming. Your life project does not have to be significant in any public way. Indeed, it can be deeply private, something that matters only to you and may be noticed by nobody but you. You don't need to be battling for the future of a business, or for some noble cause. You can simply be battling for somebody you care about, or even for yourself. But whatever it is, just making it into a personal project lends it real significance and a quiet heroism.

Best of all is to have a range of projects:

- one that relates to your work
- one that relates to your family or friends, and
- one that relates to a personal interest.

## *Life projects in action*

Before delving a little more into the psychological thinking that explains why having life projects is good for you, let me introduce you to a number of people who show how this works in practice. These are examples of successful but very different life projects ranging over work, family and more individual concerns.

*Eamonn: 'Making the impossible possible'*

Eamonn Sinnott, Intel vice-president and the plant manager of Intel Ireland, always seems to have several projects on the go in his life. He brings a kind of vital energy to whatever he does; he is clearly flourishing in his life and also runs a flourishing business. The Ireland Intel plant is regarded as one of the most successful of the worldwide network of Intel 'Fabs' which manufacture computer chips. This is no mean feat, given the strong competition between factories. He has no difficulty coming up with examples of life projects. Some were initiatives he took on voluntarily, out of interest or passion. Interestingly, however, he chose to describe a project that arose out of necessity – underlining, again, how flourishing so often arises in response to a challenge.

> One of the biggest challenges I faced was when we had to ramp up our factory to full capacity. We needed all the equipment to perform significantly better than it was doing – all the way from a 30 per cent level at the time to more like 70 per cent. Was it doable to expect that this would happen in the time frame that was required? Absolutely not! My boss at the time offered the following, now immortal, words of advice when I explained the magnitude of the challenge: 'Good luck!'
>
> I can't say in truth that I 'chose' to pursue that goal. It was a must-do in many ways. I had no option but to take it by the scruff of the neck and turn it into a personal mission. Was what we were trying to do reasonable? No! I'm reminded of the George Bernard Shaw quote: 'The reasonable man adapts himself to the world; the unreasonable one persists in trying to adapt the world to himself. Therefore all progress depends on the unreasonable man.'
>
> But isn't 'doable' just a state of mind? Nobody thought what we needed to do on the equipment performance was really doable. Perhaps, better stated, nobody knew what was 'doable'. But the success of the factory depended on it. The success of the factory was one and the same as my success. So, with that burning need to be successful, off we went.
>
> I sought advice from wherever I could. I knew about the impact

of 'lean manufacturing' techniques.[1] We took on those techniques with a vengeance; everybody got behind them. To cut a long story short, we were not only successful but have continued the performance improvement to this day, blowing way past any and all operational challenges that were set for us.

Personally, I learned a great deal from this experience. Henry Ford said something like: 'If you believe you can or if you believe you can't, you're right.' Well, I'm not sure about that; but there is a grain of truth in it. When I look back on it now, on that project, I can see that I needed to have more belief that I – or, rather, we – could achieve that goal. To this day, whenever I am presented with something that I initially think is difficult or impossible or whatever, I ask myself: 'Is it really just about believing that I can?'

When I look back, I feel a bit annoyed with myself that I wasn't more certain that we could achieve it. That's what makes a leader. I keep reminding myself that I need to learn more and more about how to be less realistic about the future, and to save that realism for the present.

### *Susan: 'Getting my daughter over the threshold'*

Susan is an energetic and cheerful working mother with three children ranging in age from six to sixteen. She has a demanding job, yet manages to live a full and flourishing life, investing time and energy in her job and her family life, but also working to keep in regular touch with her women friends. She has at least three life projects on the go at any one time, but chose to talk about a family project.

My daughter Nan was starting secondary school. I knew it was going to be difficult for her to move from the small all-girls national school she was attending, where most things were organized for her, to a large, mixed secondary school. She would have to take responsibility for organizing herself in a completely different way, as well as make new friends, deal with boys, and study. Not to mention coping with puberty. It was a big agenda for a thirteen-year-old. She's a really great kid – very hard-working, but very disorganized.

At the time, I was really busy myself at work. I was in my new job only eight months and was still trying to establish myself. My husband was also really busy and under a lot of pressure at work.

But I decided that this year was going to be a crucial one for our daughter, and I decided very consciously to devote time and effort to making this transition as easy for her as I could. To get her safely over the threshold. I suppose, looking back on it, it qualifies as a 'life project', even though I did not think of it in those terms.

It was really hard. I couldn't tell you the number of times she would call me from school telling me she had forgotten something crucial, like sports gear, or her art material, or even her lunch money – even though I tried to get her to check these things the night before. And sometimes I had to down tools to fetch stuff for her and deliver it. Initially I would be exasperated and annoyed, but then I would remind myself of why I was doing this. I would say to myself: 'This time in her life won't come again. I won't always be able to help her in this direct way with the challenges she will face as she gets older. But I can help her now, and it will count.' Then I would feel much happier about doing whatever I needed to do.

I spent a lot of time at weekends just chatting to her. Even though it started out as an effort, it actually became something I looked forward to. I really got to understand how she was changing, and how she was thinking, and just what an interesting person she was turning out to be. I tried to make a point of us all going out together on Sundays so we could have some connection point in the middle of our busy lives.

And it worked.

Really, by the middle of her first year of secondary school, she had found her feet, she had made friends, she was doing well at school and she was even reasonably organized. I think she felt very supported and loved. I know that some of her friends had a hard time of it that first year. So I don't regret a minute of all that time. Apart from helping her, I felt much better about myself. I used to say to myself: 'You know what? You're not a bad mother!'

### *Sarah: 'The "adding ten years to my life" project'*

Sarah, a quiet reserved woman, runs her own business which she built up single-handedly and is the centre of her life. She is also an intrepid traveller, each year venturing into ever more exotic and remote areas. Surprisingly, she chose not to describe her many projects at work or travelling. Instead, she focused on her project to add ten years to her life.

Two years ago, my life was going really well – or so I thought. Then I went to the doctor for something trivial and she suggested having a general check-up. We discovered that my blood pressure was really high. She told me starkly that either I took myself in hand, changed my diet, lost weight and started becoming more active, or I almost certainly would suffer a heart attack or stroke. I was really shocked. For a while, I did nothing. Then I decided that I had to take responsibility for myself and make my health my number one priority.

My first goal was to get active. I started small. I got up an hour earlier each morning and jogged around the neighbourhood for thirty minutes. I went at barely above walking speed. It was agony! I was in a lather of sweat after five minutes and I thought that my chest would burst with the effort of breathing. But I kept it up – rain or shine, busy or not busy. After six months, I had graduated to jogging at a reasonable pace for forty-five minutes. Any time I felt discouraged or demotivated, or just felt like staying in bed, I thought to myself: 'You're going to spend the whole day doing things for other people. This is your chance to do something for yourself.'

The fitter I became, the more aware I was of the weight I was carrying. Almost without effort, I began to become much more conscious of how much I was eating, and so it was easier to cut down. Every time I was tempted to eat something I shouldn't, I told myself: 'You will have to carry the effect of all those extra calories around tomorrow on the run.' Interestingly, at this stage I became really interested in the whole fitness thing and I decided to join the local running club. At first I could hardly keep up, and was trailing way behind. But I found just being with other people raised the game for me. I became much more motivated to get really fit, and I found that the other club members were really supportive. So it became much more of a group enterprise. I ran my first mini-marathon exactly a year later.

Now running and the club have become hugely important parts of my life. Not just the physical fitness any more – even though I have lost 17 lbs and my blood pressure is normal. Now, I work on my fitness because it makes me feel really good about myself. I am a more relaxed person. I do what I have to do more effectively. I feel more energetic and motivated about things in general. That part of my day is now really important to me.

## *Understanding the psychological architecture of projects*

Meaningful projects have a recognizable momentum:

1. needs
2. goals
3. values
4. emotions
5. action.[2]

The more closely all the links in this chain are connected, and the more keenly aware you are of those links, the more motivated you will be – and the more effectively you will pursue the project.

Eamonn, Susan and Sarah all had different goals. They were motivated by different values. But they all had the essential links in the chain, most particularly the strong, positive emotional investment.

### *1. Needs*

Each of the 'needs' that drove the life projects I've outlined above could have been driven by negative emotions – anxiety, irritation, guilt. But Eamonn, Susan and Sarah, each in their own way, focused on the positive emotions aroused by the need – pleasure, excitement, love, caring, achievement.

### *2. Goals*

In order to thrive, human beings have to keep setting and pursuing goals. At the most fundamental level, your brain is a machine designed to pursue goals and to monitor what progress you are making in achieving them. In fact, the essence of intelligence is the pursuit of goals in the face of obstacles. 'Without goals,' says Steven Pinker, 'the very concept of intelligence is meaningless.'[3]

You might well ask: 'If we are wired to achieve goals, why do we need to turn them into projects? What is the difference?'

Well, there is an important distinction between the two.

Most of the time, life chooses our goals for us; they arise from basic human needs. We have to take care of our physical needs for food, water, rest, warmth. We have to fulfil our psychological needs for basic pleasure, for self-esteem, for status, for relationships with other people. And then there are the more general goals that come at different stages of the life-cycle: becoming more independent of our parents; finding someone to love; taking care of children; advancing to a more senior position in our career; taking care of our elderly parents; finding a renewed purpose in retirement.

Achieving these goals is simply coping with the basic needs of living.

You can do what's required in a routine or dutiful way – that brings a certain kind of satisfaction. To flourish, you have to turn a few of these goals into personal projects. But you will flourish only if you actively *choose* to take on the challenge. Instead of going through your day (and your life) being poked and prodded by necessity, you too can take that need 'by the scruff of the neck' and put it firmly in front of you.

This is a profound change in perspective. Instead of reacting, you act freely.

But there is another distinction – goals become projects when they are driven by a strong personal value.

## *3. Values*

Needs and goals are the seedbed – the necessary, but not sufficient, condition for any life project.

At any one time we have any number of needs. What motivates us to turn one of them into a project?

The answer is: our personal values.

If we valued everything equally at any given moment, we would be unable to make a decision about which path to follow. Each of us has a set of personal values, but we each arrange those values in a unique hierarchy. Without a hierarchy of values, we simply could not make any choices.

Take an average Saturday morning for you, as a working parent:

- Your son wants you to spend time with him. You know you *need* to do that.
- You also feel really tired. You know you *need* to catch up on your sleep.
- You are also under pressure to finish a work project that is overdue. You *need* to do that.
- You have taken no exercise for a week. You also *need* to do that.

So, how do you decide which need to follow? It is your internal value hierarchy that will determine what you eventually choose to do. What is the value that is most important to you: caring for somebody, work achievement, or caring for yourself?

Of course, you will try to juggle all of those values, but there is still an underlying priority that determines what you do first and how much time and effort you put into it. What you prioritize – the things you choose to spend your time and energy on – reflect your true hierarchy of values, not what you say your values are. We often obscure this choice by ignoring what we say we value and pursuing something which we tell ourselves we 'have to' do.

When a goal becomes fused with your most cherished value, it becomes a personal project. Now, there is a lot more riding on it than just getting the job done. Eamonn says, 'The success of the factory was one and the same as my success.' Getting the job done was closely linked in his mind with the high value he puts on personal achievement. For Susan, getting her daughter over the threshold was driven by the value she puts on being a caring person, and also a competent parent. For Sarah, her strong value on taking personal responsibility – a value that also drove her business success – infused her personal project to get healthy.

Values are not airy-fairy theoretical concepts that are the preserve of preachers – religious or corporate – and worthy discussion programmes. Values are immensely practical. Your motivation for a life project may originate in a need, but it is your values that determine what you choose to turn into life projects.

### *4. Emotions*

Emotions are the real lifeblood flowing through projects. Thankfully, nature has arranged it so that when we are making progress towards a goal, we feel happier, more satisfied with our lives and more personally fulfilled. In fact, a large part of how we feel day-to-day about ourselves and our lives is profoundly influenced by where we judge ourselves to be in relation to our personal goals. We are constantly monitoring whether we are achieving what we set out to achieve, what progress we are making, and often also comparing where we are in relation to our peer group. Having a life project that we are fully engaged in delivers regular happiness boosts, because it puts our happiness under our own control.

Emotions are also intimately linked to our values.

At the most basic level, how do you actually *know* you are acting out of a value?

You know it, because you *feel* it.

It is your emotional reaction that reflects and signals what you truly value. When you feel excited and interested in something and you are eager to engage more with it, it is because it is related to what you value. I always feel happy when I am learning something – from what I am doing, from other people, from books and research – because understanding new ideas is one of my core values. On the other hand, I generally feel bored when trying to fix machines of any kind because solving technical problems is low down on my value chain. The only exception is anything to do with cooking – I will happily learn how to use any cooking device, because I value good cooking and good food so highly.

Emotions also signal your distress when something violates, or does not connect to, what you value – you immediately feel an impulse to withdraw or avoid it. If you put a high value on security, you will react negatively to any project involving risk – no matter what the possible gains are. Even more strikingly, you will become upset when your values are under threat. If integrity is a top value for you, engaging in or even hearing gossip will be upsetting, and the immediate impulse will be to withdraw from that conversation.

You certainly will not thrive in any project that violates a core value.

So, emotions provide the reward of pleasure when you achieve or live your values – and the punishment of pain when you don't. Thus, you feel good when you are doing things that reflect or promote a deeply held value, and you feel bad when you are ignoring or acting against a core value.

And this applies to *everybody*– not just people who profess to have values. It is part of our nature.

If caring for your family is top of your value hierarchy, it will feel right and often pleasurable to do that. If achievement is your top value, then you will experience a surge of pride when you finish something and a surge of anxiety when you don't. The more important the value is to you, the stronger your positive emotional response when you are working towards it and the stronger your negative emotional response when it is under threat. Without emotions, values would be experienced as dry, abstract and intellectual concepts.

Finally, as Sonja Lyubomirsky and Ken Sheldon have shown, we don't get used to the pleasures of pursuing and achieving our goals as rapidly as we do to the pleasure of improved life circumstances.

There is no treadmill effect.

This is particularly true if we strive to keep the effort and activity involved fresh, meaningful and positive.

### 5. *Action*

Finally, there is action.

Without action there is no project – there is just aspiration. Your goal has to be turned into a set of practical sub-goals – plans and strategies to achieve the outcome you want.

You have to get started, keep going and know when to stop.

Here, again, emotions are your best friend. Knowing the facts – the rational reason why something should be done – may convince you that you should act. But it is your emotions that supply the impetus and the motivation to get going and keep going in the face of obstacles.

And it is your emotions that signal when you have reached your goal.

## *How to choose a life project*

In the light of what you know about the psychological architecture of projects, and keeping in mind the examples described above, let's set out and take a look at the criteria for choosing a worthwhile personal project.

- It must be freely chosen.
- It must mean something to you.
- You must believe that it's doable.
- You have to set goals in relation to it.
- You must put in enough time and effort to achieve those goals.
- You must have adequate resources to pursue it. (The main resources are your personal commitment, and your ingenuity in relation to making things happen.)
- There must be a reasonable chance (but not a guarantee) that you can achieve your goals in a specified time. (That 'reasonable chance' of success is to be found in your own mind – in your commitment and enthusiasm – rather than in objective fact.)

### *A project that is freely chosen*

Ideally, a project is something you want to do.

My husband, John, is an avid gardener. And, like most gardeners, he is forever planning projects to improve the garden. He is so happily engaged with each project that, before he goes out to work in the morning, he walks around the garden, noting what is blooming (and thanks to his planning there is something blooming every month of the year). When he comes home from work, and again before he goes to bed, he repeats his routine.

John's is a life project that is pure choice.

All of us, with some thought, can choose projects like that. You will learn more about such projects in the chapter on vital engagement (see Chapter 15).

But I am going to concentrate on projects that are more bound up with the iron obligations of life, because so much of our life is like that. So, in the examples given by Eamonn, Susan and Sarah earlier, their projects were not initially freely chosen. As they showed, the key to transforming a necessity or duty into a life project is turning what you *have* to do into what you *want* to do. Eamonn Sinnott's observation captures this mental transformation: 'I had no option but to take it by the scruff of the neck and turn it into a personal mission.'

The first, and most difficult, step in this transformation is to stop fighting what you have to do and to focus strongly on what you *can* do.

Second, you have to realize that both together – what you 'have to do' and what you 'can do' – are the best possible, and perhaps the only possible, action that can be taken in the circumstances, given the needs of the situation.

The third step in the transformation is to *embrace* what you need to do. I really mean 'embrace' – metaphorically putting your arms around the project and surrounding it with an active, positive and caring energy. In a manner of speaking, the project becomes your baby. That is the act of *committing* yourself to something.

That process of commitment may happen in seconds, or over a long period. It may even happen without you being aware: you may plan to do something small, but see with some surprise that you have become deeply committed to a much larger project than you had realized.

This is important to remember, as we often feel daunted when we hear of people successfully completing very big projects. We think: 'How could I take on something that big?' But remind yourself that the successful person you admire may not have initially realized the scale of the challenge. The great upside of commitment is that, once made, it boosts motivation and mobilizes enough energy to get the job done.

You grow to match your commitment.

### *A project that is personally valued and meaningful*

Choose a project that resonates with what you truly value. That way, you will be more motivated and committed to it. However, it also works the other way round. Once you commit yourself to something, that something automatically assumes meaning and value for you just because of that investment. It becomes bound up with the way you define yourself.

We all experience this phenomenon in a trivial way, day to day. We start doing something relatively unimportant – trying to fix something or solve a crossword puzzle – but the more time and effort we invest in it, the more importance it assumes.

This transformation is particularly likely when the project you choose is a good personal 'fit' with:

- what really motivates you
- your core values, and
- your personal strengths and interests.[4]

So, it's worth considering those elements in determining how you choose your life projects.[5]

#### WHAT IS MY BASIC PATTERN OF MOTIVATION?

We all have three basic psychological needs: for connectedness to other people, for autonomy, and for expressing our valued competencies. But we each have our own individual mix of these three needs, and this must be taken into account in choosing a project.

Some people put a lot of emphasis on connectivity, others on autonomy. The more directly connected your projects are to your individual pattern, the more likely you are to flourish. But it can also work the other way round. If you are somebody who puts a very high value on autonomy and working on your own, involving yourself in a project that calls for a lot of connectivity can add a whole new dimension to the way you think about yourself and the way you work.

Best of all are projects that combine the three things. They:

- connect you more strongly to people
- give you the opportunity to act independently, and
- enable you to do what you are good at doing.

Sarah's running project started off as an act of autonomy ('I knew I had to take charge of my health'). The very act of running soon became a means to carve out a piece of the day for herself – another act of autonomy. Along the way, it also met her need for expressing her valued competencies ('Once I put my mind to something, I am very determined!') and ended up connecting her to other people in a very enjoyable way.

### WHAT ARE MY CORE VALUES?

You may know right off what your core values are. Or you may have to think for a while. Most people start to answer that question in very general terms: family, hard work, honesty, success.

But what we *say* are our values are sometimes not the real values that motivate how we act. The real values may be hidden, even from ourselves. Most values – conscious or otherwise – originate from three sources: early experiences in the family, early experiences of personal success, and early experiences of loss or deprivation.

It helps to clarify what your real values are if you ask yourself three questions.

1. When you were a child, what was the most reliable way to get your parents' attention, love and respect?
2. What brought you your biggest successes, particularly in early adolescence as you tried to establish yourself as your own person?
3. What did you feel most deprived of in childhood and adolescence?

If you reliably got your parents' attention (positive or negative), approval and love by achievement, then achievement is likely to be high up in your value hierarchy. Or it may have been helping others, or being well behaved and conscientious, or always trying to please. As a child, you do what you can to survive – and your parents' attention, approval and love are what you need to survive. Gradually, all these early survival behaviours become transformed into your values.

You also learn your values by copying what your parents value. Of course, you can rebel against those values. But the evidence is pretty strong – by the time you get to adulthood, you will most likely be similar to your parents in terms of your values, although you may express them differently. Your mother may never have worked outside the home but was a perfectionist about how she performed her household duties. You may be working in a totally different domain but find you are just as much of a perfectionist.

Most of all, whatever brought you early success or a feeling of uniqueness in adolescence is likely to be transformed into a core value. The job of adolescence is to find and create a new identity, so any experience that helps you do that has great meaning attached to it. For many adolescents, an early success in a particular academic area – in sport, in a volunteering project, in helping a friend, in being popular in a peer group, in fixing things, in artistic work – can function to create core values of high achievement. This may translate into 'being a team player', 'being a leader', 'having a good time', 'being a problem-solver', 'being a thinker'.

Finally, what did you feel most deprived of in childhood and adolescence? Was it love? Independence? Affirmation? Being treated fairly? Social status in the community you lived in? Financial security? Personal achievement? A sense of really belonging to a peer group? These losses are keenly felt, and we often spend the rest of our lives seeking to find what we did not have in childhood, trying to plug that hole in ourselves. Whatever we lacked becomes a core, driving value.

When you have answered the three questions, you will find out how you have crystallized the core experiences in your life into your core values. These values will tend to remain top of your value hierarchy – even though they may be outside your conscious awareness.

In later years, you may come to reflect on these values and change them. This sometimes happens at major life transitions: the end of adolescence; or when you become a parent; or during a personal crisis. At these transition points, you may find yourself dissatisfied and unhappy with the way your life is going and begin to question the values that are driving you. Or you may feel you are now at a turning point – when you have the opportunity to shape your life in the way you want to, rather than the way you have had to up to now.

But however it happens, the change is often a matter of reinterpreting your core values in a more positive way, rather than replacing them completely. For example, you may reinterpret success as being not just about earning lots of money but also being of real service to others.

Changed or unchanged, the more your life project is allied to your true values, the more you will enjoy it and the more successful it will be.

### WHAT ARE MY SIGNATURE STRENGTHS?

Most of us are aware of our 'signature' strengths, what we think of as uniquely characteristic of ourselves.[6] Many of these originate in our genes and our temperament – natural fluency, empathy, the ability to think spatially, open-mindedness. But some emerge from and are honed by our efforts to pursue our values.

Ask yourself a version of the three questions above.

1. What strengths and talents did I develop as I tried to get my parents' attention, approval and love?
2. What strengths or talents did I find in myself as I tried to establish myself as my own person in adolescence?
3. What strengths and talents did I develop as I tried to secure what I was most deprived of in childhood and adolescence?

Again, like values, the more your life project utilizes these unique strengths, the more enjoyable and successful it will be.

### WHAT ARE THE KINDS OF ACTIVITIES THAT GENERALLY MAKE ME HAPPY?

You can most easily answer that question by looking at what genuinely interests you. For example, extroverted and highly sociable individuals do better and feel happier when they choose a project that involves interacting with other people.

Some people enjoy the intimate rather than the sociable aspects of relationships. For them, selecting a project that involves working closely with one other person is more likely to make them happy and keep them motivated, rather than a project that involves joining a group.

Some people derive great pleasure from intellectual activities – projects that involve thinking, reflecting, analysing, planning. Others love more physical 'hands-on' activities.

One of the reasons that older people are generally happier than younger people is because they have developed the experience and ability to select more enjoyable life projects.[7]

### *A project that is doable*

In reality, we very rarely know for sure whether something is doable until it's finished. While we need a minimum level of resources to embark on a project, it is the so-called 'softer' factors – belief, passion, high expectations of yourself and others and, most of all, optimism – that actually make things happen.

Eamonn captured that mix of realism and optimism that is required for a successful project. From where he was standing (the present), he was crystal clear and realistic about the scale of the challenge he had to face and what was required to deal with it. But he was also aware of the equally realistic need of the factory to survive and compete in the future. So, mentally positioning himself in the future gave him a different perspective as to what was required to get there – an *unrealistic* leap of faith and optimism.

It was that potent emotional mix of realism and optimism married to a strong personal commitment to make it happen that made the project 'doable'.

### *A project with specific goals*

Before you embark on a life project, you must be clear about the outcome you want or have to achieve. Otherwise, you will lose focus and motivation. Even if your project is a very ambitious one that is likely to take a long time, such as setting out to transform the culture of an organization or to transform how things have always been done in your family, it is critical that you set goals and sub-goals that need to be achieved within certain time limits – a month, a year, a three-year period – even though these targets may have to be adjusted now and then.

Sometimes, you can't do this at the beginning. You don't know enough. But once you engage with the project, the sub-goals start to emerge. Unless you set time frames, you deprive yourself of one of the critical components of a successful project (and a critical component of happiness) – getting regular feedback as to whether you are succeeding or not. In some projects, the feedback is obvious. In other projects, this may be more difficult.

For example, setting out to support a teenager making the transition to secondary school is potentially a vague project. But Susan formed a set of goals and sub-goals: giving reminders to her daughter in the evening; helping in a practical way when the reminders did not work; setting aside time on Saturday; planning family outings on Sunday. Even though she did not articulate how she judged whether she was succeeding along the way, almost certainly she had a certain set of criteria in mind and a particular way of monitoring success – for example, by carefully observing her child's progress in making friends in her new school; by monitoring how she was doing in her schoolwork; by listening carefully to how she described her days in the school and tracking her moods day to day.

Assuming that you have the required basic skills and personal commitment, the higher you set your goal, the better you will perform. A goal that is set too low generates low effort and low performance. But, however ambitious the project, the more specific the goal and sub-goals, the better the result.

The only way to eat an elephant is bite by bite.

### *A project carried out with the required time and effort*

When you freely commit yourself to something, you are creating an unconflicted state of mind. The actual tasks involved become more meaningful, and therefore more bearable, even enjoyable. In the absence of that commitment, the work can never be made easy enough.[8] Everything is an effort.

One of the greatest obstacles to confident and successful action in any domain of life is ambivalence – simultaneously 'wanting' and 'not wanting' to do something. Ambivalence fatally traps your energy and generates a host of negative feelings – anxiety, guilt, resentment, boredom, annoyance at yourself. These feelings are reflected, in turn, in half-hearted action or inertia. Making a commitment, on the other hand, mobilizes all your internal resources to respond – including your will, your thoughts, your feelings, your memory, your creativity. It brings a sense of coherence and internal unity, as all your energies are now heading in the same direction.

And best of all, this happens automatically, without you having to think about it.

Your brain goes into goal-mode.

### *A project that you have adequate resources to pursue*

This is perhaps the rock on which most projects perish.

There is a minimum requirement for every project we undertake in life. When it comes to the material resources we will need to get the project going – money, equipment – we usually make a reasonable estimate of what is needed. But when it comes to more subjective resources – for example, the amount of time we will have to give it – we often seriously underestimate what is required.

When choosing any life project, it is vital to keep competing projects in mind. Choosing projects that are in conflict with each other – for example, creating a work project that will entail long hours at work, and at the same time setting out to spend more time with your children – is a recipe, not for flourishing, but for increasing stress.

Bear in mind that the most valuable resources you will need are not necessarily material ones, but are far more likely to be psychological – for example, somebody who will encourage you or support you in your efforts. You may need many different kinds of support: emotional support, advice, practical information, somebody to 'open doors' for you. Count up those resources when you are deciding what project to choose.

But perhaps the most valuable resources are those within yourself – if you can psychologically connect to them. That is why it is crucial to take the time to do the 'Your Best Self' exercise that I described in Chapter 1 – to recall in a systematic way the successes you have already clocked up in your life, however minor and in whatever domain, and to psychologically reconnect to the personal resources that enabled you to achieve those successes. Those personal resources have not gone away. They are still there, still available to you. They may just need to be dusted off and brought back into commission.

*A project with a reasonable chance (though no guarantee) that you can achieve your goals in a specified period of time*

This is important because human beings like a beginning, a middle and an end to something. It is very daunting to commit ourselves to a project requiring significant effort with no end in sight. In fact, when we do, it is often a way of fooling ourselves, because with no end in sight, it is very difficult to measure progress.

The critical thing here is 'reasonable chance'. That is as much an emotional as a rational judgement. Optimism is as important as due diligence in making that assessment.

When you follow these guidelines, and pay attention to the basic architecture of life projects, you will significantly increase the positive side of the flourishing ratio. In the most immediate way, you will be happier. In fact, personal projects satisfy nearly all the needs of the conscious self – exercising your skills, feeling in control, expressing your values, personal interests and personality, meeting your needs for connectivity, autonomy and using your most valued competencies.

Not only that, but personal projects also meet some of the needs of your higher self. Projects provide structure and meaning in your day-to-day life. And, as you will learn in Chapter 16, feeling that your life has meaning is a very significant part of flourishing.

We can all too easily become trapped in a blur of 'busyness' that is disconnected from any vital purpose or intention, or we may feel trapped by inertia. We are all susceptible to feeling like a stick in a river – either caught up in an uncontrollable current, or stuck going round and round in a sluggish eddy. Having deliberate life projects provides us with a boat, complete with oars or an engine, which we can use to navigate the river and get to where we want to go.

When you have clear life projects, they constantly connect your moment-to-moment activities to form a coherent course of action that has a purpose and that makes sense to you. You can connect what you are doing in the minute – poring over data, helping with homework, or pounding the treadmill (boring and demanding activities on the surface) – with the positive purpose of your project, with its real value and significance for you. In that way, you transform a negative into a positive.

Projects also strengthen resilience and help you rebuild your life after major setbacks – losing your job or your business, a failed relationship, a grievous loss of one kind or another. There is good evidence that these experiences can serve as a catalyst for creating and committing to a new 'life project', by forcing us to search for new ways to give structure and meaning to our lives.[9] In fact, the art of giving up goals that are no longer possible and establishing new ones is one of the foundations of resilience and happiness.

The very act of thinking of a new meaningful project will immediately increase positive feelings and personal control.

The more adverse or extreme our circumstances, the more important life projects become. The accounts of people who had to recover from appalling injuries, or who survived long-term incarceration in prison, or even concentration camps, show that despite their loss of physical freedom, they maintained their psychological freedom and spirit by setting and working on daily 'micro-projects' for themselves.

In less extreme circumstances, creating micro-projects also helps us cope.

If you feel that you have lost all control over your day, take on an item from your endless 'to do' list: tidy your desk or a cupboard; sew on a button; pay a bill; book a theatre ticket. (But don't be tempted to telephone a call centre or your insurance company – you need to be in the full bloom of your psychological health to take on those 'projects'.)

The benefits of projects also apply to personal relationships, to teams and to organizations. When friends and partners are mutually engaged in collective projects – planning a holiday, doing something new together, pursuing a goal – it brings a sense of vitality to the relationship, it deepens their engagement with each other, and it builds their capacity for cooperating with each other and weathering setbacks together.

Similarly, the best teams and organizations are those who are constantly identifying, planning and delivering joint projects. Yet, astonishingly, many teams and organizations are not defined in any meaningful way by the projects they are engaged in. The most ineffective and demoralized teams are those who just talk – ostensibly working towards some goal, but in reality having no definite purpose or direction. The most effective organizations are those whose mission and strategy are clear, lively, engaged, and immediately translated into individual and team projects, so that every single person in the organization knows their precise contribution and their worth to the organizational 'life projects'. Indeed, unless somebody knows and feels that, they are either being poorly managed or their role is actually meaningless and redundant.

Whatever life project you choose, and however well planned it is, there are times when you get discouraged or even bored. It is easy to start off with a burst of optimism on any project, but you must also learn how to keep going.

Here are four strategies that have been identified as helping people to keep going on projects:

- keep 'owning' the goal
- concentrate on making it enjoyable
- keep a balance, and
- remember the big picture.

Creating variety in what you are doing – whether it's varying the level of challenge, or the pace of activity, or the people you involve – is one way to keep a project fresh and enjoyable.

It also helps to vary the 'weight' of each of your chosen projects. If you're engaged in a high-pressure project at work, consider taking on something you've been meaning to do for yourself, or with your family, that has a lighter and more fun side to it. Try to maintain a balance between projects so that you can develop your physical, emotional and intellectual functioning.

If you do that, not only are you more likely to succeed, you are also more likely to feel happy and to experience a significant increase in self-esteem, self-efficacy and well-being.

In short, you will flourish.[10]

## STRATEGY THREE

# *Control your attention*

'What we are today comes from our thoughts of yesterday, and our present thoughts build our life tomorrow: our life is the creation of our mind.'

Buddha

# 9. What you pay attention to becomes your life

Attention is probably our most underestimated capacity and, paradoxically, we pay remarkably little attention to how we use it.

But we should.

Attention is a crucial gateway between us and the world around us, between the events that happen *to* us and what happens *in* us. It is not the stream of events in the course of the day that registers in our consciousness; it is only what we pay attention to. What registers in our consciousness then determines what we *experience*. So, our experiences of the day are not the things that happen to us. Rather, our experiences are what we *create* and *recreate* by how we direct our attention and our thinking throughout the day.

As the days pass, those accumulated experiences become our life.

Therefore, paying attention to how we pay attention is a crucial step in learning to flourish.

We wake up every morning with only a limited quantum of attention – the psychological currency of the day. How we use that currency has a very significant effect on how the day goes – and how life goes. Whatever we pay full and careful attention to gets noticed and gets done. Whatever we don't pay attention to languishes. The power of full, undivided and devoted attention can, and often does, move mountains.

If we can obtain control over the way we use our attention, we can achieve a very large measure of control over our minds and over our lives – over how we feel, how we think and how we act in the world.

One of the most efficient men I know, senior Intel manager Sean O'Reilly, is fond of referring to his 'daily units of attention' – units he guards and spends with great care.

Some of our units of currency are already spoken for. They have to be spent on meeting the daily needs of survival: eating, commuting, meeting obligations, the practical tasks of living and earning a living. But that still leaves a lot of currency in the bag.

Do you want to use those remaining units of currency on things that you neither want nor value?

Do you want to spend them carelessly, without even noticing?

Or do you want to spend them on the things that *you* choose?

Your answer is crucial in determining the kind of life you're going to have.

Think about a really good day you had recently, a day that was satisfying and happy. You may remember a day when you relaxed completely or one when you achieved something important to you – whether it was finishing a work project, having a meaningful conversation about something you were worried about, organizing your wardrobe or your files, solving a bothersome technical problem, playing a lively game of tennis, or reading a good book on holiday.

Now recall a day when you felt unhappy and deeply dissatisfied. You may have been engaged in exactly the same type of activities – but, somehow, nothing worked. Your efforts to achieve anything never got off the ground. Or you felt listless, unable to relax but equally unable to motivate yourself to do anything else. At the end of the day, you felt deeply frustrated.

Since nobody sets out to have a bad day, the question is: How do you manage to have such days?

The key difference between a good and a bad day is that on good days you manage to focus your attention and act *intentionally* – whether or not you actually do what you set out to do. On good days you spend your units of attention in the way you want and intend. You do not get distracted. Not a minute of your day is wasted – yet you feel relaxed and happy throughout the day. Gaining control over your attention allows you to unite your will, thoughts, feelings and behaviour into a single effective force.

A good day is when your 'executive self' is acting like a good manager should – in charge, paying attention to all the right things, setting goals, making choices and taking decisions. By contrast, bad days are when you are *reacting* constantly – to external events, to your own distracting thoughts and feelings. Indeed, you often have no idea at all what you are reacting to.

Increasingly, we find ourselves in that kind of uncontrolled reactive mode, our attention scattered to the winds.

## *A new disorder – Attention Deficit Trait*

Most of us have no idea of the stress and suffering endured by those with the condition known as Attention Deficit Hyperactivity Disorder (more commonly known as ADHD) – a neurological disorder with a strong genetic component. People with this condition have a constant struggle to control their attention because it is so easily captured by external distractions and by internal negative preoccupations, creating a host of problems for them in trying to manage their work and their lives.

Edward Hallowell is a leading expert on the clinical disorder ADHD, but his research is showing that a growing number of adults with no neurological disorder are being driven to behave in ADHD-like ways. They are experiencing an inner frenzy of distractibility, impatience, difficulty in setting priorities, staying focused and managing time. Edward Hallowell calls this ADT – attention deficit trait.[1]

There is a fundamental truth about attention: you can only pay attention to one thing at a time. We *know* that we can't talk to a child, type a report, answer the phone and remember to make a list all at the same time, because each of those activities uses up most of our capacity for attention in the moment. But this does not stop us from trying. Women especially like to believe that the laws of attention do not apply to them. They pride themselves on their ability to multitask. While it is true that women are better than men at multitasking, what they are actually better at is *switching* their attention rapidly and smoothly from one thing to the other and back again.

However, there is only so much switching you can do before you overload your brain circuits. This phenomenon of ADT is now being driven by the frantic, multitasking world in which we all live – a world that creates a kind of brain overload.

Your working memory – the amount of information you can keep track of at any one time – becomes overwhelmed. As Hallowell vividly puts it: 'When you are confronted with the sixth decision after the fifth interruption in the midst of a search for the ninth missing piece of information of the day, when the third deal has collapsed and the twelfth impossible request has blipped unbidden across your computer screen, your brain begins to panic . . .'[2]

He is describing the typical experience of an overloaded business person or manager. But this could just as well describe a similarly pressured teacher, call-centre worker, junior doctor or parent. Instead of your attention acting like a spotlight so that you can focus on what is happening, you are using your attention more like a weak torch, waving it around aimlessly in a very agitated state. It never settles on anything long enough or steadily enough for you to actually *see* anything, nor for your mind to focus and engage fully with it.

In that overloaded state, your negativity bias is triggered and your tendency to pay more attention to the negative becomes even more exaggerated. The brain goes into crisis mode as you try to get the situation under control, often acting in a 'mindless' way, dancing more and more to a tune that you can't even hear. Every memo, every task, every email, every reaction and interaction appears like an incoming missile, sending you spinning in one direction or another. Your attention is fragmented and your capacity to understand what is actually happening, to stay connected to the big picture and to the goals you had intended to pursue, is fatally undermined.

You go into meltdown.

In a world where attention is under ever-increasing pressure, your executive self has a harder and harder job controlling your most precious resource – your attention.

It pays, then, to understand exactly how your attention works.

## *How attention works*

At every moment of the day, you are being bombarded by information coming at you – from sensations, thoughts and emotions *inside* you, and from the stream of events happening in the world *outside* you. You would be overwhelmed by it all if you allowed all of this into your mind. So, your brain has set up access routes, ways of processing all that information traffic.

Your conscious attention route is the most direct way that you allow information access to your brain. It is this capacity – what psychologist Steven Pinker calls the 'narrow, movable window'[3] of attention – that allows information to enter your conscious mind and be processed in the most complex way. Conscious attention can take three forms, and your executive self needs all three working together smoothly if you want to flourish.[4]

- The first is *alerting attention*. This is the kind of attention that keeps you mentally open and ready to respond to what happens throughout the day – to threats and to opportunities.
- The second is *orienting attention*. This is the ability to orient or direct your attention so that you can select out the important information from all the rest.

- The third is *executive attention*. This is the ability to devote your attention to getting things done – to planning, to making decisions, to overcoming obstacles (including old habits or mindsets) and to learning new responses, particularly in conditions that are difficult or complex.

When all three kinds of attention work together, you get optimal functioning. You have a good day.

The more you train your mind to attend to the right set of signals, and to filter out irrelevant information, the more you succeed and excel in any area. That is the essential nature of expertise. People who are experts in any area of life – parents, technical experts, highly skilled clinicians, technicians, lawyers, communicators, or artists – *notice* things that other people don't pay attention to. Their attention is automatically directed towards picking up and interpreting particular sounds, words, images, facial expressions and reactions. They also automatically filter out what's not relevant to the task at hand.

People who are flourishing have mastered how to do this. They have learned to control their attention and to achieve what they intended. The more they can focus their attention, the more they can weld their thoughts, feelings, intentions and will into a single effective force. The result is a feeling of being 'together', of being in control and happy.

In order to do this, you need to understand something very important about how attention works.

While the conscious attention route leads you to where you want to be, it is not a free road – it exacts a toll on your inner mental resources. And the problem is that attention feeds off that same basic resource as a lot of other important mental processes do.

## *Attention is easily depleted*

Every day we not only have to pay attention to things, we also have to:

- concentrate hard on some things
- avoid distractions
- manage our impulses
- resist temptations
- keep going in the face of obstacles
- make choices.

These are what are called 'heavy' mental processes. All these activities require self-control and all draw on a common inner resource of brain energy that is limited and easily depleted. Psychologist Roy Baumeister and his colleagues have shown just how heavy a toll such heavy mental processing takes on us – particularly our capacity for exerting self-control or willpower.[5] Baumeister has come to the startling conclusion that we can call on this inner reserve as little as 5 per cent of the time.

However, we call on this resource much more often than we think in the course of a normal day.

In a series of intriguing experiments, Baumeister and his colleagues have shown that the smallest exertion of self-control leaves us psychologically depleted and impairs our performance, including our ability to pay sustained attention.

### *The effort of concentration leaves us depleted*

We are all familiar with the depleting effects of having to concentrate hard on something.

After listening to a complex presentation, writing a detailed report, helping a child with homework, sifting through bills or listening to a friend's problems, we feel mentally exhausted. Not only are we unable to concentrate on something else afterwards, but we find ourselves unable to summon up the energy to take the initiative or take action on anything, *especially* if it requires making any effort.

Any parent, teacher or manager, stressed after a long day, knows the feeling.

Somebody is nagging you for something. You know you should say no, but you just go along with it because you feel too depleted to muster the energy to resist.

Baumeister showed that even the most minimal effort is too much for us. In one experiment, people who had just concentrated on a problem-solving task felt so oppressed by the resulting inertia that they subsequently kept watching a boring film, unable to rouse themselves to press a buzzer to stop.

### *Acts of self-control affect our ability to solve problems*

Even a minor effort to resist temptation affects concentration.

The Baumeister team did an experiment where, before participating in a test of problem-solving ability, some volunteers had to resist the allure of chocolate and chocolate chip cookies, while others were free to indulge.* Those who had to resist eating the chocolate did worse on the problem-solving test and gave up much faster. In fact, a mere five minutes of having to resist a temptation reduced by *half* the amount of time volunteers spent trying to solve the problem. They also reported being more tired and having to force themselves to keep going.

Something as apparently trivial as using enough self-control to resist eating a chocolate cookie exacted a significant psychic cost.

### *Having to exert control over our feelings takes a high toll*

Every day, we have to suppress our feelings – dealing with our children, our intimate family and friends, our colleagues and the general mass of humanity. On top of all that, there is the craziness caused by demands such as having to call service providers and getting caught in the torture of automatic phone systems.

All these efforts to control our reactions exact a cost.

In experiments where people watched film clips that were chosen to evoke negative or positive emotions, those who were asked to suppress their spontaneous emotional response subsequently reported greater difficulty concentrating. They performed significantly worse in problem-solving tasks, compared to those who could freely express their feelings. That is why, if you have to sit through a meeting, a social occasion, or a family occasion where for some reason you have to suppress feelings of irritation, disappointment, anxiety – or even happiness – afterwards you will feel emotionally exhausted and perform below par when tackling problems.

* A word first about how social psychologists typically approach studying how people react. Usually in these experiments participants are not made aware of the real purpose of the study. If you want to find out how somebody reacts to having to resist temptation, and whether that will affect their subsequent ability to solve problems, you don't tell them that (in case that knowledge itself might affect their performance, making them too self-conscious, or might even become a self-fulfilling prophecy). The purpose of the study is disguised. What the researchers want to study, such as the subsequent problem-solving task, is typically presented as a non-related piece of research – for example, as a way to help the researchers collect data for a future research project.

*Just taking responsibility for making a choice depletes our inner resources*

Perhaps the most surprising of Baumeister's discoveries is that in a culture where endless choice is so highly valued and promoted, actually making choices does not come without a cost.

Take the following scenario (which is a version of one of Baumeister's experiments).

> You are asked to participate in a debate about a controversial topic close to your heart – how schools are run, or taxation, or crime policy, or the national football team. Some people in the debating team are free to choose which side of the argument they take, others are pressured to take a particular side but are told that it is ultimately their choice, and the remainder are given no choice about which side they have to argue.
>
> Afterwards, you are all given problems to solve.
>
> You might think that having *no* choice would be most the most stressful option. In fact, those who have had to make a choice – either freely or after persuasion – will show the lowest level of persistence and the worst performance in the problem-solving task afterwards.

In other words, the very act *of having to take responsibility for a choice*, even when you are choosing something that you want, depletes your inner resources.

Baumeister equates using anything that requires self-control to using a muscle. You know that if you keep lifting a weight in the gym, after a number of repetitions, the strength in the muscles you are using is rapidly and dramatically depleted. You then experience a sudden weakness – you can hardly lift up your arm, never mind the weight – and you have to wait until the muscle recovers its strength before you use it again.

In the same way, we easily use up our self-control muscle. Baumeister calls this phenomenon 'ego depletion'. Much of our problem in trying to manage our attention is explained by the depletion of this muscle. All of these small acts of self-control during the day – resisting the temptation to say something we should not, suppressing our true feelings, deciding what to do and what choices to make, trying to start or finish a difficult job, concentrating at a boring meeting – all call on the same limited mental resource that we need to call on when we are trying to pay close attention to something important.

Small wonder, then, that the executive self can process only so much information using the heavy-duty options of conscious attention.

However, nature has provided a relief route – a way for the brain to process an enormous amount of information, direct your attention and get things done without any conscious awareness.

And without using up your limited mental resources.

That route is the automatic system in the brain.

## *Being on automatic*

Think of the morning routine. Most of us get up, shower, dress, eat, gather up our belongings and start the duties of the day using very little conscious attention. We occasionally focus in a conscious way – deciding which shirt or blouse to wear, or manoeuvring the car out of the parking space and into the stream of traffic. Then, more often than not, we go into automatic. We find, to our amazement, that we are pulling up at our destination without any conscious memory of the journey – apart from those moments when we had to consciously concentrate on something.

Without any conscious effort, we have 'outsourced' our attention to automatic systems in the brain that are paying attention on our behalf to a huge range of things happening inside and outside ourselves. When we drive, our eyes are registering a stream of information about the road and the surrounding traffic. Our ears are attuned to the sounds around us, both inside and outside the car. Our muscles move without having to direct them. All the information coming in is being processed automatically in different parts of the brain, ready to trigger an extremely rapid and efficient reaction to any surprises that arise. When these surprises pop up in our consciousness, we make subtle adjustments in response – sometimes unconsciously, sometimes with only a dim awareness of doing so.

This outsourcing of attention is the automatic route in action. It is the brain's way of relieving the executive self of some responsibility. Going 'on automatic' uses little energy and requires no conscious effort. While using the 'heavy' mental processes of self-control and willpower is like driving an old banger of a car, with every gear change and turn of the steering wheel requiring major effort, using the 'light' mental processes of the automatic system is like driving a car with a powerful engine that purrs into life, with the gears shifting smoothly, silently and automatically into place.

Once we go on automatic, we are free to think and do other things. The most obvious example of this occurs when we learn a new skill. In fact, the very definition of 'skill' is that we can do something at a very high level without thinking too much about it – such as typing, or riding a bicycle, or driving a car.

The learner driver, for example, is acutely conscious of every small action and has to concentrate hard and make a series of decisions. But if a skilled driver is asked to describe what precise choices and movements they are making as they drive round a sharp bend or negotiate traffic lanes, apart from articulating some general strategies, they will have to think hard before they can describe what they are actually doing in the moment.

This is the essence of being on automatic – what we are doing does not require full conscious guidance. In contrast to the heavy mental processes of paying full attention and concentrating, automatic processes are instantaneous, effortless and use up little brain energy.

In fact, they use a third less effort than conscious thinking.[6]

Just like the expert parents, managers, clinicians and artists referred to earlier, your attention is automatically directed to the right information and away from the wrong information.

But, the automatic route is not just there to help you get skilled.

The automatic system runs the meter that is clocking up the positives and negatives that determine whether you are flourishing, just managing or floundering in your life.

It also determines to a significant extent:

- how you make judgements about people
- what attitudes you adopt
- what choices and decisions you make
- what you remember
- what goals you set out to achieve.

It does all this because it acts as a major access route for information entering your brain – without any conscious awareness on your part that you are registering that information.

This powerful automatic process can work for us and against us.

If we learn to exercise control over it, it is a powerful aid to attention – automatically directing our attention to the right things without depleting us. But if the automatic system becomes too dominant, it can hijack our precious attention.

This effortless toll-free route can lead us where we don't intend, or want, to go.

### *We are on automatic more than we think*

One of the leading researchers on the automatic system, John Bargh of New York University, has shown us that attention works by responding to cues from the environment.

In his research, Bargh presents people with words or images designed to automatically 'prime' or activate certain ways of thinking and reacting. Sometimes these cues are conscious (people see or hear a word or image on a screen), and sometimes cues are presented in a way that bypasses awareness altogether (such as a flashing word or image seen so quickly that it is only registered subliminally).

We are affected as much by unconscious as by conscious primes, and what we attend to – consciously or unconsciously – determines the subsequent choices and decisions we make and how we behave. For example, the simple act of *seeing* something automatically influences how we behave.

In one of Bargh's experiments, people were given lists of words to form into sentences. Some were given lists which included words related to rudeness. Others were given lists that included words related to politeness. The rude and polite words were the primes or cues. A third group was given lists that contained neither. Afterwards, the groups were observed as they interacted with another person. A full 67 per cent of those who were exposed to the rude words were observed to actually behave rudely, interrupting the person quickly and frequently. In comparison, only 38 per cent of those who were exposed to the neutral words acted this way, and a mere 16 per cent of those who were exposed to the polite words acted rudely.

Just seeing rude or polite words acted as a cue for people to behave in that way.

Not only are we affected by the behaviour we see in the environment around us, but we can be primed to act in the way we *think* other people act. For example, when students are primed with words such as 'elderly', 'wrinkle' or 'forgetfulness' they start to *behave* in the way they expect the elderly to behave – walking more slowly, and being forgetful. The primed students could not recall as many features of the room in which the experiment was held as could students who were not primed by those words.

You can even be primed to pursue a goal without realizing that you are doing so, by triggers that are completely outside your awareness. Moreover, you will behave in just the same way when you are in pursuit of that unconscious goal as if you had chosen it consciously. So, as Bargh has demonstrated, you may think you are simply having a pleasant conversation with somebody, but if you have been primed to judge that person (perhaps words such as 'assess' or 'evaluate' were planted in your brain in advance), that is exactly what you will do.

Yet, when questioned, you will have no awareness of having formed an intention do so.

Similarly, in problem-solving tasks, people who had been unconsciously primed to succeed significantly outperformed those who had not been so primed. Despite the fact that they were unaware of their intention to succeed, they behaved in exactly the same way as if they had formed that goal consciously. They persisted in trying to achieve their goal in the face of obstacles and interruptions. They were so motivated to succeed that, even after the signal to stop, over half of them persisted on the task.

Those who had been primed also reacted emotionally to success and failure in exactly the same way as if they had been consciously pursuing a chosen goal. If they failed, their mood became more negative and their performance was worse on a subsequent test. Only a fifth of those who had not been primed behaved in this way.

If such subtle and unconscious cues can trigger these kinds of responses, we can begin to understand the effects on us of consistent and high-intensity cues – for example, living or working in a very negative and depressing environment where we are constantly exposed to negative messages. Because of the way in which the automatic system works, we are much less able to resist the force of such messages and are much more susceptible to contagion than we like to believe.

But, the good news is that working and living in a positive and encouraging environment can automatically help us to flourish.

Bargh's findings have real implications outside the laboratory. They show that we are much more influenced by subtle cues from the external environment than we might imagine. They go a long way to explain why what were once external 'primes' – the way our parents or other authority figures, such as teachers or bosses, spoke to us – can become transformed into automatic thoughts that continue to influence our behaviour, positively or negatively.

Being frequently told, 'What's the point? You will never succeed,' or, 'Don't give up. If you persist, you will achieve what you set out to do,' become internalized as automatic thoughts that pop into our minds every time we find ourselves in a situation where there is a choice to persist or to give up – to be positive or despondent.

In Chapter 10, you will learn how to become conscious of those automatic thoughts – and how to change those that may be causing you to act in ways that are preventing you from flourishing.

## *The way forward*

The work of psychologists such as Baumeister and Bargh has revealed some of the fundamental ways in which attention works – and why it is so hard for us to pay high-quality attention to the things that we want and need to pay attention to.

The formula for success is:

- first, learn to maximize the power of your conscious attention – to widen that narrow and moveable window and bring it more under the control of the executive self, and
- second, learn to use the great power of the automatic system – in a way that helps, rather than hinders, you.

But before you start, you must become aware of how you are currently using or outsourcing your attention.

### *Become aware of how you are spending your units of attention*

Tomorrow evening (if tomorrow is a typical day) devote fifteen minutes to finding out how you actually spent your units of attention.

Divide a page into four columns.

In the first column, divide the day into hours from the time you woke up.

In the second column, opposite each hour write down what you were doing.

In the third column, note the quality of attention you brought to bear on this activity.

Was your attention fully engaged, distracted, or absent altogether?

Were you fully 'present' to what you were doing, or were you absent?

You will probably be surprised to discover that there were whole periods of time when you have no memory at all of what you were doing. You *know* you were at a meeting, or walking somewhere, or doing something. You were physically present, but psychologically absent – on automatic. With some effort, you can probably recall what was mentally preoccupying you during that time and what may have sparked that preoccupation.

Finally, in the fourth column, note your emotional state during that period – positive (happy, engaged, interested, excited, contented) or negative (anxious, sad, irritable, bored, stressed).

If being on automatic allowed you to feel positive and get things done effectively, that is fine.

However, what you will most likely find is that going on automatic is more often associated with negative feelings and preoccupations, and with less than optimal working. You were 'pretend working' – going through the motions. Your units of attention were absorbed by your negative emotions.

This exercise is worth doing – not least because it helps you switch out of automatic mode and primes your brain to be more alert the following day, to notice how your attention is being deployed or distracted. If you repeat the exercise for a few days, you may discover even more surprising things about your life – such as how little actual time and attention you may be giving to people or things that you say are very important to you.

For example, how much time every week would you say you spend one-to-one with each of your children, doing things together or really listening to them? Parents are often dismayed to find just how little.

You can do the same exercise in relation to other important people and tasks in your life.

You may say you want to spend more time thinking and planning, or more quality time with each member of your staff. So, go and find out how much time you actually spend doing those things – and how you would judge the quality of your attention when you do.

### *Gain control over your attention by exercising control over your emotions*

As you already know, your emotions exert a powerful effect on what you pay attention to and what goals you pursue. That is why emotions can capture, redirect and fragment your conscious attention in a very significant way.

You may consciously want to attend to what is happening during a conversation or a meeting, but emotions – particularly negative emotions – can undermine that attention. Feeling anxious makes you surreptitiously check your phone or your emails when you should be listening. If you feel under pressure, you may not be able to stop thinking of the next task and, as a result, find that you have missed crucial information in the moment. You then feel frustrated and unhappy, which further occupies your attention – and on it goes.

Getting control over your attention necessarily means exercising control over your feelings – reducing the frequency and intensity of negative feelings, and increasing positive feelings.

Emotions are also intimately connected to intentions. Forming an intention to do something, to pursue some goal, is not a purely rational process. Emotions play a crucial role. You may be rationally convinced that you should act in a particular way, but it is your emotions that will motivate you to do so. It is emotions such as interest, anxiety, hope, anger, enjoyment, disappointment and passion that motivate, rather than a grand assembly of facts. That is why emotional intelligence, rather than a high IQ, determines so much of your life success.

Positive emotions push you out of your comfort zone and into your stretch zone – motivating you to 'broaden and build' your attention and perspective. Negative emotions do the opposite.

Remember, the brain is designed to pursue goals – as long as you help it along. Once you form an intention to do something, your brain does the rest. You can work this 'emotion–intention' system to help expand your attention and unite it with a positive intention – a highly effective route to flourishing.

Creating such a positive purpose is the subject of Chapter 12.

### *Use the automatic system to your advantage – prime yourself*

If we can be primed by cues in the environment to behave in certain ways, we can use that capacity to manage our behaviour.

The trick is to learn to associate an external cue with the desired internal or behavioural response. That is how to build a habit – and good habits are an important part of flourishing.

Parents know the power of habit. Every time a toddler runs towards a particular door, the parent says, 'Be careful of the step. Slow down.' The toddler slows down – not always, but often enough to associate the step and the warning (the external cues) with slowing down (the internal and behavioural response). Soon the toddler forms the habit of slowing down without any warning. Just *seeing* the step triggers the desired behaviour.

In the same way, we can use the automatic system to change our own behaviour and to achieve our goals – by bringing what we intend to do under the control of external 'primes', so that we no longer have to use heavy mental processes such as willpower.

Whether you want to study for an exam, train for a marathon, finish a report, or learn to think more positively, you don't have to keep remembering your intention, or cranking up your motivation. Instead, by doing something consistently and frequently, it becomes a habit – an automatic way of responding that bypasses consciousness. The external cue can be a certain time of day, a particular room, a visual reminder – whatever works to automatically start the process of achieving your goal. In that way, you no longer have to consciously think about it.

You just do it.

That is why I try to run at the same time of the day, and why I am (uncharacteristically) meticulous about where I keep my running gear. It is easily accessible – right inside the cupboard where coats, briefcases and keys are kept. That way, every time I open the cupboard, I am reminded of my intention to run. All of these cues automatically activate my intention and put me in the right frame of mind for what I want to achieve. Eventually, even the thought of going running will start the process.

Habits, once they become automatic, are extraordinarily powerful, as illustrated by this example.

> A few years ago, in our house, we changed the way the door opened from the hall into the kitchen. This involved changing the position of the handle. It took me nearly three months to unlearn the habit of reaching out to the (now) wrong side of the door. Virtually every time I approached it, I made the same mistake. That is the power of habit – and that is about how long it takes to change a habit.

Once changed, a new habit will unfailingly direct your attention to where you want it directed.

The way to unlearn bad habits is to bring them under the power of cues from the environment. That's why little reminders, such as putting a rubber band on your wrist, or changing your watch to your left wrist, can help you resist doing things that you want to stop doing – for example, interrupting, or checking your email every few minutes – and remind you of what you need to do – for example, listening attentively, or checking your progress so far on a task.

You can also use a related technique – *preselecting* cues to attend to that will help you pursue more complex goals.

Take the goal of changing your eating patterns. Rather than stating your goal in general terms ('I will eat more healthy foods'), you need to think in advance of the cues that automatically trigger eating and then decide in a very specific way how you are going to respond to those cues ('When I eat out and am presented with the dessert menu, I will refuse it and always order fruit'). You are preselecting a cue (being offered the dessert menu) and deciding in advance how you will respond. Note how specific the visualization of the cue needs to be – actually being presented with the menu.

This makes you much less vulnerable to temptation. When you are in a restaurant, your eating behaviour is primed by multiple cues from the environment – smells, tantalizing menu descriptions, even seeing what other people are eating. When you mentally anticipate these cues and how you will respond, this makes it more likely that you will consciously attend to these cues (and their effect on you) when you are in the situation – even if your attention is occupied by other things. By mentally rehearsing your responses in advance, you are more likely to respond in the way you intend to.

This process can also be used to bring more complex behaviour under your control, such as a tendency to overreact to certain people. You can also use it to help you develop desired behaviours. For example, if you want to act more assertively, or use your influence more positively, go through the same exercise. Identify in advance the situations where you want to behave in this way (an important staff meeting) and the likely cues that will either undermine your intention (a colleague who constantly interrupts you or gets in first with suggestions) or present you with opportunities (when the agenda is being set, immediately when somebody else stops speaking, when there is a stalemate in the discussion), and then mentally rehearse your responses.

Then, when these cues appear, however fleetingly, you are ready to take advantage of the opportunity.

## *De-clutter your life*

Edward Hallowell, who identified Attention Deficit Trait, offers useful suggestions about how to creatively engineer your environment in order to manage too many demands on your attention.

- Create a positive, calm atmosphere where you work and live.
- Make time every few hours for an unhurried, pleasant face-to-face connection with somebody else.
- Get enough sleep and exercise.
- Avoid high-sugar foods that will make you even more hyper.
- Keep even a small section of your workspace clear and tidy at all times.
- Do your most important work at the time of the day when you know you function best.
- Keep a part of the day free from email, phone calls and other distractions so that you can think and plan.

When your mind is frazzled, slow down what you are doing and do something that will clear your mind – a routine, neutral task that you can do almost by rote. For example, water your plants, tidy your files, put reminders in your diary.

Follow the OHIO rule (Only Handle It Once) when you pick up a piece of paper – a bill, a letter, a report. Act on it, file it, or throw it away.

At the end of every day make a list of no more than five priorities that will require your attention the next day.

These guidelines can also be applied in organizations to enable high-quality attention. Visual cues matter: cheerful reception areas; orderly meeting rooms; relaxing spaces scattered around the building, with comfortable, colourful armchairs, if possible in front of a window, where people can sit comfortably and discuss things. All these promote a positive atmosphere that cues positive behaviour. This, in turn, makes a big difference to the productivity and work culture of an organization.

Similarly, at a societal level, seeing clean, well-maintained neighbourhoods – where every piece of graffiti is erased and every broken window fixed – cues positive civic behaviour. Indeed, these practices were fundamental to the first highly successful Zero Tolerance programmes in run-down New York ghettoes.

### *Build in recovery and renewal routines*

Your attention has to draw on the same limited inner resource as many other mental processes.

In order to maximize your available capacity, remove as many temptations and distractions as possible, and reduce any unnecessary occasions where you have to exercise self-control. Rearrange your desk so that you are not facing something (or someone) that distracts you. Avoid unnecessary encounters with people who irritate you. If you have to attend the same meetings, sit where you can't easily see them. Don't take calls during mealtimes.

But that still leaves a lot of ordinary day-to-day stresses that will drain away your precious attention, and many relentless calls on what is left.

For organizational consultants Jim Loehr and Tony Schwartz, time management is no longer a viable solution to managing those demands.[7] We can all manage our time better, but allocating a particular time slot to something won't solve the problem if by the time you get to it, you are too exhausted or distracted to deal with it properly. Based on their work with elite athletes, they have found that the best solution is the proper management of energy, not time. This requires building up routines that will expand, sustain and renew the physical, mental, emotional and spiritual energy you need in order to perform the tasks in your life.

Your aim is to maintain a rhythm between expending energy and recovering and renewing it.

This insight chimes with Baumeister's findings about how easily the brain is depleted by psychological effort. That is why recovery routines are so important, as seen in this example.

> I once worked with a very successful but highly pressured company where managers were complaining of burnout. I discovered that their attention and energy were at their lowest ebb not during periods of high pressure, but at meetings, particularly back-to-back meetings. So I suggested that no meeting should last longer than fifty minutes with a ten-minute 'recovery period' afterwards to enable people to mentally process what had happened, to clear their minds and arrive refreshed for the next meeting.
>
> Management took up the suggestion, and the results were impressive in terms of more effective engagement and crisper decision-making at meetings.
>
> Different recovery routines worked for different people. Some people liked to chat. Others liked to relax alone. Others preferred to take a quick walk outside.

At the end of a working day, when you are at your most depleted, often there is little attention left over to positively re-engage with those you love. The trouble is that your partner may be feeling the same way. If you meet each other in this state, the result is likely to be that great torment of married life – cross-complaining, or a kind of stress competition ('You would not believe the awful day I had' 'You had an awful day – it could *not* be as bad as the day I had').

It's a good idea to develop 'threshold routines' – routines that help you focus and rebuild your attention and make a calm re-entry into your private life – particularly if you have children.

Start on the journey home from work.

Find out what is the most effective way for *you* to clear your mind and lift your mood: listening to your favourite music or an audio book; humming or singing to yourself; listening to the radio; or just pure silence. In general, anything rhythmic works well to calm your thoughts and your feelings. Better still, try to walk a part of the journey. Try to avoid using up energy on phone calls; the point now is to conserve what energy you have.

When you arrive in the house, put your bag down and approach your partner or child in an attentive way. Notice whether they are waiting expectantly for you and ready to engage, or whether they are in the middle of something and not ready for interruptions.

If they are ready, *register* the encounter, make something positive of it – by sitting down together, being (even briefly) affectionate, and engaging positively with what is occupying or interesting them.

Some parents react almost with horror to that suggestion. 'What about the dinner?' they say. 'Or getting a wash on?' They say they want to get the evening routine going so that they get all the tasks out of the way and then, finally, relax. But by the time they do relax, the children are often in bed and the adults' attention is depleted.

When parents do try the 'threshold routine', they report that it really works. They can attune themselves better to their partner or child's needs and moods, so the interaction becomes more harmonious. They feel calmer and better about themselves and each other.

Offering those you love and care about the unsurpassed gift of your calm, undivided, full attention is surely the best buy for your precious units of attention.

# 10. Rewiring your brain to make the best use of your attention

Your brain learns from experience. It adapts and develops automatic response patterns.

This means that every time you see or hear something new, you don't need to expend too much time or effort trying to understand what it is. Based on your past experience – what you have stored in your memory – you jump to conclusions.

'This is a friendly face.'

'This is something I could do.'

'That is somebody I won't like.'

'This is not going to work out.'

Very often, you are right in your instant automatic reaction and need not detain yourself any further.

But not always.

If you over-rely on such automatic processing, it dulls your capacity to detect subtle differences from what you expected. You act literally 'mindlessly', without any awareness of why you are thinking, feeling or behaving in a particular way.

Neuroscientist and clinician Daniel Siegel of the UCLA School of Medicine defines living like this as 'on automatic' – overly influenced by 'top-down' brain processes that filter how you understand your experiences.[1] These automatic preconceptions, beliefs and reactions shape and sometimes overwhelm the 'bottom-up' information coming in from what's actually happening. For example, your automatic reaction to any new situation may be to fear that somebody will not like or approve of you. Or perhaps you expect that everybody will agree with you. These expectations prevent you from paying full attention, or being fully 'present', and may distort your understanding of what is *actually* happening.

Even more problematic, since many of our most embedded and unconscious expectations are formed in early life, any early experiences that are negative can trap us into dysfunctional emotional patterns and tired routines of thinking and behaving. This means we can't attune correctly to a rapidly changing environment, and our ability to think and act in a creative way is diminished.

The good news is that there is accumulating evidence that the brain can change, that it is more malleable and 'plastic' than we once thought. This can even happen in adults. Because of this plasticity, we can retune our brain and break the power of these automatic reaction patterns.

Let's look at how these patterns are established in the first place.

## *How automatic reaction patterns are formed*

Neural connections in the brain are laid down by our genes but also by experience. Every time we have an experience of any kind and respond in a certain way, specific neurons fire in our brain and become connected.

As neuroscientists say, 'Neurons that fire together, wire together.'[2]

With each firing, these connections become thicker and stronger, and so a particular response becomes our default option. We lay down patterns of reacting that can take us over and diminish our freedom to act as we want and intend.

For example, suppose as a child you were exposed to a lot of harsh criticism from a parent or teacher and you could never seem to please that person, no matter what you did. As a child, your menu of possible responses is very limited. Depending on your temperament, you may have responded with any of the following.

- Fear: 'I'm afraid to tell the truth or try doing this in case I get criticized.'
- Appeasement: 'Please, I'll do anything you want. Just don't criticize me.'
- Depression: 'There is no point trying to get this right. I am no good.'
- Defensive anger: 'I'm not going to listen to you. You don't know what you are talking about.'
- Defiance: 'I'll prove you wrong about me.'

When these responses get repeated over and over again, they become automatic – your default option not just to the person giving the criticism, but to everybody.

## *How automatic reaction patterns are sustained*

These repeated responses also affect the structure of the developing brain. Each time you respond in a specific way, parts of the brain are activated. If you continually respond in the same way, the same parts are activated over and over again, and they become thicker and bigger. This may be because the neurons in that area branch out to make connections to other neurons, or increase the number of cells in those areas or the blood flow into them.

These densely connected areas are readily activated in our day-to-day lives – for better or for worse. This is because they have been strengthened by our early habitual responses. Once they are activated, we respond in patterned ways. In the case of criticism, if our response to early criticism 'works' – and we avoid further criticism – we will repeat the response again and again. And before long, we will do it automatically.

The more often we respond in a particular way, the more it becomes part of how we think about ourselves. That is why we even resist changing something that is causing us a lot of pain – such as low self-esteem, or succumbing to pressure – because it *feels* like an integral part of our identity.

And yet, intuitively, we know that beneath these automatic response patterns there is a truer version of who we are waiting to be discovered.

This is where the work on brain plasticity comes in. While neurons that fire together do, indeed, wire together, Siegel takes this one step further. Crucially, he says, 'Where attention goes, neurons fire. And where neurons fire, they can rewire.'[3] It is this neuroplasticity – this capacity for the brain to be rewired – that opens up the possibility for real personal change and flourishing.

We can wake up from living life on automatic, if we learn to respond to what life throws up in different and more positive ways.

If we practise new ways of responding, the old connections in the brain become weaker, and new connections grow.

The most powerful way to modify and train the capacity to control attention is to learn to become 'mindful'.

Being mindful is not just being more aware of what is going on around you. It means becoming aware in the moment of how your mind is actually working, and being more attuned to what is happening to your attention.

When we are mindful, we break up our automatic patterns of thinking and of behaving. Instead, we look at the world in a fresher, more novel way.

Mindfulness, Daniel Siegel says, is 'waking up from a life on automatic'.[4] He uses the term 'mindful brain' to capture the idea that being mindful is intimately related to 'the dance between our mind and our brain'.[5]

In other words, we can use our minds to better manage the way our brain works.

When we are mindful, we become aware of the flow of information that is coming into the mind and being generated by it – the 'flow of consciousness'. Being mindful activates that higher part of the brain, the prefrontal cortex, which enables us to:

- observe ourselves and what is going on in our minds
- see the bigger picture
- pause before we act
- modulate our responses
- resist the pull of those powerful automatic processes.

The practice of mindful awareness allows us to rewire the brain in such a way that we can find, strengthen and defend our better selves.

The heartening news is that changing your brain is not complicated – and does not require surgery. There are two effective ways to become more mindful – practising meditation, and thinking in a more flexible way.

Practise either or both of these, and you will be less caught up in patterns of thinking and feeling that no longer serve you.

## *The practice of meditation*

Jon Kabat-Zinn, former professor of medicine at the University of Massachusetts, has been largely responsible for bringing the concept of mindfulness through meditation into mainstream medicine and science.

He defines mindfulness as 'the awareness that emerges through paying attention on purpose, in the present moment, and non-judgementally, to the unfolding of experience moment by moment'.[6]

Although there are many different techniques, the essence of meditation is the training of attention. You do this by sitting still, closing your eyes and becoming aware of what is happening in your mind. You become aware of the thoughts coursing through your mind and the sensations in your body, but you try not to get snagged by them. Most of all, you try to switch off the internal meter that is constantly judging everything as good or bad, likeable or dislikeable.

The goal of meditation is to develop a state of pure awareness. But, along the way, you learn complex cognitive skills.

- You learn how to concentrate and to deal more effectively with distracting thoughts.
- You become better at monitoring what is going on in your mind, and especially what is happening to your attention.
- One of the most striking things you learn is just how powerful are the automatic processes in your brain, and what it takes to reclaim your precious attention and the freedom of your mind.

These skills are vital for being more in control of yourself and your life, and are at the heart of flourishing.

People who practise meditation consistently report a heightened sense of physical and psychological well-being.[7] They report feelings of greater serenity, compassion and joy – even bliss on occasions. Regular meditation makes people measurably happier. Many neuro-imaging studies of people's brains as they meditate (especially if they are long-term meditators) have corroborated people's own reports of the effects.[8] But even people who take part in meditation training programmes lasting only a few weeks show long-term benefits.

During meditation, activity decreases in the part of the brain that arouses the fight-or-flight response, with a corresponding decrease in negative feelings and physiological stress responses. Blood pressure decreases and the release of stress hormones is slowed down. There is a corresponding increase in activity in the parts of the brain that trigger relaxation and calm, that enable you to pay sustained attention, that allow you to experience positive emotions such as joy and happiness, and that soothe negative emotions. In fact, if you keep practising meditation, these parts of the brain will show an increase in grey matter, a marked thickening of the cells. There is even evidence that the normal thinning of the cortex that occurs with age is slowed down.

During meditation there is also a marked increase in the levels of dopamine, melatonin and serotonin. These neurohormones play a crucial role in helping you to:

- become motivated
- experience positive emotions
- better manage and stabilize your moods
- prevent stress and depression.

And, if that were not enough, melatonin also stimulates the immune system, thus helping you to fight illness and delay ageing.

### *What is it like to meditate?*

Anybody can practise meditation.

All you need is a quiet space and the freedom to spend a certain amount of time (between ten and twenty minutes at the beginning) sitting in silence with your eyes closed.

You must sit rather than lie, to avoid becoming drowsy and falling asleep. It helps to sit up straight, so that you can breathe more easily and deeply.

You can start with trying to focus your attention on your breath. When you notice your attention wandering, you gently return your focus to the breath. This capacity to focus your attention is the first step in mindfulness training.

You do this over and over again, for as long as the meditation session lasts.

Captured as we are by the non-stop flow of automatic signals from the brain that creates the 'stream of consciousness', this simple exercise can be surprisingly difficult.

You discover that your mind is full of mental chatter, has a 'will' of its own, and wanders off like an untrained puppy, heedless. Your first attempts at meditation might go something like this.

> . . . I feel a twinge in my back. Oh, I'm not concentrating properly. OK. That's better. I feel tired. That's because I did too much today. Did I bring home that stuff I need? I hope I didn't forget it. Concentrate on your breath. Oh God, I dread this thing tomorrow. No point worrying, I suppose. What's that noise? Next door? I don't know why they have the TV so loud. Ignore it. Breathe in and out. My leg muscles are really stiff again. I must stop getting distracted.

> Judith. Why am I thinking of her? Oh, I remember. She will be at this thing at the weekend. So smug. I shouldn't let it get to me. But I always react. Oh well. My stomach is bothering me again. No more fries for a while. These poor people in Africa – how can they keep going after such a disaster? I wonder, is my standing order still working? What time is it? Probably not time to stop yet. Back to breathing. Mmm, I feel more relaxed now. I'd love to change my car . . .

This automatic stream of consciousness – what Eastern cultures call the 'monkey mind' – often prevents us from being fully aware of what is happening in the moment.

How often have you found that your mind has wandered and that you have missed a critical part of a conversation or a meeting?

The more stressed and under pressure you are, the more frequently this happens. Despite the initial difficulties, practising meditation will allow you to gradually get control over this.

Siegel identifies four streams of awareness flowing into consciousness:

1. sensations from your body
2. thoughts and ideas from your mind
3. an awareness of observing yourself, and
4. what he calls 'knowing' – realizing in some deep way how you are.

The more practised you are at meditation, the better you become at avoiding losing concentration and the more easily you can sink into each stream of your awareness, without getting sucked into any one stream.

Suppose, for example, you have had a recent disappointing experience. Your mind is likely to return to it when you meditate. You will become aware of the accompanying bodily sensations (a heaviness in your chest, a sinking feeling in your gut) and thoughts ('I really wanted that' 'I feel so sad' 'Why did this happen to me?). You will also observe yourself reacting ('This is really affecting me; I'm finding it very hard to concentrate'). But you also 'know', in a wordless way, the essence of that experience of disappointment, inside you.

As you meditate, all the elements of your mind and body – sensations, observations, thoughts, feelings – become more united and in balance, no longer fighting each other for your attention. You experience, in the deepest sense, that your Self – the real and core you – is more than each one of those streams. The result is a feeling of openness and greater insight. The more you can immerse yourself in awareness in the moment, the more you can disengage from the automatic system.

This capacity to be aware in the moment will extend from your periods spent meditating – to your relationships and to your work.

### *Meditation promotes better integration of both sides of the brain*

Most of the time, when you are trying to solve a problem, you use the left side of the brain. The left hemisphere of your brain 'thinks' in a verbal, analytical way:

- it pays attention to details
- it sorts things into categories
- it actively defines and tries to solve problems in a step-by-step way.

The right hemisphere of the brain 'thinks' in a non-verbal way:

- it focuses on the more general context of an issue, on the big picture
- it pays attention to process and ambiguity
- it uses imagery and emotion, rather than language.

The brain is thinking visually all the time and producing images. However, unless we are painters, poets, architects or designers, we tend not to pay attention to these images and lose half the information.

When you meditate and use both sides of your brain, you become aware not just of your thoughts (left brain) but of images too (right brain).

After I meditate I draw the images that pop into my head. These are always full of revealing knowledge that I did not know I had, as in the following example.

> Once, I was really stuck on a project. During meditation my thoughts went round and round ('Did I really understand this project properly? Am I missing some crucial information?'). Then an image popped into my mind – of a woman trying to play the piano in the dark. But she was sitting so far back that her hands could not reach the keyboard. There was a bright light shining, but it was somewhere far off.
>
> I suddenly 'knew' what was keeping me stuck: I could not do what I wanted to do and 'make the music' or reach the light of

inspiration because of the distance that had grown, separating me from my original purpose and my own real hands-on experience.

Now that I had this insight, I knew how to solve my problem. I needed to lift my head up from the detail of what I was doing and go back to what had originally motivated me to embark on the project.

I listed the original ideas I had had, and my own intuitions and insights about the project. Something loosened or shifted in me, and I finished the project in the way I had intended.

### *Meditation makes you more attuned to yourself and to other people*

Meditation is a very powerful way not just to become more attuned to our feelings and thoughts, but to get nearer to our authentic experiences and true selves.

This effect is probably directly related to the better integration of both sides of the brain. For example, we store the details of our experience in the right side of the brain, whereas we create the narrative of our lives (the 'story' we tell ourselves about what happened) in the left. The more the two sides of our brain are joined up, the more coherent that narrative becomes. There is a better connection between how we sum up the quality of what happened to us in the past, and the actual detail of what happened. This has real consequences for our capacity to form secure intimate relationships.

This ability to construct a coherent narrative of our lives – and its importance for our well-being – can be seen most clearly in research psychologists' work on attachment. People who enjoy a secure attachment with their parents in childhood are capable of forming deep, intimate relationships. They can be depended upon emotionally and are themselves comfortable depending on others. And yet, they are strikingly free and autonomous in their thinking and feelings.

Leading expert in attachment, Mary Main of the University of California at Berkeley, has found that people who were securely attached in childhood show great coherence in how they describe themselves and their childhood experiences.[9] When they recall their childhood experiences, and their relationship with their parents, they can convincingly back up their general descriptions of such relationships (whether loving or rejecting, critical or intrusive) with anecdotes and memories.

In contrast, people who had an insecure attachment with their parents in childhood cannot create a convincing narrative of their experiences. Some tell a generalized, idealized story of their childhood but they cannot back up general statements ('I had a very happy childhood' 'My mother was a very loving person') with any real memories. Or the actual memories they recount are at odds with their idealized picture. They have detached their actual experiences (stored in the right side of the brain) from their narrative about themselves (generated by the left side of the brain).

Others offer accounts that are incoherent, disorganized and fragmented. A negative memory ('My father was really hard on me') is immediately followed by a positive statement ('But he was really a loving person') followed by another negative statement ('Not with me, though. He always favoured my sister'). The reason insecurely attached adults cannot create a coherent picture of their childhood is that as children they had to repress or deny their own experiences – especially of anxiety, longing or sadness. Instead, their experience was filtered or overwritten by their parents' view of things ('No need for this. Stop crying. Stop hanging on to me') or their parents' own needs ('Stop being so demanding. If you had my problems, you'd know about it').

The result is that their parents' view dominates their general narrative, and their actual experiences and memories are excluded. A large part of psychotherapy is helping people who have had unhappy childhoods to make sense of what happened – helping them to move forward and not remain preoccupied by the past.

Practising meditation is another way of developing insight and developing a more authentic sense of self. It allows you to let your raw experience surface, as well as the 'voices' of your parents in the past, so that gradually you can separate the two and come to your own authentic summing up of your life.

Consciously or otherwise, you spend a huge amount of brain energy trying to second-guess the mind, the feelings, the intentions and the attitudes of other people. As you become more attuned to yourself, you also become more attuned to other people, particularly their non-verbal and emotional signals. Being correctly attuned to another person – in tune with what is going on in the other's mind – is at the heart of all effective relationships, whether they be with an infant, a teenager, a lover, a friend, or a work colleague. Becoming mindful is an effective way to achieve that. You are better able to understand how they see and experience the world.

Being mindful not only connects your thoughts and feelings in the moment, it attunes you to your higher self – the essential self that is there behind your thoughts, your emotions, the routines and habits of your life, and even the everyday story that you use to explain yourself to yourself.

Being mindful helps you get close to the essential you – and to your natural and abundant capacity for happiness and flourishing.

### *Meditation helps you deal with negative emotions and moods*

When you meditate, the negatives in your life – the setbacks, the disappointments, the frustrations – are not denied. Rather, you feel better able to deal with them and not to let them overwhelm you. You can detach yourself sufficiently from the automatic firings of your brain, so that you can meet any negative thoughts at the door of your mind and decide calmly whether to let them in or not.

Being mindful can, in writer Elizabeth Gilbert's attractive description, allow us to decide which ships we give harbour to in our minds. Thus, while we may not be able to prevent 'ships' turning up laden with envy, resentment, anger, self-hate, depression, helplessness and hopelessness – the endless cargo of negative and self-destructive thoughts – we can prevent them from dropping anchor.[10]

Mindfulness allows you to do that in two ways.

First, the more attuned you become to the working of your mind, the more you become aware that your negative thoughts are not the whole of what you are.

Second, when you are mindful, and you experience something negative, you are better able to stay with the bare bones of the experience ('It happened. It is disappointing, and I am aware of that'), rather than immediately setting up a cascade of angry reflections ('I don't deserve this') or distressed thoughts ('I am no good. Nothing is ever going to go right').

It is this cascade of secondary thoughts and reactions that leads to the worst of human suffering.

### *Meditation and the treatment of psychological disorders*

Because of how it helps us deal with negative thoughts and feelings, mindfulness – and, specifically, meditation – is being used more frequently in the treatment of psychological disorders.

The research is still in its early stages, but a handful of studies looking at the effect of practising meditation on the symptoms of obsessive-compulsive and eating disorders, stress, anxiety and depression shows a significant reduction in symptoms and an improvement in general mental health. A recent study of children suffering from ADHD showed that after six weeks of meditation training in addition to their usual treatment regime – some were on medication, some not – the children showed a significant reduction in the main symptoms of hyperactivity, impulsiveness and inattention, irrespective of the other treatments they were receiving. Increased self-esteem and better parent–child relationships also followed.

Furthermore, a full 50 per cent of the children previously on medication were able to reduce or stop taking it, and still maintained their improvement.[11]

Another treatment programme for adolescents and adults who suffer from ADHD that trained them in basic meditation techniques over eight weeks showed that their capacity to focus their attention and resist impulses improved markedly, and their general well-being increased.[12]

In sum, what's not to like about meditation? An investment of twenty minutes a day at least three times a week will:

- significantly increase your capacity to pay full and engaged attention to what you need to pay attention to, and
- free your thinking and behaviour from patterns that are no longer working for you.

When you open your eyes after meditating, the world seems fresher, more colourful, and more full of vital energy and possibility.

So too with your life.

## *Developing a flexible state of mind*

The second way to become more mindful is to develop a flexible state of mind.

This version of mindfulness has been defined by renowned Harvard University psychologist Ellen Langer as a style of thinking and learning that involves actively keeping your mind open to the novelty and uncertainty inherent in all situations, rather than approaching things as fixed.

Instead of seeing things as absolute ('This is the way it always/never is'), you take a more conditional view ('This is the way it *might* be, or the way it *sometimes* is').

Langer has shown that an open, conditional approach results in:

- more engaged, effective and enjoyable learning
- greater competence
- more positive feelings
- greater creativity
- less work burnout
- better health, and even
- increased charisma.[13]

Langer focuses in particular on what she calls 'the tyranny of evaluation' – the automatic meter that judges every experience instantly as good or bad – and the resulting cascade of thoughts, feelings and actions. While this instant judgement has the advantage of efficiency and speed, we pay a big price for it because, as Langer wryly observes, we are frequently in error but rarely in doubt.[14] The 'advantages' are based on our assumption that the environment is stable, that our understanding of things is complete, and that we have found the best way to react. In an ever-changing world, these assumptions are not sound. Everything changes – children, the demands of work, intimate and social relationships, our own needs. To be effective, and to respond in a creative way, we have to notice these changes and adjust our responses.

We have to become mindful rather than mindless.

### *The characteristics of a mindful style of thinking*

Langer's work has identified four characteristics of a mindful style of thinking.

#### FOCUS ON WHAT IS HAPPENING IN THE MOMENT

Focus your attention on what is happening *now*, in the present moment, not on how you think or expect it to be.

This prevents you from making premature judgements.

#### FOCUS ON NEW ASPECTS OF WHAT IS HAPPENING

Focus particular attention on what might be *new* about the situation or interaction you are encountering.

- In what ways is it different from the last time, or different from what you expected?
- Is what is being said subtly different?
- Is the mood or emotional tone different?
- Is the way the information is being presented different – a different order, different priorities?
- Are there any omissions or additions?

### FOCUS ON THE CONTEXT

Focus your attention on the *particular context* of the situation or interaction.

For example, instead of judging someone (including yourself) as good or bad, efficient or inefficient, lazy or productive, focus your attention on remembering or finding out whether they (or you) only behave in this way in certain contexts. Recall, find out or even imagine how they (or you) behave or might behave differently in other contexts. This stance will alert you to what it is about the *context* rather than the *person* that is shaping their behaviour.

You change context more easily than personality.

### FOCUS ON OTHER PERSPECTIVES

Focus your attention on what other possible *perspectives* you might take. The more perspectives you can actively keep in mind in any situation, the more effectively you will respond.

Most of us are not very good at this. We get locked quickly into a particular way of seeing something, which appears self-evident to us. As a consequence, we overestimate the extent to which other people think the same way as we do. We also cut ourselves a lot of slack. We focus on our intentions ('I was trying to help') rather than the actual outcome. We are far more judgemental with others, focusing on what happened rather than on what they intended to happen.

When you think in a more flexible way, the quality of your thinking and learning improves dramatically. You reduce the automatic tendency to jump to conclusions.

Crucially, this kind of mindful thinking forces you to create new ways of understanding information. That is why mindfulness is associated with innovation and creativity – which are at the heart of a flourishing life.

Becoming mindful like this is helpful when you find yourself in a stressful situation, particularly when you are involved in a relationship that is going through a bad patch – with a partner, a child, a work colleague. Adopting a mindful approach – for example, deciding to be fascinated by the next encounter, to be a rapt and genuine observer – will have several positive effects.

- It will calm your mind and your feelings.
- It will unleash the full power of a fresh perception.
- It will inevitably alert you to subtle aspects of the situation that you hadn't noticed before.

There is a more than even chance that this new information will provide you with a gateway to approach the problem between you in a more constructive way.

### *Practical steps to developing a mindful thinking style*

#### ADJUST YOUR FOCUS

It is worth memorizing or writing down the four key areas of focus:

- on what is happening in the moment
- on new aspects of what is happening
- on context, and
- on other perspectives.

Keep these in mind so that you can use them in important situations or interactions.

#### BE CONDITIONAL

Learn to use more conditional words, such as 'might be', 'can be', 'could be', 'may be on occasion', 'could have been'. Use these in place of absolute words, such as 'is', 'was', 'always', 'never'.

Conditional words appear to prime a mindful state, a more active and open listening and engagement. They enable a kind of creative uncertainty.

Adopting such an approach can help us change our behaviour, as in the case of a man I once coached.

> Ed was a man who was a very high performer in his job, but who was having trouble getting on with colleagues. It emerged that the core of the problem was his belief in the value of confrontation. He held the firm view that confronting somebody you disagree with is

*always* good, and he reacted out of this belief in every situation where a disagreement arose.

Rather than trying to persuade him to drop this belief and adopt other ways to handle disagreements, I simply asked Ed to spend a week finding out the answer to four questions and to report back his experience of doing this the following week.

What are the kind of situations in which confronting somebody *may* be useful?

What are the kinds of situations where it *might* be counterproductive?

What *type* of people are amenable to confrontation?

What type of people are not?

Ed was less than convinced, but agreed to try.

The following week, he came back and reported that he was surprised how interesting and enjoyable the experiment had been. As he tried to gather the information to answer the questions, a whole new world of perception and possibilities had opened up to him. He had discovered that instead of having to drop his core belief in the value of confrontation (something he was very unwilling to do) he could adopt a more *conditional* form of the belief: 'Confronting *some* people *may* be useful in *some* situations but not in others.'

The result was that Ed remained identifiably himself but, by adopting this mindful stance, gradually developed a more flexible style of interaction.

According to Daniel Siegel, the reason this type of mindful learning may be more effective and more enjoyable, and keep our brains more active as we age, is that the brain stores such 'conditional' learning in a different way than it does absolute statements.

When information is presented as an absolute fact, it goes straight into the memory and is stored as a fact, a part of our knowledge of the world that we can access rapidly (as Ed stored the 'fact' that it is always good to confront people). When information is presented in a more conditional way, it has to be stored in the brain in a different way so that it can be connected to many possible conditions. Ed, for example, had to store away in different parts of his brain his insights into how different types of people react to confrontation and the range of situations where confrontation is effective or not effective. This way of storing information requires a more complex set of neural connections, so the brain has to be more active, nimble and flexible.

Clearly, there are many similarities between the two kinds of mindfulness – practising meditation and thinking in a more flexible way.

Both involve a form of 'thinking about thinking' – becoming aware in the moment of how your mind is actually working – that attunes you better to what is happening inside you and in the environment around you.

People who are mindful are more aware of their thoughts and feelings without getting lost in them. In difficult situations, they are able to pause without immediately reacting. They have a great gift of staying focused on what is happening in the present, and are less susceptible to distraction and lapses in concentration. Because they are emotionally attuned to themselves, they find it easy to express exactly the thoughts and feelings they intend to express. They are less likely to be judgemental and critical of themselves or other people. Being mindful strengthens the immune system, increases the body's capacity to handle stress, and is accompanied by a general increase in physical well-being.

Both forms of mindfulness involve engaging and enjoyable ways to learn about and manage ourselves, quite unlike the effortful application of willpower that exhausts us. Both result in more effective learning, greater competence and more creativity. Both result in greater overall well-being – reduced physical and psychological suffering, better immune functioning, faster healing, and more brain plasticity.[15]

Not bad for two practices that do not take up a lot of time and cost nothing.

These practices build our capacity to pay attention to the things in life that we want and need to pay attention to if we are to flourish.

# STRATEGY FOUR

## *Always know your positive purpose*

'The mind is its own place, and in itself
Can make a heaven of hell, a hell of heaven.'

John Milton, *Paradise Lost*

# 11. The eight-step dance to feeling positive or negative

As far back as the fifth century BC, Buddha said: 'Our life is the creation of our mind.'

In this observation lies a most intriguing fact about human nature: events do not 'cause' positive or negative feelings. We create our feelings ourselves. When something happens, what enters our minds is neutral information that does not necessarily have a positive or a negative value. It is the meter in our brain that automatically interprets that information and instantly assigns it a value – good or bad, positive or negative. It is that initial interpretation that triggers a cascade of responses in our body, in our thinking, in our feelings and in our behaviour. With the developments in our knowledge about how the mind and brain work, we have a much clearer understanding of how exactly we create our lives in this way.[1]

These developments show that feeling positive and feeling negative are not necessarily polar opposites, nor are they mutually exclusive: you can feel happy and unhappy, positive and negative at the same time; and you can choose to attend to either. The actor Christopher Reeve, who suffered a severe spinal injury that left him totally paralysed, remarked that if his injury had occurred a few millimetres to one side of his spinal cord, he would have merely suffered a concussion; a few millimetres to the other, he would have died. He chose to focus not on the negative – 'if only' – but on the positive: he was not dead.

For Christopher Reeve, who had to make such a massive adjustment, this process of 'choosing' his focus probably took a long time. In the normal course of events, the process of judging whether something is good or bad happens extremely rapidly and automatically. In fact, we are hardly conscious that it is a process at all. But if we want to learn how to pay attention to the positive – so that we have more choice over the end result – we first need to better understand that process.

## *The steps to feeling positive or feeling negative*

The route to feeling positive or negative has eight defined steps. They happen in rapid succession, but also loop back on each other. What's important to note is that it is not the event that causes your physical, thinking and feeling responses. It is what you *pay attention to* at each stage of the process that determines whether you will ultimately experience it as positive or negative.

Understanding this process is vital to flourishing, as it opens up the possibility of intervening and managing your responses more effectively.

### *Step 1: The event*

Life is full of events.

- Your wife calls you at work.
- A colleague that you expected to hear from does not call.
- You eat lunch.
- Your car gets clamped.
- Your son tells you he got four As in his exams.
- You find out that you did not get the job you applied for.
- Your toddler has a temper tantrum in the supermarket.
- You arrange to meet your best friend.
- Someone tells a joke.
- You catch sight of your partner or your teenage daughter.
- You watch a programme on TV.
- Just as you are falling asleep, you think about something that is happening tomorrow.

'Events' include not just the external things that happen to you, but also thoughts and memories that occur to you. In the middlc of a conversation, you suddenly think of something – and that can change your mood and behaviour just as dramatically as an external event.

### *Step 2: The onset of an emotion*

Immediately after the event comes the emotional response. You might think it's easy to identify the event that triggers a particular emotion.

Sometimes it is. Loss of any kind usually causes sadness. Anger is usually caused by being treated unfairly or witnessing an injustice done to somebody else. Achieving something usually makes us feel relieved or proud.

But even as you read the list of events in Step 1, you are aware that it's not always so simple.

It is probably safe to say that your car being clamped will make you angry or distressed. But how you feel when someone calls you or does not call you depends on whether you really want to hear from them. Lunch will depend on the quality of the food and the company. Your son's four As may be a source of delight or disappointment. You may be relieved you did not get the job because you felt pressured to apply for it and are neither interested in it nor qualified to do it well.

Seeing your spouse or your teenage daughter or your friend may just as easily provoke irritation, sadness or worry as joy and affection – depending on what's going on between you.

You might react with embarrassment and irritation to your toddler's tantrum, but you might just as easily respond with compassion because you know that he has been trying to be good all day.

The thought that occurs to you might be about a meeting that you know will be enjoyable – or one that you dread.

### *Step 3: Automatic interpretation*

Every event, every new piece of information that enters your mind gets interpreted. Instantly, you interpret what is happening and assign a meaning to it. And the very first judgement you make on it is: 'Is this good or bad?'

Psychologists call this process 'appraisal'. Often this interpretation is done automatically and without you being aware of it.

Immediately interpreting an event as good or bad, negative or positive, is one of the most powerful of our 'top-down' brain processes – those automatic patterns of activation in our brain that we looked at in Chapter 10. Since these responses are strongly patterned by our previous experiences in life, this can work for or against us.

### *Step 4: Physiological response*

The instant your brain has interpreted what is happening as good or bad, it activates a series of changes all over your body – in your hormonal glands, in your muscles, and in your heart and blood vessels. Your physiological response is exquisitely tailored, with each emotion having a distinct biological 'signature'.[2]

Negative emotions such as fear and anger release the stress hormone cortisol into your bloodstream, and that in turn activates your heart and muscles to get you ready for 'fight-or-flight'.

Positive emotions such as love and affection trigger the 'tend-and-befriend' response, releasing the hormone oxytocin into your bloodstream, getting you ready to become attached to another person, stimulating sexual arousal and reducing anxiety. In women, it stimulates their wombs to contract and, when pregnant, their breasts to produce milk.

### *Step 5: Signalling*

Parallel with these physical changes, your emotions start to communicate themselves in a particularly powerful way to everybody around you.

Facial expressions, however brief, are the most rapid and powerful clue to emotions. Minute changes in a few muscles of the face appear a few fractions of a second after your interpretation of an event. Psychologist Paul Ekman and his colleagues have shown how a whole range of emotions – anger, disgust, fear, sadness, surprise, happiness, contempt, embarrassment, amusement, pride, shame, awe, love, sexual attraction – are signalled by quite distinct facial expressions that other people can instantly identify.[3]

Facial expressions are accompanied by equally rapid changes in your tone of voice, in your eye movements and your gaze, in your gestures and your posture, as well as in your other nervous system responses – for example, going pale or red, or feeling weak.

### *Step 6: The specific feeling*

All of the steps just described are about the effects of emotions. A 'feeling' is what you call the end state – the label you give to how you now experience all those changes in yourself.

You may call the end-state feeling love or joy, gratitude or contentment, interest or hope, pride or amusement, inspiration or awe, surprise or fear, anger or disappointment, contempt or disgust – or any one of their many subtle variations.

### *Step 7: A distinct set of thoughts*

Specific feelings have very particular effects on the way we think. This, in turn, affects how we make decisions and behave.

- Anger provokes thoughts such as: 'I'm not going to put up with this.'
- Love and affection provoke thoughts such as: 'I really want to get closer to him, to help and support him.'
- Fear provokes thoughts such as: 'I don't want to be here. I want to escape this. Please, somebody, help me.'
- Contentment and satisfaction provoke thoughts such as: 'I want this to go on longer.'
- Sadness provokes thoughts such as: 'I feel really deprived. I wish the situation could be changed.'

### *Step 8: Action*

The final step is action. Each emotion – and its accompanying thoughts – sets up a specific 'action tendency'.

When we feel positive emotions, we feel the urge to approach, to engage, to have more of the experience or event that triggered that emotion.

When we feel angry we feel a strong urge to act to put things right. When we feel afraid, or sad, we want to withdraw. We want to flee for protection to somewhere we feel safe, or tend to our own scared or bruised feelings.

The more frequently you process events in a particular way through the eight steps, the more patterned your emotional response becomes.

If you frequently process a challenge in such a way that the end-state feeling is confidence, this gradually becomes your default option in the face of any challenge. Similarly, if every time someone disagrees with you, you interpret it as personal criticism, and the end-state feeling and action are defensive or angry, that will become your default option.

Let's call this your 'Eight Step Emotional Processing'. The implication for flourishing is this: the more aware you become of your Eight Step Emotional Processing, and the more you can bring it under your conscious control, the more you are in charge of – rather than the victim of – your internal meter, which is clocking up the positive–negative ratio.

Achieving more control over the eight steps starts with becoming more aware of each step as it happens – and this brings us back to being mindful. The practice of meditation or of a mindful thinking style makes us generally more able to:

- step outside of ourselves
- observe what is *actually* happening, and
- become attuned to what is going on in our minds.

The more you develop that capacity, the easier it is to get control in the moment over the Eight Step Emotional Process in your daily life. In particular, it gives you the capacity to *pause* without immediately reacting. If you keep attention focused on what is going on in your mind during each of the eight steps, you will begin to see that there is more scope and more freedom in how you interpret each stage and how you react to it.

If you can change one step in the dance, you can change the whole choreography of your emotional responses.

## *Changing a step in the dance*

### *Steps 1 and 2: The event and the onset of an emotion*

You can do relatively little about many events in your life. Nor do you have much control over the initial onset of your emotions. Emotions tend to come unbidden. Sometimes you are conscious of the emotion, sometimes not.*

It is how you react to the emotion that really matters. The essence of limiting the power of negative events is to stay with the bare bones of the event. One of the simplest and most powerful ways to do this is to say, in the immediate aftermath of a negative event: 'OK. I don't like it, but it happened.' This deceptively simple sentence acknowledges the event, but psychologically it throws a cordon around it and places it firmly in the past.

Similarly, you can try to stay with the bare bones of your initial negative emotional reaction ('I feel disappointed, and I am aware of that'). Again, this gives your emotion full respect but also, paradoxically, when you say, 'I am aware of it,' you are separating yourself from it. You are

* Remember, however, that when people regularly practise meditation, their brains begin to function differently – even when they are not meditating – so that they show less neural and physiological reactivity to negative events.

casting it as a reaction, not immediately identifying with it or letting it sweep over you. You are effectively saying, 'I *have the experience* of being angry or sad,' rather than, 'I *am* angry or sad.'

You are asserting that your emotion is not the whole of you.

What this prevents – or, at least, slows down – is the triggering of an automatic cascade of negative thoughts ('This should not have happened. I don't deserve this' 'I am devastated. I will never get anything right'). That, in turn, slows down the automatic reaction to defend yourself or to give up.

It is this deluge of secondary thoughts and reactions that rapidly escalates the ratio of negatives.

### *Step 3: Automatic interpretation*

This is the really decisive step.

How you interpret events determines the next steps: how your body reacts; what thoughts come into your mind; what feelings and action are generated. As your brain is trying to interpret an event, to decipher its meaning, it runs rapidly through the following checklist.

- Is this event good or bad?
- How much attention should I give this?
- How certain am I about what is going to happen? About how negative or positive the outcome will be?
- How much control over this do I have?
- Who is responsible for this? Me or someone else? Or is it the situation I am in? Is this fair or unfair? Did I deserve this or not?
- How much energy must I expend to respond to this?

#### IS THIS EVENT GOOD OR BAD?

We are mildly predisposed to judge events as neutral or mildly positive (on the basis that no news is good news), unless we are already in a negative state or are predisposed to worry.

People who score highly for the trait of neuroticism – the tendency to worry and self-doubt – are more strongly disposed to judge neutral events as negative. If that is your temperament, you need to focus on developing the habit of questioning your initial negative response ('Is this interpretation of what is happening more to do with the way my mind works than the event itself?') and developing your capacity to let yourself imagine good outcomes.

The work of neuroscientist John Cacioppo and his colleagues suggests that we don't have just one system in our brain to judge things as good or bad, positive or negative.[4] Positive and negative are not a single dimension where being positive cancels out being negative, or vice versa. Rather, we have two specialized systems that process events in parallel and, to a large extent, independently.[5] The defensive or avoidance system processes all information that might contain threats to us, while the opportunity or approach system processes the positive information.

When an event does not provide much in the way of positive or negative information (for example, passing a stranger on the street), you remain emotionally indifferent. When the positive information is overwhelming ('Hmm. She is an attractive person and she is making it clear she is really interested in me'), your reaction is positive. When negative information dominates ('She is very loud and over the top'), your initial reaction is negative. But many events – even these examples – provide both positive and negative information ('She is interested, but do I really want to get involved in this?' 'She seems over the top, but maybe that is her way of flirting because she finds me attractive?').

For the most part, we are strongly motivated to judge things overall as good or bad because it makes life simpler.

So, when we feel ambivalent about something, we manipulate the two systems so that we can come down on one side or the other. We either deliberately pay more attention to the positive ('He is really very handsome and seems to have lots of friends') and downplay the negative ('Maybe he will look better in daylight') and decide to engage. Or we reverse the process and pay more attention to the negative and decide to pass.

This would be fine if the two systems were equal, but they are not. The negative channel is more dominant. What this means is that at this very early stage of judging an event as negative, we quickly abandon and forget any positive information about the event that we have also registered. We stop paying attention to it.

The moment we judge something to be good or bad is decisive because it determines how we answer the next set of questions.

### HOW MUCH ATTENTION SHOULD I GIVE THIS?

If an event is negative, you will inevitably give it more attention and assign it more weight.

For example, when you experience an event that makes you fearful, you will automatically interpret this as a threat, and you will judge it to need your maximum attention. That is why a worry keeps such a hold on your mind. When an event makes you angry, you interpret this as unjustified, an offence against you or what you value, and you then give it a lot of your attention. On the other hand, an event that is interpreted as good and leaves you satisfied and contented requires very little attention. That is your *automatic* brain reaction. But you do have a choice about this. You don't necessarily have to spend your precious units of attention on the negative event. You can learn to temper the urge to devote your full attention to the negative, in particular to ruminate over it.

The trouble is that we never pause long enough to make that choice.

### HOW CERTAIN AM I ABOUT WHAT IS GOING TO HAPPEN? ABOUT HOW NEGATIVE OR POSITIVE THE OUTCOME WILL BE?

Events are stressful, to the extent that we are certain that the outcome is going to be negative for us. But certainty is often a mental filter that can overwhelm the 'bottom-up' data that is coming in from our actual experiences in the moment.[6]

This habit of being certain about how negative things will be, or even that they will be negative, is a huge source of stress and unhappiness. Yet, we continue to be certain despite our repeated experiences that what we thought was going to be positive often turns out to be unexpectedly disappointing, and things we were sure would be a disaster turned out to be fine.

We are very attached to being right – even about events that are not self-evidently good or bad.

Developing a stance of 'creative uncertainty' is a way of escaping the tyranny of certainty. Remind yourself that there is always more than one perspective on any event. Each event has its positives and negatives. So has every course of action. As Ellen Langer points out, each disadvantage is simultaneously an advantage from another perspective, and vice versa.[7] Not getting a promotion may be an advantage if you look at it from the perspective of your family life. A relationship break-up is very painful, but afterwards you realize that you have recovered your self-esteem and sense of self.

In the middle of a crisis that seems overwhelmingly negative, the positive potential is often hidden, as I have experienced in my own life.

Many years ago, when my father was diagnosed with terminal cancer, treatment and pain relief were not as well developed as they are today. His doctors told us he would probably live for a few months, but that his condition would continue to deteriorate, that it would be hard. And indeed, his last few months were so difficult that he often wished for an end to his suffering – as did we, for his sake.

And yet, those few months turned out to be unexpectedly positive. That time gave us all a precious opportunity to talk about things, even to get to know each other in a deeper way. Would any of us, least of all my father, have wished for this opportunity? No. Would any of us, least of all my father, have wanted to miss it? No. It was a bittersweet experience.

But then, many of life's most important moments are.

As a way of reminding ourselves to remain creatively uncertain, it's worth absorbing this fable, quoted in the film *Charlie Wilson's War*.

There's a little boy, and on his fourteenth birthday he gets a horse. And everybody in the village says, 'How wonderful. The boy got a horse.'

And the Zen master says, 'We'll see.'

Two years later, the boy falls off the horse, breaks his leg, and everybody in the village says, 'How terrible.'

And the Zen master says, 'We'll see.'

Then, a war breaks out and all the young men have to go off and fight. Except the boy can't, because his leg's all messed up, and everybody in the village says, 'How wonderful.'

And the Zen master says, 'We'll see.'

### HOW MUCH CONTROL OVER THIS DO I HAVE?

The more certain we are of our judgement, the more control we feel we have over the situation. That is one of the reasons why we want to be certain – it gives us that desired sense of control, and leads to confident action.

This is all very well when we are right and we actually know what to do. But that is not always the case. When we feel angry, for example, this brings with it a strong sense of certainty about what caused the situation, a strong urge to act and a strong feeling of control. On the other hand, when we feel afraid, we feel we have very little control over things – even though we may have far more control over the actual outcome than we are aware of.

The point here is that emotions carry with them a certain perception of control that may not reflect your actual control, or lack of it, in reality.

Unless you are aware of that, you will assume that your *perception* of control equates to real control. It is a very good idea to remind yourself of that when you are experiencing any strong emotion. For instance, when you get angry with someone, you have very little control over – or even certain knowledge about – how they will react.

Reminding yourself that perception is not reality will orient you to look for *disconfirming* evidence for your *felt* sense of control. When you do look for such contradictory evidence, you may discover that your perception of control has a shaky basis in fact. The righteousness of anger may blind you to the things that might spiral out of your control – in yourself or others. Or you may find out that, despite your fears, you have more options to protect yourself, and therefore more control, than you thought.

Looking for disconfirming evidence is one of our least favourite actions. We are mightily motivated to do the opposite – to form a hypothesis and then busy ourselves finding evidence to confirm it.

But, making a habit of checking out any disconfirming evidence is vital for wise functioning as an individual or as a group.

### WHO IS RESPONSIBLE FOR THIS? ME OR SOMEONE ELSE? OR IS IT THE SITUATION I AM IN? IS THIS FAIR OR UNFAIR? DID I DESERVE THIS OR NOT?

I put the questions of responsibility, blame and fairness together because they are so often linked in our minds.

We spend a great deal of our time and attention assigning responsibility and blame for the situations in which we find ourselves. How we answer these questions has big implications for how we subsequently act. And, unfortunately, we make systematic errors in how we do that.

When it comes to accounting for our negative behaviour and our mistakes, for example, we are much more forgiving of ourselves than we are of others. We take a judicious view of why we might have acted as we did, pay a lot of attention to our good intentions and how we were thinking and feeling, and we draw attention to the context for our actions. Yet, when judging others, we dispense summary justice. We focus on their actions and on the outcomes. We pay scant heed to their intentions. Instead, we blame their mistakes and negative behaviour on their character.

These are just a few of the biases in our automatic thinking about ourselves and others, and they cause a great deal of disagreement, conflict and communication breakdowns in our interactions with other people.

HOW MUCH ENERGY MUST I EXPEND TO RESPOND TO THIS? The stronger the negative emotion and the greater the urge to act, the more energy we will use.

The tendency to expend a lot of effort responding is shaped by temperament and personality. Some people are predisposed to be overreactive: confronted by a threat or a possible opportunity, they immediately go into overdrive. This may be a good strategy on some occasions, but it is rarely good on all occasions. However, we are not bound by our predispositions. Indeed, sometimes in psychotherapy people are surprised, and vastly relieved, when it is suggested to them that they don't always *have to* expend maximum energy on responding to the events in their lives.

For example, when you feel angry, it might be better to expend energy on learning to soothe yourself instead of taking action – or, at the very least, before you act. So too with always feeling compelled to *do* something when somebody asks you.

### *Steps 4 and 5: Physiological responses and the signalling of emotion*

I take these two steps together because you can do relatively little to influence your physiological reactions – apart from breathing deeply and slowly. But, in parallel with bodily changes, your emotions start to communicate themselves in a particularly powerful way to everybody around you. And you can do a lot to modify some of that signalling.

Facial expressions are the most rapid and powerful way we signal an emotional reaction. They provide reliable clues to what someone is really feeling because they are so hard to fake. Deploying a tight smile – closed lips, no involvement of the muscles around the eyes – to mask a negative emotion is not only unconvincing, it may actually cause a negative reaction (even some heart dysrhythmia) in the person at the receiving end.[8]

Qualities of your voice – including how quickly, slowly, softly or loudly you speak, whether you speak fluently or hesitantly, whether you make errors (using the wrong word, slurring, mispronouncing familiar words), as well as the frequency and length of pauses – also reveal your emotional state. In fact, people listening can make judgements about what you are feeling with accuracy rates of about 70 per cent.[9] Your feelings are not only on view on your face, but 'on view' in your voice. And, like facial expressions, however much you want to, it is extremely difficult to control your voice when in the grip of strong feelings.

Touch is also a powerful signal of emotion. In one experiment, volunteers were divided into pairs, with each pair sitting at a table separated by a black curtain that prevented all communication between them except touch. Each person was asked to try to convey a specific emotion to the other by a brief touch. Remarkably, they succeeded in reliably communicating the emotions of anger, disgust, fear, love, sympathy and gratitude to each other by touch alone. They had less luck communicating pride, embarrassment and sadness.[10]

Touch plays a central role in soothing. Women in stressful situations showed decreased stress-related activity in the brain when their hand was held by their husband (though not by a stranger).[11] A friendly touch results in more cooperation and reciprocity, even among strangers.

While the *onset* of an emotion and the accompanying physiological changes happen rapidly and outside your conscious control, you do have some control over the intensity and duration of your response. As Charles Darwin observed, when an emotion is freely expressed, this expression intensifies the experience of the emotion. When its expression is inhibited in some way, the emotion softens.[12] So, we can modulate a negative emotion, or even trigger a positive emotion, by changing the way we express ourselves bodily.

Remember the tight combination of body–feelings–thoughts in every emotional response. When you are in the grip of a strong emotion, it is very difficult to change the feeling. You can't simply direct yourself not to feel the way you do, or to feel something else. You *can* change your thoughts – although you have to practise doing this when you are not very emotionally aroused. But it is relatively easier to change some of your bodily reactions. And changing even *one* aspect of your physical response can be surprisingly effective in changing your feelings. This happens because of the rapid feedback loop between your body, your brain and your feelings.

For example, if you adopt the facial expression and gestures characteristic of a particular emotion (even if you are not aware of doing so), the feedback that goes from your body to your brain is that you *are* experiencing that emotion. Your brain then triggers the appropriate response, so you end up actually feeling that way to a small but reliable extent.[13]

If you adopt the facial expression of happiness, you will feel a little bit happier. In experiments where people are instructed to smile, or even induced (without being aware) to adopt a smiling-like expression, their mood actually improves. (In Chapter 7 we saw how women who were injected with Botox experienced significant mood improvements because they could no longer frown.) While you may not be up to a beaming eye-crinkling genuine smile, you can at least manage a self-deprecating or wry smile. Or, you can smooth out your forehead and cheeks with gentle rhythmic hand movements – surprisingly effective in reducing a tense expression, and a good way to remind yourself that you do have a body that is reacting. Placing your hand across your stomach (just below your ribcage) is also a very effective way to soothe a feeling of distress caused by hearing upsetting news or somebody being aggressive towards you – perhaps because it mimics the way mothers hold their babies in their laps, triggering that very old feeling of security.

Similarly, when you feel angry, extra blood flows into your hands and the temperature in your fingers actually rises to get you ready for combat. Your face reddens. You furrow your brow. Your head juts forward and you glare. Your nostrils flare. You clench or bare your teeth. The veins in your neck become distended and throb. Your chest heaves and your breathing becomes more laboured. Your gestures become more frantic. In an outburst of anger, all these changes may happen in a few seconds. While you can't change some of these physical responses, you do have some control over others.

For example, unclenching your hands, and placing them palms-up on your lap, one resting in the other, will calm you down. This is a gesture of openness and repose. Adopting that gesture sends feedback to your brain that you are *feeling* receptive and calm, so you begin to actually feel that way. The combination of embodying and feeling that way makes it more difficult to act angrily.

Try this for yourself.

If you sit in that open position, and then imagine you are getting ready to confront somebody angrily, you will find that you begin to 'organize' your body in a particular way in readiness. You will begin to sit forward, to jut your head out. You will feel the urge to pull your hands apart and start using them in some way – pointing, tapping the table, waving them around. If you stay resolved to keep your hands in the palms-open resting gesture, you will find it harder to organize yourself to become properly angry, and the feeling will damp down.

Smoothing out your brow, slowing down your breathing, or stretching out your fingers, also helps break up a negative response. When in dispute with somebody you care about, and the discussion is looking like it will end in an argument, it is sometimes better to stop talking for a while and just to touch the other person tenderly. This may be enough to trigger the memory of the affection between you, and to trigger that actual feeling again.

Now let's take a look at fear.

When you feel afraid, blood remains near your chest, to get you ready to move quickly away from threat. Your face pales. Your eyes open wide and may protrude; the pupils become dilated. Your nostrils flare. There is a sharp intake of breath, or a gasp. Your breathing quickens. Your hands may sweat. You may clench them or raise them wide open to cover your face. Most of these responses are outside your conscious control. But, for example, you can change the rhythm of your breath, slowing and deepening it. This is very effective at reducing anxiety and is the basis of most treatment programmes for panic attacks.

When you feel anxious and nervous, it also helps to adopt the body stance that characterizes self-confidence: standing straight, shoulders pushed back, head lifted. When having a difficult conversation (in person or over the phone) with somebody who intimidates you, it is better to do it standing up, with your shoulders pushed back and your head lifted.

Managing your bodily responses in the moment is hard. That is why it is really useful to practise when you are not in the grip of an emotion.

Recall a vivid memory of a particular time when you felt a negative emotion. Close your eyes and see yourself at the peak of that emotion. Now, try to reproduce in your body how you were then.

What was your stance?

What gestures were you using?

What facial expression did you adopt?

How were you breathing?

What was the tone of your voice?

This exercise demonstrates how you organize your body to 'do' a particular emotion. The more aware you are of how you do it, the more effectively you can 'un-do' it and the more control you have in shifting out of negative and into positive mode.

### *Step 6: The specific feeling*

All of the steps just described are about emotions. Remember, a 'feeling' is what you call the end state, the label you give to how you now experience all those changes in yourself.

Some of us have a broad and subtle palette of emotional descriptions ('I feel some slight reluctance, I'm just hesitating, about what you are suggesting'). Others use a more restricted or extreme range ('I hate that idea'). How we label the emotion, in turn, affects how we signal it. We may start by feeling light and happy, or down and out of sorts. But once we label the sensation 'delight' or 'depressed', our signalling intensifies accordingly – and so does the feeling.

The better you are at distinguishing the subtleties of feeling, the more control you have over your own feelings and the better you are at reading and managing the feelings of others. That is the basis of emotional intelligence.

In the case of positive emotions, in some situations it won't make a huge difference if you misread mild contentment for deep happiness – although you may end up overestimating how happy your wife is, or how highly motivated your team is about your pet project. But in the case of negative emotions, accurate reading can have very significant consequences. There is the world of difference between labelling your emotional reaction 'dread' rather than 'concern'; between labelling it 'indignation' rather than 'anger'; between 'disappointment' and 'dejection'; between 'aversion' and 'disgust'; between 'embarrassment' and 'humiliation'; between 'regret' and 'remorse'.

The more extremely we label our feelings, the more the feelings escalate and the more strongly they provoke a torrent of related thoughts.

### *Step 7: Distinct set of thoughts*

Specific emotions have very particular effects on the way we think. This, in turn, affects how we make decisions and behave.

How anger affects our thinking provides a particularly clear example. Since anger is one of the most frequently experienced emotions – most people report becoming mildly to moderately angry anywhere from several times a day to several times a week – this is another reason to look at its effects in more detail.[14]

Jennifer Lerner of Harvard University is a leading expert on emotion. She shows that anger primarily triggers thoughts of blame. The more somebody thinks angry thoughts, the angrier they actually become, which then provokes even more blaming, in an endless loop. But the effect of anger on our thinking is even more extensive than that. Anger narrows our thinking, making it harder to think or deal with anything except what is making us angry.

At the most basic level, it distorts what we pay attention to. We become particularly attuned to anything that reflects our own angry state. We pay more attention to angry arguments generally and find them more convincing. In turn, we are more likely to resort to angry arguments ourselves to promote our case. We begin to think in a more careless way, paying less attention to the quality of the argument that somebody is making and being more influenced by the superficial characteristics of the person making the argument.

When angry, people expect life to throw even more annoyances at them. Compared to their non-angry counterparts, they believe that the chances of being ripped off or disrespected are higher. Angry people become ever more judgemental and indiscriminately punitive. Their threshold for provocation is lowered. This has a particularly pernicious effect on interpersonal and social relationships. Angry people feel less trust in their co-workers and acquaintances, even when those people have played no role in making them angry in the first place. Anger provokes a kind of siege mentality. Angry people are more likely to be negative about people who are not members of their own social, work or ethnic group. They are more likely to stereotype them and to want to act against them. This kind of anger is often linked to the expression of contempt – the single most predictive factor in the breakdown of relationships, whether personal or in civic society.

Jennifer Lerner has done a lot of research on how anger affects the way we make decisions. People who are angry become very certain about who is to blame for the situation that has arisen, but they are equally certain about what needs to be done. Anger makes them highly optimistic that what they decide to do will achieve the desired outcome. They become more eager to make a decision and to *act* decisively, and they become reluctant to think about alternative actions. They feel they don't need to gather more information about a situation before they act, and they process the information they already have while paying attention only to what suits their version of events. They begin to feel more confident, in control and convinced of their rightness. They are more prone to attribute the cause of the problem they are dealing with to individuals, rather than to more complex situations. They underestimate risks, are eager for action, and feel indiscriminately optimistic about their chances of success. (Interestingly, when Lerner first published this research in 2006 – in a paper called 'Portrait of the angry decision maker'[15] – it was regarded by many people as an uncanny description of George W. Bush's behaviour leading up to the invasion of Iraq.)

Fear and sadness also have their own characteristic set of thoughts. Anxiety, for example, provokes loops of 'what if' thinking.

What if I make a mistake?

What if I get into trouble because of that?

What if I lose my job as a result?

What if I become unemployed and can no longer pay my bills?

What if all the stress makes me sick and I die?

And so on.

Sadness, particularly if it spirals into depression, triggers a deadly 'cognitive triad' of beliefs:

- I am bad (no good at anything, useless, etc.).
- The world is bad (dark, unfair, etc.).
- My future is hopeless.

These negative thoughts, in turn, trigger memories that fit with them. You recall all the other times you have been sad or fearful – further intensifying your negative thoughts.

### TWO STRATEGIES FOR DEALING WITH NEGATIVE THOUGHTS

First, meditation (as described in Chapter 10) is a powerful way to become attuned to the working of your mind, and to manage negative thoughts. It trains you to see them not as the whole of what you are, but rather, as Daniel Siegel suggests, 'as waves at the surface of the mental sea'.[16]

The second strategy is more active, based on the techniques of cognitive behavioural therapy. For a week, carry around a small notepad. When you notice yourself feeling negative, pay attention to your thoughts and write them down exactly.

Just the act of doing this has a freeing effect. It externalizes the thought on to the page and loosens its hold. You will be surprised by how often the same thoughts recur – even in very different domains of your life ('You never get anything right' 'I should have done something else' 'You are an idiot' 'Everybody hates me' 'You can't trust anybody' 'Something awful is going to happen') – all revealing your negative 'internal working model' of yourself, of other people and the world.

This negative internal working model produces your particular pattern of 'automatic thoughts'. You begin to understand them in this way – not as objective truths, but as subjective emotional reactions and not necessarily true.

The next step is to mentally challenge your automatic thoughts.

What evidence do you have for thinking in this way?

Is there some other way you could interpret it or think about it?

The important thing here is not just to rehearse the few examples you have (which will come readily to mind) to prove your point, but to actively look for contrary examples. For instance, if you think you are unlucky in life, you can cite all the evidence for this. But now list all the times you were lucky and all the times you avoided bad things happening to you. This evidence will not pop into your mind, because your internal working model automatically excludes it. You have to work to find it.

Examining your automatic thoughts will reveal your underlying (and often unarticulated) assumptions about things.

Sometimes, some of your assumptions are true. Suppose, for example, your dilemma is that you have just accepted a major new job, but now you are having big doubts about the decision. So, what assumptions are you making about the problem?

'It would be a lot of work and stress to now undo all the preparations that are in place.'

That assumption is true.

'A lot of people would be very annoyed with me.'

That assumption is also somewhat true.

'My reputation would be damaged.'

Certainly, it would raise questions about you for a while. But could you live with all these consequences?

'Yes,' you say, 'I probably could, because enduring all that stress would be better than being stuck in a situation that is wrong for me and that will cause me long-term unhappiness.'

So, what is holding you back?

Finally, after much probing and discussion, you will come to your bedrock assumption. *That you are not allowed to change your mind.*

Why are you not allowed to change your mind?

'Because,' you say, 'only losers change their mind.'

Even as you say it out loud, it may sound a little strange to your ears. That is the fundamental, bedrock assumption that is trapping you. It has assumed an emotional truth for you, but it is not true in any objective way.

Leadership and coaching consultant Nancy Kline calls such a belief the 'limiting assumption' – the one that limits our imagination and most gets in the way of what we want to positively achieve.[17] Our limiting assumption is what most often prevents us from taking the positive road.

Your bedrock assumptions most often originate early in your life. They are the opinions of a dominant parent that you have internalized or the lessons you learned from your own experiences of trying to please that parent ('You must be perfect to succeed' 'You must be in control to be happy' 'You must always be right' 'Only losers change their minds'). These assumptions are part of your internal working model:

- 'Am I somebody who is lovable and worthy of respect?'
- 'Can other people be trusted?'
- 'Can the future be shaped in a positive way?'

This can be a wholly or partially positive cognitive triad:

- 'I am a good and worthwhile person.'
- 'Other people are generally well intentioned and will cooperate if you understand them properly.'
- 'The future can be and must be shaped by all of us individually.'

Or this can be a wholly or partially negative triad:

- 'I am not a very likeable person deep down.'
- 'Other people can't be trusted and always let you down.'
- 'The future is frightening and out of our control.'

The limiting assumption emerges from a negative triad and is usually related to a specific fear.

Having identified your limiting assumption ('I can never be wrong'), Nancy Kline suggests that you ask yourself what you think its *positive opposite* is in your mind. You have to think about this for a while. The positive opposite of, 'I can never be wrong,' is not, 'Always be right.' That's just another version of your limiting assumption.

Only *you* know what the positive opposite is, because only you have the knowledge of how it originally arose in your mind.

I once worked with a man called Robert whose limiting assumption was just that – that he could never be wrong.

> Robert recalled that his father, who was a very authoritarian and critical personality, could never bear to be contradicted by anybody and was intolerant of mistakes. 'There was no openness in our family. It was right or wrong all the time.'
>
> In Robert's mind the positive opposite of always being right was being open. He eventually formulated a new assumption in a way

that worked for him: 'I can be open to what other people say but still respect my own opinions.'

Once you have identified your new assumption, Nancy Kline then suggests asking a final question that incorporates the new assumption and really liberates your thinking: 'If you truly believed [*insert your new assumption*] how would you go about achieving what you desire? How would you act in the world?'

In Robert's case, once he posed the question in that way to himself ('If I truly believed I could be open to what other people say but still respect my own opinions, how would I go about achieving what I desire? How would I act in the world?'), he could immediately think of multiple ways to be more open, multiple ways to respect his own opinions in his own mind – and in how he expressed them to others.

No longer locked in the old 'either right or wrong' assumption, he could generate his own tailored solutions in a way that was perfect for him.

### *Step 8: Action*

The final step in the Eight Step Emotional Process is action.

Each emotion, and its accompanying thoughts, triggers a specific 'action tendency'. When we feel positive emotions, we feel the urge to approach, to engage, to have more of the experience that triggered that emotion. When we feel afraid, or sad, we want to withdraw. We want to flee for protection to a place where we feel safe, where we can tend to our own scared or bruised feelings.

Take anger: when we feel angry, the 'action tendency' is the urge to put things right, to obtain justice (as we see it). We try to defend ourselves or exact revenge – physically or verbally. Anger is designed for short-term action sequences.

Someone grabs your ball.

You feel angry.

You act to get it back.

You remonstrate with the wrongdoer to give it back.

If he doesn't, you grab it back.

Justice is done and you feel happy.

But life does not always work out in a happy little tableau like that. When we can't right the wrong, the 'action tendency' can't complete its full cycle. But the urge to act does not go away. Instead, we are very likely to carry it over to the next situation we encounter, but be totally unaware of doing this. We seek justice elsewhere.

You may feel badly treated by your boss (or your mother, or your partner) who did not give you a fair hearing (i.e. justice) as you see it. You feel powerless to set the matter to rights. But, unconsciously, you may seek out a chance to vindicate yourself elsewhere. You get disproportionately angry in a subsequent encounter with a colleague, or with your child, or with a random member of the public. You perceive a slight where none was intended. Anger erodes the capacity to overlook any mitigating factors before attributing blame and acting on it.

But, while strong emotions prompt an action tendency we are not destined to act automatically. How we deal with each of the preceding steps – how we interpret the event, how we express the emotion, and the way we think about it – all strengthen or lessen the final urge to action.

In the end, we have a choice in every situation.

We can act or not act.

We can act positively or negatively.

To act wisely and positively requires more effort and skill than to act negatively.

Or, to paraphrase Aristotle, anybody can act – that is easy. But to act with the right person, and to the right degree, and at the right time, and with the right purpose, and in the right way – that is not easy.

# 12. Identify what you want to achieve – and make it happen

If attention is a precious and undervalued resource, so too is the power of forming an intention. In Daniel Siegel's vivid phrase, the brain is 'an anticipation machine', always readying itself for the next moment.[1] When you supply your brain with a particular intention, it automatically does half the work of implementing that intention – alerting you to opportunities to do what you set out to do, and rapidly processing any information that might help or hinder your purpose.

In other words, when you form an intention to do something, it 'primes' your brain to organize itself in very particular ways.

What this means in practical terms is that your brain directs your attention not just to what you *can* do now, but to what you *could* do next. It alerts you to opportunities to carry out your intention and motivates you to avail yourself of these when they arise. It helps you react faster to what is unfolding. It taps into your memory, your fund of tacit knowledge, to identify the emotional and social skills that you need to use, and gets them ready for action so that you automatically know the right thing to do as the situation unfolds.

In this way, your brain, your whole nervous system, all your senses, become attuned to achieving your intention. Your whole approach becomes more unified, more coherent.

Suppose you are about to have a conversation with somebody, and I ask you, 'What is your positive purpose?'

If you are like most people, the chances are that you will tell me what you are about to *do*.

'I am going to meet with a colleague about some plans.'

'I am going to have a talk with my daughter; she's been very moody recently.'

'I am going to tell my boyfriend that we need to talk.'

Embedded in each sentence is some purpose: to agree a plan; to find out what is going on in your daughter's life; to communicate better with your partner. But if the goal remains unarticulated, it is more vulnerable to being forgotten, or being displaced by other issues that may arise in the conversation.

Now, suppose I ask you to tell me not what you are about to *do*, but to articulate clearly not just what your specific purpose is but what your *positive purpose* is in having the conversation.

This step requires a bit more thought.

So, if you're about to meet your work colleague, you might say, 'Well, my positive purpose is to persuade my colleague to join me in exploring a plan that will be worthwhile for each of us and for the team generally.'

If you're about to talk to your daughter, you might say, 'My positive purpose is to make it possible for my daughter to talk about what is going on in her life in a way that she finds helpful.'

If you're about to talk to your partner, you might say, 'My positive purpose is for us to get closer to each other.'

When you articulate your positive purpose in this explicit way, how you then conduct the conversation will be radically different. With your colleague, say, you will set out not just to have a conversation in the sense of exchanging information. Instead, you will look for opportunities to persuade him of the benefits of the project for him and for the team. Your brain will activate a range of persuasion tactics and will monitor how effective each is proving. Similarly, your brain will prime you to activate questions that will help your daughter open up, or to activate actions that will create a feeling of closeness with your partner.

Once you supply your brain with a specific mandate, it will do most of the rest of the work – automatically anticipating and seizing every opportunity to further that positive purpose. You will be less easily distracted by things that are irrelevant or unhelpful to your purpose – for example, getting drawn into an argument, or trying to ferret out information, or defending yourself.

Correspondingly, the absence of a positive purpose is a major drawback, putting you at risk of drifting into conversations and projects without any clear idea about what you want to achieve. One or both partners starting the interaction without an explicit positive purpose is one reason why discussions between two people who are in dispute can get stuck in endless predictable sequences that always end the same way. Having your say, making accusations, or defending yourself – this is not a positive purpose. If, on the other hand, you make it your positive purpose to try to get more clarity about the other person's position, or to make a positive suggestion, or to explore the room for compromise, then you can monitor if the conversation is achieving or not achieving that purpose. If it is not, you can end it and suggest trying again at some other time.

You can make interactions, particularly those that are potentially difficult, more engaging and productive by trying to find out what the other person's positive purpose might be. If you know what it is, you can set about trying to help them find good ways to achieve it. This works particularly well with people who have a tendency to be negative, to find fault with every proposal.

Generally, people don't set out to be negative. Most people want to be good and do good, as they see it. For example, a chronic naysayer at work may be genuinely motivated to ensure that only excellent work is done. They may positively want to make a good impression on their colleagues and to be helpful. But that positive purpose can get tangled and distorted by all kinds of things – their insecurity, their way of expressing themselves, or their unhappy experiences of always getting on people's nerves because of the way they go about things. But if you can help that negative person to recall and articulate their original positive purpose – to get the best results, to be helpful – it becomes easier to get them to examine whether the strategies they are using are achieving that purpose or not.

If they are not, you can help them devise more productive strategies.

## *Getting to the heart of motivation: Approach or avoidance*

Having a positive purpose is related to having what is known as an 'approach goal'.

Our basic motivation to do anything in life is either to approach a challenge or avoid it. Our primary purpose is either to seek success or avoid failure. For example, you get a job, or you fall in love. You can frame these events in an 'approach' way – motivating yourself by imagining the pleasure ahead. Or you can frame them in an 'avoidance' way – motivating yourself by imagining what might happen if you fail in the relationship or the job.

Which psychological stance you adopt has a major effect on what you do and how you feel.

An approach goal will focus your attention on what you *can* do to achieve your hopes, what opportunities you can set up to make it happen. You will pursue your goal with energy and eagerness. You will pay particular attention to any information that indicates whether you are succeeding or not. You will be most concerned to guard against errors of omission – things that you could have done that you didn't.

An avoidance goal will focus your attention on what you *should not* do, in case it might end badly. So, you will pursue your goal with caution. Your state of mind will be vigilance rather than eagerness. You will pay particular attention to any signals that anything might be going wrong. You will be most concerned to guard against errors of commission – making mistakes or doing things you should not do.

Adopting an approach goal generally leads to greater persistence, especially after a setback or failure. It motivates you to make more effort to look for other ways to achieve your goal and to generate many different alternatives. Consequently, you have a much higher chance of achieving your goal in the long term. In contrast, an avoidance goal – precisely because your primary desire is to avoid making a mistake – inhibits your ability to persist after a setback or failure. You will be more inclined to stick to your initial strategy, rather than risk trying a new strategy. Your efforts will have a repetitive rather than an innovative quality, thus reducing your chances of succeeding in the long term.[2]

## *Positive purpose and flourishing*

Framing your purpose in a positive way affects how you feel about yourself.

It gives you a greater sense of autonomy, of vitality and of general satisfaction. It gives you an immediate sense of control and a feeling that you can influence what actually happens, when it happens and how it happens, so you engage with the world in a more vigorous way. A sense of control becomes a self-fulfilling prophecy. It makes you feel more personally effective. Things that initially looked like eluding your control seem more controllable.

In short, having a positive purpose builds a flourishing sense of self.

This has long-term effects on how you feel about yourself.

For example, when people are asked to recall what are known as 'self-defining memories' – episodes from their past that remain especially vivid to them – those who recall trying to achieve positive goals showed high levels of positive feelings about themselves. In contrast, people who reported a high number of goals involving avoiding undesirable outcomes, were more negative generally about themselves. The implication for flourishing is clear: if your list of personal goals contains a higher proportion of approach goals rather than avoidance goals, if your life is characterized by a strong sense of positive purpose, you are more likely to experience success in life and to enjoy a high level of personal well-being.[3]

When you are feeling positive, you are more likely to use approach goals because positive emotions trigger approach behaviour in general – increasing the urge to engage with the environment around you; to explore new things, new people, new situations and new opportunities; to continue doing what you've started. This behaviour broadens and builds your thinking and range of responses and induces a generally more open, optimistic, receptive frame of mind – all of which are compatible with approach goals.[4]

Positive emotions also act as a very efficient antidote to stress.

Suppose, for example, what you set out to do has turned out to be much more complicated and difficult than you anticipated, or that you experience a setback. If you can generate some positive emotions – a pleasant feeling derived from remembering a pleasant experience, a feeling of confidence derived from reminding yourself of a previous success or of the people who love you – this will speed up your recovery from the physiological and psychological effects of stress and put you back on track for achieving your goal.

It also works the other way round – if you use approach goals, you are likely to feel more positive. The nature of approach goals is to focus your attention on opportunity and possibility. You will pay more attention to signals and information that you are achieving your goal, and you will be less thrown by negative or threatening information.[5] You will persist longer and will keep generating new ways to achieve your goal, so you are more likely to succeed – all of which will increase your positive feelings.

Of course, there are occasions when an avoidance goal is preferable. When you are in a high-risk situation – when a child is ill, or there is a crisis in a relationship or in a business – your purpose has to be firmly focused on reducing the level of risk and avoiding any further damage being done. But, outside of these crisis situations, an approach goal, a positive purpose, is the better option. That is why individuals who have a temperamental tendency to self-doubt and worry, and are thus more inclined to form avoidance goals, must work harder to create a positive purpose.

However, all of us, irrespective of our temperament, will very often find that many of the purposes we are pursuing are not our own. They are being dictated by others, either explicitly (because they require us to do something), or implicitly (coming from our own internal pressure to please). When we are doing what we 'should' or what we 'ought' to do, or are motivated by shame or guilt, it is very difficult to work from a genuinely positive purpose.

You can transform obligations by imbuing them with your own positive purpose. You may be finishing a project, or taking care of somebody, or trying to fix a problem because you have to. But, you can add a positive purpose – for example, 'I am doing this task because my positive purpose is to do it better than I have ever done it before.'

## *Escaping the white bear*

Many of the examples above are about having a positive purpose to *behave* in a certain way. But flourishing is also about creating a *state of mind* that is positive, happy, confident, energized, optimistic, resilient.

Trying to achieve a positive state of mind is a bit trickier. Many of our attempts to control our thoughts and our feelings in order to achieve a certain state of mind – to be happier or less depressed, for example – are not very successful. In fact, we often end up feeling exactly the opposite of what we intended. Psychologist Daniel Wegner has discovered why exactly this happens.[6]

When you form any intention or purpose, your brain initiates two powerful processes to make that happen. The first is a conscious 'operating process', the job of your 'executive self'. The second is a powerful 'monitoring process' that automatically checks if you are not achieving that purpose. When the two systems work together well, you achieve your purpose. Generally, when your purpose is to *do* something – get the dinner ready, or produce a thousand widgets a week – these two systems work in tight harmony. Your executive self has to make that happen. Meanwhile, your monitoring system is looking for any negative information on your progress ('Potatoes not peeled; table not set' 'Already Wednesday, and not on target'). That information is sent to the executive self, who then has to try harder, or change tactics and get back in control.

However, when it comes to trying to control your thoughts and feelings rather than your behaviour, it gets a bit trickier. The two systems can work against each other and you can end up in exactly the opposite state to what you intended.

We are all familiar with the phenomenon.

- The more you try to feel sleepy, the more wide awake you become.
- You try to stop worrying and end up worrying about worrying.
- You are anxious in case you say the wrong thing, and end up saying the thing you least wanted to say.
- You want to be positive, but every single reason not to be happy floods into your mind.
- You instruct yourself to stop being anxious, and immediately find your heart is fluttering, your neck muscles are rigid and your stomach is in turmoil.
- You set out to stop being depressed or insecure, yet you end up feeling even more depressed and insecure.

Wegner calls these 'ironic effects'.

If you were a volunteer in Wegner's laboratory, he would demonstrate this 'ironic effect' by instructing you not to think about a white bear. But, despite your best efforts, your brain will do exactly the opposite and will produce a fully formed image of – what? Well, of a white bear of course. And the more you try to banish the bear from your brain, the more persistently he will return.

We are all aware of this phenomenon in our ordinary lives. Sometimes, to our utter bafflement, as we walk gingerly along a cliff edge with the firm purpose of *not* falling off, the thought, 'Jump off!' pops into our mind. Or, as we are carefully drying our very best crystal vase, the perverse thought occurs, 'Go on, drop it!' Or, in a tense social situation where we need to be on our best behaviour, we feel an overwhelming urge to say something completely inappropriate. Mercifully, most of us succeed most of the time in not actually saying or doing the things we want to suppress.

Why are we afflicted with what Edgar Allan Poe called this 'imp of the perverse'?

It is the unfortunate by-product – and a brilliant illustration – of how the two powerful processes in your brain are working to help you achieve your purpose.

For example, when your purpose is *not* to think of the white bear, your brain's operating process tries to help you do that by constantly instructing you to put the thought out of your mind, or by generating other thoughts to distract you from this image. But, your brain's monitoring system is simultaneously examining your progress ('Am I succeeding in not thinking about the white bear?') which, of course, immediately introduces the image back into your mind again. You try even harder to banish the beast, and on it goes. Eventually, your executive self gives up the effort and allows the white bear permanent squatting rights in your mind.

We frequently have this 'white bear' experience when we try to stop a particular worry.

Your teenage son is late coming home.

You worry he may have had an accident.

You tell yourself not to worry.

Your monitoring system checks your progress ('Have I stopped worrying about him having an accident?').

Instantly, an image of him walking home alone along a dark road pops into your mind.

You try even harder to banish that thought.

But now, an even more alarming image appears in your mind.

A car driven by a drunken driver is careening towards him.

On and on . . . until eventually you give up and allow your mind to flood with the most lurid images.

The fundamental reason why this happens is that the two brain processes you use to achieve your purposes are not equal. Your operating process relies on your executive self, who is like the manufacturing manager in a complaints department – it is his job to keep a lot of people happy in a very pressurized environment. He has to use up a lot of effort and conscious control to achieve that. But, as you already know, your poor executive self is easily exhausted from this kind of effort.

Your monitoring process, on the other hand, is like the security CCTV camera that just rolls along, effortlessly searching for any lapses in the manager's operation. Every piece of negative information is logged and is sent to the manager. The more stressed the manager becomes, the more your monitoring process floods his exhausted mind with information that he is failing.

There are three ways of avoiding the 'white bear' effect.

- You can define your desired 'state of mind' behaviourally.
- You can frame your purpose positively.
- You can avoid mental overload.

### *Defining your state of mind in positive actions*

The executive self and the monitoring system work better together when they are trying to produce actions, rather than thoughts and feelings.

When you want to achieve a specific state of mind – such as being happier, or calmer, or more open-minded – close your eyes and visualize in your mind's eye what you would look like and sound like and act like if you achieved that desired state.

Where are you when you visualize this?

Who are you speaking to, or listening to?

What are you saying?

Are you asking questions?

What expression is on your face?

What gestures are you using?

The more detail you imagine, the better. If you have trouble visualizing any aspect of this, pick someone who seems to you to be happy, calm or open-minded in the way you desire, and observe them carefully. How exactly are they behaving? Then visualize yourself copying those actions. In that way, you are using your capacity to 'mirror' someone to help you achieve your positive purpose.

What this exercise does is link your desired state of mind with real behaviour. In this way, when you remind yourself of your positive purpose, it will be automatically converted into behavioural goals. Your executive self can immediately go to work to make that behaviour happen, and your automatic monitoring system will happily oblige with a constant read-out of your progress – not 'white bears'.

### *Framing your purpose positively*

Wegner found that when people express what they want to achieve in a positive way, the two systems in the brain work better together.

Suppose, for example, that your positive purpose is to be 'less critical' (even though it is expressed negatively, it is still a positive purpose). Now, suppose you express that positively – 'to be open and positive'. Your executive self then concentrates your attention on searching for positive evidence that you are succeeding ('Yes, I really listened positively to what he said and did not jump to conclusions'). Meanwhile, your monitoring system now has a much bigger job – to search for any thoughts and actions that are 'not open and positive'. Looking for anything that is 'not' something is a very broad-ranging search, covering not just thoughts and actions that are the opposite of what you want to achieve (being defensive, prejudiced, opinionated) but a whole range of other thoughts that are neutral or irrelevant to being 'open-minded' (being curious, interested, bored, hungry, sexually aroused). So, in a manner of speaking, you keep your overactive monitoring system so busy that it has no time to be creating 'white bear' effects.

In contrast, if you frame your purpose negatively ('Be less critical'), you hand over power to the automatic monitoring system. Now, your executive self has to divide its efforts into 1) trying not to be critical, and 2) figuring out ways to be the opposite – that is, more open. Meanwhile, your monitoring system has a much simpler job – checking out if you are succeeding in being 'less critical' – and is now focused like a laser on searching out every last critical, defensive, intolerant thought. The result is a barrage of those very thoughts. You have the same perverse imp whispering in your ear, 'I don't agree with that. Nor that either. That's nonsense. Go on, contradict him. Tell him he is all wrong and you are right. Ah, go on.'

Setting out positively to *create* a particular state of mind is much more likely to succeed than setting out to *eliminate* a negative state of mind. That is why my two principles of flourishing are both framed positively:

- actively build the positive, and
- actively contain (not eliminate) the negative.

### *Avoiding mental overload*

When our purpose is to change the way we think and feel so that we can achieve a desired state of mind, Wegner discovered that what determines whether we succeed or not is our capacity to pay attention, to concentrate, to give time to something.

That mental capacity is substantially reduced and depleted by mental overload, time pressure, too many distractions and stress. When we are mentally overloaded, our capacity does not just decline. Rather, our efforts often end up producing exactly the opposite result to what we intended. That cognitive load fatally undermines our struggle against an unwanted state of mind – depression, worry, irritability – and turns it into an invitation for those states to overwhelm us.[7]

When you suffer from mental overload, this tilts the control away from your executive self and hands it over to the automatic monitoring process. To regain control, you have to reverse that by replenishing the supplies your executive self most needs – time to step back and reflect, an opportunity to recover using some of the techniques outlined in Chapter 10. However, in the long term, emergency measures are not enough. The very best way to strengthen your executive self is to build a capacity for mindful thinking.

The second resource your executive self needs is discipline and habit.

Given how easily distracted we are, we have to bring our positive purpose under the control of time, place and ritual. The more we associate practising our positive purpose with a particular time, place and ritual, the more successfully we will implement it.

For example, if your positive purpose is to become an especially attentive listener to your children, select:

- a time of the day (in the half-hour after the children come home from school), or
- a place (their bedroom), or
- a ritual ('talk time' after the bedtime story).

In that way, you lend your purpose the power of discipline and habit. It becomes less susceptible to distraction, or forgetting, or negative mood.

## *Selecting your positive purpose*

There is virtually no limit to the kinds of positive purposes you can form. They tend, however, to fall into two categories:

- those related to day-to-day activities, and
- those to do with building our characters and being better people.

### *Creating a positive purpose in day-to-day activities*

As we go about our normal day, there are two layers to every task and interaction.

The 'external' layer is what we have to do. Take any conversation. What we are saying is conveying the 'message' of the interaction: giving feedback to a work colleague; telling somebody to do something; asking for a favour; looking for information. But there is also an 'internal' layer to the conversation, what psychologists call a 'meta-message'. Unconsciously, we pay as much attention to this meta-message as we do to the message. In particular, we constantly monitor two kinds of meta-messages – those conveying closeness, and those conveying status.

Is what the other person is saying, or how they are behaving, making us feel closer to them or pushed away?

Are we feeling equal and respected, or put in a one-down position?[8]

Every interaction offers the opportunity to create a sense of closeness and liking, or equality and respect – preferably both. That makes a very useful positive for daily interactions.

But there are also other layers in everyday activities. Recall again our four basic drives that we looked at in Chapter 5, to:

- bond
- achieve
- learn, and
- protect what we value.

Each of these can be recast as a positive purpose.

As well as creating opportunities to *bond* with others in a way that is mutually caring and respectful, you can look for opportunities to create a sense of achievement in the most modest of daily activities. For example, you can try to slice a carrot, do a presentation, tidy your filing cabinet, walk to the bus or cut the grass better or faster than you ever did it before. Or you can set out to make it a *learning* experience, to note three things you never knew before about this task.

Thinking about and finding a positive purpose can transform an acquaintance into a close friend and collaborator, a simple task into an interesting one, a neutral day into a great day – and a routine life into a flourishing life.

*Learning to get along with Kevin*

Once, at a week-long course I was attending, each person was paired with another person for a full day to work together closely on a project. To my dismay, I found myself paired with Kevin, a man who had already made clear his strongly held opinions on a certain issue – opinions I definitely did not share. I groaned inwardly at the prospect of spending a whole day working with him.

But then, in a moment of lucidity, I decided that instead of resisting the experience, I would embrace this opportunity to get to know somebody I would never willingly choose to spend time with. I thought, 'I will be fascinated by the differences between us, rather than irritated.'

This then became my positive purpose.

I really observed him and listened to him, so that I could understand the way his mind worked. As a consequence, I noticed things about him – and about the way I normally respond – that I otherwise wouldn't have, and these observations set off other questions in my mind. I wanted to find out more about what motivated him, what experiences in his life had shaped his values, what experiences and values we shared.

Kevin responded in kind to my efforts. Our interaction became more positive, more engaged. As the day progressed, what had started as an unwelcome challenge turned into a day-long, totally absorbing and enjoyable experience. At its end, each participant was asked to write down the most worthwhile experience they'd had on the course – the one they had learned most from – and to share this with the whole class. Quite independently, both Kevin and I nominated our day working together as that experience par excellence. I was touched by what he said about me and how much he had learned, and it was clear from his response that he was equally touched and pleased by what I had to say.

At the end of the day, our fundamental disagreements remained, but were respectfully contained within the positive and interesting relationship we had built with each other.

### *Creating a positive purpose to become a better person*

A flourishing life is not just about 'feeling good'. It is also about 'being good' and 'doing good'.

Being good is what we once called 'character building'. Over the past few decades, we have largely forgotten the concept of character building because of the focus on the softer, more expressive idea of personality. However, psychologists Christopher Peterson and Martin Seligman, both major figures in the Positive Psychology movement, have gone some way to changing that and make the case for building character strengths – or plain, old-fashioned virtues – as a central component of a flourishing life.[9]

Conscious of the need to redefine and agree what we mean by character strengths, they set about examining how the major world religions, philosophers, writers, psychologists and psychiatrists defined these strengths. Based on that extensive trawl, they came up with a workable classification of six character strengths and values:

1. wisdom and knowledge
2. courage
3. humanity
4. justice
5. temperance
6. transcendence.

All are defined in very practical behavioural terms.

### 1. WISDOM AND KNOWLEDGE

Building this strength requires:

- creativity (devising novel and productive ways to think about and do things)
- curiosity (having an interest in things for their own sake)
- open-mindedness (weighing all the evidence fairly, not jumping to conclusions)
- love of learning (mastering new ideas, new ways to understand things)
- perspective (a way of looking at issues that is broad and balanced).

### 2. COURAGE

Courage is the emotional strength to accomplish goals in the face of opposition. It requires:

- bravery (not shrinking from a threat or a challenge, standing up for what is right)
- persistence (finishing what you have started despite obstacles)
- integrity (taking responsibility for your actions, being sincere and genuine)
- vitality (approaching life with excitement and energy).

### 3. HUMANITY

Humanity is the strength to care for others. It requires:

- love (valuing close relationships with others)
- kindness (helping others)

- emotional intelligence (being aware of your own motives and feelings and those of others; knowing how to relate in different social situations).

### 4. JUSTICE

This is not just a personal character strength but a civic strength that is the basis of a healthy community. It requires:

- being socially responsible (doing your share, being loyal to a group, being a team player)
- fairness (treating everybody fairly, not letting personal feelings bias decisions about others)
- leadership (inspiring and encouraging your group to get things done; seeing that things happen, but also maintaining good relationships within the group).

### 5. TEMPERANCE

This is almost like a word from another age, so forgotten has this strength become. It is the virtue that we have least interest in – and yet, arguably, it is the one that human beings need most in modern society. Temperance means having the strength to protect against excess. It requires:

- forgiveness (accepting the shortcomings of others; forgiving those who have done you wrong and giving people a second chance)
- modesty (letting your achievements speak for themselves; not always seeking the credit or the spotlight)
- prudence (being careful about your choices; not taking undue risks; not saying or doing things that you might later regret)
- self-control (being self-disciplined; tempering your feelings and actions).

### 6. TRANSCENDENCE

This is the strength that allows you to forge connections to the larger universe and create meaning in your life. It requires:

- appreciation of beauty and excellence (noticing and appreciating not just great work and skilled performances, but also the wonders of life, the beauty in things)
- gratitude (being thankful for the good things that happen)

- hope and optimism (expecting the best in the future, and working to achieve that)
- humour (being playful, seeing the light side of things, making other people smile)
- spirituality (having a coherent set of beliefs about the higher purpose of life; knowing where you fit in within the larger scheme of things; having a set of values that shape and guide how you behave and that give you comfort).

These six character strengths are most probably grounded in evolutionary biology – they are the best ways we have found to survive as a species and to live together as sustainable communities.

They are 'corrective' in that they help us to counteract negative behaviour and weaknesses that are inherent in the human condition and that cause a lot of misery: selfishness, intolerance, cowardice, rigidity, dishonesty, loss of meaning and despair. These strengths are universal and at the core of most of the major religious traditions. Many prayers and religious practices are expressions of gratitude, hope and forgiveness – or, at the very least, pleas to God to bestow such virtues on us.

When we follow these principles, they contribute hugely to a good life for ourselves and for others. Not least, they are the strengths that allow us to survive and transcend adversity and suffering. These are the character strengths that most of us would like to be described as having. They are what we hope to instil in our children. Increasingly, they are vital for integrity and excellence in the way we run organizations.[10]

Most poignantly, they pass what Peterson and Seligman call 'the deathbed test'. This means that if you were asked on your deathbed to complete the sentence, 'I wish I had spent more time . . .' you are likely to mention wishing that you had:

- got to know your children better, or
- spent more time with your friends, or
- left a mark on the world so that it was a better place, or
- possessed more courage to stand up against bad things and destructive people, or
- been more grateful for the good things in your life, or
- exercised leadership when it counted, or
- spent more time thinking about the purpose and meaning of your life.

So, if you want to build a positive purpose in your life, above and beyond the positive purpose you instil in your day-to-day activities, you might consider perusing that list of character strengths again. Choose the one that strikes you as most relevant and most needed in your personal life, or in an important relationship, or in the organization in which you work.

When you find it, choose which aspect of the strength most appeals to you – how, for example, do you want to practise courage?

Which aspect is most intuitively appealing to you?

Which is most relevant and easily applicable in your life – for example, do you want to strengthen your capacity to stand up for what is right, or finish some difficult project in your life that you have started despite daunting obstacles, or take responsibility for something you have done?

The list of strengths may look impossibly daunting, but the reality is that they are all deeply interconnected. If you practise one, you tend to strengthen others.

In time, they will form the unbreakable filaments that keep a flourishing life together.

STRATEGY FIVE

# *Take charge of your mood*

'Don't let yourself get down. Either be up or getting up.'

Patty Briguglio, MMM Associates, Inc.

# 13. Mood matters

Just as emotion affects how we think and reason, what we remember and how we treat other people, so does mood. The effect may be less intense, but it is more prolonged and more global.

Unlike emotions, which are right at the front of your consciousness, moods are more free-floating, diffuse, hovering at the back of your mind. While emotions demand immediate attention and action, moods are more subtle, not associated with any particular urge to *do* anything. Rather, they are capable of affecting *whatever* you are doing, affecting you in a more global way.

Sometimes you are aware of your mood, sometimes not. You may have forgotten the event that evoked an emotional reaction, but suddenly your mood has darkened or brightened without you noticing it. You may sometimes find yourself in a mood and have no idea what caused it.

Moods are influenced by many things:

- time of the day
- natural sunlight
- the weather
- hormonal changes
- positive and negative ions in the atmosphere
- the safety and pleasantness of the environment
- personality.

Unhappily for them, people who are temperamentally high in neuroticism are more prone to negative moods.

Those who are temperamentally high in extroversion, luckily for them, are more prone to positive moods.

Most often, moods are provoked by an emotional reaction to an event – the residual emotions left over from something that made us happy or upset us.

Moods are not just watered-down feelings. While both may be instigated by the same event, they are very different processes and serve different psychological needs. Emotions alert us to threats and opportunities; they are the generals calling for action. Moods are more like the Quartermaster General, in charge of the supply lines: 'Have I enough personal resources – physical, psychological or social – to take on this challenge / get up and tend to my crying baby / motivate the people who work for me / be sociable at this party?'

If the answer is yes, your mood will be positive.

If the answer is no, it will be negative.

Moods, then, give you a constant read-out of how resourceful or depleted you feel: biologically, psychologically, socially, materially.[1]

If you understand mood in this way, you can understand why mood varies throughout the day. Positive, active feelings track natural biological rhythms, increasing rapidly from early morning until about midday and then remaining at much the same level (but peaking every few hours) until about 9 p.m., after which they fall sharply. They also reflect individual biological rhythms – whether you are a day or a night person. No such daily rhythms are found for negative feelings, which are more influenced by specific events – although, for those who are depressed, the peak moments of sadness occur early and late in the day.

Moods are also affected by the seasons, with people generally reporting more negative moods in the winter, which is also the time of the highest levels of Seasonal Affective Disorder (SAD), a type of depression that comes on in the winter months. This makes evolutionary sense. Our mood system evolved to encourage us to be less active during times of fewer resources – when there is less light, poorer vision, the days are cold and short, and sources of food are less freely available.

For the average adult, a mood lasts for about two hours. Mood changes can be subtle – from mildly positive to feeling a bit down, or vice versa – or they can be extreme – going from elation to wild despair.

When your mood changes, your entire consciousness changes with it.

- What you pay attention to changes.
- How you make judgements and decisions changes.
- The way you remember things changes.
- The way you interact with people changes.

All of these changes have real consequences for how you see the world, how you react to it and how you behave. The more intense your mood, the bigger the effects.

You use your current mood as 'diagnostic' information ('How do I feel about this?) when you have to make a judgement or decision. Of course, the more objective information you have, the less you need to rely on your mood to make a judgement. If you know that you want to buy a particular car that is available in two garages with a €500 price difference, you don't really need to ask yourself, 'How do I feel about this?' in order to make your decision. Having said that, you may still pay attention to your mood. If being in the cheaper garage makes you feel uneasy, you may decide not to buy the car there.

But many decisions we face in our lives are not that straightforward.

Should I trust him?

Will I invest in this new product?

Will I continue going out with this person?

Will I vote for this person?

Will I take this new job?

Will I have a baby?

Will I tell her what I found out?

Will I take a chance and let my son go on that holiday with his friends?

Will I promote her?

These kinds of decisions have a lot riding on them. Almost certainly, you will not have all the information you need. Or what you do know may be uncertain or ambiguous. Or the situation may be changing rapidly. For these kinds of decisions, you rely more heavily on the diagnostic information provided by your mood to make the decision – what you call your 'gut instinct'.

In making a decision in this way, you are falling back on our old friend the amygdala. It takes note of your mood and immediately scans your archive of experience.

What happened the other times when I felt in this mood?

How did it work out?

Was it dangerous or safe?

Was it good for me or bad for me?

This comparison is done by way of association, not in a logical way. This means that if an aspect of the new situation matches an old memory in any way, the two experiences become associated in your mind and the amygdala reacts as if they *are* the same, mobilizing you to react to the experience now as you did in the past – even though you may have no conscious memory of how you reacted then.

## *Mood affects the way we think*

When we are in a good mood, we think fast and effortlessly. Provided that we are diligent and take reasonable account of the objective facts that we have, positive mood improves the quality of our thinking. We come to decisions faster and are more confident about them, which makes it more likely we will follow through on them. If we are reasonably self-aware, and know our typical blind spots, positive mood also gives us more confidence in our gut instincts, allowing us to use the vast amount of personal experience we have accumulated in our emotional memory – much of which may be unconscious.

When we are in a low mood, thinking becomes slower and more effortful. We pore over every piece of information. Negative mood undermines our confidence in using impressions, intuition, 'rules of thumb' and other thinking shortcuts. But this more effortful way of thinking and making judgements does not make us any more accurate. In a study cleverly titled 'On being sad and mistaken' researchers found that when people in a sad mood were shown brief samples of people's behaviour, they made less accurate judgements about them than people in a positive mood. They were also less able to make judgements about the meaning of non-verbal behaviour or what type of relationships there might be between people. However, when they were distracted while they were trying to make these judgements, thereby disrupting their low mood and slow, deliberative approach, their judgements actually improved.[2]

Mood also affects how we think about ourselves. When people in a good mood are given positive and negative feedback about themselves, they pay more attention to the positive feedback and consider it more informative. But when people are in a bad mood, they rate the negative feedback as equally informative. This is known as 'depressive realism' – giving more weight to negative information, with a corresponding diminution in willingness to give ourselves the benefit of the doubt.

## *Mood affects what we remember*

When you are in a positive mood, you tend to remember other positive things stored in your memory. Ask someone in a positive mood how their life is going and they will judge that most things are working well –

including even their car or TV set! They have to try harder to remember any negative things.

When you are in a sad and defeated mood, you will more readily access all your sad memories. This makes you feel even sadder and more defeated. When you are in a bad mood, you rapidly access and recall a host of other negative memories and experiences before concluding that life is going badly.

'My job is lousy. But then again, it is no worse than the last job. God, I won't forget what happened there in a hurry. You can't rely on people, even people you think of as friends. Wish I'd known that before I invested all that time in my girlfriend . . .'

And on it goes.

The effects of negative mood are much more powerful if you are unaware of your mood. The opposite is also true – when you become aware of your mood, its effect on you is lessened because you can take it into account.

'I know I am in a bad mood, so maybe I shouldn't overreact.'

Not surprisingly, the effects of negative mood are also much stronger if your self-esteem is low. Even more interesting, for those who have high self-esteem, the effect of mood works the other way: the more negative their mood, the more *positive* memories they recall.[3] It is as if, in the face of a threat, self-esteem acts like a reassuring parent within – immediately reminding you of your talents and achievements, of all the pleasures you have had in life and will have again.

The most cheering news is that the effects of positive mood are also powerful. While bad mood interferes with your access to positive memories and increases access to negative memories, the effect of positive moods is to substantially increase your access to positive memories that improve the quality of your decisions and help you recreate the world around you in a more positive way.

## *Mood affects our ability to pursue our goals*

When you are in a good mood, most goals seem possible.

When you are in a bad mood, everything seems too much.

Positive moods make you feel you can do what you need or want to do. You can recall past successes and have a much higher expectation of success. As a consequence, you will act in a more personally effective way. You are more likely to work at your best: to make good decisions, to be creative and problem-solving. Interestingly, when you are in a positive mood, you will find it easier to decide when you have done enough at a particular point and be more comfortable with what you have done. This is not because positive moods encourage you to reduce your standards; they just give you a more confident sense of what is actually required.

In a negative mood the pattern is exactly the opposite. You have a reduced sense of personal efficacy and a lowered expectation of success, particularly in relation to solving personal problems. You set high standards for yourself – but these act as a drain. You feel more burdened. You are more susceptible to perfectionism. Sometimes you set the bar so high that you have unconsciously prepared your excuse if you don't succeed ('I knew it was too much for me') – a self-handicapping strategy. You focus less on what needs to be done, or on understanding the detail of the task, because almost all of your energy is devoted to managing your negative feelings. Taking these effects together, your negative mood is telling you that you are not likely to succeed in your goals any time soon – creating a great deal of psychological pain, and becoming a self-fulfilling prophecy.

When you're in a negative mood – particularly when you feel anxious, sad or low – you're more likely to want to be alone, more focused on yourself. This intense self-focus is counterproductive, because it makes you less inclined to actively engage with the situation and to respond effectively. In the face of a threat, or after a setback, a certain amount of self-reflection is very productive. The trouble with negative mood is that it can very easily turn reflection into downward spirals of worry and rumination.

Negative mood directs your attention to all the problematic features of the situation and away from whatever opportunities there may be to deal with it. That is why one of the most successful ways to change a negative mood is to deliberately distract yourself from it by focusing on something outside yourself.

Positive mood has the opposite effect. Your good mood is telling you that you are ready for action. You have the urge to get things done, and so you engage more vigorously with the environment. Even when all you want to do is relax, in a good mood you are more likely to organize yourself to relax more effectively.

## *Mood affects our relationships with other people and is highly contagious*

When you're in a positive mood, you're more likely to want to be with other people and to have a good time with them. That, in turn, heightens your good mood. In a positive mood, you are better company. You are more motivated to cooperate with other people and to want to help them. You are better at managing, motivating and inspiring others. While nobody likes negative feedback about themselves, when you are in a positive mood you are better able to tolerate it.

Positive mood has such powerful effects on the way we interact with others, because it makes us more likely to trust them. Indeed, it is emotions and mood as much as, or maybe even more than, reasoning that determine our level of trust in others. Positive mood does not make us more trusting in some gullible way. Rather, it alerts us to information and cues about the other person that indicate whether the other person is trustworthy. Only when we find that information or those cues are we ready to trust.[4]

When you are consumed by a very powerful negative mood, all these effects are reversed. You feel less inclined to be with others – and when you are, you may be irritable, uncooperative, distrustful, demanding or needy.

It is worth considering the average duration of an adult mood – a full two hours. Two hours is a quarter of the average working day. For most of us, it is the time we spend with family and friends during a day. For working parents, it probably represents almost all the time they will spend with their children after work. Our mood will significantly affect the quality of these vital interactions.

Take this example of how her mother's moods had a lifelong impact on Martina.

> I used to dread coming home from school in case my mother would be in one of her 'moods'. You could just sense it the minute you went in the door. She would have this look on her face like, 'Don't even think of getting in my way.' Stuff would be banged down – well, not exactly banged down but let's just say put down with some force. My sister and I would try to be really quiet and stay out of her way but then we'd have to ask her something, and she would answer like you had goaded her beyond endurance. I used to find myself grinding my teeth from the tension – a habit I still have to this day. When

my father would come in from work, it would get worse. There would be these silences. If he heard her banging stuff, he would say, 'Oh, your mother is in one of her moods.' It seemed to roll off him like water off a duck's back. But really, it blighted my childhood.

### *The contagion of moods*

The power of moods to affect relationships is a persuasive argument to become more aware of your mood and better at managing it.

But here is another powerful argument: moods are highly contagious. They transfer to other people and can have the same far-reaching effect on them as they have on you.

You don't even have to know somebody else for their mood to affect you. Your mood becomes 'entrained' by somebody else's mood.[5] Mood can be transferred from one person to another via tone of voice alone.

Take, for example, an experiment when people were asked to listen to a speech about a neutral topic. They thought it was a test of comprehension. Some heard it spoken in a slightly sad voice, others in a cheerful voice. Just listening to the speech put them in the same mood as the speaker. Moreover, when they were required to repeat what they had heard, they spontaneously imitated the speaker's emotional tone.[6]

In another experiment three strangers were left sitting facing one another for two minutes. They were told that they could look at but not speak to each other. After two minutes, the most emotionally expressive of the three had succeeded in transmitting his or her mood to the other two – even though not a single word had been spoken.[7]

We don't know exactly how moods become contagious, but part of the explanation lies in one of the powerful automatic processes in the brain – our tendency to 'mirror' each other. A new type of neuron, called a 'mirror neuron', has been identified in monkeys and more recently in the human brain.[8] When we watch somebody do something, the same neurons start to fire in our brain as are firing in the person performing the action.

For example, when we see somebody pick up an object, our brain 'mirrors' the reaction and gets the same hand muscles that we would use if we were picking up the same object ready to move.

Watching a football match on the TV, we see a player leap high into the air and our brain mirrors his actions – our adrenaline surges and our heart races as if we were on the pitch.

We witness somebody telling a very sad story, and our own eyes prick with tears.

We see somebody receive a blow, and we automatically recoil.

In any of these instances, if a neuroscientist was doing an fMRI (functional Magnetic Resonance Imaging) scan of the brain, the activity in it would mirror that of the person doing the action.[9] This mirroring mechanism – whereby we instinctively imitate the actions of others – is involuntary and automatic. We don't have to *think* about what other people are doing or feeling, we simply *know* what's involved and unconsciously mimic it. This mirroring is a primitive form of empathy – an immediate and instinctive reading of another person's thoughts, feelings, intentions and reactions. And it explains how we 'pick up' others' feelings and moods so readily.

This tendency to mirror is deeply embedded in the human psyche. From birth, babies imitate the facial expressions of the adults who are caring for them. This tendency continues right throughout our lives as we unconsciously mirror the body posture, hand movements and mannerisms of people we are interacting with, especially if we are getting on well with them.

Not only do we mimic their gestures, but we come to *feel* as they do. This can have powerful consequences – both positive and negative.

In a positive way, it can help us bond closely with the other person. As we unconsciously mimic them, it increases feelings of rapport. In turn, when we like people, we are more likely to mimic them, further quickening the pace of bonding. Just observe young couples who are deeply in love 'mirroring' each other's every movement and gesture. Look around the staff room, or cafeteria, or wherever people meet in pairs to discuss work-related issues. The pairs that are physically 'in sync' are much more likely to be having a productive discussion. Those in physically awkward alignment – one sitting far back in the chair, arms folded tightly, the other leaning forward, shoulders hunched, hands moving jerkily – are unlikely to be having a positive conversation.

The important point here is that this social mimicking – and the behavioural consequences – occurs without conscious choice.

### *Emotions, moods and 'physiological linkage' in close relationships*

One of the most dramatic examples of 'mirroring' is the physiological linkage that becomes established when women live together – in families, shared apartments or college dormitories – when their menstrual cycles gradually become synchronized.[10] For men, this explains the enduring mystery of why the women in the household all seem to go into emotional meltdown together – and why the bathroom is always engaged.

As you might expect, the closer, more intimate and more important the relationship – irrespective of whether it is positive or negative – the more powerful the mood contagion. Couples in love or at war with each other, parents and children, close siblings, friends or work colleagues are especially interlinked physiologically and emotionally.

Recall when you were a child how in milliseconds, literally a heartbeat, you could pick up your mother or father's mood – just like Martina in the earlier example.

Recall the dizzy excitement of falling in love – the dizziness mainly caused by the fact that the slightest look or touch from the beloved, even an image of them coming into your mind, could send surges of hormones coursing all over your body that could, literally, leave you feeling weak.

Like in music, we take our emotional note from others and become attuned to them – for better or for worse. The more emotionally engaged we are with somebody with whom we are interacting, the more powerful the contagion and the physiological linkage between us. And the more emotionally negative and stressful the interaction is, the stronger the link.

Take a couple having a row.

At the beginning, each partner's body is operating to its own individual rhythms.

Within fifteen minutes, their physiological profiles begin to resemble each other more and more.

As her heart rate quickens, so does his.

As his blood pressure rises, so does hers.

As stress hormones rush through her body, they also rush through his.

They have become physiologically linked, as if they were hooked up to some *Mad Max* machine.

The more negativity there is between them, the more matched their bodies become. Something similar happens when they are having a positive, pleasant encounter – but the linkage is much less marked (although during intensely enjoyable sex there is a high degree of positive physiological linkage).[11]

### *Emotional contagion in groups and at work*

Let's take another example.

A group of teenagers are out with their friends on Saturday night.

There is an air of restless excitement, a buzz of energy crackling through the group: they joke, tease, jostle, interrupt and poke each other good-humouredly.

The noise level rises.

There is a sense of letting go, of being swept away by the group mood, of having a brilliant time together.

Everybody feels free to say or do anything – every word and action gets an enthusiastic response, as others respond with something even more crazy and exciting, each member of the group following some unspoken agreement that this high-intensity interaction must be kept going.

There is a state of high elation, manic glee.

What the couple arguing and the teenagers enjoying a good time have in common is that irrespective of the 'event' that started the episode (the disagreement between the couple, the decision to go out for a good time with friends), the interaction develops a life of its own, powered by the emotional contagion between the parties.

Emotional contagion also happens at meetings, among people working in the same department or work team, among members of a board or a committee, and among players on the same sports team. For example, over a period of weeks, the mood of each player in professional sports teams becomes more synchronized with the moods of the others – irrespective of stressful events or how well they are doing in matches.[12] Skill and discipline are important for team success, but the ability of a team to feel 'as one' is probably even more important. A wave of determination, optimism and courage sweeping contagiously through a team lights a fire that will carry them through a tough tournament. Similarly, a wave of defeatism can spread through a team like a virus.

The more emotionally interconnected a group is, the stronger the contagion effect. This phenomenon has been observed among work groups as diverse as policemen, teachers, nurses, people who work in call centres or on assembly lines – even accountants. Across seventy different work groups the same contagion was found, and the same set of circumstances predicted the strength of the contagion. The more the group members depended on each other to get the work done and for social interaction or support, the longer they had worked together, and the stronger the moods expressed by individual members, the more contagion there was.[13]

Mood at work is influenced by many factors.[14] As always, personality counts. Those high in temperamental neuroticism are, unhappily for them, more prone to worry, anxiety and guilt about work. Those with a temperament high in extroversion are likely to be more cheerful, enthusiastic, confident and energetic at work. Stress at home can spill over into a negative mood at work. Being treated unfairly also has a big impact on mood.

Whatever your personality and life circumstances, work can and does change your mood. If the mood of the organization you work in is positive and upbeat, your mood will improve, irrespective of other stresses in your life. In that sense, work can become a sanctuary if things are going badly in other areas of your life. On the other hand, even if your life is going really well, your good mood in the morning will quickly dissipate when you enter a workplace that is negative and debilitating.

Mood at work counts – not just to the individual but to the productivity of the organization. When people are in a positive mood at work, they are:

- more cooperative
- more generous with their time and expertise
- more attentive and helpful to colleagues and to customers
- less likely to indulge in interpersonal conflict
- better at creative problem-solving.

There is also less absenteeism, and reduced staff turnover. As a consequence, the people the organization serves – the pupils, the patients, the customers, the citizens – get better service and are more satisfied.

When a negative mood sweeps through a group, the performance of an entire department or team can be affected.[15] For example, in a cardiac unit where the nurses' general mood was described as depressed, there was a death rate among patients four times higher than on comparable units.

## *Mood affects our ability to be highly effective leaders*

Wherever we group together with other people, everybody inevitably catches the mood of the other. This is particularly important when the other is someone we depend on – for emotional support, or for job security and success.

The mood of parents and leaders is particularly contagious, because others are depending on them. Like our primate cousins, we watch the leader of the group more carefully than anybody else.

This starts early in life. Watch how a baby or a young child, when uncertain about what to do or when confronted by something new, will instinctively look up at the parent's face, as if to ask, 'Is this OK?' Psychologists call this 'social referencing', and adults do the same with authority figures – albeit somewhat less obviously. We look carefully at the leader ('How is he responding to this?) and then we take our cue from that.

Because of this attention, the mood of the leader is very contagious. A leader's status can come from formal position, or from expertise, experience or popularity. When their mood is positive and upbeat, the group's mood improves, and vice versa. Leaders also behave in ways that further strengthen this contagion.[16] They use up more psychological space at meetings. They are usually the first to speak, and their remarks are taken seriously and taken up more frequently than the remarks of others in the group.

When leaders of organizations are in a positive mood, the positivity cascades down the organization. Everybody around them sees things in a more positive light. This, in turn, makes them more optimistic about achieving their own goals, better at absorbing and understanding information, more creative and flexible, and more effective as decision-makers. The more frequently and consistently leaders themselves experience and express positive moods, the better the people who work for them perform.

Leaders influence the mood of an organization in two other ways:

- how they lead, and
- the organizational culture they create.

A leader's emotional style sets off a chain reaction and drives everybody else's mood and behaviour.

To lead a team or an organization effectively, you have to perform a number of fundamental tasks.

- Develop a persuasive vision of the work and the organization ('Why does it matter?').
- Get people to develop a collective sense of what needs to be done and how to do it ('This is the way we do things round here').

- Convince people not just of the importance of what needs to be done but of their crucial role in this ('This is why my work matters round here').
- Create an atmosphere of cooperation and trust, enthusiasm, confidence, excitement and optimism ('We can do this together and we can succeed').
- Encourage flexibility in decision-making, and openness to change ('We are constantly learning and changing').
- Establish a meaningful identity for the organization ('This is who we are').[17]

When leaders are positive, they perform these tasks more easily and effectively, and the result is a very positive organizational culture.

One teacher describes the culture or 'feel' of her school in this way.

> What we are doing here really means something – to the children, to the parents, to us, and ultimately to the economy, I suppose. And I feel I am helping to make it happen. The principal is brilliant – she makes sure we all feel part of the whole challenge. So you feel good about yourself, no matter how hard you are working. Everybody here feels like that. All of us here can rise to whatever challenges we have to face, and we help each other out to achieve things. You never feel you are carrying the load yourself.

That's a school where the leader's mood clearly has a major positive impact – not just on the people, but on the work they do.

Denis Dempsey, a senior manager at Intel Ireland, describes the culture of that organization in similarly positive terms.

> The different major start-ups in Intel Ireland have all been major projects for me as I felt that I was part of something much bigger, not just in Intel Ireland. You had the sense that you were sitting on the crest of a wave that was getting bigger and moving faster. There was a huge buzz about that, and it was coupled with incredible growth of share price at one stage which made us all paper millionaires for several years! You could see the clear link between working hard, learning, seeing the success in Intel Ireland, and Ireland as a whole, and financial outcomes.

These leadership tasks are just as relevant for a parent taking charge of a family. Children – and parents – flourish when parents succeed in:

- creating a vision of why family and close relationships matter
- organizing a harmonious and equal way of getting family duties done
- promoting an atmosphere of high standards and high support
- encouraging flexibility, open-mindedness and a strong sense of identity.

Whether leader or parent, each of these tasks is more easily and effectively performed when you are in a positive mood. This is because positive mood widens your mental horizons, making it easier to integrate a lot of information from different sources and to extract yourself from the ordinary day-to-day routine. Positive mood makes you more optimistic, more alert to the possibility of opportunities and good outcomes. You are then more likely to feel confidence in others and in their ability to make the vision happen – and to express that confidence.

Positive mood makes you:

- a more constructive thinker
- better at creating an atmosphere of generosity, cooperation and trust
- better able to develop and maintain high-quality interpersonal relationships, and
- more creative at resolving conflicts when they arise.

Negative mood has exactly the opposite effect, keeping you constrained and focused on threat rather than opportunity.

## *Mood affects the 'culture' of organizations*

The culture of an organization (a school, a hospital, a government department, a business, a voluntary body) can be broadly defined as 'the way things are done around here' – the 'feel' or mood of the place. The culture of an organization operates at three levels.[18] Each of these levels can determine whether an organization flourishes or languishes.

The first, most obvious level is what you can see and hear – the physical look of the place:

- the environment (bright, cheerful and well maintained, or gloomy and uncared for)
- how people dress (formal or informal clothes, tidy or sloppy)
- how people address each other (by titles or first names)
- how meetings are run (regularly and efficiently, or unpredictably and chaotically)
- how decisions are made (transparently and with care, or by cliques, or carelessly)
- communications (open, frequent, engaging, clear or random, confusing, boring)
- social events (frequent and informal, or once-a-year events)
- how conflict is handled (in a timely and skilled way, or poorly handled, or avoided)
- jargon (lots of insider language, or not)
- routines and rituals ('We always do it this way').

You can observe these aspects of a culture, but their meaning may not be clear.

Why are decisions made like that?

Why do people take such care of their surroundings?

In order to understand, you have to look to the next level of the organizational culture. This second level consists of the values that the organization *says* it subscribes to, expressed in its:

- strategies
- goals
- standards
- philosophy.

These can be real or just paper exercises. (Is there anything quite as depressing as waiting for some service in a gloomy, untidy room, with dispirited or indifferent staff, while you gaze at a 'charter' on the wall telling you 'We highly value your custom' or 'We aim to please'?)

In order to really understand the culture of an organization, you have to go to the third level – the shared, unspoken understandings about what is *really* important to the organization. These are assumptions about:

- people and what motivates them
- who is important and who is not
- how the work gets done

- how success is really achieved
- how failure is dealt with.

The expressed values may not be consistent with these assumptions.

For example, the organization may *say* they highly value risk-taking and innovation but the reality may be that conformity is rewarded and failure punished. 'Team work' may be trumpeted as a core value, but the people who actually get ahead are those who work fairly ruthlessly in their own self-interest. To truly understand the culture – and to change it – requires engaging with these assumptions.

The culture of an organization (including a family) develops gradually over time. Sometimes, especially in new organizations, it is formed in a deliberate process. The founders (or first leader) have a set of values and assumptions they believe are key to make the organization successful, and they try to embed these in how they shape and run the organization. However, leaders are often unaware of the extent to which their own behaviour is the most powerful mechanism in creating the organization's culture. Most leaders are familiar with the 'What gets measured gets managed' axiom. But they are less familiar with an equally true (if less elegantly expressed) axiom: 'The reaction of the leader to emotionally charged incidents is what shapes the real culture of an organization.'

Emotionally charged incidents at work are the critical incidents or crises that arouse a high level of anxiety, disappointment or anger, usually in response to a setback or failure.

A new product or service fails.

Somebody makes a big mistake or takes a risk that does not work out.

There is a threat of redundancy or lay-offs.

Such incidents arouse strong negative emotions, and strong negative emotions make us hypersensitive to what is happening. All eyes are on the leader.

How will he or she react?

We lay down deep lessons in those moments of high emotion. When leaders are positive, they react strongly and decisively to such incidents, including doling out appropriate sanctions. But they manage to maintain the right ratio of positivity to negativity. They maintain an air of calm. They focus on the positive message of lessons learned. They set out clearly and positively the standards that have to be met – but they also give people opportunities and the expectation that they can meet these standards. Each element of that response then becomes embedded in the culture.

A leader prone to negative moods is likely to overreact to such incidents, to say and do things that he or she may subsequently regret and that will be remembered and embedded in the culture.

Leadership, mood, organizational culture and effectiveness are tightly linked. When the formula works, the results are impressive. When people who provide services are positive and cheerful, they make much more effort to please customers and actually achieve better results. For every 1 per cent improvement in service to customers, there is a 2 per cent increase in revenue.[19]

Results from a range of industries show that in 75 per cent of the companies, a positive work culture was what differentiated high-profit, high-growth companies from those that were less successful. The formula is actually quite exact. The emotional style of the leaders accounts for between 50 and 70 per cent of a company's work culture (how people feel about working for a company). This, in turn, accounts for between 20 and 30 per cent of business performance.[20]

We often try to disguise the fact that we are basing our behaviour and decisions on our moods, pretending to ourselves that we are taking account only of 'the facts'. But the reality is that when it comes to managing important relationships and making decisions, the effect of mood is very strong.

It follows, then, that being aware of our mood and its effects is critical to flourishing.

What is encouraging is that once we become aware of how our mood may be influencing us, we can modify and even stop its influence if we need to.

In the next chapter, we look at how to do this.

# 14. How to manage your mood

We like to think of ourselves as stable entities: good at this, average at that, weak at the other. But abilities, talents and personal qualities are not fixed quantities we carry around inside us, waiting to be let out. They can expand and shrink – depending on how we *perform* them.

Mood is a big, big factor in how you express your portfolio of strengths and weaknesses. As we have seen in Chapter 13, it affects virtually everything you do and everybody you interact with. You can't leave your mood at the door of your life. You can't care for your family, go about your day's work, manage relationships, make plans, or just generally get on with things *as if* your mood does not matter.

Your mood matters – a lot.

Your mood is not something mysterious that descends on you. Yes, good and bad things happen in your life. But events by themselves do not 'create' your mood. *You* create your mood. This means you can manage and change your mood.

If you were to take that fact seriously, it could revolutionize your life.

Learning to effectively manage your mood depends on being aware of how moods work – and, in particular, how *your* own moods work.

What prompts your moods?

How do your moods affect yourself and other people?

How skilled are you in changing them?

Those with a temperamental tendency to neuroticism – the tendency to worry and self-doubt – are particularly susceptible to the effects of negative mood. They have to work harder to prevent their negative mood taking hold and to learn to help a positive mood take hold instead. They have most to gain from learning to manage their moods.

But, for all of us, the ability to understand and manage our moods is a critical component of a flourishing life.

Our emotions are our reactions to what happens to us, particularly when faced with unexpected events. Negative emotions are reactions to threats of any kind – the prospect or reality of physical or psychological pain, of losing something we value, of our goals being frustrated. Positive emotions are our first reactions when confronted with opportunities – the prospect or reality of pleasure, of bonding with other people intimately or socially, of learning something new, of achieving our goals.

The more unexpected the opportunity or threat, the stronger the emotion.

Each emotion sets in train changes in our brains, in our bodies, in our attention and in our thoughts – all designed to help mobilize us to deal with the opportunity or the threat. So, each emotion sets up 'an action tendency', a specific urge to think, decide and act in a particular way. When we feel love, our goal becomes to move closer physically and emotionally to the beloved, to lavish them with care and tenderness. How much progress we are making towards that goal then provokes further emotions. When we feel we are making good progress, we experience a positive emotion – happiness, contentment, excitement, interest. When we feel we are making little or no progress, we experience a negative emotion – frustration, anxiety, irritation, disappointment, anger, sadness. In this way, emotions act as signals as to how much progress we are making towards our goals.

But emotions, no matter how intense, don't last very long – minutes rather than hours. Gradually, they decrease in intensity. Otherwise, they would exhaust us. Sometimes emotions provoke 'emotional episodes' that are more extended. Anger can set up an episode of disagreement and conflict that can last for hours. Joy and excitement can set up a whole evening of engaging, lively social interaction. In the course of the episode, emotions can flare up again momentarily and then subside.

Emotional episodes include not just your emotions but also those of other people. The episode assumes a life of its own, driven by feedback loops between your emotions and the other person's. The stronger the emotions, the more rapid and powerful the feedback loops become. The episode will continue until one party physically or psychologically 'exits' and brings the episode to an end.

However, emotions and emotional episodes provoke moods – and moods last much longer, extending over hours or even days. The more intense the emotion or emotional episode – positive or negative – the longer-lasting the effect on mood afterwards. A particular interaction with somebody may provoke intense anger that slowly dies down. But the anger can trigger a mood of irritability that lasts the rest of the day and right into the evening.

At a general level, actively managing your mood means following the flourishing principle:

- increasing the frequency of positive moods, and
- limiting the frequency and intensity of (unnecessary) negative moods.

Sometimes negative moods are necessary and useful: if you have endured a recent loss or setback, it is natural and useful to feel down, to conserve your resources and take stock. But what you have to actively manage is the intensity and duration of the mood, so that it does not become counterproductive and self-perpetuating.

Actively managing your mood means being able to mobilize the necessary psychological resources to get things done and to pursue goals that are important to you. You need to be able to summon up and marshal the specific emotions required in any given situation – interest, enthusiasm, confidence – but also sufficient anxiety, and even indignation.

If you can do that, the emotion will prime the right thinking and behaviour in response to the situation – open-minded exploration, high-energy action, determination, persistence.

## *Actively tune into your mood*

The crucial word here is 'actively'. While you create and recreate your mood, you often do this with no awareness.

The first guideline to managing your mood is to become actively aware of the mood you are in. In this way, you can use your good mood to advantage, and take account of your bad mood and its likely effects on you.

When you sense yourself in a positive mood, it's a good time to get things done – particularly difficult things. When you are in a negative mood, do the opposite. Try to put off difficult tasks – particularly those involving somebody else, such as having a discussion about a contentious issue, or making a verbal complaint, or giving somebody negative feedback. A negative mood makes you more likely to misread neutral responses from the other person as negative, and so to overreact. Your mood is also likely to infect the other person, making the whole interaction more fraught.

One of the consequences of becoming more aware of your negative mood is that the effects on your performance diminish. You are less likely to act out the mood. This means, for example, that if you can't avoid taking on a difficult task, you can at least take account of your negative mood and try to contain it. Thus, if you are aware that your mood is irritable, you can be vigilant about avoiding getting into conflict with somebody – or, at the very least, try to circumscribe it.

When you are in a negative mood, it's a good habit to have a few holding sentences ready, such as: 'I'd like more time to think about this.'

Return to the issue later – hopefully in a better mood.

### *Count your resources*

Remember, the function of a mood is to assess your perceived supply lines: 'Given what I need to do, do I have enough physical, psychological, mental and social resources to deal with it?'

If the answer is, 'Yes, I have enough resources to deal with what I have to do,' a good mood follows.

If the answer is uncertain, or a definite no, a negative mood follows.

For example, a big disappointment can make you feel very sad. But this will not necessarily develop into a low, depressed mood if you feel you have very supportive family, friends or colleagues. In fact, just actively recalling that available support will cheer you up, reminding you how lucky you are, or how beloved. In that way, the mood provoked by a negative event can actually be positive.

Similarly, a bad mood can follow a positive emotion. If you are given a big opportunity, it may provoke a negative mood if your perceived resources are judged to be insufficient to take advantage of it. You may not feel confident enough, or you may feel that you don't have the support of somebody critical. Or you may judge that you have many people supporting you, but you will have to pay too high a price for their support. The problem with much of the actual support provided to people in times of need and stress is that it is too little, too late, or even irrelevant to actual need.[1]

The important word here is 'perceived' resources. We can, and regularly do, misread the resources available to us because we don't go to the trouble of consciously counting them. Developing the habit of doing a conscious, systematic audit of your resources is an effective strategy to manage your mood. That is why developing a regular habit of mentally counting your blessings pays dividends when you are daunted by a challenge.

- Do I have enough physical resources – energy, skill and strength?

- Do I have enough psychological resources – confidence, competence and control?
- Do I have enough mental resources – understanding, ideas, focus and concentration?
- Do I have enough social support – a network of people who can offer practical help, advice, information, connections and emotional support, if I need it?

If the answer to any of these questions is no, ask yourself why – and be prepared to sometimes think again.

Do you really need to have that person's approval?

Is this just an old habit that you are bringing into every situation?

What can you do to secure at least some of what you need?

If you do an audit like this, you are reminding yourself of what you do have going for you, and that will lift your mood. If you identify a deficit, you can do something to counter it.

For example, a negative mood is often exacerbated by physical tiredness – even though you may experience it as a loss of confidence or focus, or a wave of despondency. If you become aware of your lack of physical energy, you can address it. If you are not in a position to take a rest, taking a short break – five minutes sitting somewhere quiet (even the bathroom) with your eyes closed – will help. Stepping outside into the open air and breathing deeply will help. Getting enough sleep will do wonders for your mood.

### *Develop a habit of being grateful*

Learning to be grateful for the resources you have turns out to be a very powerful antidote to negative mood.

In one experiment, people were asked to record once a week for ten weeks reasons to be grateful in their lives. At the end of the ten weeks, they were found to feel better about their lives as a whole, to have fewer physical symptoms and to be more optimistic about the future. In short, their general mood had improved.

In contrast, another group who had been asked to simply record the major events of the week or the hassles and stresses of their lives showed no such improvement. This was despite the fact that the 'grateful' group experienced as much stress and as many negative emotions as the others.[2]

Gratitude is a sense of appreciation, what psychologist Robert Emmons calls 'an interior attitude of thankfulness, regardless of life circumstances'.[3] The word to focus on here is 'regardless'. It's easy to be grateful when things are going well and you are in a good mood. But it is when things are going badly, and you are in a negative mood, that gratitude is most important. Happy people seem to have the knack, or have developed the habit, of being able to appreciate over and over again the good things in their lives. As a consequence, they feel that their lives are fulfilling, meaningful and productive.[4]

When you develop a habit of gratitude, you notice other people's generosity. You are more inclined to appreciate their good intentions, you feel more indebted to them in a positive way, and you are more likely to want to reciprocate their generosity. The habit of gratitude is not just a powerful antidote to negative mood but is the very best antidote to a culture of entitlement – a culture that promotes destructive feelings of hostility, envy, resentment, bitterness and greed.[5]

As researchers Robert Emmons and Charles Shelton observe, 'Gratitude has a special place in the grammar of moral life.'

The essence of learning to be grateful is to learn to *want* what you *have*. You can develop the habit of gratitude, or teach it to your children, by following four simple steps.

- Learn to identify non-grateful thoughts – combat a culture of entitlement.
- Take time to formulate grateful thoughts in a way that appeals to you.
- Learn to substitute the grateful thoughts when you feel surly or negative.
- Then translate your feelings of gratitude into actual behaviour.[6]

Another reliable way to increase your positive mood is to record once a week the three good things that happened to you during that week. This deceptively simple exercise has been found to be remarkably effective. If you persist for six weeks, you will feel considerably happier and less depressed.

Doing it more often than once a week won't help and is not as effective – most probably because it will lose its freshness and become boring.

### *Use distraction*

One of the most effective ways to manage a negative mood is to distract yourself. Doing something mildly pleasant – such as going to a film, or doing a crossword puzzle, or even tidying up your wardrobe or your desk – will make you feel better.

Better still, take some exercise.

The evidence is now overwhelming on the benefits of exercise in lifting negative mood – or even depression.[7] Even though you may be tempted to sit and nurse your negative mood, a brisk twenty-minute walk, a half-hour of gardening, a swim, or a session in the gym will work its magic and lift your mood – as well as making you healthier.

If I am stuck and unable to see my way through something, I distract myself by going for a run. Sometimes, especially for women, plumbing the depths of a problem is counterproductive.

I have come to respect distraction as a great strategy for happiness.

### *Try being kind*

Whether you are in a good or a bad mood, committing yourself to doing five acts of kindness in one day will make you feel much happier. An act of kindness is anything that will benefit another person or make them happy, and that involves at least some small cost to yourself – in terms of time or effort.

In one experiment, participants were asked to perform five acts of kindness per week over a six-week period.[8] They could choose to perform all five acts in one day or they could spread them over the week. At the end of the six weeks, those who had done their five generous acts all in one day showed significant increases in their happiness. Spreading out the acts of kindness over the course of a week seemed to have diluted the positive effect on mood.

It appears that if you limit yourself to performing one act of kindness per day, you run the risk that its positive impact just gets swallowed up by everything else that is happening in your life. In contrast, ensuring that you do five acts of kindness in a day requires devoting your time and attention, making you more aware of what you are doing and more aware of the effect on you and on other people.

### *Make a plan*

Planning a new exercise regime, organizing to meet up with your friends, or to go on a short break or holiday will immediately boost your mood and vitality.

Try making a list – there is something very soothing about lists. It gives you a sense of control, a feeling that you are back in charge of your life.

Better still, tackle something on the list immediately – particularly some job that you have been putting off for a while, such as paying a bill, subscribing to a magazine, sending a card or an email to somebody, arranging photos in your family album.

### *Learn to savour your positive moods*

In an effort to prolong or intensify your positive moods you might be tempted to think about them, to analyse why you are in this good mood.

Don't.

The one question most likely to destroy a good mood is: 'Why can't it always be like this?' You will find yourself being instantly reminded of all the reasons why it can't.

This, unfortunately, is a question that women seem to be particularly susceptible to asking after a rough patch in a relationship has just righted itself, inevitably reminding themselves and their partner of the negative things that provoked the original conflict.

What you *can* do is learn to savour your good mood.

The essence of savouring is to live fully in the moment and to relish it. Savouring is near to gratitude and is rather a lost art, caught up as we are in the endless round of tasks and activities. But it is an art worth practising.

In my own case, I try to savour the moment and, in memory, those moments that remind me of the inexhaustible abundance of life: the effortless affection of my children; our summer trips to the west of Ireland with our friends, when we climb the stunning Twelve Bens or Maumturk Mountains – and occasionally dance around the kitchen to the music of The Eagles.

These are the moments of pure grace that I want to hold for ever.

At the very least, there is always a small immediate pleasure to be found using your five senses.

I look at our lovely garden where my husband, John, has something flowering every month of the year.

I listen to the Benedictus from *The Armed Man*.

I breathe in the smell of an old book.

I eat toast and some of my homemade cherry and orange marmalade.

I touch the old, smooth, mellow wood of our banister.

Or I simply remind myself of those things in my mind's eye, because evoking happy memories results in almost as intense a feeling of happiness as the original experience.

Occasionally, I try looking at or listening to something as if it is the first time – or the last time I will ever see or hear it.

When you do this, that something reveals itself to you in a wondrous way. You see and hear it like never before.

Recall in your mind, for example, someone you love. As you look at that mental image of a familiar face, certain features will stand out. But many others will remain blurry. You will struggle to recall them.

Now, really look at the person in a new way. Savour every feature and detail.

I once watched each of my two children in that way – the shape of their faces, of their hands, the arch of their necks, the distinctive way they moved. It evoked a great wave of feeling – love, affection, pride, gratitude.

Whatever else was going on in my mind, this surge of feeling washed it away.

It has remained vividly in my memory – always available, always full of pleasure, no matter what my mood.

STRATEGY SIX

# *Master the art of vital engagement*

'When finally you achieve something, then you are alive and you did something that only you can do. And if you don't do it – if you don't push yourself to do it, and look for the best way to do it – then you don't wake up.'

Sylvie Guillem, dancer
(interviewed by the *Telegraph Magazine* in 2011)

# 15. The joy of losing yourself in everything you do

We all know people who seem to be deeply and enjoyably involved in their lives. Some have a single overriding passion – soccer, science, theatre, teaching – that completely absorbs them. Others seem to have the knack of consistently finding many things that give them scope to develop their talents and skills. They rarely seem bored or overwhelmed by what they have to do. Looking at such people, it is tempting to think that they must have some very special abilities or personal qualities, or have been given exceptional opportunities – and sometimes they have. But the real explanation lies elsewhere.

They are flourishing because they have mastered the art of vital engagement.

Psychologist Mihaly Csikszentmihalyi* probably knows more about the science and art of vital engagement than anybody else in the world. At the core of vital engagement is the capacity for what he calls 'flow' – the experience of full and deep, enjoyable involvement in what you are doing.[1]

Csikszentmihalyi and his research team have spent the last four decades investigating the phenomenon of flow. His interest was sparked by observing how some people – painters, athletes, sculptors, dancers, rock climbers, musicians, chess masters, surgeons – became so totally and enjoyably engaged in what they were doing that nothing else seemed to matter. No effort seemed too much. They were stretched to the limit in trying to achieve something that they thought worthwhile. Yet, despite the time and effort involved, they seemed energized and happy, in full control of their actions, masters of the moment. Csikszentmihalyi called these experiences of vital engagement 'optimal experiences' or being 'in flow'.

He found that these experiences, although prevalent in certain activities such as sports, the arts and surgery, were not confined to them. People reported experiences of flow or optimal functioning while playing chess,

* Pronounced 'chicks-sent-me-high' – we knew him simply as 'Mike' when he taught me as a young graduate student at the University of Chicago.

designing software, participating in group discussions, reading to a child, swarming around in a motorcycle gang, doing routine assembly-line work, and dealing with a major crisis. In other words, people can experience deep enjoyment, or flow, while at work or at play, while doing a wide variety of activities, but the personal psychological experience tends to be described in almost identical terms.

The more a person reports experiences of flow in their average week, the more likely they are to describe themselves as strong, active, creative, concentrated, motivated and happy – the way most of us would like to describe ourselves. Yet, just about 20 per cent of people report experiencing flow on a daily basis (the same proportion as describe themselves as flourishing). About one third of people say they rarely or never experience flow.[2]

Research with thousands of people worldwide has demonstrated that optimal experiences of flow are described in the same way by men and women, young and old, regardless of social class or cultural differences.

For example, my friend Michael Bourke is a man who has many moments of flow in his life. He loves cooking, he loves art, but most of all he loves singing – and in between the delights of his life (and delighting his friends) he manages a successful career as a lawyer. This is how Michael talks about his passion for singing.

> As children our mother sang to us and we learned to sing naturally. In my late twenties I started to take singing lessons, to learn about breath control, resonance, diaphragm control and all the other things that go with having a trained voice. I used to practice – never enough, of course. I would sing a particular verse or song over and over, with different nuances and emphasis on particular words or phrases.
>
> When people listen to me sing and are attentive, they look into my eyes and I know they are touched by the music, and I am carried along by their response. I am in a heightened state of delight, even when singing the saddest songs, especially when I feel people are responding and involved. The song, the music and the human connection lasts and lasts for me. I invest large amounts of emotional and nervous energy in the physical production of the sound and the interpretation of the song. To an extent my body is the instrument producing the music. Because of the resonances in my body, and the emotion of the song, I am extremely fulfilled.

> When I sing, I am taken out of the mundane world into another place – and it is always a pleasure to return to that place.

What Michael describes is finding flow in expressing himself creatively, but there is potential for flow in even the most routine work.

Csikszentmihalyi cites the case of assembly-line worker Rico.[3] He had to perform the exact same operation every 43 seconds or so, nearly 600 times over the course of his normal working day. Astonishingly, Rico experienced regular flow in his work. He constantly set challenges for himself. He tried to beat his own record by cutting down the time he took to perform each operation. He worked out private routines about how best to move his hands and use his tools. In part, he tried to improve his performance in order to earn a bonus and the respect of his supervisors. But his primary motivation was his deep satisfaction in beating his own record and in working at full stretch.

Anticipating that he would eventually exhaust the challenges in his current job, Rico took evening courses so that he could get a more demanding job that would allow him to set further challenges for himself and become more deeply immersed in what he was doing.

He intuitively knew how to transform those daily experiences of flow into a life of vital engagement.

## *The eight elements of flow*

You will recall from the last few chapters that what distinguishes 'a good day' from 'a bad day' is whether your executive self is in charge. The capacity for being in flow is intimately connected to your ability to control your precious units of attention and to strengthen your executive self.

Flow has eight major components. It happens when:

1. you take on an activity that is challenging and requires skill
2. you are concentrating fully on what you are doing in the moment
3. the activity has clear goals
4. the activity provides immediate feedback
5. deep involvement removes from your awareness the frustrations and worries of everyday life
6. there is a sense of control

7. self-consciousness disappears
8. the sense of time is altered.

People mention at least one – and often all of the above – when they describe such experiences.

Let's look at each of the elements in turn.

### 1. *You take on an activity that is challenging and requires skill*

You are most likely to enter a flow experience when you take on something that stretches you, when both the level of *challenge* and the level of *skill* required are above your average level.

You play tennis, or poker, or chess with somebody who is more experienced than you.

You take on a job in a completely new domain.

You become chair of a highly political Parent Teacher Association.

The challenge may be initially taxing, but it turns into enjoyment at a very particular point – the moment when you perceive that your skills are equal to the challenge ('Ah, I can actually do this!').

You are stretched, but not stressed.

This kind of 'good stress' is characterized by this perfect balance between challenge and skills. You feel 'stressed' in the sense that you are physiologically aroused in readiness for the challenge ahead – adrenaline is flowing, you are hyper alert, maybe feeling a bit jittery or giddy. You may feel twinges of anxiety, but the predominant feeling is positive. If you had to sum up the totality of your feelings, you might use words like 'excited', 'interested', 'eager to get started'.

But that balance between challenge and skills is inherently fragile. If the challenge begins to exceed your level of skill, anxiety builds. If the challenge gets too easy or too routine, you lose interest.

### 2. *You are concentrating fully on what you are doing in the moment*

The moment when the balance between challenge and competence is reached is also the moment when your attention becomes completely absorbed by the activity.

People in flow describe that feeling of complete absorption in the same way, even if the activities are very different. The mind is no longer wandering, or preoccupied by something else. It is completely and effortlessly focused on the next move. The experience is poised at the sweet spot between conscious (but not effortful) concentration and being on automatic.

Despite the physical or mental exertion involved, people in flow report feeling relaxed, at ease, energetic. Their concentration is so complete that they no longer think of themselves as separate from what they are doing. They no longer have to think about what to do next; each action carries them forward effortlessly. They are so involved in what they are doing that there is no psychological energy left over to process any information that is not relevant to the task at hand.

Flow screens out the kind of doubts, uncertainties and distractions that interfere with peak performance and full *enjoyment*.

### *3. The activity has clear goals*

Flow happens – or, rather, you make it happen – when the activity you take on has three features:

1. clear goals
2. rules about how to achieve those goals, and
3. special skills required to achieve those goals.

When you consider those three features, you can immediately understand why playing games and sport so often lends itself to flow.

Surgery also meets these requirements. The goals of surgery are clearly defined – remove a tumour, set a bone, get a specific part of the body working again.

Virtually any skilled activity can be structured to have clear goals and rules and to require ever-increasing skill – for example, designing a software program; making an inspiring speech; amusing a child; writing a poem; preparing a report; painting a room; pruning a tree. You just need to think about it in these terms.

1. What is my goal?
2. What are the rules for achieving that goal (rules that already exist or that need elaborating)?
3. What skills do I need to achieve my goal?

When you structure an activity in this way, you engage in it differently. It becomes more interesting, more complex, more absorbing.

For example, I like reading poetry. But what adds immeasurably to my enjoyment is reading about the 'rules' of different kinds of poetry, the different ways the effect of the poem can be created, and the skills the poet uses to achieve that effect. When Seamus Heaney deconstructs a Philip Larkin poem to reveal its hidden architecture, I am drawn vicariously into the flow that Larkin himself must have experienced while writing that poem.

But even the simplest and most routine of activities can be transformed into a flow experience by setting up goals and making up rules. For example, I run most days. Like most runners, I set goals for myself – to complete each round of the park in a specified time (or, at the very least, to keep up with my husband who often runs with me). I also make up 'rules' to keep me engaged. I run as fast as I can for three minutes and then jog for the next five. Or I try to reach a particular landmark in the count of thirty. And when I succeed (occasionally), I feel ridiculously pleased with myself.

The important point here is that you can find flow in almost any activity. It is how you *perceive* the challenges and the skills involved, not their objective difficulty, that influences the quality of flow.

### *4. The activity provides immediate feedback*

For an activity to flow, you need immediate feedback as to whether you are succeeding or not. By attending closely to the immediate feedback, you know what the next move needs to be.

If you are onstage, or giving a speech, how is the audience reacting? Do you need to speed up or slow down? Give more data or tell more stories?

If you are rock climbing, how secure is your foothold on the rock?

If you are analysing a problem, is the data telling you what you need to know?

If you are reading to your child, how fully and enjoyably is he attending to the story? Do you need to keep going or stop to explain?

If you are doing a business deal, how is the other person reacting? Do you need to ask more questions or make your move now?

To be in flow, you must attune yourself to that feedback. You have to train yourself to pay attention to the right signals. That ability is at the heart of being highly skilled. The better you can pay attention, the more you will build flow into your life; the more you build in flow experiences, the better you will train your attention.

Sometimes feedback is easy to notice, but at other times – in activities that are more complex – it is less well defined. People who are highly skilled in their field develop a knack for 'knowing' when things are 'right'.

> My children attended a nursery school run by a woman called Elizabeth Maloney. What most struck me about Elizabeth was how highly attuned she was to the goals of the preschool – enabling and teaching children to learn enjoyably through play. She wanted the children to be in flow, and she was constantly attuned to the stream of feedback from them. She seemed to sense when it was the right time to let them play undisturbed and when it was the right time to intervene, and her interventions were always exactly right.
>
> I once asked her how she did this so well, and she said: 'My ears are trained. I can tell from the sounds if things are going well or if the excitement is beginning to get slightly out of control. I can hear boredom. I can hear tension.'

Skilled parents are similarly attuned. For example, they set out with a clear vision of what a responsible, successful, loving eighteen-year-old might look like and then seem to 'know' what feedback to look out for along the way – at, say, ages five, eight, twelve or sixteen. They are constantly monitoring progress against their long-term goal and then making adjustments.

These are parents who regard what they do as a highly skilled activity and turn it into that. They are also the parents who are so enjoyably absorbed in what they do that they have frequent experiences of flow.

### 5. *Deep involvement removes from your awareness the frustrations and worries of everyday life*

There are always some worries – about your life, your relationships, your work, your children – loitering at the edge of your attention, waiting until there is nothing else demanding your concentration to sneak into your mind.

When you are deeply involved in what you are doing, when you are in flow, you don't have to actively shut out your cares and worries, they just drop effortlessly out of awareness.

In flow, what you are doing becomes your whole world in the moment.

### *6. There is a sense of control*

We can never be fully in control of an activity – any number of things can go wrong. But as Csikszentmihalyi discovered, people in flow are engaged by the enticing *possibility* of control – of getting on top of what they are doing so they attain some kind of perfection in the moment.

What brings the sense of excitement and enjoyment, then, is not actually *being* in control but trying to *exercise* control by using your skills to the utmost.

The paradox is this: the possibility of full control only arises when there is also the risk of failure; and the alluring possibility of control only arises when you move out of your comfort zone.

### *7. Self-consciousness disappears*

Most of the time, we spend a lot of time thinking about ourselves.

What am I thinking?

What am I feeling?

How are they reacting to me?

How are things going today?

How is my life going?

This uses up a lot of mental and emotional energy. When you are in flow, you need all your available energy for the task at hand, so there is none left for self-scrutiny. In the middle of a totally absorbing and challenging activity, the stream of consciousness dies down. Yet, at another level, you remain exquisitely aware of everything you are doing. In fact, you are hyper aware, in full control of your psychic energy.

Perhaps that is the most mysterious aspect of flow – the combination of loss of self-consciousness with hyper awareness.

Once you lose self-consciousness, something else rather mysterious happens. The boundaries of your self begin to expand. In flow, you get a sense that you have become part of some greater presence.

A yachtsman may begin to experience himself as 'at one' with his boat, the sea and the elements.

The surgeon may experience an intense feeling of oneness with her operating instruments and her team.

The painter feels himself literally part of nature.

The person who is in flow while praying or meditating may feel part of some divine or spiritual dimension.

It is an experience of elation.

When the period of flow ends, your conscious self 'comes back', but it feels stronger, more self-confident, more authentic. You feel a greater sense of unity and mastery within yourself, and in the world around you.

*8. The sense of time is altered.*

One of the features of being in flow is that time no longer seems to pass in the ordinary way. Hours seem to pass in a minute, but at crucial points when the challenge is at its highest – when you have to reach the high note, as it were – what actually took seconds can seem to stretch into minutes.

You are living in the moment, in the fullest possible sense.

That is why the experience of flow is the nearest we come to the experience of pure happiness.

## *Why flow makes us happy*

Human beings are notoriously susceptible to swinging between being bored and being anxious.

If the challenge of what we are doing falls below our level of skill, we begin to relax and then become bored. If the challenge exceeds our level of skill, we become anxious and immediately self-conscious, fragmenting our energy between the task at hand and trying to manage ourselves and our feelings. Being in flow is what helps us navigate between the twin dangers of anxiety and boredom.

To chart a successful course, we need to develop a set of psychological skills for ourselves, and to help people we care about, people we manage – and especially our children – to do the same.

These skills include the ability to:

- recognize when you are in flow
- know how to find challenges in your daily activities
- learn how to set appropriate goals for yourself and to monitor your progress
- develop disciplined attention and concentration
- develop rituals that help calm your mind
- learn how to enjoy immediate experience, and
- develop your capacity for commitment – a fundamental skill.

A great deal of your productive and creative energy would be available to you to flourish, if facilitating flow became a real part of your daily agenda.

Flow facilitates commitment, and commitment has the effect of stabilizing your behaviour so that you are less likely or tempted to give up. It keeps you focused on the opportunity, as well as the threat. If you learn to sustain that commitment, it draws you further into the flow experience. It gives you momentum. Once you commit to the challenge, you reach that perfect balance between automatic and conscious behaviour. Your behaviour gets into an automatic rhythm without you having to consciously pay attention to each detail of the execution. Yet, at the same time, you are focused like a laser on the next move.

Look at any skilled soccer or rugby player – totally absorbed by the rhythm of the game yet hyper alert to opportunity and threat.

The late Philip Brickman of the University of Michigan describes commitment as a way to consciously automate things, to put them out of awareness but at the same time keep them in focus – what he calls the perfect combination of mindless and single-minded behaviour, which produces the experience of irresistible momentum in the activity.[4]

You are vitally involved in the activity itself, not just in the goal. The means to the end becomes suffused with positive energy. Winning *and* how you play the game are in perfect balance.

Colleen Barkley, a senior manager at one of the Intel sites in the USA, is an avid rock climber. Virtually every weekend she sets off to climb the Rockies, setting herself ever more challenging climbs. Every weekend, she returns exhilarated, full of enthusiasm for the next challenge. Recalling one recent climb, she captures clearly that perfect balance of being 'on automatic' and being single-minded, and the perfect balance of threat and opportunity.

> There were times when I was just not sure where the next move was going to come from. So, I honestly took a deep breath and said out loud, 'Where are the opportunities here?' I was amazed that when I did that, and actually looked around, I could always find a place for my feet to move up to, or a way to traverse a tricky crossing. I could always find something I could climb on to. I probably did that about seven or eight times throughout that day. It just became effortless, automatic. And yet, I was totally concentrating. It was incredibly empowering. It helped me get past the survival-based

'I can't do this – this is too hard' thoughts and into a space of working with the rock instead of trying to 'conquer' it. The mountain would win anyway.

To develop a sustained commitment to something, the activity has to be not just enjoyable but meaningful for you. You may engage in some activity or work because you believe it is a very worthwhile endeavour. You can run on a treadmill to get fit, or join an association that is doing good things, or take on work that is important to your organization. But if you don't enjoy it, your commitment will wane, and if you force yourself to continue, you will risk boredom and burnout. Neither will you build a life of vital engagement if you take on activities that are simply enjoyable.

For example, you might become enjoyably absorbed by doing a crossword puzzle, or playing on a Wii, but you are not likely to turn either activity into a life commitment. To build that commitment, you have to see what you are doing as having a deeper meaning and value.

It is this developing sense of the meaning and value of what you are doing that turns a flow experience into a vital engagement in your life.

## *Building flow in your life*

Surprisingly, many of us turn out not to be that good at identifying what creates flow experiences for us. We rely on our retrospective accounts of what we *thought* we found deeply absorbing and enjoyable, and these accounts are often flawed by distortions in memory or by what we think we are expected to or *should* have enjoyed.

We recall the sunshine on holidays, but edit out the stress of travelling, the mosquitoes, the interpersonal tensions.

To get a more accurate picture of actual enjoyment and flow experiences, Csikszentmihalyi and his team developed the Experience Sampling Method. They supply survey volunteers with a paging device programmed to bleep at random times over the course of a week or so. They also give them report sheets. When the beep goes off, people are asked to record what they are doing at that moment, and to rate:

1. how challenging the activity is
2. how much skill is required to meet that challenge, and
3. how they are feeling.

You can do this for yourself by programming your watch or mobile phone to bleep at certain times over the course of a day and recording your experience in a notebook. Or just stop on the hour, every two hours or so, and make a note.

What exactly are you doing?

On a scale of 1–10, how challenged do you feel?

How much skill are you using to meet that challenge?

How happy do you feel?

How engaged and motivated?

You may be quite surprised by the results. You may discover, as the researchers did with the majority of people they studied, that your *idea* of what you find enjoyable is at variance with your actual experience. This is particularly the case when it comes to work and leisure.

### *Rethink work and leisure*

When Csikszentmihalyi's researchers paged their sample group at work during those times when they were actually working (as opposed to day-dreaming, gossiping, or being engaged in personal business), they were found to be in flow for a full 54 per cent of the time. They reported themselves as feeling active, cheerful, satisfied, happy, creative, concentrated, motivated and strong.

In contrast, when they were paged while engaged in leisure activities – reading, watching TV, socializing, eating out – they were in flow only 18 per cent of the time. For 52 per cent of those leisure times, they described these experiences as involving neither challenges nor skills, and reported themselves as feeling passive, apathetic, dissatisfied.

Yet, despite their actual experiences, people still held fast to the idea that leisure was more enjoyable than work. The puzzled researchers concluded that we seem to ignore the evidence of our own experience. We forget or discount how often we experience deep enjoyment when working, and how relatively infrequently we do when relaxing. Instead, we continue to cling to the idea, or stereotype, that work is hard (something we 'have to' do) and that leisure is more enjoyable (something we 'want to' do).

The second reason we mislead ourselves about the enjoyableness of time off is the type of leisure we choose. Work lends itself to flow experiences more often because it is structured with built-in challenges, rules, requirements to use your skills, immediate feedback. In contrast, much leisure time is often unstructured and passive, and leaves us feeling low in energy and motivation. This is particularly the case with watching TV, one of the most common leisure activities.[5] When watching TV, metabolic rates slow down and people feel passive, drowsy and less alert.

On the other hand, leisure involving the pursuit of a hobby or interest that demands skill, investment of time and attention, inner discipline and engagement pays the greatest dividends in terms of producing flow experiences – real enjoyment and happiness.

And when leisure involves the company of fellow enthusiasts, it is even more rewarding.

### *Build your capacity for 'serious play'*

One of the most striking characteristics of people who frequently experience flow in their lives is that they make very little distinction between work and play.

When working, they seem to recognize opportunities for challenge that colleagues in the same type of job either don't see or don't want to see. They get a kick out of becoming more skilful at things – even small things. They seem to have the capacity to make their work resemble a good game, full of:

- variety
- challenge
- clear rules for success
- clear goals, and
- immediate feedback.

The border between work and play disappears. This is what Csikszentmihalyi calls 'serious play'.

People who have that capacity find their work and play exhilarating. I witnessed this at first hand on a trip abroad.

> I had landed at a very busy international airport after a long and tiring flight. I joined the long queue for the shuttle buses to the different hotels. Everybody looked glum, resigned to a boring wait. Then a man appeared with a walkie-talkie and announced in very poor English, but with great enthusiasm, that he was our contact man for the different shuttle buses. He went down the line, asking us which hotel shuttle we were each waiting for, and then proceeded to organize us

into relevant hotel groups – the Sheraton group, the Hyatt group, the Hilton group, and so on. As he received messages through the walkie-talkie he immediately announced the news, 'Sheraton shuttle here in three minutes.' But, rather than waiting for a message through the walkie-talkie, he took it upon himself to run up the path and round a corner so that he could catch the first glimpse of each bus arriving and then rushed back, announcing breathlessly which one was in sight.

The effect on the waiting people was remarkable. People started smiling and talking to each other, remarking on the man's obvious enjoyment of and pride in his job.

By investing his routine job with minute-by-minute challenges and rules, this man with a very modest job was clearly in flow.

### *Develop your passion*

Some people have no trouble identifying their passion in life.

They love the GAA or the Munster rugby team.

They are vitally interested in what they do at work.

They love gardening – the cycle of planting, growing and harvesting.

They are completely absorbed by the theatre, or by art.

For many, this interest starts early in life. For others, the passion develops gradually, and often out of necessity. As children, they 'had to' play sports in school, or 'had to' help out at home with cooking. Bored to tears on a family holiday, they started reading 'proper' books.

Or, as adults, they are inveigled to join a drama group by a friend and do so with little enthusiasm. Yet, from that unpromising start, they gradually develop an interest, then a passion, for what they once 'had to' do. As soon as they develop some basic skills and see how challenging the activity is, they begin to enjoy it – and then to love it.

Sometimes we all need encouragement and a certain amount of gentle pressure to make the effort to start something new. But, once we start and persist, we gradually build up the skills to meet the progressive challenges the activity throws up, and then one day that magic moment arrives when our skills and the challenge facing us are perfectly matched. This is the beginning of deep enjoyment, the experience of flow. Building this capacity for 'serious play' is a foundation block for building a flourishing life.

The more we are drawn onwards by our interest, the more meaningful an activity becomes. As our interest develops, we will feel the urge to seek out people with the same interest, to join a network of fellow enthusiasts or practitioners.

What started as an individual interest can then become a lifelong passion embedded, in an ever-deepening way, within a community of interest.

### *Learn to pay full attention to what you are doing in the moment*

Virtually any activity can become intrinsically interesting and motivating and a source of flow.

The key is attending to the activity in such a way that you can identify what challenges it can hold for you, and what goals you might set for yourself. Even in the absence of any immediate challenge, you can practise paying full attention to each of your five senses. Try looking, or listening, or tasting or touching something as if it were the very first time you have experienced it, or the last time you ever will. This is the moment when you start *actively* engaging with the experience, rather than passively consuming it.

This engagement is what transforms a routine experience into a deeply sensual one.

Take touch, for example. Touch is central to really good sex, yet is often experienced within a very narrow range. When you become enjoyably absorbed by touch, you become aware of the range of sensory experiences available all over your body, of the range of intensity and duration in touch. As you and you partner experiment with that range, you make up private 'rules' and sequences and you become more skilled.

That is when sex goes into flow.

### *Learn to find challenges and set goals in your daily activities*

If you don't routinely find challenges in what you are doing, try making a habit of asking yourself two questions before you do something.

- What skill does this activity require?
- Is there any way I can make this activity more challenging for myself?

You can use this approach with any activity – from the most routine to the most complex.

Setting *any* goal in relation to an activity has the effect of revealing the sequence of challenges involved in it. As these unfold, the level of skill demanded of you will increase. This draws you in further. You begin to 'feel' your way around the problem you are trying to solve. The more you understand what you are doing, the more enjoyable the experience.

When you extend your interest in this way, you are involving not just your senses, but your feelings and your mind as well. This ability to unify what is happening in your body, your feelings and your mind significantly increases your capacity to concentrate and to screen out distractions. Every time you do this, you are building your capacity for concentration, and that increased capacity makes it easier for you to build flow experiences in other areas of your life.

### *Learn to be disciplined*

It is not enough to *know* what puts you in a flow experience, you have to develop the discipline of setting challenges for yourself every day and the discipline of developing your skills to meet those challenges.

And you have to practise.

If you avoid challenge, or won't persist in learning new skills (particularly at the beginning of any activity), you may indeed have an easy life. But the price you will pay is a life that is less enjoyable and lacks vital engagement. That is why it is important for parents and teachers to keep setting new and enjoyable challenges for young people – challenges that will keep stretching their abilities – but also to give them the practical and emotional support to persist and stay disciplined.

Discipline for discipline's sake, as a way of developing character, is no longer fashionable. But it has its place, not as a set of rigid rules, but as a vital practice – a way to build concentration, to control attention, to learn to do something for its own sake rather than to reach some end goal.

### *Develop private rituals to calm your mind*

Starting any activity that requires high concentration is difficult until you establish a rhythm – physical or mental. Writing, running, playing a game, making a presentation, having a conversation – each of these activities requires a rhythm before it flows.

Initially, you may experience a block.

When you do get going, every effort is 'lumpy', all over the place. You feel distracted, out of sync with what you are trying to achieve.

That is why we need warm-up routines – done in the same order every time. The content of the routines is not important. All that is required is that they must be familiar and reassuring and help to exclude distractions. These routines gradually assume the status of rituals, or even superstitions – things that bring 'good luck' or prevent 'bad luck'. Athletes are notoriously superstitious – for example, attaching huge emotional importance to wearing a particular item of clothing or making a call to a particular person before the game. The real benefit is that the routines progressively involve them in the rhythm of the activity, giving it their undivided attention.[6]

Similarly, surgeons have preparatory routines. For example, here are the routines of ophthalmic surgeon Pat McGettrick.

> I have two routines, one before surgery, and one if something goes wrong during surgery. No alcohol for twenty-four hours before surgery day. No tea or coffee on the morning of surgery. Eight hours sleep before surgery. I do a short ten-minute meditation before I start the list. I eat a banana for energy mid-morning.
>
> Most of my patients have surgery under local anaesthetic, so they are awake and acutely aware if there is any delay, or if something goes wrong during the procedure. For example, if an instrument is not available or is faulty and has to be replaced, there is a delay. During this delay period, I reassure the patient first. Then I calm myself by sitting quietly and doing my meditation and yoga breathing, even if the interruption is as short as a couple of minutes. This switches me off from the potential chaos around me and keeps me focused on the task in hand.
>
> Actually, this routine of mine has a positive effect on my scrub nurse and assistant also, because if I am calm they will remain calm.

The role of routines in getting us absorbed in the activity is why it is important for all of us to develop what Csikszentmihalyi calls 'micro-flow' activities that get us ready to take on a challenge that requires concentration. Pat's routines are a classic example of micro-flow activities. In the same way, routines that involve putting things in order externally – tidying your desk, laying out your clothes or your tools in a set order – are particularly effective because they help you impose order in your mind.

*Learn to enjoy immediate experience*

A central component of flow is the ability to live completely in the moment.

In the world we live in, that ability is under assault. No sooner do we register enjoyment than we feel compelled to move on to the next thing, or capture the moment on our camera phone, or text or tweet about it. The moment you do that, you break the spell and disrupt the flow experience because your attention is already on the future – on what you have to do, or on the possible reaction of the person who receives your photograph or text.

There is nothing wrong with wanting to capture or share the moment – but *not* at the expense of savouring to the fullest the deep enjoyment of total absorption in what is happening in the moment, and *not* at the expense of disrupting the rhythm of the activity and the rare experience of inner peace.

*Develop more 'flow-friendly' characteristics in yourself and in the people you care about*

Everybody is capable of flow. But those who experience flow most often in their lives have particular characteristics. They are more curious, more open-minded, less self-centred, more willing to do something for its own sake rather than for any expected reward.

Children and adolescents who experience flow tend to come from families that encourage such traits in them.

- They *play* a lot together as a family – board games, sports, word games, lively discussions – or just hang around a lot together, enjoying each other's company for its own sake.
- They encourage their children to be curious and open-minded about taking on new hobbies and interests, and they support those interests and hobbies practically and emotionally.
- They encourage their children to develop their skills and persist at things.

In short, they help their children to develop the capacity for serious play.

## *When flow becomes vital engagement*

There are great benefits when you achieve flow in your life.

- You become less dependent on the external environment for rewards.
- You become capable of finding purpose and enjoyment in what you do day-to-day, even when it is difficult or tedious.
- You are more open to a variety of experiences.
- You keep on learning every day.
- Your relationships improve.
- You manage better the challenges that life throws up.

Even more important, flow keeps you growing and developing.

In order to continue experiencing flow, you have to identify progressively more complex challenges, and then develop the skills to master them. Experiencing flow in any area of your life, work or leisure, is a natural motivator for personal growth. That is why flow is the gateway to a life of vital engagement: a way of being in the world that is characterized by a deep and enjoyable commitment to something over a long period, something that has become very meaningful to you and that you believe has real value in the world.[7]

The more knowledgeable you become, the more value you put on what you are doing, and the more connections you see between what you are doing individually and achieving the higher goals in life – to create a more prosperous and flourishing society and a better world.

When that happens, lawyers see what they are doing day-to-day as directly connected to defending liberty and justice.

Gardeners, farmers and bee keepers see themselves as practising one of the most ancient human occupations, and defending the natural environment.

A businessman sees a direct and vital connection between what he is doing and helping the economy, and the country's growth and prosperity.

People in the arts see themselves as the guardians of a great tradition, and the source of a vital energy in society.

Teachers see themselves as the vital link between the rich depositories of scientific and cultural knowledge, and the next generation.

That is vital engagement. People who are vitally engaged in life see what they do as a calling. Vital engagement is what distinguishes a calling from a career or a job.

### *A job, a career or a calling?*

Amy Wrzesniewski of Yale University and her colleagues found that people in a wide range of occupations see their work as falling into one of three categories – job, career or calling.[8]

A third of people describe their work as a job, primarily a means to an end. They work because they have to, for financial reward. Whatever interests they have, they are not expressed through their work.

Another third see their work as a career. They have a deeper personal interest in what they do. But for them, the real achievement is advancement within their career, which will bring not just greater financial reward, but also higher status, greater self-esteem and more power. Work is a stepping stone to higher status.

The final third see their work as a calling. They describe their work as a deeply enjoyable end in itself and as not just personally fulfilling, but socially valuable. They describe their calling as one of the most important things in their life. They like talking about it to other people. They encourage others to consider such work. They say if they did not have to work, they would still want to continue what they are doing, even if they were not being paid.

Not surprisingly, people who describe their work as a calling tend to work in higher-status occupations, where work tends to be more interesting, challenging and better paid. But this is far from the whole story. In one study of people who all worked in modest-status clerical jobs as administrative assistants, there was roughly the same proportion (a third) in each of the job, career and calling categories as there were in the original larger study.

Deep enjoyment and satisfaction in your work and your life may be more to do with the quality of vital engagement you bring to it than the nature of the work itself.

For example, surgeons who frequently experience flow emphasize that what makes surgery so special for them is the *feeling* they get from the activity itself, some even saying that nothing else in their life quite compares with it in terms of enjoyment. That is almost the danger of flow – the possibility of becoming addicted to an activity because it is so enjoyably absorbing.

Just like somebody who suffers from obsessive-compulsive disorder, you can become dependent on a particular experience of flow to reduce anxiety and create a certain type of order in your mind. Work that you enjoy can become addictive, particularly in hyper-competitive organizations. The external pressure becomes intertwined with the internal enjoyment of flow and contaminates it.

In these situations, people can become addicted, constantly needing new challenges, wanting to perform at such a high level that they finally can't meet the expectations they have set themselves.

At the other extreme are people who become burdened by the drudgery of their job. Some people have difficulty finding a match between the skills they really value in themselves and the work they have to do. They can't act with autonomy. They feel micro-managed and hemmed in. They may be emotionally disconnected from the purpose and mission of the organization they work for, or have settled for well-paid but boring work that requires little real engagement from them. Bit by bit, the tedium eats into their soul and they become depressed, self-loathing, vulnerable to obliterating the tedium by drinking or gambling.

This happens most frequently in organizations that over-specialize jobs and don't build in opportunities for variety and a certain amount of experimentation. Such organizations fail to emphasize innovation and learning.

Of course, the nature of your commitment and vital engagement in your work will depend, to some extent, on the state of your field of interest or profession – on whether *it* is flourishing or not. Throughout the 1990s, many professions underwent profound shifts as global market forces and technological developments such as the Internet began to change the world. These included professions essential to individual and social well-being, including medicine, law, the arts, education, philanthropy, genetics and journalism. All were confronting to varying degrees the new corporate power of the markets; the decline in traditional ethical and religious principles that used to guide the behaviour of professionals in the field; fewer heroic role models; and a very uncertain future.

A study looking at how practitioners were coping with trying to do good work and exercise their calling in two rapidly changing areas – genetics and journalism – produced some intriguing insights into the importance of aligning the demands of work and inner values.[9] The changes in these sectors have produced outcomes with profound consequences: genetics has the potential to control what is happening in our bodies, and journalism to control what is happening in our minds.

In journalism the researchers found a profession in deep crisis. Journalists who had entered the profession full of ideals about the freedom of the press and the public good found themselves under increasing pressure to blur the boundary between news and entertainment, to abandon investigative journalism in favour of providing celebrity gossip and scandal that would generate huge profits for newspaper owners and shareholders. Journalists were found to be deeply demoralized and disillusioned, fearful for the future of their profession – and this study was conducted over a decade ago, before the Murdoch crisis (or even before the Internet and 'citizen journalists' posed an even bigger threat to the traditional media).

Geneticists, in contrast, were buoyant. They were excited about the developments in their field and optimistic about the future of the profession.

The critical difference between the two professions was alignment. In genetics, all the relevant stakeholders – scientists in the field, investors, and the general public – substantially agreed on the same goal. They all wanted to produce the highest-quality work, with the potential to be converted into procedures and products that could transform healthcare and longevity. There was no pressure on scientists to compromise the quality of their work.

In journalism, all was misaligned. The pursuit of profits and sensationalism was at war with the core values of the profession. The result was constant tension, confusion, and self-doubt – all threatening the profession's vital engagement in their work.

Needless to say, no field enjoys a golden age or endures a crisis for ever. A crisis in a profession may provoke vital engagement in a different sense – powered not by a sense of belonging and satisfaction, but by a reforming zeal. But what *is* true is that when there is alignment between a field's core values and its status and success in the world, it readily lends itself to a life of vital engagement for its practitioners.

The capacity to be vitally engaged is an important part of a flourishing life.

Watching people who have that quality in their lives, and imagining creating a life like that for yourself, can appear daunting. But that journey can start with small experiences of flow, with the willingness to take on an activity with a challenge, just for its own sake. It does not matter much what that challenge is – whether it is in your work, your leisure, or your daily routine. All that matters is that you concentrate enough to stretch your body and mind as you try to master the challenge.

When you do, you will enjoy a tremendous feeling of enjoyment and satisfaction.

And, if you persist, out of that small core of joy, you can build a life of purpose and meaning, a life of vital engagement.

STRATEGY SEVEN

# *Know the meaning of things*

'We live our lives going forward but only understand them looking back.'

Kierkegaard[1]

# 16. The crucial importance of making sense of your life

The pursuit of meaning is woven into every aspect of flourishing. People pursue their goals and projects more vigorously and face challenges more courageously when they believe what they are doing has a purpose. In turn, the more vitally engaged they are in what they are doing, the more meaningful the activity becomes to them. It becomes a virtuous cycle. Correspondingly, when people feel that their lives lack meaning, they languish. They drift along on the wave of events or become bogged down by deadening routine and effort.

Meaning can be said to book-end flourishing – being both a motivator and an outcome. However, it is when adversity strikes that we seek meaning most urgently. If our entire lives were centred solely on things going right, it would leave the meaning of our lives prey to chance. So, while adversity is not necessary to create a sense of meaning, a more solid and enduring sense of meaning is based on a combination of pursuing the good *and* transforming the bad into good.

The essence of meaning is being able to make connections between things.[2] Doing this allows us to impose order on the varied events of our day and of our lives. Making connections is what allows us to make the link between our actions and their consequences, and between past and present – allowing us to learn from experience and plan for the future. Meaning is what binds events and time together, and what ultimately binds life into a coherent whole.

The search for meaning happens at multiple levels.[3] At the simplest level, we look to understand the *significance* of things in our everyday lives.

When you hear your baby crying, or a peculiar noise from the engine of the car, or when you get an email summons from your boss, or you see something that surprises you, the automatic response is: 'What does that mean?'

Is the baby hungry, in pain, or just bored?

Has the fan belt broken?

Is it good or bad that the boss is looking for you?

What is *she* doing here with *him*?

Until you believe you understand the meaning of something, you can't fit it into the way you think, and so you can't frame a response.

A second way in which we look for meaning is by trying to figure out other people's *intentions*.

Why didn't she return your call?

Is she ignoring you?

Or did she not get the message?

Understanding our own and other people's intentions are an important part of managing our day-to-day lives, because intentions signal the true purpose behind actions. We pay a lot of attention to whether people mean what they say, looking for signals that they will behave in a congruent way, so that we can proceed on that basis in responding to them.

## *Making sense of life's questions*

Apart from people with a philosophical bent, or suffering from depression, we are generally untroubled by big questions about the meaning of life. However, at major turning points in life – adolescence, midlife, moments of crisis – we ponder the bigger questions.

'What is the meaning of life?'

'What is the purpose of my life?'

'Why is there so much suffering in the world?'

The more intense the emotional experience, the more intensely we seek this higher-level meaning.

Our instinct is to find a personal meaning in things. Even when an unexpectedly positive thing happens – such as winning the Lotto – people often attribute this random event to their actions (how they chose the numbers), or to 'being lucky' (as if this were a personal quality), or to God personally looking out for them.

Mostly people expend energy on looking for meaning when bad things happen.

If you are diagnosed with a life-threatening illness, or somebody you love dies unexpectedly, or your house gets destroyed by a flood or a fire, you want to know, 'Why did this happen to *me*?' You may know *rationally* that the universe is random, generally dangerous and indifferent to individual life and welfare, and that many of the things that happen are equally random. Yet you feel singled out ('What did I do to deserve this?).

This tendency to look for personal meaning in things reflects a basic human dilemma. How can we explain how human beings, with our immensely complex consciousness and free will, find ourselves in such a random universe?

Despite the dazzling achievements of science, a stubborn majority takes a jaundiced view of the fact that their precious and unique existence is due to pure chance – attributable to their parents having had sex together at a particular moment in time. They turn to religion to account for their existence, believing that their life is part of a divine plan, that they were created by God, who endowed them with a soul, the capacity for free will and a unique moral worth. But, as every student debater knows, that explanation just raises further questions – such as where God came from, and whether He can interfere with the laws of science on our behalf – that end in further mystery. For those with a strong religious faith, they are content to live with that mystery.

The more scientifically minded seek to explain human consciousness – the distinctive way we think, reflect and imagine – as the consequence of evolution, or what Stephen Pinker calls 'magnificent contrivances of the natural world'.[4] However, evolution still cannot account for our unique capacity for free will, or the unique quality of individual experience. Even the most ardent scientists concede that the human mind is not yet evolved enough to understand how it works – or why it is there at all.

Perhaps Mihaly Csikszentmihalyi sums up the situation best. The answer to the old riddle, 'What is the meaning of life?' turns out to be astonishingly simple, he says. The meaning of life *is* meaning – whatever it is, wherever it comes from.[5]

Meaning, then, is not something that is automatically 'given'. Rather, we have to *make* meaning ourselves. Happily, we are well equipped to do that – our brain being designed to make connections and 'see' meaning in things.

This facility in our brain has been beautifully illustrated by the work of neuroscientist Michael Gazzaniga. He has identified what seems to be a hard-wired capacity in the brain's left hemisphere to interpret and give meaning to things by making connections between them – even when there is no actual connection.[6] This 'interpreter module' in the brain was discovered while studying the effects of 'split-brain' surgery, a procedure to sever the connections between the two sides of the brain used in the treatment of people suffering from severe epilepsy.

In his experiments, Gazzaniga flashed information to the patient so that it registered on just one or other side of the brain. For example, the left hemisphere was shown a picture of a chicken claw and the right hemisphere a snow scene. Then the patient was shown a number of additional pictures and asked to choose which were connected to what he had seen. The patient's right hand (which is controlled by the left hemisphere) selected a picture of a chicken (related to the chicken claw) but his left hand (controlled by the right hemisphere) hovered over a picture of a shovel (associated with the snow scene). Even though neither side of the brain 'knew' what the other had seen, the interpreter module in the left hemisphere (which saw the chicken claw) had to make a connection with the shovel (associated with the image registered in the right hemisphere). So it obliged. The patient 'explained' the connection by saying that you need a shovel to clean out a chicken shed. This was ingenious – but the connection and its meaning were totally fabricated.

## *Shifting between different levels of meaning*

Day-to-day, we shift up and shift down between the different levels of meaning.[7]

At the lowest level, people are concerned with 'the how' of what they are doing ('I am making a stew this way / writing a report like this'). As they move up to a higher level of meaning, they are more focused on 'the why' ('This is one of my household duties / this is my job') or higher again ('I am nurturing my family / responsible for the success of this project' or 'My work is my personal passion'). Virtually everything we do is capable of having these different levels of meaning.

The level of meaning you attach to what you are doing has important consequences. When you think what you are doing is an expression of an important personal value – such as caring, or passion, or competence – you are much more personally motivated and involved, and are less likely to give up, even when frustrated. You are much more likely to feel that you matter and that what you do matters.

The more you shift up your meaning, the more positive you feel. But to flourish, you also have to be able to shift down quickly. The downside of operating at a very high level of meaning ('What I am doing is really important to the world') is that you may attribute so much value to what you are doing that you fail to notice that it has become irrelevant or counterproductive. You may fail to notice internal cues, not realizing how stressed or exhausted you are.

People who are consistently operating at a very high level of meaning can burn themselves out, or become messianic and arrogant. And if things go wrong with their plans, they can become despairing.

When people encounter problems, they need to make a rapid shift down to a level of meaning where they can more easily make changes and solve problems ('Do I really need to do it in this particular way?').

## *Meaningless suffering*

Perhaps the best way to understand the importance of making meaning is to reflect on the distress we experience when we are unable to figure out why things are happening.

You have been passed over for an important job at work, even though you are the best qualified. But nobody will tell you why.

A friend or relative stops speaking to you and refuses to explain their reasons.

A company persists in billing you for a service you never signed up for, and despite your every effort to deal with this, does not return your calls or answer your letters or emails.

The organization you work for insists on endless form-filling that leads to no action and gets in the way of getting anything done.

We become distressed by such events because we perceive them as meaningless.

Meaningless suffering is the cause of endless human misery and wasted energy. It robs us of a sense of control over our lives and is a major factor in developing 'learned helplessness'.[8] This phenomenon was discovered when laboratory animals were exposed to stress that they could neither control nor avoid. The animals were confined in 'shuttle' boxes and subjected to mild electric shocks. Some animals were able to escape the shock by jumping over a low partition, and they quickly learned to do this. But others were immobilized and unable to escape the shocks. When these animals were put into boxes where they could actually escape the shock, they didn't even try. They had learned to be helpless, and they carried that helplessness into every new situation – including situations that they could change.

Similarly, if somebody is in a relationship or an organization that is characterized by chronic meaningless suffering, it can lead to learned helplessness and passivity. Unsurprisingly, learned helplessness is a major factor in depression, anxiety and in many other kinds of dysfunctional behaviour in individual lives, in relationships and in organizations.

The key to reducing or eliminating meaningless suffering is to realize the importance of explanations. When people are given meaningful explanations, most have the capacity to adapt to almost anything and to cope much more effectively with even very stressful situations. And the less control people have over situations – for example, when undergoing a medical procedure – the more important meaning becomes.

The worst kind of meaningless suffering is caused when there is no explanation for it at all. Only marginally better are explanations that start from the perspective of the person from whom you are seeking the explanation.

'I am just following the rules.'

'You think you have problems . . . let me tell you about mine.'

## *How we make meaning in our lives*

Psychologist Roy Baumeister identifies four main ways in which people try to make sense of their lives.[9] These four needs are for:

- purpose
- values
- efficacy, and
- self-worth.

They apply not just to our individual lives but to work teams, organizations – and indeed whole societies.

### *The need for purpose*

Having a purpose is about believing that we are heading towards something that we desire. It imposes a certain order on our lives, linking what we are doing now to some future outcome.

It is that connection to the desired future that gives meaning and purpose to what we are doing now. Even the smallest thing can become meaningful when it is related positively to our goals.

### *The need for values*

You need values because they give you a sense of goodness and positivity about your life and help you decide whether what you are doing is right or wrong. Values connect your external actions with your internal self.

When your decisions and behaviour are shaped by values, you feel anchored in your life. Your decisions and actions are imbued with meaning for you, and that shields you from the debilitating effects of uncertainty, guilt, anxiety and regret. Your actions become irredeemably part of yourself so you take responsibility for (or 'own') what you do.

That is what it *feels* like to be authentic, to have personal integrity.

### *The need for efficacy*

Efficacy is the belief that you can control and influence things in order to make a difference.

We want to feel that we can get important things done – in our families, in our work, in the wider community. If, despite our best efforts, we don't feel that we can make things happen, we become deeply frustrated and our lives begin to feel meaningless. For example, when our repeated efforts to please a boss or a family member fail, we cry: 'This is pointless!'

This is the angry, despondent exclamation of meaninglessness.

### *The need for self-worth*

Consciously and unconsciously, people look for reasons to believe that they are good and worthwhile. They look to their engagement in the different domains of their life – family, friends, work, community – for sources of self-esteem, status and belonging. When they are successful in that regard, they feel their lives are meaningful. In turn, the more they engage, the more meaningful their life becomes.

When we have purpose, values, efficacy and self-worth, we experience our lives as deeply meaningful.

When one – or more – of these needs is blocked, we are correspondingly unhappy and unfulfilled.

Our lives feel empty and adrift.

We become prey to alienation, cynicism and even despair.

## *Is there a single source of all meaning in our lives?*

We can rarely find a single domain in life that will enable us to meet all four needs.

Both religious faith and having a sense of vital engagement provide meaning across the three levels of your existence – in your thoughts, in your feelings and even in your body.[10] You *know* what you need to do. You know what is wrong and what is right, not just in your mind but in your gut.

For example, very religious people may feel physical disgust at the prospect of doing something that is taboo.

Someone deeply engaged in an artistic or work project can feel in their gut when something is 'wrong'.

Correspondingly, when things feel 'right', this deepens the meaningfulness of what they are doing.

In modern societies unity of meaning is becoming harder to find. The enormous diversity of activities and the freedom of choice that we now enjoy make it relatively easy to find purpose, efficacy and self-worth in our lives. However, it is harder to find a set of values that is shared by everybody – except, perhaps, the value we put on equality and tolerance.

But as we try to respect other people's values, which may be very different from our own, this can have the effect of making our own values seem more arbitrary. Consequently, many people find it hard to identify a reliable and convincing set of values to give meaning to their lives.[11]

Most of us manage to meet our four needs for meaning from a combination of sources – from family, work, personal achievements, friends, religion and spirituality, sport, social activism, politics, art, and our personal projects. There is one advantage to this: people who commit themselves utterly to a single cause or person in such a way that the object of their devotion is their sole source of purpose, values, efficacy and self-worth are very vulnerable when that cause turns out to be misguided, or that person betrays them. Drawing meaning from various sources, we protect ourselves if one domain fails us unexpectedly – such as the loss of a job, or the breakdown of a relationship.

But the meaning we get from such sources is not static or assured. We get stuck in routine, and things lose their freshness. Our commitment wanes ('Is this worth all the effort?') and if we want to revitalize it, we have to find ways to rediscover its meaning again.

## *The story of your life*

We are a storytelling species, and this applies to ourselves too: in order to make sense of our lives, we turn them into stories. Psychologist Dan McAdams shows that, as we go about our day-to-day lives, we are constantly constructing a story that we tell ourselves about ourselves. In fact, research in cognitive science suggests that the fundamental architecture of stories – with their beginning, middle and end, their characters and plots – may provide the basic structure for much human thought.

This means that the other important source of meaning in our lives is our life narrative.

Your 'narrator within' is housed in the left-brain interpreter centre, issuing a constant stream of commentary on what you are doing, as if you are being accompanied by a TV documentary maker, shadowing your every move and asking you questions.

Why are you doing what you are doing?

How are you feeling about it?

What do you think is going to happen next?

Your life narrative includes not just the stories that you act out in your life, but also those that you could have, or wished you had, lived. It includes the stories that important others – parents, siblings, friends and colleagues – tell about you. All of these stories – real and potential – coalesce into one, becoming the fundamental mental structure that holds everything together. This narrative then becomes your identity – representing the most private way you feel about yourself, and also the public self you present to the world.

In this half-conscious, half-unconscious story, you feature as the main character and you organize the material into 'chapters' ('When I was at primary school' 'When I first got married' 'When I lost my job' 'When the children were young' 'After the break-up' 'When I was very unhappy' 'When life was good' 'After I got sick' 'When I was promoted to my present job').

To a large extent, how you define those chapters is determined by how well you think you succeeded in attaining the major goals of that particular period ('My forties were a really bad time for me because my marriage broke up' 'The day I got my degree results was the best day of my life. I knew then that I had proved myself to my father and, for the first time, he actually praised me to my face').

Around the central theme of each chapter, you construct stories with plots and a cast of characters – parents, siblings, teachers, bosses, good guys and bad guys, friends and adversaries. You attribute motives and intentions to each of them – including yourself. These motives, as well as the external events that happen, drive the unfolding plot.

In every life narrative there are high points, low points and turning points. But running through it like connecting threads are your fundamental assumptions or 'wordless blueprints' about yourself, about other people and about how the world works.

Are you worthy of love and respect, competent and in control of your destiny?

Or is the opposite true?

Are other people trustworthy?

Is the future full of opportunity or threat?

Are events capable of being shaped, or completely outside your control?

These basic assumptions act as a kind of mental scaffolding that gives your life meaning and purpose. They provide coherence to your experiences and help you define your identity as you move through the different phases of your life. Once established, you then view much of what happens day-to-day through this frame.

We use our life narrative and its fundamental assumptions to make sense of things – to interpret and respond to everyday events, and to anticipate what may happen to us. Sometimes we are aware of this, but most of the time this process is working outside our consciousness – yet it is still affecting how we think, feel and behave.

For example, if you construe yourself as the character who never gives up, or who always rescues people, or who always gets a raw deal, consciously or unconsciously you are disposed to act in this way in every new situation you encounter – and to find evidence as to why that is the only or best way to act, further reinforcing your story about yourself. The more often you act out that story, the more dominant it becomes – for good or bad.

Stories count.

They can help you to flourish, or keep you in a cycle of languishing.

### *Re-imagining your story*

Life narratives have such an important influence that it pays to become more aware of the story you are telling yourself about yourself and your life. There is a complex relationship between what objectively happens in your life and how you *choose* to recall and interpret what happened.

You exercise a great deal of choice over:

- the particular events or experiences you highlight as significant
- how you account for the causes and consequences of your experiences, and
- what conclusions you draw from them.

It is a very worthwhile, and absorbing, exercise to write your story.

Put aside some time (although it is unlikely you will finish the exercise in one sitting) and start from the beginning. Try starting with a classic opening line, such as 'Once upon a time . . .' or 'My story starts . . .' and see where that takes you.

Do you start with your birth?

Do you start with your parents, or even with your grandparents?

Do you skip to some major event that happened to you and work backwards?

Next, segment your life narrative into different chapters, with each defined by the major goal you were trying to achieve at that time.

Describe the major characters in that chapter, and your relationship with them.

Describe how you recall thinking and feeling, why you acted as you did and not in some other way.

If you prefer, you could start by describing the defining moments in your life to date, and write a page or two about each one. In the process, you will become aware of the choices you are exercising about when a certain 'chapter' started and when it ended.

Try to find links between the different periods and episodes of your life.

How did your experiences in your family affect your subsequent life?

Are there recurring patterns – either good or bad?

Are you always shaping your own destiny, or are other people or events shaping it?

Are you at your best when acting independently, or when working closely with other people?

Which decisions worked out well and made you happy, and which did not – what is the difference between them?

The more causal links you can make, the greater the psychological benefits. Writing your narrative allows you to zoom in on particularly important details, or to pan out to view the larger life patterns in which issues are embedded.[12]

Now, the most important part: skip ahead and write the last chapter. You can skip to the end of your life, but most people prefer to end the account five, ten or twenty years from the present.

What do you want to be doing then?

Who are the people you hope will be in your life, and what kind of relationship do you want with them?

What is the most important thing you want to have achieved by that point?

What are the things you most want to experience?

Try not to censor yourself too much. Even if you know that some of your dreams are unlikely to happen, it is important to connect to them in order to get clues about your deepest needs and motivations. You will begin to see if there are other ways to meet those needs.

Next, start the work of connecting where you are now with where you want to be.

What do you need to be doing *now* to make your future happen?

What changes do you need to make in yourself, your work and your relationships?

This part of the exercise is the moment of truth – when you become aware of the real constraints in your life and the real possibilities. Unless you have that balanced picture, you are at risk of living in a fantasy or giving up on your actual power to change things.

Writing your story not only helps you shape your future, it helps you to make sense of what may otherwise seem random and disordered. It is a powerful reminder of your need to:

- create or rediscover a sense of purpose
- reconnect to the values that drive you
- act effectively to shape your destiny, and
- remember why you are a good and worthwhile person.

The more you weave purpose, values, efficacy and self-worth through your narrative, the more you will experience your life as deeply meaningful.

Finally, for those who are in any kind of leadership position, doing this exercise will greatly assist you. Virtually every study of leadership identifies the crucial role leaders play in creating a collective culture – a set of standards and values, a way of doing things, a 'story' – that binds people together in their collective efforts. This is what enables every member of a team to understand the connection between what they do and the overall mission of the organization.

This is not just a 'feel-good' strategy. The culture of an organization accounts for between 20 and 30 per cent of performance.[13]

Constructing and telling compelling stories is a key part of successful leadership. According to Robert Dickman, the founder of the executive coaching company FirstVoice, stories are facts wrapped in an emotion that can compel us to take action to transform the world around us.[14] And it is much easier to construct an emotionally compelling story about the organization you are leading if you have a compelling narrative or story about yourself.

Dickman says that all good stories follow a common arc: a guiding passion that helped you break from the bondage of the past and create a more promising future; the biggest obstacle (in yourself or in the situation) that you had to overcome; the resulting transformation in yourself; and the lessons learned.

The more effort you put into constructing your own story, the more capable you will be of doing the same for the organization you lead.

## *Disruptions in our life narrative*

When people's life narrative is flowing forward, they are generally happy and productive. Life makes sense to them.

But sometimes it veers off course.

Psychologist Robert Neimeyer has shown that such disruptions can take a number of forms.[15]

### *A narrative dominated by somebody else's view of you*

Sometimes a life narrative is dominated by somebody who is very significant in your life – a parent, an older sibling, a friend, a boss – who insists on seeing you in a particular way, one that is at odds with how you privately see yourself. Usually their view is simplistic ('Joe is afraid of nothing; he will take anything on' 'Maria will never make much of herself because she is lazy'). If the person who sees you like that is in a position of power in your life, formally or emotionally – particularly if you fear them in any way – their view of you can marginalize your more nuanced account of yourself.

Joe knows that he is often afraid, but he is even more afraid to acknowledge it.

Maria knows that it is lack of confidence, not laziness, that is holding her back.

Gradually, the person's own private view of themselves becomes undermined. They find themselves following the script set by the other person's view of them, thus further reinforcing it – the classic vicious cycle. People with a disability, or suffering from cancer or other serious illnesses, can become victims of such dominant narratives, where their disability or illness comes to wholly define them.

People who insist on holding such dominant narratives of us, in Neimeyer's resonant phrase, steal the authorship of our life.

### *Dissociated narrative*

Sometimes people have experiences that they can't face, because they find them too painful. These experiences provoke so much shame or guilt, anxiety or rage, that they are unable to acknowledge them to anybody, even to themselves. Being a victim of child sexual abuse, or being involved in fraud, or conducting an affair can cause people to block out the experiences, or compartmentalize them, in an attempt to prevent that painful private event or story from finding expression.

The price to be paid for that compartmentalization is high. To keep something compartmentalized requires vigilance and self-monitoring, plus a ruthless segregation of any memories, images or associations related to it. Harbouring a secret means curtailing intimate conversations to avoid the risk of self-disclosure.

All this requires considerable mental effort and self-control. Since the capacity for that kind of 'heavy' mental processing is so limited, people in that situation can find themselves exhausted, depleted, distracted.

Their overall life narrative can't develop in the ordinary way, so it becomes dissociated and fragmented.

### *Disorganized narrative*

The most dramatic and far-reaching disruptions in a life narrative are caused by a severe adversity or trauma, when people are overwhelmed by intensely emotional experiences that overload the brain, disrupting how they think and understand themselves and make sense of the world.

These traumatic experiences can be so radically inconsistent with their previous assumptions about themselves, or about particular people, that they can't fit them into their story.

Traumatic experiences can float apart from your normal life narrative and threaten its very foundations.

You think of yourself as a loving and competent mother – then one of your adolescent children gets into serious trouble.

You see yourself as an experienced and talented manager – then your business goes bust.

You build your life around what you believe to be a loving, intimate marriage – and then discover that your partner has been having a long-term affair with your best friend.

Of course, these events will not necessarily disorganize your sense of self. But the more strongly identified you are with a particular role – the more dependent you are on it for your sense of self and for the meaning of your life – the more vulnerable you are when a crisis undermines that role.

Correspondingly, if people manage to reconstruct their life narrative in the face of stress, setbacks and failures, they can build resilience and flourish under fire.

That is the subject of the next three chapters.

## STRATEGY EIGHT

# *Build your resilience*

'The world breaks everyone and afterward many are strong at the broken places.'

Ernest Hemingway, *A Farewell to Arms*

# 17. Good stress, bad stress

Resilience is high among the qualities we most admire in others, long for in ourselves and hope for in our children. Setbacks, failure, disappointments, betrayals and suffering are inherent in life. Resilience is the ability to bounce back and to go on with life. In fact, without going through a crisis, large or small, we can't claim to be resilient.

Building resilience is at the heart of a flourishing life.

Being alive demands constantly adapting to what is happening around and inside us – we have to meet the demands of physical, emotional and economic survival. For much of the time the pressure to meet these demands creates good stress. It revs up our physical, mental and emotional energy to get the job done. We feel interested, motivated, eager, even excited. Even if we feel nervous, it's a giddy 'butterflies in the stomach' nervousness, the pumping of adrenaline that gets us ready for the race ahead, ready to step decisively on to whatever life stage on which we have to perform.

At other times, we feel overwhelmed. We feel the demands on us are too many and our resources too limited to deal with them. But at the same time, we feel those demands can't be ignored or resisted. This is bad stress.

It is the stress you feel at 3 a.m. when you are awoken – again – by your baby crying. You are exhausted and sleep-deprived. But the demand can't be resisted. You must get out of bed.

*But you can't get out of bed.*

It is the stress you feel when you are assigned another work project on top of an already unsustainable weight of commitments. You don't have the time or mental resources to do it well. You must complete it by tomorrow.

*But you can't get it done by tomorrow.*

In these bad stress scenarios, you are torn between competing values.

Will I be a caring parent? Or do I need to get enough rest to keep going tomorrow?

Will I get the job done so that I feel more competent and keep my job? Or is it more important to safeguard my health and maintain some kind of sane balance in my life?

Bad stress is when you know that one of these valued goals will be harmed by whatever choice you make.[1] You feel powerless. And stress and powerlessness are a deadly combination.

In addition to routine stress, we have to manage unforeseen stress. At one time, psychologists believed that there was a simple way to measure such stress. They got people to rate how much adjustment was required to deal with a list of key life events – the more adjustment needed, the more stressful the event was rated.[2] Thus, out of a maximum score of 100, the death of a spouse was rated 100; getting married 50; changes in your business 39 . . . and so on. But it soon became clear that there was a huge variation in how people reacted to the same type of event.

It turned out that it was not the events in themselves that determined the level of stress, but how people *coped* with them.

How you cope depends on many things, but it boils down to two main factors:

- how you think and feel about yourself, and
- what personal, practical and social resources are available to you.

Let's take the example of a child leaving home.

If you are a mother who has devoted her life to full-time homemaking, if you have had few opportunities or little motivation to build a life for yourself outside your family, and if your partner is distant and unsupportive, your beloved last child leaving home is likely to be extremely stressful.

On the other hand, if you have been chafing at the bit to have more time for yourself and to return to your career; if you have well-developed personal interests, a happy marriage and a wide network of friends, your last child leaving home is unlikely to be experienced as stressful.

Similarly, a change of job or having to make changes in your business could be a nightmare or a dream come true – depending on how you think about it.

Do you see the change as a setback or an opportunity?

Do you think of yourself as the kind of person who has a strong need for stability or who relishes a challenge?

## *The twin pillars of coping with stress*

A useful way to understand the relationship between good stress, bad stress and coping is to imagine yourself as a bridge with two supporting pillars. Let's call one the 'Self Pillar' – how you think and feel about yourself, as well as your skills, personal qualities and emotional competencies. The other pillar is the 'Resources Pillar' – the information, money, equipment, practical help and emotional support you have available to you. The demands on you make up the 'traffic' that passes over that bridge. A large part of the traffic is routine – the equivalent of commuter traffic, school runs, deliveries. But there is also the unexpected traffic that causes disruption and delay, or even the occasional emergency – the equivalent of a caravan that is too wide, a tractor that is too slow, a juggernaut that barrels on to the bridge too fast.

When the bridge is strong, it can support the volume of expected and even unexpected heavy-duty traffic. But if the traffic becomes too heavy, the bridge becomes stressed. Sometimes, the stress is caused by the sheer volume of traffic. At other times, one major crash inflicts severe damage. The supports weaken and begin to crack. Unless the volume of traffic can be reduced, or the structural weaknesses repaired, the bridge will eventually collapse.

At other times, the problem is not the volume of traffic but a fault line in one of the pillars. Maybe it's the Self Pillar – a lack of self-confidence, a crippling fear of failure, a willingness to let our lives be sucked dry by somebody else. Or the weakness can arise in the Resource Pillar – lack of the right information, of opportunity, of practical or emotional support.

Just like the bridge, we need a certain amount of 'traffic', or good stress, in our lives if we want to live up to our potential. If the traffic is too light and the bridge is underused, it becomes isolated, overgrown, sidelined and loses out on opportunities for improvement. In just the same way, when we don't have enough good stress in our lives, we languish and become vulnerable to depression, free-floating anxiety, and a range of vague symptoms – fatigue, disturbed sleep, aches and pains – that are hard to pin down.

Coping entails either regulating the traffic of demands, or building strong pillars of support – or both. In psychological terms, coping is the sum total of all these efforts. When our efforts are successful, we show resilience. The more often we succeed in coping successfully, the more we grow that quality of resilience in ourselves.

Resilience starts as the successful outcome to coping well with stress. But if you do this often enough, resilience becomes internalized as an enduring personal quality.

This will substantially reduce your vulnerability to future stresses. However, when we don't learn to cope with stress, we remain vulnerable to bad stress and put ourselves at risk of illness, and even premature death.

## *The effects of 'bad' stress*

Eva's description below captures vividly how bad stress negatively affects body, feeling, thinking, behaviour, relationships – and how it depresses functioning.

*Eva's story*

It was the worst time in my life. My marriage was falling apart. Every time I tried to discuss things with my husband, it ended in another huge row. I could not sleep, I started having palpitations. I was sure I was going to have a heart attack. My work was shot. As soon as I tried to focus on something, my mind would wander back to my problems and I would find myself making whispered phone calls – to my solicitor, my mother, or friends – when I should have been finishing projects. And I was so irritable some days that I ended up making problems for myself. Once my secretary burst into tears because I snapped at her, and it took me days to get our relationship back on an even keel.

My friends were great, but I was conscious that I was leaning on them a lot and I suspect that they got sick of the whole saga. Sometimes, when we met, I would see them laughing and having a good time, and then they would spot me coming and adopt this kind of guarded expression: 'How are you?' And you would know that they really hoped that maybe the news would be good – not just for my sake, but so that they didn't have to get into sympathy mode again.

So, I would try to put on a cheerful front. But that made me feel even more alone and, when I got home, I would burst into tears. My mind would go round and round: What is happening to me? Why did this happen to me? Why can't I handle it better? I am a competent person, I am strong – or, at least, I used to be!

My self-confidence took an awful battering during that whole period.

When we are very stressed, the negative overwhelms the positive. We experience ourselves functioning at our worst. It's as if all our strengths suddenly turn into weaknesses.

The drive to do things well turns into a punishing perfectionism.

Competence and efficiency turn into hyper-controlling behaviour.

The sensitivity that used to help us react with subtlety becomes a propensity to be overwhelmed by every little change we notice in ourselves or in other people's reactions.

The capacity to reflect turns into endless rumination.

The ability to handle things ourselves becomes an insurmountable barrier to asking for or accepting help.

As the negativity mounts on all sides, we feel our sense of control over ourselves and our lives slipping away. We are painfully conscious of our physical symptoms and distressing thoughts and feelings, but are less aware of the insidious damage that bad stress is doing to our immune system – our irreplaceable defence against injury, illness and disease.

### *Bad stress wears down and wears out the immune system*

A major 'study of studies' that examined thirty years of scientific research – nearly 300 studies involving almost 19,000 people – showed just how stress affects the immune system. It revealed that while short-term stress (such as an examination) revs the immune system to get us ready to do battle, chronic stress drives the system to breakdown.[3]

Most of us get stressed in a short-term way when we are sitting an exam, or asking someone out on a date, or facing a minor medical procedure, or making a presentation at work or a speech at a wedding (good stress). To get us ready to meet that stress, our body gets geared up for 'fight-or-flight'. It delivers extra oxygen and glucose to the heart and to the large muscles. Our heart beats faster and we feel adrenaline coursing through our body.

Meanwhile, the immune system also gears up. It activates the body's all-purpose 'natural immunity' response – which does not use much energy – as if preparing for an attack from infection or injury. And it suppresses its other line of defence – the heavy-duty, energy-sapping 'specific immunity' system – which targets more serious invaders such as cancer.

While this readjustment frees up your energy to rise to the challenge you are facing, it leaves you vulnerable to particular viruses and diseases. This is the price you pay for being revved up and ready to deal with the immediate challenge. If the stress is short-term, this is generally a price worth paying. However, when the stress continues and becomes chronic, this adaptive change works against you. To deal with the chronic stress, your body continues to divert energy away from your specialized line of defence. Sooner or later, you are left dangerously exposed. It is a bit like a commander using his highly specialized bomb disposal personnel for ordinary trench warfare. Then, when exposed to a lethal bomb threat, they are not available to deal with it.

The chronic stressors that are the most damaging are events that change our identity or our role – the loss of a job, the breakdown of an important relationship, becoming a full-time carer. These events call for multiple adjustments in how we think about ourselves and how we live our lives. We don't know when, or even if, the stress and distress we feel will end, leaving us feeling out of control and without hope.

The effects of bad stress on health are stark and clear. In Chapter 6 we saw how the rate of healing of cuts among student participants in a study was 40 per cent slower during exam periods than during holiday time, and that levels of immune cells fell by 71 per cent at exam time. This is one of many such studies involving participants young and old, male and female, signalling the link between stress, depressed immune function and a range of illnesses and vulnerabilities, such as upper respiratory infections or elevated PSA levels in men (prostate-specific antigen, suggestive of prostate cancer).

High levels of anger and anxiety – what Richard Suinn of Colorado State University calls 'the terrible twos' – are particularly toxic.[4]

Why?

Because when you frequently feel anxious and angry, you go into a highly aroused emotional state – hyper vigilant, constantly scanning for further threats on the horizon. Your body responds by keeping your sympathetic nervous system in a constant state of activation – with adverse effects on your heart and cardiovascular system, your immune system and a host of other body functions. Longitudinal studies that followed hundreds of law and medical students for up to 30 years have shown that hostility was associated with a higher rate of heart disease – and, in the case of older adults, this was irrespective of age, health status, smoking and blood pressure.

A stress response that takes the form of high levels of resentment, suspicion and aggression also substantially increases vulnerability to a wide range of illnesses, including asthma, internal organ disease, and rheumatoid arthritis. It also reduces the tolerance for pain – which, in turn, can affect recovery.

In addition, chronic anxiety and anger lead to behaviour that adversely affects health – overuse of alcohol, smoking, disturbed sleep, poor compliance with medical regimes, and distrust of doctors and other professionals.

## *Developing an effective coping style*

Strong, effective ways of coping with stress form the foundation stone on which resilience is built.

If you ask people how they handle stress, they give a bewildering variety of answers.

'I make a list of what I have to do.'

'I burst out crying.'

'I go off by myself to think.'

'I try to find out as much as I can about the situation I find myself in.'

'I ask for help.'

'I go for a smoke.'

'I pray.'

'I try not to think about it.'

'I go for a run.'

'I make myself a stiff drink.'

'I call my mother.'

'I go into overdrive.'

Despite the differences, these are variations of a few underlying strategies.

Until relatively recently, psychologists understood effective coping largely in terms of managing the negative emotions that accompany stress. And indeed, having an effective coping style does mean having a few well-practised techniques. But, the new research about positive emotions has forced a radical rethink.

Knowing ways in which to generate and maintain positive feelings and thinking – even under great pressure – is also a crucial part of effective coping.

The heart of resilience – like the heart of flourishing – depends fundamentally on the ability to actively rebalance the positivity and negativity in your life. Setbacks and crises inevitably increase negativity – and you have to work hard to limit its intensity. But you also have to actively and simultaneously increase the positive, so that you will not fall below that critical threshold and tumble into a downward spiral of languishing.

Returning to the metaphor of the bridge, an effective coping style* means being able to balance the load on the bridge – the demands on you – using the supports you have available.

That requires nurturing certain 'resilience-friendly' personal qualities, and modifying 'stress-prone' qualities.

## *Knowing when to engage with a challenge and when to disengage*

When it comes to coping, we are all instinctively 'engagers' or 'disengagers'.

Active engagement is a type of fight response. Once engagers are confronted with any issue, they feel an urge to 'move towards' the problem: to find out more about it, take it on and get some control over it. They want to *fix* what's wrong.

Disengagement is a type of flight response. Disengagers are motivated to move *away* from the problem. Their main focus is on avoiding the issue – or, at least, avoiding dealing with it for a while. They are not inclined to talk about it, or think about it, any more than they have to. They try to keep away from the issue – physically or mentally. They try to distract themselves by thinking about other things, or becoming immersed in some activity. They may even deny the problem altogether. They are highly focused on trying to control their own physiological arousal and negative feelings.

Men are particularly focused on this aspect of emotional coping. They don't want to get so worked up that they risk being overwhelmed by their feelings of anxiety, anger, loss or powerlessness. (The crucial importance of managing overwhelming emotion, and techniques for doing so, are explored in Chapter 18.)

Leading researchers Susan Folkman and Richard Lazarus were the first to distinguish between what they called 'problem-focused' and 'emotion-focused' coping.[5]

Problem-focused coping does what it says – you cope by trying to

* I say 'coping style' because no one coping strategy is effective in every situation. An effective coping style means learning to use a wide variety of coping strategies that match the nature of the challenge.

tackle what is causing the stress. For example, you notice some disturbing symptom – a lump, a rash, a pain. Straightaway you try to find out more about what it might mean. You go on the Internet. You call a friend. You go to the doctor. If you find out that it is nothing, you draw a sigh of relief and resolve to live a healthier life. If the doctor tells you that there is indeed a problem, you then try to find out as much as possible about treatment options. You consult with your family and friends. You make a plan and act on it.

Problem-focused coping, then, always involves engaging actively with the problem. It is directed mainly at the *external* situation.

Emotion-focused coping, on the other hand, is directed *inwards*. It is aimed at trying to manage how the stressful situation is affecting you. You focus on relieving your feelings of anxiety, anger, loss. You do what you think will relax you and soothe your feelings. Emotion-focused coping can mean actively engaging with the problem, or disengaging from it. You can engage with the feelings and physical reactions to the stress by going for a walk, or breathing deeply for a few minutes. You can call someone for reassurance, consolation or advice. You can disengage by seeking distraction in work, or watching TV, or playing some sport. You might have a stiff drink – either to relieve your stress symptoms, or to blot them out.

Engagers use both problem-solving and emotional coping. They spend time and effort examining how they really feel, or they try to manage the situation. They seek out opportunities to talk to family, friends and colleagues, or to anybody who will listen ('What do you think I should do?).

Disengagers are less inclined to try problem-solving until they have first done a lot of emotion-focused coping. They want to get their feelings under control before they act.

Extreme disengagers use the most avoidant kind of emotional coping.

### *Which coping strategy is better?*

Well, as Susan Folkman and fellow researcher Judith Moskowitz point out, that depends.[6] The effectiveness of any coping strategy depends on the *cause* of the stress and, crucially, on how much *control* you have over it.

It depends on what you hope your coping strategy will achieve.

It depends on what type of personality you are, and the 'fit' between your style of coping and the situation you are trying to deal with.

It depends on what stage you are at in dealing with the issue.

A sudden bereavement, or a health crisis, or a relationship breakdown may require a very practical problem-solving approach at the beginning. But, sooner or later, you will have to switch to emotional coping in order to work through your feelings.

All of the provisos above, far from complicating your understanding, actually provide a set of solid guidelines to make your coping more effective.

In general, trying to cope by actively engaging with the issues that confront you is a good life strategy. But, like all strategies, it has positive and negative forms.

Engagement in the sense of gathering information, making systematic efforts to understand what is happening, trying different ways to solve the problem, seeking advice and support – all these can have positive consequences. You get a better handle on the nature of the problem and how to resolve it. You develop competencies as you try out solutions. The more engaged you are, the more alert you are to any change in the situation – so you can adapt your response if necessary.

Active engagement as a coping strategy works, if you have some *control* over the issue that is causing the stress. But there are many situations where you have little or no control.

For example, if you are a child caught in the middle of warring parents, trying to solve your parents' problems is likely to have very bad consequences for you. It draws your attention and energy into something that you have little or no control over, making you feel distressed and powerless.

The same is true if you are trying to actively please somebody who can't be pleased, or trying to make somebody love you who clearly can't or won't. Trying to actively engage in such situations is counterproductive. It diverts your precious attention from dealing with things you *do* have control over.

It is generally a good thing to persist in trying to get something you want, or believe you are entitled to. But, in many situations, there comes a point when you have to recognize that it is not going to happen and that your high engagement is exacting too great a psychological (and health) cost.

That is the point when you have to switch to a disengagement strategy.

### *Why disengagement is not always bad*

Disengaging from the problems in your life – in the sense of trying to deny or avoid dealing with them – is generally not an effective coping strategy.

If you have a worrying symptom, or a failing project, or somebody important in your life is behaving destructively, denying the issue or repressing any thoughts and feelings about it will allow the problem to grow, making it more difficult to deal with eventually – and more likely to spiral out of control. Avoidance in the form of shifting responsibility for the problem on to somebody else, escaping into drugs or alcohol or overeating are also unproductive ways to solve a problem, and are likely to cause additional problems.

Trying to eliminate anxious or angry thoughts is like trying not to think of a white bear – your mind will flood with unwanted thoughts and images. Indeed, trying to suppress strong negative feelings can result in disturbing dreams and nightmares. It can raise your blood pressure. In addition, denying your negative thoughts and feelings creates significant stress for the people around you. They are getting mixed signals and are unable to deal effectively with what is going on in the interaction between you. Your forced positivity ('I am not upset') creates dissonance in *their* central nervous system, and they start to feel stressed.

A more benign form of emotional avoidance may sometimes be necessary, and productive – particularly when you have very little control over what is stressing you.

For example, when somebody is confronted with an overwhelming loss, they may be simply unable to take it in initially. A certain amount of avoidance coping – denial, distancing, fantasy and wishful thinking – may be necessary, giving them time to build up their resources. That is why doctors sometimes face a dilemma when they have to give a patient bad news about their health – particularly in the case of a terminal illness. They are ethically obliged to be transparent and honest about the seriousness of the problem, so that the patient can make informed choices and put their affairs in order. But sometimes the patient will refuse to take in what the doctor is saying.

I have personal experience of this.

> My mother was diagnosed with a serious form of cancer when she was fifty-nine. The surgeon told us that the prognosis was poor, with only a 20–30 per cent probability that she would live more than two years. She endured severe and invasive surgery. Yet, she resolutely avoided any discussion about her condition. Soon afterwards, she started referring to the surgery jokingly as her 'bypass'. As it happened, around that time our town got a new bypass and there were quite a few accidents on it.

So, when we phoned to see how she was doing, my mother would say, 'More trouble with the bypass.'

And she made us wait to hear which one.

It was a classic denial strategy. But it appeared to suit her personality, and allowed her to recover and make plans for the future. Many years later, my brother finally asked her what she thought she had been suffering from.

She thought for a while and then said, 'Cancer, I suppose'.

My mother's story illustrates her coping strategy – whereby she simultaneously 'knew' and did not know what the problem was. Thankfully, she survived and is now a lively 87-year-old.

## *Flexibility is the secret to coping with stress*

Most of us know somebody who, on first appearance, looks very vulnerable. Let's call her Sally (even though it could just as well be Sam). She has lots of physical and psychological symptoms that distress her. She complains a lot and often makes dire predictions about how much strain she is under, and the likelihood of a premature end. She elicits lots of attention and care from people around her. Yet, after a while, you notice that Sally is a pretty tough cookie, a real survivor and, you suspect, someone who will long outlive you.

What accounts for Sally's resilience is the great variety of coping strategies she uses. Undoubtedly, her all-time favourite is looking for sympathy and support. But, when she senses that the support is thinning out, she may book herself a weekend break, or decide to get professional advice, or take up squash or yoga. She may change how she is working, or her style of interacting with somebody significant. She may announce that she now sees her situation in a new, more positive light. It is the sheer variety of her coping repertoire that accounts for her resilience.

And yes – she probably will outlive you.

Now compare Sally to Fred (who could be Frieda). Fred is known for being strong and decisive, with a no-nonsense 'let's get on with it' attitude. He likes to be in control and is admired for being independent-minded, not given to worrying about other people's opinions. Fred is regarded as very successful in whichever domain of his life – work or family – he invests with his energies. But then a crisis begins to brew in another domain. His marriage begins to deteriorate, or things begin to go wrong in the team at work. Fred redoubles his efforts to cope as he always has: he becomes even more decisive and independent-minded.

After all, these are the strategies that have always worked.

But as his wife or colleagues increase their demands for a deeper examination of the crisis, Fred's approach creates even more difficulties. The more they press for a change in how he is dealing with things, the more he resists, until a significant gap in understanding and empathy develops. The original crisis is displaced by a new central problem – how Fred is *coping*.

The importance of flexibility in coping throws a different light on what we see as vulnerability. Someone who normally appears strong and resilient may turn out to be vulnerable in a crisis situation because they rely too heavily on one single coping strategy – and it just doesn't suit the specific situation they now find themselves in, or the people they have to cope with.

Managers are often mystified as to why an otherwise competent person is rejected by the team members and negatively affects the work of the team. But group 'fit' is not just about common purpose – it also depends on being flexible in how a team member copes with the inevitable stresses that arise in any group.

To help yourself develop some awareness of your own favoured coping response, ask yourself two questions.

- What is the *first* thing I always, or nearly always, do when I am stressed?
- What is the thing I never, or very rarely, do when I am stressed?

The answer to the second question will indicate which class of coping strategies you might consider developing.

For example, if you are a consistent 'engager', consider the positive disengagement strategies that you might try, and vice versa.

### *Horses for courses – how men and women cope with stress*

When it comes to flexibility, men and women have a lot to learn from each other. Men and women tend to respond differently to their own and other people's stress.

For example, men have a stronger tendency to use fight-or-flight strategies. They either want to deal with the problem, in which case they move quickly into action, or else they want to escape it. They try to steer clear of the emotional content of a problem and to stay focused on action. They show a strong preference for working things out for themselves – even when they are very stressed and could do with help. They are good at compartmentalizing things, not letting a worry from one area of their life leak into other areas. They 'zone out' as a way of relieving stress, or distract themselves by watching something on TV. Or they stare into space or doodle.

Women, on the other hand, tend to use a 'tend-and-befriend' strategy.[7] They are focused on relieving psychological distress. They have a strong tendency to engage emotionally – and verbally – with problems. They like to talk about them, to share the detail with their partner and friends. They think a lot about what caused a problem and how they can solve it. They seek support, reassurance and advice.

These gender differences originate in hormonal differences (women produce more oxytocin, which facilitates bonding), in different values, and in different wiring in the female and male brain. For example, at any one time, women's brains show more neural activity than men's, and even when the female brain is resting, it shows as much activity as the active male brain.[8]

The strategies favoured by men and women are all effective.

However, overusing preferred strategies can exacerbate the problem you are trying to solve. Too much support-seeking can become mentally and physically exhausting – and may wear out the patience of your partner or friends. Too little support-seeking can leave you isolated and very vulnerable when stress becomes too intense and chronic, overwhelming your own capacity to deal with it. Thinking can tip over into chronic worry and rumination. But constantly distracting yourself from the problem can make the problem worse in the long run.

To increase their coping flexibility, women and men could learn from each other.

Men could try looking for support in a way that protects their self-esteem by, for example, reframing the search for advice as an exercise in competency – seeking out the right expert who can help them, or a good listener who can enable them to talk through (and think through) the way they see things.

Women may not find zoning out – say, watching sports on TV – as effective as men do, but they might find going for a walk or pottering around the garden fulfils the same function. They could try compartmentalizing things by writing a list of the issues they will think about later in the day, or week, and then put the list into a drawer which they close firmly – thus consigning the worries to another place and another time.

### *Develop 'resilience-friendly' personal qualities and modify 'stress-prone' qualities*

Of the so-called Big Five personality characteristics, only extroversion and openness to experience are associated with greater resilience.[9]

#### EXTROVERSION

Extroverts like to engage with other people, making it more likely that they will have a wide network of people to support them, which is a vital component of resilience. Crucially, intimate and non-judgemental listening enables us to express and confront distress and bewilderment and to retell our whole sorry tale, until eventually we have no more to say. Being listened to – and being asked questions (sensitively) – helps us to clarify our thinking, examine our assumptions and consider the options. Only then are we ready to move on and implement solutions. A trusted listener helps us untangle and clarify things, and prevents us falling into the private hell of worry and rumination.

The link between extroversion and resilience is that extroverts are generally optimistic. When optimistic people face stressful situations over which they have little control, they make more use of coping strategies such as reframing – trying to see the situation from another perspective, looking for something good in the situation and learning from it. Or they try to accept what has happened.[10]

But, as you will learn in Chapter 23, it is important to distinguish between naive optimism – the belief that *somehow* things will turn out OK – and more active optimism – the belief that things will turn out OK *because* of your efforts to ensure that they do.[11] Only this more active, constructive form of optimism is associated with resilience.

#### OPENNESS TO EXPERIENCE

Openness is the other quality associated with resilience. Openness is the disposition to be interested in new situations, ideas and experiences. When faced with stress or a crisis, open-minded people are readier to process its emotional impact, analyse their feelings and attempt to change their reactions. They are more likely to succeed, because they are also open to trying different approaches. They are also more likely to be imaginative, creative, emotionally responsive and intellectually curious.[12] These characteristics make it easier for them to cope with adversity, because they are more willing to reconsider their assumptions and beliefs and are less daunted by the prospect of rethinking their lives.

### HARDINESS

In her innovative research on stress, Susanne Kobasa, of City University of New York, found that what makes people 'stress-resistant' or resilient was what she called 'hardiness'.[13]

Hardiness has three components:

- commitment
- control
- challenge.

Commitment means having a general sense of purpose – a sense that you are involved in an enterprise that you believe *matters* and where *your* part in it matters. The more you feel that the enterprise really matters, the greater your commitment and the more effectively you can motivate others.

When you have such a commitment, no stress is insurmountable.

The opposite of having a strong sense of commitment is feeling alienated – as if nothing really matters. And, even if it does, you have no part in it, anyway.

The second component is control – having a sense of control over those things in your life that are important to your well-being.

The third component is challenge – a belief that change is an opportunity, rather than a threat. Despite setbacks and stress, you feel that life is full of possibilities and that change will open up those possibilities. You are open – to experience, to feedback, to learning from others.

The opposite is a personal style that is rigid, distrustful and wary of change.

You can cultivate the commitment and challenge elements of hardiness by adopting some of the strategies of flourishing that I have already described.

These are:

- having three life projects
- having a positive purpose, and
- living a life of vital engagement.

You can cultivate control by focusing on the small things that you can control in a stressful situation. Try breaking down the task into smaller parts and biting them off one chunk at a time.

You can sustain your courage by recalling previous challenges you have faced. It is crucial to remind yourself of success in the past – to counter the tendency to automatically dredge up negative memories when you are stressed. You can help yourself do that by talking to someone who is supportive, who appreciates your strengths and can remind you of them.

Finally, remember that while some people may find it easier to bounce back from stress because of their temperament, *everybody* can increase their resilience.

It just takes discipline and practice.

You may not be extroverted by disposition, but pushing yourself to engage with other people despite yourself pays huge dividends. You can deepen your relationships and be ready to help and support other people.

All of us can learn to be more open-minded, and any kind of mindfulness exercise will help that.

But, most of all, it is important to remember that most resilience is learned – it is the outcome of every successful attempt at coping.

Of course, fundamental to building resilience is the ability to manage the emotions that may overwhelm you when dealing with a stressful situation. When you disengage from a problem as a way of coping, that does not mean that you disengage from what is going on inside you. Equally, when you engage with a problem, in order to do so productively, and to deploy the right coping strategies, you need to avoid being blindsided by your emotions.

For that reason, the next chapter is devoted to managing your emotions in a crisis.

# 18. How to handle unruly emotions

Even for those with a strong predisposition towards practical engagement with problems, managing their emotions is fundamental to dealing with stressful situations successfully. This is because high physiological arousal and heightened emotions, particularly negative emotions, can interfere with the quality of your judgement and decisions, and your attempts to manage complex relationships – all crucial components of problem-solving. In high-stress situations, poorly managed negative emotions have a long shelf life and leave unpleasant static in relationships for a long time afterwards.

Leading expert on coping, Annette Stanton, divides emotional coping into two components – processing and expression.[1]

Emotional processing means figuring out *what* you are feeling, and *why*. Focusing on understanding your feelings – both positive and negative – can help you clarify not just why you are feeling as you are, but what is truly important to you.

You may realize you are angry or distressed about something going wrong, not just because of the frustration it is causing, but because of just how much it matters to you when it is going *right*. This insight may motivate you to put more effort into trying to resolve the situation constructively. You may realize that your feelings are ambivalent – you feel angry and want to express that, but you also see that your anger is covering up love and longing. Or perhaps you feel anxious but realize that your fear is obscuring your strong desire to take a risk, to put yourself forward, to reach out to someone or something. When you realize that, you are much less likely to act in an impulsive or destructive way, or to miss a real opportunity. You will be more considered and more likely to stay with your feelings until you have resolved them in a way that prepares you for positive action.

Emotional processing can be distressing, especially at the beginning. When I worked as a therapist, clients would often complain that in the beginning it was making them feel worse, not better. As they talked about painful memories, their minds flooded by upsetting images, they would sometimes be overwhelmed by tears and rage.

Similarly, at the beginning of a stressful situation, you can feel overwhelmed. But then, just like the client in therapy, as you gradually sift through your feelings and your thoughts about them, you can order things in your mind and the intensity of the feelings declines. Then, one day, you realize that the stressful situation has lost its power over you. You no longer feel angry or afraid. Instead, you feel more neutral – or even indifferent. With a little smile, you realize that you are happy again.

The other component of emotional coping – expressing your feelings openly and freely – sometimes happens at the same time as you are processing your feelings, sometimes afterwards, or sometimes in the absence of any processing at all. Each stage – processing and expression – feeds into the other. When both processing and expression work well together, the results are impressive for people facing a wide variety of stressful situations.

For example, emotional coping has been found to be of real benefit to women faced with the trauma of breast cancer or a diagnosis of infertility, and to young adults dealing with a parent who has a serious illness or psychological disorder. Women with breast cancer who work through and express their feelings report more positive views of their health, more energy, less distress, and they make fewer medical visits for pain and other cancer-related problems.

The effectiveness of emotional coping also depends on how – and in what order – you use the two stages of understanding and expressing your feelings. If you make only a half-hearted effort to understand and work through your feelings, and then only partially express those feelings, you will have more difficulty adjusting to what has happened in the long term. Equally, if you are too intense in your efforts to understand your feelings and give too free a rein to expressing them, it bodes as badly as doing the opposite – acting out strong emotions without any attempt to understand what is going on inside you.

The best strategy is to do the emotional processing bit first – to spend time trying to understand and sort out what you are feeling – but in a moderate, balanced way. Then, when you have gained some understanding of what is going on inside you, you are in a better position to express your feelings – also in an appropriate and balanced way.

## *The dark side of emotional processing – worry and rumination*

Too much emotional processing can turn into worry and rumination – which are connected but different.[2]

Worry is provoked by anxiety, and fuelled by imagining all the bad things that might happen. When you worry, you are actively *engaging* mentally with what is stressing you – but in a negative way. Worrying draws you ever deeper into the problem, setting up a chain of negative thoughts and images, each feeding off the other. The trademark of worrying is 'what if' thinking.

'What if I mess up the presentation I am making tomorrow? What if I then get a bad review at the end of the quarter? What if I lose my job? What if I then can't make my mortgage payments? What if I end up losing my home?'

Rumination is slightly different – involving endless, repetitive focusing on negative thoughts and feelings, and on their causes and consequences.

'Why did he say that? Why did the relationship turn so sour? Why do all my relationships end unhappily? What am I doing wrong? What is wrong with me? What must people think of me? I just can't get over that he actually said what he did. Why would he do that?' And so on . . .

Rumination is strongly linked to depression.

Both worry and rumination prevent you switching your attention away from the negative event. Both interfere with performing well in life, coming up with good solutions to a problem, and translating solutions into effective action.[3] Both are very self-focused.

When people worry, they think they are solving their problem by preparing for the future – or even preventing it happening.

When they ruminate, they think they are solving their problem by gaining insight.

But they are not.

Both absorb energy and are extreme examples of trying to cope emotionally – by turning attention inwards, and getting completely stuck at the emotional processing stage.

Unfortunately, women are particularly prone to both.

### *What happens in your brain when you worry and ruminate*

Remember the amygdala, the little watchtower in the brain – the ancient part that processes fear and anger. People with a tendency to ruminate – those with a temperamental disposition towards neuroticism – have an overactive amygdala.

When your brain is wired like that, your amygdala goes into overdrive at the slightest whiff of negativity, frantically signalling danger so that it grabs your attention. Since negative experiences are stored in your memory in a particularly vivid way, you find it harder to attend to the positive, or to distract yourself – even when you know this would help. However, just because you are wired this way does not mean you can't gradually rewire your brain to respond in a less distressing way.

The key issue when you worry or ruminate is your difficulty in inhibiting a negative image or thought once it strikes you – even when it is irrelevant to your immediate concerns.[4] It is this difficulty in suppressing the negative that starts the chain of other negative thoughts and images, gradually sucking you deeper into the whirlpool of worry and rumination.

Resilient thinking is characterized by a very different response pattern.

We can see the difference by looking at what happens when people are facing potential threats. Psychologist Christian Waugh demonstrated this in an experiment in which each participant was told that one of two simple shapes (say, a triangle or circle) would appear on a screen.[5] One shape would signal that an unpleasant and disturbing image *might* follow it – so this shape constituted a signal of a potential threat. The other shape would signal that a neutral image would *always* follow. The experiment was a clever way of reproducing the everyday experience of dreading something that might or might not happen.

Before the study, a questionnaire had established the individual participants' levels of resilience. While the participants were viewing these images, their brain activity was scanned. The study found no difference in how people with a high or low level of resilience reacted to the disturbing image when it appeared – all showed spikes in activity in the areas of the brain that react to and manage emotions. So, being resilient does not mean you are immune to threats, or do not react strongly when the threat materializes.

The telling difference was in how participants reacted to the *possibility* of threat. When they were presented with the shape signalling that something negative *might* follow, participants with both high and low resilience showed a lot of brain activity. But once the threat did not materialize, the increased brain activity in highly resilient people levelled off more quickly and more completely than in those with a low level of resilience. In contrast, their brains showed prolonged arousal – irrespective of whether the disturbing image appeared or not.

Indeed, from the outset, once low-resilience participants were presented with a possible threat, their brain reaction started earlier and showed greater arousal than in the high-resilience group. This suggests that people who are low in resilience are more burdened by memories of negative experiences and by negative expectations of what *might* happen, and that they react to those internal cues rather than to what is *actually* happening. In the study, the more participants anticipated and worried about what *might* happen, the slower they were to recover when the disturbing image did not appear.

The brains of highly resilient people show much less activity in the part associated with worrying and 'what if' thinking. They are more responsive to what *is* happening in reality – good or bad – rather than to what *might* happen.

Tellingly, they also show more activity in two areas of the brain – the area that deals with expectations of threat, and the area that deals with good outcomes. In other words, when confronted with a threat or a challenge, they simultaneously activate both positive and negative expectations and interpretations of what might happen. This co-activation helps them to be highly attuned to what is actually happening, and makes them ready to react appropriately. If the threat materializes, they can mobilize their energy to deal with it; if it does not materialize, they can relax and conserve their energy. Actively generating possible good outcomes to the uncertain situation also helps them to soothe themselves while dealing with it.

The differences in brain activity between people who have high or low levels of resilience are not major – a matter of seconds in some cases. Yet, as Waugh points out, 'this small difference in the duration of neural activity may be sufficient to influence thinking, feeling and downstream physiological responding'.[6]

### *Positive self-reflection and the role of distraction*

To prevent emotional processing turning into worry and rumination, it is wise to approach life with a reflective mode of thinking that is more open and curious about experience ('I am really interested in a positive way in understanding more about the way I think and react'). The focus, then, is on solving problems by opening them up positively.

But first, you have to distract yourself from the temptation to ruminate. Researcher Susan Nolen-Hoeksema found that getting ruminators to do something that distracted them from their mood and preoccupations for just eight minutes had very positive effects. Afterwards, people felt more in control and thought about the causes of their problems in a more optimistic and constructive way.

Distracting yourself with a short-term activity – going for a walk, watching a film or TV, playing or watching sports, looking through a magazine, tidying a drawer – provides a respite from stress and particularly from the effects of over-thinking. When you return to the issue, you will find that you are less distressed, thinking more positively about the problem, and are better able to come up with solutions to solve it.

When you rebalance your ratio of positive to negative, you can then regain your foothold on normal functioning. (The key words here are 'short-term' and 'return' – losing yourself in distracting activities and not re-engaging with the issue only creates further problems.)

If you then successfully implement even one of your solutions, your ratio of positive to negative will increase further, and will initiate an upward virtuous cycle.

### *Positive self-reflection is linked to mindfulness*

A major aspect of rumination is that it is judgemental ('This is really bad' 'I am hopeless') and characterized by abstract analysis ('Why is life like this?' 'How can things like that happen to me?').

Positive self-reflection, on the other hand, is more open, curious and non-evaluative. It has a quality of pleasant surprise and possibility about it. When you have reflected on yourself in a positive way, you are likely to say things such as, 'Isn't that really interesting?' or 'I found that really revealing.' It has a flavour of mindfulness about it.

Remember Ellen Langer's rules for mindfulness: attend to what is happening directly in the moment; forget about broad generalizations; suspend judgement (particularly negative judgement). Instead, cultivate 'creative uncertainty'. Applying these rules to your reflection will open it up in a positive and effective way.

This kind of 'mindful experiencing' is a powerful way to combat rumination, because it builds up your capacity to control your attention.[7] If you develop a habit of mindfulness in your ordinary life, it will pay huge dividends when stress strikes, allowing you to observe negative thoughts without letting them take hold or activate a network of associated negative thoughts and memories.

Freed from this downward pull of worry and rumination, you will be able to think more effectively about how to deal with your problems.[8]

## *Too much or too little emotional expression*

Knowing how to express negative emotions in the right way is a key emotional intelligence competency. Daniel Goleman describes the experience of being so overwhelmed by anger or fear that you explode emotionally as 'neural hijackings', a temporary takeover of the brain by the amygdala.[9] Such hijackings can end in tragedy – assault, murder, mass panic, suicide. But they also happen in less dramatic form in everyday life, when we 'vent'.

Many people still think it is healthy to give full vent to their negative feelings, that it's good to get things 'off your chest' or 'out of your system'.

The evidence proves the contrary.[10]

Negative feelings, particularly anger, feed on themselves. Indeed, expressing anger in an intense way increases it, and intense anger distorts our thinking and can destroy relationships. Anger is also toxic to the heart. If you tend to be a hostile person, easily roused to anger, you are more likely to suffer high blood pressure and coronary heart disease. If you suffer from heart disease, an angry outburst is more likely to provoke a heart attack than other kinds of stress.[11]

Too intense expression of other negative emotions can also work against you. For example, expressing every anxious thought can escalate anxiety into panic. While expressing your sadness by crying may help, intense and prolonged crying can exhaust you physically and psychologically, and will exacerbate rumination.

The other extreme – repressing your negative feelings – is also problematic.[12] People who have a repressive coping style tend to deny *any* negative feelings. They can only achieve this over-control by developing a rigid, defensive style, not allowing themselves to express negative feelings such as anxiety and anger. In response to threat, they insist that they are dealing with it 'rationally' and are 'not easily upset'. Yet even as they make such assertions, when monitored in a laboratory, they show all the physiological signs of stress – rapid heartbeat, sweating and muscular tension.[13]

## *The right style of emotional coping – and why it's good for you*

Dealing with intense negative emotions is not easy, but there is one relatively simple method: putting a name on them. Naming your feelings can calm you down, allowing you to put some distance between your intense emotions and your sense of self. This is because, as brain scans have revealed, when we put labels on our reactions it not only decreases activity in the amygdala but increases activity in the right prefrontal cortex, which is involved in regulating emotion.[14] We are recruiting our higher brain to help us.

This technique works even better if you use the formulation, 'I *have* this feeling of anger,' rather than, 'I *am* angry.' In this way, you don't identify yourself wholly with one feeling. You recognize coexisting feelings – say, a twinge of guilt that may be provoking your anger, or a feeling of anxiety about the consequences of acting on that anger, or a feeling of loss of control.

You may also identify positive feelings you are experiencing independently at the same time – recalling a recent burst of happiness at good news, or how much somebody loves you. That awareness may temper your anger, and you will be less inclined to either be so overwhelmed that you say things that will harm your relationships or repress it and harm your heart.

Annette Stanton's work suggests that the overriding purpose of effective emotional coping is to positively engage with your feelings, so that you are moving *towards* something: towards greater understanding and an open expression of your thoughts and feelings about what has happened; towards a positive reinterpretation, trying to see what happened in a more constructive light; or towards active acceptance when the situation can't be controlled.

For example, your positive purpose can be:

- to *regulate your reactions* – the 'Composure Index'. Sometimes that means concentrating on damping down your physiological arousal, your thoughts and your feelings, so that you maintain or regain a sense of composure and calm. In other circumstances it may mean mobilizing your thoughts and feelings, your confidence, your courage and your determination, so that you can confront something (or someone) that needs to be confronted – but just enough to do this constructively and not lose your composure.

- to *get a better understanding* of what is going on inside you – the 'Insight Index'. This includes discovering what may be really motivating your reactions, or uncovering any mixed feelings. This prevents you from overreacting in a way that would work against your best interests.
- to *devise solutions* that are fit for purpose – the 'Solution Index'.
- to *improve your relationships* with the people around you – the 'Relationship Index'.

When you start to use any kind of emotional coping, ask yourself if your strategy is going to further one or all of these positive purposes.

If your answer is no, *stop* what you are doing – because it is making the situation worse.

Stop:

- crying, or
- arguing, or
- making frantic phone calls, or
- drinking another glass of wine, or
- thinking of yet another 'what if', or
- trying to get agreement or cooperation.

Just stop.

Do nothing for a while and allow your mind a rest.

You will then allow your great and complex brain to come up with a better strategy.

## *Learn to generate and sustain positive feelings during periods of high stress*

Inevitably, during periods of high stress, negative emotions increase rapidly. They can set off a cascade of negative thoughts and interactions. Yet, because the positive and negative emotional systems operate independently, even in the middle of a crisis we can still experience positive emotions.

The trouble is, we don't often pay attention to them.

So, the first step in dealing with times of high stress is to seek out those positive emotions. Let them register fully in your consciousness.

Then you can start to find ways to grow and strengthen them.

In the white heat of stress, especially at the beginning, positive emotions may be hard to identify. But within a relatively short time, positive emotions reassert themselves. You may continue to feel bad but, bit by bit, your positive emotions are returning. They are just waiting for you to notice their return.

Resilient people continue to work actively to decrease the *duration* of their negative feelings, but they also have the habit of simultaneously paying attention to any positive feelings.[15]

They pay attention to the ordinary pleasures of everyday routines.

They relish the comfort of friends and the consolation of support.

They remind themselves to feel grateful that the crisis was not worse.

They are inspired by how other people are coping.

They remain interested and curious about how things are unfolding in themselves and in the situation generally.

They work to stay hopeful about the future.

It is this capacity to feel positive *even* when feeling negative that is at the heart of resilience.

In the grip of a frightening crisis, you may be tempted to ignore or dismiss such positive experiences as making little difference to the magnitude of your problems. But any positivity – no matter how small – matters when you are very stressed. Positive emotions don't just give you a temporary boost and stop you plunging into unmanageable stress, depression and despair. Barbara Fredrickson's work (described in Chapter 3) shows that they actually *undo* the damaging effects of stress.[16] Moreover, this 'undoing effect' can happen within seconds.

Just as stress raises your blood pressure, experiencing *any* positive feelings immediately afterwards returns your heart rate and blood pressure back to your baseline resting levels. Without that input of positivity, there is no rebound. This input of positivity need not be dramatic, nor the feeling intense, to achieve this undoing effect. A reassuring touch from somebody, particularly from somebody you love, a humorous remark (even if it's black humour), looking at something soothing or beautiful (for example, a favourite family photograph), a glimpse of nature, a phone call from a friend – all can act as a powerful reset button.

*Select a coping strategy that will help increase positive feelings*

Some coping strategies are more effective than others at helping you increase positive feelings. Research has shown that accepting the reality of what is happening and trying to distract yourself temporarily are very effective in helping to reduce negative feelings. But when researchers looked at a range of coping strategies – direct action, expressing deep feelings, distraction, redefining the situation, acceptance, social support, relaxation, prayer, positive reframing – two coping strategies were particularly effective: trying to see things in a more positive light ('I look for something good in what is happening, and try to learn from the experience'), and direct action to tackle the problem were particularly effective at increasing positive feelings.

*Remind yourself of your values and goals*

One of the most powerful ways to build positive feelings is to remind yourself of who you are and what is really important to you.

Are you the kind of person who is open to learning something from every experience?

Do you pride yourself on your ability to find practical solutions to problems?

Is deepening relationships by sharing your experiences important to you?

Now ask yourself: How can this stressful event help me to be the person I am and to express more deeply what is really important to me?

This exercise in reflection will immediately increase positive feelings – because just the act of remembering your important values is a reaffirmation of yourself and what you stand for.

It will also remind you of what you are like 'at your best'.

*Be receptive to joy*

Paying attention to the positive is *not* about instructing yourself to be positive. In the middle of a crisis, any pressure – from yourself or other people – to cheer up and think positively is likely to be counterproductive. Rather, the principle is to be receptive to joy.

Stress disrupts your normal routine, your conditioned patterns of thoughts and reactions. But this also has an upside. It allows you to break free of them, even for a while. It allows another dimension to break through. You may be feeling that the world is not as safe and predictable and controllable a place as you thought. But you also discover that, for all the stress, life goes on.

The sun still rises and sets.

You still enjoy the taste of fresh crusty bread.

The waves still break magnificently on the shore.

Children still laugh uproariously.

And, when you take the trouble to notice these things, you feel less alone and instead feel supported and held up by the universe.

# 19. Flourishing under fire

Nobody can teach us more about resilience than those who have experienced profound suffering. Think of those who have to deal with adversities such as a violent or traumatic bereavement; rape and child abuse; catastrophic injuries; chronic and debilitating illnesses; conditions such as addiction or infertility. Consider survivors of fires, major accidents, natural disasters, military combat and terrorist attacks. Sometimes we wonder how people caught up in such situations can go on.

Over the past few years, psychologists have studied those who have endured such traumas and how they have coped. Unsurprisingly, they have found that in a small minority of people great adversity depresses normal psychological functioning and they succumb to the crisis that has befallen them. Their confidence is shattered and they become depressed, chronically anxious or develop post-traumatic stress disorder.

However, most people respond in one of three ways.

Some just survive, trying desperately not to fall below the level at which they are now functioning. They carry on, but in an impaired way.

Others focus on trying to get back to something like their original state of functioning. They recover and carry on much as before.

But a third group takes a different path. Far from being depleted, these people are profoundly transformed in a positive way. They manage not just to survive and recover, but to turn what has happened into an opportunity to thrive, to get to a higher level of psychological functioning than ever before. They achieve this not *in spite of*, but *because of* what has happened. This phenomenon has been variously termed post-traumatic or stress-related growth.[1]

I prefer to call it flourishing under fire, and it is the subject of this chapter and the next.

It is tempting to think that people who flourish in response to severe adversity are innately invincible. But they are not. They are just as vulnerable as the rest of us. Rather, it is the quality of their psychological engagement with the new reality of their lives that makes them flourish. This engagement gives them a kind of super-resilience, a quality Ann Masten at the University of Minnesota calls 'ordinary magic'.[2]

The most heartening aspect of the research on this phenomenon is just how ordinary it is, how easily within our grasp if we learn one crucial lesson – the very experiences that we most dread, the crises and failures that are uncontrollable and that can render us helpless, are also the very experiences that are most likely to precipitate personal growth.

It would be a mistake to think of this ordinary magic as just about coping or damage limitation. Rather, it is an unquenchable expression of our instinctive drive to keep growing and developing as individuals.

As long as we stay connected to that instinct, we can turn the lead of adversity into pure gold.

## *The journey to flourishing under fire*

Thankfully, most of you reading this book will not face severe adversity in your lives.

But, no life is without its share of suffering – the breakdown of a relationship, worry about a troubled child, the loss of a job or a failing business, the small and wounding betrayals of family and friends, debilitating illnesses. It is worth learning how we can, in our own modest way, make good – or even greatness – come from suffering.

Psychologists Richard Tedeschi and Lawrence Calhoun have been at the forefront in identifying the phenomenon of stress-related growth.[3] They liken the initial stress to a psychological earthquake, a seismic event that severely shakes or reduces to rubble many of the basic assumptions that had up until then guided people's understanding, decision-making, and the meaning of their lives. This seismic event ruptures their life narrative, which is for ever after divided into 'before' and 'after' the crisis.

The process of dealing with a traumatic event is like reconstruction after an earthquake. After an earthquake, engineers investigate which roads and buildings have collapsed, which have withstood the shock, and why. They try to apply the lessons to the design and construction of new structures so that they will be sturdier and more quake-proof in the future.

Psychological rebuilding proceeds on the same basis. You have to take account of the changed reality of your life, of what you have learned – positive and negative – about yourself, about other people and about how the world works. The work is to incorporate these lessons into a new framework for living.

The disruption often extends beyond the particular cause of the crisis. When you have a heart attack, or your marriage breaks up, or your business fails, it is not just your assumptions about your health or your spouse or how to run a business that are undermined. The crisis may also shake to their very foundations your sense of identity, your purpose in life and your hopes for the future.

If you have built your life around trying to be a good spouse, the discovery of infidelity may be as traumatic as a diagnosis of a life-threatening illness – although objectively such an illness is more of a threat – and divorce initiated by your partner can be devastating.

If you have devoted yourself to being a loving parent, a teenager 'going wrong' can severely undermine your sense of self-worth.

If you pride yourself on your business acumen and your business fails, it can destroy your confidence.

If you have devoted a huge part of your life to an organization or cause, its collapse can rip the meaning out of your life.

When adversity strikes, and we are forced to adapt to a painful new reality, the more radically our old view of ourselves or of other people is disrupted, the more adaptation is required. In order to adapt, we are faced with three immediate psychological tasks:

- to manage our emotional distress
- to fully comprehend the meaning of what has happened, and
- to fit what has happened into our life narrative, or construct a new one to meet our changed circumstances.

### *Managing the emotional distress*

Immediately a crisis befalls us, we are faced with the challenge of managing very distressing feelings – fear, bewilderment, extreme disappointment, anger. Stress symptoms such as muscular tension, headaches, gastric upsets are common. We may suffer sleep disturbances and feel emotionally exhausted and irritable. Our thinking can be disrupted by intrusive thoughts and images. We may try to avoid any person or situation that reminds us of the trauma. The more unexpected the event, the more enduring the feelings of disbelief and psychological numbness. Attempts to adapt to the new reality may be undermined by persistently wishing for things to be different.

Sooner or later, we are faced with the task of working our way out of denial and through the rest of the classic stages of grief:

- anger ('Why me? I did not deserve this')
- bargaining ('OK, I will accept that I have lost his love / a lot of money, but not my marriage / my whole business')
- depression ('It's all over. Nothing will ever come right again'), and finally
- acceptance ('It happened. Now I have to deal with it').[4]

These are not stages that happen in some orderly way. It is a messy process as we cycle back and forth between different reactions. A minority of people can become stuck for a long time in depression or chronic anger, and this can cause significant psychological or even psychiatric difficulty.

### *Comprehending what happened*

When we face severe adversity, we are presented with powerful and disturbing new information about ourselves – and sometimes about people who are important to us. We must integrate this new information into our existing mental models.

At first, we just try to comprehend what happened in a factual way, painstakingly making connections between what happened, what preceded it and what this might mean for the future. This urge to assimilate the new information comes from our instinctive 'completion tendency', the brain's natural tendency to reach a goal it has set itself.[5] In this case, a crisis has interrupted the way we were going about life and how we think about ourselves, another person, or the way the world works. Our brain's goal is to integrate this information and 'complete' our understanding of it. This triggers an endless preoccupation with the event.

While this is happening, all of the new information is kept in our active memory waiting to be processed. It churns round and round, intruding into our consciousness – sometimes when we're in the middle of unrelated matters – in the form of flashbacks, images and unwanted thoughts. We can be at a business meeting and suddenly realize that we have been so mentally absent that we have taken nothing in. Because these intrusions create distress and emotional exhaustion, people go into temporary states of avoidance or denial. Typically, intrusion and avoidance fluctuate in tandem, allowing us to keep the new, disturbing information to tolerable levels.

The completion tendency is why some people want to recount details of a seismic event over and over again. Others, particularly men, may be unable or unwilling to talk about what happened. They may try to handle it alone. The paradox is that in their desperate attempt to maintain control in this way, they may end up even less able to come to terms with the new reality and take control of it.

When not talking, people may ruminate a lot on what has been lost, going over the details again and again. 'What if' thinking is common.

What if I had gone earlier?

What if I had not said what I did?

What if he had not reacted like that?

What if they had told me earlier?

This kind of counterfactual thinking is a desperate attempt to gain some sense of control over the situation. And sometimes it helps. Once someone has identified what they could have done, they feel a bit better – less a victim of uncontrollable circumstances. At the very least, they feel they have learned a valuable lesson. But when this form of rumination continues over a long period, it is distressing and counterproductive.

It is particularly destructive in situations where the person had no control – for example, when a beloved, well-cared-for child dies as a result of an illness or accident, or a business goes bust because of a recession. Then, 'what if' thinking can lead to a crippling sense of guilt or remorse and keep people psychologically bound to the trauma.

At some point, we have to be ready to say, 'It happened,' and confine it definitively to the past.

When, finally, we are satisfied that we have a comprehensible account of what happened, the road forks and we have new choices and decisions to make. Major life crises almost invariably involve a severe disruption to one or more of our life goals. The more embedded these have been in our lives, and the more connected to our sense of personal identity and purpose in life, the more painful and complex the process of modifying or disengaging from them.

If you keep trying to achieve your goal in the old way, you will feel distressed and powerless. This is not to say that, if you're facing a crisis, you must give up on the goal of, say, having a loving relationship, or being a good parent, or running a successful business, or being a devoted activist. It's just that you need to redefine and revitalize that goal.

You have to ask yourself: 'Knowing what I now know, what does trying to love again / be an effective parent / run a good business / be a successful activist look like?'

### *Reconstructing your life narrative*

In Chapter 16 we saw how we make a framework of meaning in our lives through our life narrative – the set of basic explanations and assumptions we have about who we are and how the world works. A major life crisis profoundly disturbs this life narrative and divides it into 'before' and 'after', with the traumatic event – 'When my marriage broke up / when my business failed / when my son tried to commit suicide / when I got sick / when the Celtic Tiger came crashing to an end' – as the dividing line.

After a crisis, everything has to be reassessed. We have to start the process of rebuilding our internal mental models and our private world of meaning. We have to decide if what we now know fits with the previous assumptions we had about ourselves, about other people and the way the world works.

Must these assumptions be radically revised?

Sometimes we manage to convince ourselves that little change is needed, that we can continue *as if* we have not experienced a serious health crisis, or a significant betrayal. This may have the effect of immediately reducing feelings of distress, but there is a cost: if we maintain our old assumptions and live life as before, we may be at risk of a recurrence.

The harder road is to accept that we must significantly modify one or more of our previous assumptions.

The task is to figure out the implications for:

- how you think about yourself
- how you lead your life
- your relationships with other people
- your life philosophy
- your future.

Another fork in the road then opens up.

As you puzzle out the answers to those questions, you can take the low road – your conclusions can be negative ('I am a failure' 'People can never be trusted' 'Taking a risk always ends in disaster' 'The world is random and can't be controlled'). This low road is a cul-de-sac of hopelessness and helplessness.

Or, you can take the high road. Your conclusions can be positive ('I am a strong and courageous survivor' 'I have learned a lot from this experience' 'It is always worth taking a risk, as long as you know you can live with the consequences' 'There are more caring and good people in the world than bad'). This high road leads to a fuller appreciation of your own strengths, and a more complex understanding of relationships, of opportunities and risks. Crucially, you recognize that while the seismic event has turned the world upside down, it can also become an engine that drives personal growth and wisdom.

Whether you take the high road or the low road, this now has to be integrated into your life narrative.

In his research on life narratives, Dan McAdams found that people respond to major crises by constructing either 'redemption stories' or 'contamination stories'.[6] These significantly affect how people actually respond to the crisis.[7] The difference between the 'redemption' and 'contamination' stories is not about the acts but about the interpretation of the facts. It is about how people imagine what might come next and the possibilities open to them.

### REDEMPTION STORIES

In her research on post-traumatic growth, psychologist Jennifer Pals found that the process of transforming a crisis into a redemption story involved two steps.[8]

First, people had to admit to themselves how deeply they had been affected by the crisis, that something of great importance to them had been lost or damaged, and that their basic assumptions about themselves and other people had to be modified. When they did this, they seemed to discover a powerful new way of thinking about themselves and achieved positive post-traumatic growth.

In contrast, those who actively resisted the process – who tried to minimize the negative impact of the crisis, or who tried to distance themselves from their feelings – bought short-term relief but severely limited their potential to grow from the experience.

The second step involved the construction of a positive ending to the story. This ending 'has to affirm and explain how the self has been positively transformed' says Pals.[9] Like the hero in a good story, people had to think of the crisis as 'the opening act in a transformative and redemptive sequence'.[10] In this way, they were able to reframe the crisis as a positive turning point, seeing the adversity that had befallen them not as some random visitation of bad luck but as intrinsic to the personal growth that followed. By reconstructing their narrative in this way, they managed to 'flip' time – repositioning the crisis not as an end, but as the beginning of something new.

'Redemption sequences' such as this are more common among people who feel that they have a 'calling'. They describe themselves as having a sensitivity to the suffering of others from an early age, and a clear and guiding set of values that has remained constant throughout their lives. They tend to recount an early life blessed by advantage – parents who loved them, or a strong community, or opportunities to learn valuable lessons. But they also recall significant adversity in early life and in adolescence.

In other words, although their lives have not been perfect, they pay attention to the positive in how they recall them. They see themselves as having turned around bad things already in their lives, and that gives them hope that they can do so again and a belief that it is always worth persisting.

What shines through these redemption stories is a strong commitment to serve others in clear, concrete ways. Not surprisingly, this is a narrative associated with high life satisfaction, strong self-esteem and an abiding sense of meaning in life.

These stories contain every element of a flourishing life and are a testament to the fact that building a flourishing life is the best bulwark against great adversity.

### CONTAMINATION STORIES

In contrast, the central theme of contamination stories is how a life that was once good went bad. After the divorce, or losing the job, or getting sick, or the business collapsing, the good was 'spoiled, ruined, contaminated, or undermined' for ever, never to be possessed again.[11]

Hardly surprisingly, people who internalize contamination narratives are found to be unhappy and despondent. They feel that their life has lost its meaning. They feel robbed of a future, their energies trapped in goals that are no longer attainable, unable to construct new goals.

Such narratives are associated with depression, low self-esteem and a sense of meaninglessness.

The key difference between redemption and contamination stories is how we reframe the crisis.

In a redemption story, coming to see the crisis as a positive turning point is not achieved by some crude mental gymnastics. The change in narrative has to be psychologically real, emerging from a fundamental reappraisal of our basic assumptions. This requires imagination, motivation and force of will.

Another important difference between redemption and contamination stories is the ratio between negative and positive.

In contamination stories, the bad overwhelms the good. People become trapped in the first phase of adaptation to the crisis, overwhelmed by the force of their negative emotions, or by destructive and dysfunctional thinking patterns. They succumb to the power of the negative and fall below the fateful 3:1 ratio between positive and negative feelings. The tragedy is often that the remedy – finding positivity anywhere they can, no matter how slight, so they can start to rebuild the positive in their lives – is the very thing they resist, rejecting it as 'trivial' or 'irrelevant'.

In contrast, with redemption stories, even as people recount the bad things that happened, in their thinking the negative always promises to give way to the positive. Even if they are stuck for a while in a 'contamination sequence', they are able to pay attention to the positive – to what they learned from the crisis, how it has transformed them and made them better people. They are able to muster sufficient positivity to harvest every small burst of hope, confidence, determination and support from others in order to keep themselves going. As a consequence, they persist in their efforts to solve their problems and to move forward with their lives. During this process, in a subtle way, they have begun to create a main 'character' who is strong, effective and good.[12]

Along the way to achieving a healthy 5:1 positivity ratio, those going through a crisis must absorb a great deal of negativity, but they correspondingly ramp up the positive to maintain the right balance – particularly the hope and anticipation of a good outcome – and that, in turn, absorbs the negative.

Businessman Brian Patterson's story is an example of how this works.

> Three years ago, without any warning or symptoms, I discovered I had renal cancer. My first reaction was surprise and shock: this was something that happens to other people, not me. My surgeon was reassuring. The cancer was at an early stage and after surgery, chemotherapy and a period of convalescence all would be well.
>
> Two months later, after a painful recovery, a scan revealed that the cancer had spread to my lungs. I was told that secondary lung cancer is very difficult to treat and that if the available treatments didn't work, I had about a year to live. I was profoundly shocked, but also angry and confused. At the age of only sixty-three, it looked as if my life was over. I endured six months of aggressive

medical treatment, which left me very depleted. And the bad news was that it hadn't worked.

This was my darkest hour. I started preparing myself emotionally and spiritually for death. Part of this was trying to reach some state of calm and acceptance. I repeated to myself, 'It is what it is.' I thought about the things that I had achieved in my life. I even planned some kind of celebration. But then I thought that all this acceptance was having a negative consequence – fatalism. I was now convinced that I was going to die, and that there was nothing I could do.

One day I woke up with a different thought: 'Acceptance is not the same as resignation.' This was the tipping point. I began to believe that, while accepting it for what it was, I could also believe in a positive outcome. I could have hope. I could be cheerful and optimistic. And I might be able to use these positive emotions to help my body to heal itself.

Six months later, after more and different treatment, and armed with positive feelings, the cancer had disappeared. I'm still not out of the woods. I have to have scans every six months. But, hey, I'm still alive and I am savouring my life with renewed vigour and enthusiasm.

In redemption stories like Brian's we see that flourishing is possible, even during the most serious life crises imaginable.

This kind of flourishing – the kind that is forged in the fire – can be utterly transformative and can be the route to real wisdom.

That is the subject of the next chapter.

# 20. The path to growth and wisdom

Understanding and finding meaning in suffering is a key part of post-traumatic growth. Few people have had more reason to question the meaning of suffering than Viktor Frankl, the Jewish psychiatrist who survived incarceration in four Nazi concentration camps, including Auschwitz. And few people have produced such a coherent and moving account of the process of making meaning. One of his most profound insights is that discovering the meaning of life in some abstract way is not what counts. Rather, making meaning comes from how we respond to the particular demands of the moment during a crisis. Reflecting on how he and his fellow prisoners survived, he observed:[1]

> We had to learn ourselves [. . .] that *it did not really matter what we expected from life, but rather what life expected from us*. We needed to stop asking about the meaning of life, and instead to think of ourselves as those who were being questioned by life – daily and hourly. Our answer must consist, not in talk and meditation, but in right action and in right conduct. Life ultimately means taking responsibility, to find the right answer to its problems and to fulfil the tasks which it constantly sets for each individual [. . .] These tasks, and therefore the meaning of life, differ from man to man, and from moment to moment. Thus, it is impossible to define the meaning of life in a general way.

At the core of this insight is the realization that there are always choices in how we interpret what is happening to us and how we respond. These interpretations and responses build meaning from the bottom up. We may be guided by an overall philosophy of life, but that philosophy only assumes real meaning through our day-to-day interpretations and actions.

One way to deepen the meaning of your life is to make a habit of asking yourself the right questions at critical times.

The first question is the one suggested by Frankl:

- What is life expecting of me now, at this particular moment, and in this particular situation?

This immediately switches your attention to yourself as an active agent in life, not its victim.

The second question is:

- What is important now?

This immediately focuses your attention on the changed situation and the new priorities. It primes you for action.

The third question is:

- Given what has happened, who do I want to shape myself to be now?

This is a recognition that you have some influence on the shape of the change you are facing.

The final question is:

- Is there anything about this situation that allows me to do something positive that otherwise I would not or could not have done?

Whenever I ask myself these questions, I notice that the answers immediately pop into my mind. Invariably, these are answers that tap into some positive purpose. They are the right answers. When I act on them, the outcome is sometimes what I wanted, sometimes not. But they are never actions I regret.

Asking myself these questions resulted in writing this book.

I had wanted to write this book for ten years. I had studied all the new research coming out on happiness and flourishing. I had been using it in my work and was constantly developing my own ideas. I was ready to go – but I was always too busy. I felt very frustrated but persuaded myself that one of these days I would finally get down to writing. Then, a job I had been doing half-time for nearly seventeen years came to an unexpected end, a casualty of the economic crisis that hit Ireland. It was a very dislocating experience. I suddenly had all this time on my hands, but for a few months I felt paralysed.

Then, one day, I asked myself: 'Is there anything about this experience that allows me to do something that I otherwise would not or could not have done?'

I knew the answer immediately – I could write the book.

So, I did.

## *Looking for value in suffering*

Suffering itself is meaningless. There is no merit in enduring suffering that can be avoided or alleviated.

But, when great crises strike, suffering can't be avoided. The most profound way we can give unavoidable suffering meaning is to find some *value* in it.

Now that I have written the book I wanted to write for so long, I realize just how much time it required. Had I continued working as I used to, I would never have written it, and I think it would be a lasting regret. So, in that sense, losing my job made this book possible. Good came from bad, and I have managed to find a real value in what happened.

Finding value in suffering is the core of post-traumatic growth. For example, in studies of breast cancer sufferers,[2] men who'd had heart attacks,[3] and people who were severely injured – even paralysed – in car accidents,[4] all showed significantly better psychological adjustment and improved health outcomes if they could find a positive meaning in their situation.

Finding value does not mean denying the import of what happened, nor the lingering sense of sadness and loss experienced. Rather, it is accepting that what has happened to you, even though it was awful and unwanted, has a value. This clear acknowledgement and acceptance of loss is the crucial distinction between post-traumatic growth and the tyranny of wrong-headed 'positive thinking', which is often just a form of denial.[5] People who are particularly anxious for social approval, and so try to impress others with their 'positive' outlook, are unlikely to report post-traumatic growth.

For me, this experience of finding value is best captured in words quoted by Richard Tedeschi and Lawrence Calhoun. Rabbi Harold Kushner, who had suffered the loss of his beloved son, says, 'I am a more sensitive person, a more effective pastor, a more sympathetic counselor because of Aaron's life and death than I would ever have been without it.' But, crucially, he adds, 'I would give up all of those gains in a second if I could have my son back. If I could choose, I would forego all of this spiritual growth and depth which have come my way because of our experiences . . . but I cannot choose.'[6]

## *Why writing and talking about negative experiences are good for you*

There is now a large body of research evidence showing that the relatively simple act of writing about traumatic experiences has many positive consequences.[7] The benefits include:

- improved immune functioning
- fewer visits to the doctor
- less distress and fewer negative feelings
- improved social functioning, and
- higher life satisfaction.

Talking to somebody else about your experiences, or even talking into a tape recorder, also has real and concrete benefits.

Whichever way is chosen, the important part of the process is that it must be:

- deliberate
- systematic
- searching
- analytical.

Sonja Lyubomirsky and her colleagues conducted experiments in which volunteers were asked to reflect on the most negative experience of their lives.[8]

Participants were divided into three groups: a writing group, a talking group (who recorded themselves) and a thinking group. Members of each group had to do the exercise assigned to them – write, talk or think privately about their worst experience – for fifteen minutes each day over three consecutive days. All participants were given the same guidelines: to explore their deepest thoughts and feelings about the experience, to reflect on its significance in their own formation and identity, and to consider any connection it might have to their relationships with parents, friends, family or other significant people in their lives. The only additional rule for the writing group was that once they began writing, they should continue without stopping – disregarding spelling, grammar and syntax – and write whatever came into their minds.

The first two groups – those who wrote about their worst experience or talked about it on tape – showed a range of short-term and long-term benefits. Those who thought privately about it showed no such benefits – and, in fact, reported reduced life satisfaction after the exercise.

The benefits to the writing group were often very concrete.

A group of engineers who wrote about the experience of being unexpectedly made redundant subsequently received more job offers than those who did not write about it.

Students who had just started university and wrote down their thoughts and feelings about that sometimes stressful experience of transition later showed increases in their grades.

Talking and, in particular, writing about upsetting and traumatic events affects three overlapping processes:

- how your body works
- how your mind works, and
- how you relate to other people.

### *Effects on how your body works*

As soon as somebody begins to disclose an upsetting experience, or immediately afterwards, they show a reduction in blood pressure, muscle tension and skin conductance (a symptom of stress).

Disclosure relieves the physical strain of suppressing your feelings. That is why confiding your feelings in writing, or to a friend, or in psychotherapy, reduces the risk of stress-related illness. For example, in a study in which people were asked to express a traumatic experience using bodily movement, only those who wrote about it subsequently showed significant improvement in physical health and academic achievement.

### *Effects on how your mind works*

Writing and talking, unlike private thinking, require us to record and document our thoughts, to put them outside ourselves. The highly structured nature of language and syntax forces us to order our thinking.[9] Words and phrases such as 'realize', 'because', 'understand', 'the reason why', 'come to terms with', 'getting past' indicate that this is an active process of cognitive reorganization.

You may be surprised to discover that once you start talking or writing you become aware of other aspects and details of an experience. It forces you to find connections between the different elements. You start to link together cause and effect, and to gain insight into yourself and into what happened. This is how to gradually construct a coherent story, with a beginning, middle and end and an understandable 'plot'. Once this begins to happen, you feel a growing sense of control and are better able to manage your feelings of distress.

Language counts in another way. The more people use causal and insight words and phrases in their accounts, the greater the benefits to them, including to their health. On the other hand, people who use a high number of negative emotional words such as 'sad' or 'angry' in their accounts of their worst experiences are the most likely to have continuing health problems.

Those who do best use a moderate number of negative emotion words and also use positive words such as 'happy' and 'laugh'. They are prepared to express negative feelings, but are not overwhelmed by this because they stay connected to the positive.

### *Effects on how you relate to other people*

Writing and talking about trauma inevitably involves a significant amount of self-disclosure – being prepared to honestly confront and express your innermost thoughts and feelings – first to yourself and then perhaps to others. This is important, because not being able or willing to tell anybody about a significant emotional upheaval disconnects you from your social world. Having even one person to support you emotionally is a buffer from the worst effects of high stress.

Effective interpersonal communication requires synchrony – what most of us call being 'in sync' or 'clicking' with another person. You feel you understand them, and feel understood yourself. That is reflected in a conversation that is comfortable and fluid. In such a conversation there is a complex but automatic mirroring of movements, facial expressions, gestures and voice tone. Keeping something bottled up disrupts this process – your brain is carrying a large and distracting cognitive load, and so your communication style becomes confused and ambiguous.[10]

For example, there may be a disconnect between what you are saying and your facial expression and tone of voice. This makes the conversation feel uneasy or odd to the other person.

People who have had similar experiences can provide a particularly valuable audience. They can help you clarify your thoughts and feelings and provide you with a new standard of 'normal' against which you can measure yourself. Telling your story becomes an interactive experience, with the other person not just listening with compassion and understanding, but supporting, extending and deepening your story. They help you try out ideas and start the process of change.

People who write about adverse experiences behave differently in social situations, compared to those who don't. They talk more to their friends, and they laugh more. They use significantly more positive emotion words in their conversation. They use more present-tense words and fewer past-tense words. And they show a significant drop in blood pressure.

In general, men tend to benefit more than women from writing – probably because women generally tend to disclose more to their family and friends than men do.[11] People who tend to become angry easily, or who have trouble in noticing, interpreting and labelling their feelings, also show significant benefits.

In fact, a common thread in all the research is that writing is of particular benefit to people who are not naturally emotionally open, or who are unlikely to talk to others about their experiences.

## *'Flipping' time – looking back from the future*

Viktor Frankl observed that one of the worst aspects of concentration camp life was not knowing if, or when, the suffering would come to an end. Life became what he called a 'provisional existence' – without a future or a goal.[12] The inmates began to think despairingly that the opportunities of life had now passed them by for ever. To survive, Frankl imagined himself in a happy future, with his beloved wife, telling the world about the camps and what he had learned from that experience. When he projected himself into that imagined future, he was able to construct a positive 'ending' to his present suffering.

You will recall from Chapter 19 how, in constructing redemption stories, people managed to 'flip' time, repositioning the crisis as the opening act in a new and transformative period in their lives. But it also helps to flip time in another way – to look back on the present from the future, and to imagine the painful present as already consigned to the past.

Imagine yourself addressing a large group of family, friends and colleagues, or being interviewed by somebody at a specific time in the future – say, five years from now.

Now, imagine (or, better still, write) what you would most desire to be expressing then. Start your imaginary address or interview with the sentence, 'Five years ago today, on [give the exact date], I began the journey that I am going to tell you about . . .' It is important to put in an exact date, as this gives a reality to the exercise.

Next, think about what you would like to be saying. Imagine describing your journey from its beginning:

- how you charted your course and what you achieved
- the goals you set for yourself and why they were important to you
- the hidden strengths you discovered and how you managed your vulnerabilities
- the setbacks you overcame
- the support you garnered along the way.

Most important of all, describe the deep motivation which kept you going.

And finally, end by talking about the most important lessons you have learned about yourself and about life, and what advice you would offer people coping with great adversity in their own lives.

What most people find surprising and deeply reassuring about this exercise is how it connects them to their innate understanding of the optimal path in life for themselves, and to the store of self-knowledge and wisdom they already possess.

It reminds you that a large part of your destiny lies in your own hands and that you can, with some thought and effort, muster enough resources to determine your fate. It makes it easier to see yourself not as a victim of your circumstances – frightened, angry and resistant because an important life goal has been blocked – but as an active agent in your life.

Paradoxically, by projecting yourself into the future, this exercise makes you more acutely aware of the possibilities of the present, and forces you to focus on the big picture.

### *Focusing on the big picture*

When people are very stressed, inevitably they become more self-absorbed. Creating a future goal forces them to turn that attention outwards.

To start the journey towards that goal, you have to connect in a more vital way with your environment. An illness or injury, a bereavement, the loss of a job, a relationship breakdown, the failure of a business, a crisis with a child – each unfolds according to its own set of 'rules'. The first step, then, is to find out as much as possible about those rules and how to manage them.

Once you do that, you inevitably begin to see yourself as part of a bigger picture, and part of a larger community of people – who are either in the same situation as you, or whose business it is to help people like you. You become very conscious of your place and the limits of your power, but also of the possibilities within this new situation.

Here is one man's account of how he dealt with just such a situation.

*Jim*

I lost my job as a manager in a construction company two years ago. Obviously, I knew that the company was in trouble because of the collapse in construction, but I thought I was the last person they would let go as I was with the company eighteen years.

I did all the usual things. I applied for every job I could. I sent out my CV to every company within a fifty-mile radius. I knew finding a new job at my age would be hard and that I would encounter a lot of setbacks. So I really focused on being flexible. I did a computer training course to upgrade my skills. I talked to as many people as possible. I kept in touch with my former colleagues and friends at work to ask them to look out for any suitable opportunities. The main thing I decided was, 'This is not just about me. There are a lot of people in my situation and a lot of things happening. I have to position myself in this new world and be prepared for any opportunities that might arise.' I made a real effort to let go any preconceived ideas I had about myself, or how things should be, and instead I responded to the possibilities as they emerged.

Finally, I got offered a job 120 miles away. Of course, it was hard on my wife and my kids. I was working shifts, so I could only get home every second week. They came down by bus the other weekends. We felt it was important that the kids could see where I was working and living, and also it made my rented apartment seem more homely.

I thought it would be much worse than it actually was. But we surprised ourselves, I suppose. We supported each other and everybody showed great endurance. I concentrated on that, rather than on what I thought I was going to feel – which was very depressed.

It all worked out in the end. I recently got a good job nearer home. I think the guy who interviewed me was impressed by how I had handled my situation, particularly the fact that I was prepared to move and be away from my family. I never thought I would hear myself say this, but I am actually better because of that experience.

### *Acceptance is an active word*

Philip Brickman describes acceptance as establishing a different relationship between 'want to' and 'have to' in our minds.[13]

When we 'have to' accept what has happened to us, the negative dominates – the painful facts of our situation hammer us into submission. This leaves us susceptible to feeling depressed and bitter. On the other hand, if we turn what we have to do into what we 'want to' do, if we 'choose to' accept our situation, the positive dominates. Needless to say, positives are hard to find in times of great hardship. But one positive that is always available is the possibility of finding meaning in the situation.

Brickman cites the awful dilemma facing the parents of children dying of leukemia. Those parents who could not accept that they had lost control over the child's survival, and who continued to focus their energies on trying to do that, were found to cope less well with their child's last days and with the grief afterwards. The parents who concentrated their energies on the meaning of those last days did better. Instead of seeing those last few days as unbearably negative, they focused on seeing them as filled with opportunity – to involve themselves in the activities of the moment, to talk and play with their child, to enhance the quality of the time that was left.[14]

Those parents came to see that what they *could* do, and what they *chose* to do, however limited, was the best possible, and perhaps the only possible, action open to them. So, they committed themselves to that course of action.

When we make a commitment like that, we immediately feel different. We experience our actions and their consequences as our own. Any possible negative consequences assume a value in our minds – they become the price worth paying, an opportunity to reveal some truth about ourselves or about the situation in which we find ourselves. Our actions have taken on a value and a meaning precisely *because* we have chosen to commit ourselves.

Alhough we may still be faced with uncertainty, suffering and frustration, we experience a unity between the way we are feeling and the way we are acting.

## *The five dimensions of post-traumatic growth*

When people have successfully re-ordered their internal world of meaning and achieved a sense of resolution, they are finally ready to move forward again in their lives with energy and commitment.

Those who show post-traumatic growth report five major changes in themselves.[15]

Let's look at each of these in turn.

### *A deeper appreciation of life and a changed sense of priorities*

There is an acute awareness of the importance of little things – or, rather, things that were once considered 'little' or taken for granted – such as the physical beauty of the world, the preciousness of the moment, the absolute miracle of love. This sense was lyrically expressed by the great English writer and dramatist Dennis Potter in his last TV interview two months before he died from cancer.[16] Throughout the interview he sipped from a cocktail of morphine to control his pain. He described seeing the blossom of a plum tree through his window:

> Instead of saying, 'Oh, that's a nice blossom,' last week looking at it through the window when I'm writing, it is the whitest, frothiest, blossomest blossom that there ever could be, and I can see it. And things are both more trivial than they ever were, and more important than they ever were, and the difference between the trivial and the important doesn't seem to matter. The nowness of everything is absolutely wondrous [. . .] the glory of it, if you like, the comfort of it, the reassurance [. . .] The fact is that if you see the present tense, boy do you see it! And boy can you celebrate it.

### *Stronger, more intimate relationships with others*

In a crisis, you find out who you can rely on – and who you can't. It can be a bittersweet experience. People you thought you could depend on may let you down at your most vulnerable moments and these feelings of betrayal can take a long time to work through. Indeed, many people find this additional wound unbearable, often repeating over and over again, 'I just can't believe that he behaved like that. How could I have got him so wrong?'

But, the negative reaction of some people to your plight is generally overwhelmed by the flood of goodwill from others. Crisis brings out the best in most people. In the wake of the September 11 disaster, the outpouring of personal heroism and community solidarity was like a shield against people's sense of shock and despair. So too, faced with personal crisis, our sense of personal vulnerability is shored up by the rallying around of family, friends and colleagues, even strangers. Gradually, through the intensity and frequency of the support, often from the most unexpected sources, our trust in people is restored – built, this time, on a foundation of stronger, more intimate relationships.

Bonds forged through crisis represent a special kind of unconditional love, an unspoken acknowledgement that we are all united in vulnerability and in strength.

*Is faoi scáth a chéile a mhaireann na daoine.**

### *A greater sense of your own personal strengths*

Although rarely even noticed in the heat of the struggle to survive, when a crisis is coming to an end the discovery of your own personal strengths comes almost as a surprise. You may initially marvel at the fact that you have survived. But then, looking back, you suddenly see why.

Helen suffered a traumatic marriage breakdown and, almost immediately after this event, was diagnosed with cancer. She recalls this time in her life.

> *Helen*
> I just found reserves in myself that I didn't know I had. I never thought of myself as a particularly courageous person, but I found out that I am. I had to be. And the great thing is that I now know – and I really mean know in my heart – that that courage will never leave me, no matter what happens in the future. That's been one good thing that came out of all this.

* Translated from Irish as: 'People live in each other's shadows.'

Tom, a businessman who had to deal with the closure of his company after twenty years described it in this way.

*Tom*

I thought I would never get through it – sorting out the financial mess, dealing with creditors and the banks, trying to explain to people why they were losing their jobs, and dealing with the terrible anxiety about my own family's future. But I did. I sorted out the whole lot eventually. How did I do it? Because I knew that if I didn't do it, nobody would or could. The responsibility was squarely on my shoulders.

And I found out that I could shoulder that burden of responsibility and not break underneath it. At the time, it gave me the will to go on.

After that experience, I figure I can handle anything. No matter what life throws at me, I know I will find a way to work it out. That gives me a great sense of confidence about taking on new responsibilities.

### *Recognizing new possibilities and paths in your life*

A crisis almost always shuts the doors on opportunities that were once open to you. Part of flourishing in a crisis is the willingness to see this as an opportunity to change direction, rather than as the end of the road.

If you go down that new road, new vistas open up and new possibilities present themselves. For example, if you are derailed from your chosen career, you can use this as an opportunity to pursue a different interest, or to develop a new competence.

The most touching instances of this come from more severe crises than losing a job or a business. For example, parents who lose a child due to miscarriage, illness, a road traffic accident, or suicide may take the opportunity to help other parents in the same situation. Despite, or because of, their trauma and grief they may raise public awareness or funds to tackle the cause of their child's death.

In that way, they wrest some goodness from their tragedy.

### *The development of wisdom*

The experience of great adversity can force us to confront the fundamental questions in life. For individuals who are religious, it can rock their faith to its foundations, or it can deepen their faith and give them a more personal sense that God is taking care of them. For those who are not religious, it can evoke a feeling of profound vulnerability, and they can feel lost and adrift.

Adversity can make us feel newly aware of just how tightly connected we are one to the other. We experience ourselves as being held securely in the universe by forces greater than us.

The truth is that, in the course of trying to wrest meaning and growth from a crisis, we experience all of those feelings – negative and positive. But finally, as we work our way through them, there is a period of settling – a new wisdom.

Our perspective widens and deepens. We begin to see our crisis in a much wider context, as part of a larger cycle of things. We may come to realize that a major personal vulnerability or mistake had its roots far back in time, not just in our own childhood experiences, but in our parents' or even grandparents' childhoods. We may come to appreciate how the ripples of vast and barely understood global forces fetched up on the shores of our individual lives.

Gradually, our preoccupation with the details of our own crisis diminishes. We come to *experience*, as opposed to just knowing, that there is, in Shakespeare's phrase, 'a tide in the affairs of men'. And that we are held afloat on that tide.

Life keeps happening.

The ebb is followed by the tide.

We recover.

The markets recover.

Good things happen.

New opportunities appear.

We keep going.

We are still standing.

We get an inkling that there is a benign inner reality underlying the chaos and randomness of life.

We get the sense I described earlier – of being held in the universe, and by each other.

This sober psychological account of post-traumatic growth hardly touches on the personal drama that goes on beneath the process.

The experience is akin to tunnelling down a dark mineshaft, and having the frightening sense of falling away from the ordinary world that you know and have taken for granted. But then, just as you feel you have reached a dead end, stripped of your pride and shaken to the core, a door opens into the light. You feel what can only be described as a sense of exhilaration. You feel lighter, opened up.

In addition, it is the great paradox of life that suffering, bravely confronted, relieves us of the most painful part of being human – the sense of being locked inside our own skins. We feel part of the common lot of humanity, an indivisible part of something much older and bigger than ourselves.

Great adversity and trauma make us aware of both the great abundance of life and its fragility.

That awareness is the very essence of wisdom.

The result is twofold.

First, a deep compassion, which is the very essence of a more developed humanity.

And second, a heightened sense of stewardship, a realization that we are all responsible for preserving and protecting what is good in this world – in ourselves, in other people, in relationships, in the organizations we care about, and in the society we live in.

What better formula for flourishing?

STRATEGY NINE

# *Stop sabotaging yourself*

'Our deepest fear is not that we are inadequate.
Our deepest fear is that we are powerful beyond measure.
It is our light, not our darkness, that most frightens us.'

Marianne Williamson, *A Return to Love*
(quoted by Nelson Mandela in his 1994 inaugural
speech as President of South Africa)[1]

# 21. You can't be driven crazy without your full cooperation

Many years ago, I was reading a book on some aspect of psychology and I came across this sentence: 'You can't be driven crazy without your full cooperation.'[2] It struck me immediately as a perfect summary of a profound truth about life: in every situation in which we find ourselves, no matter how bad, we always have some choice, no matter how limited, about how to respond.

An equally profound truth is that frequently we don't use that power and, when we do, we sometimes use it to work against ourselves, cooperating fully with whatever – or whoever – is driving us crazy.

We drive ourselves crazy in many ways. In fact, we have a particular ingenuity for inventing ways to torment ourselves. However, the self-defeating things we do generally fall into three classes:

- following counterproductive behaviour strategies
- adopting dysfunctional thinking styles, and
- sticking with rigid and unproductive 'crazy-making' behaviour.

Learning to stop thinking and behaving in these ways is the subject of this chapter.

## *Setting ourselves up for failure*

We like to think that we are rational people – and that is true, in a general sense. But, we also have a well-developed tendency to handicap ourselves in systematic ways.

Psychologists Roy Baumeister and Steven Scher surveyed the research on self-destructive behaviour among 'normal' people (those not suffering from psychological or psychiatric disorders) and found no convincing evidence that we set out deliberately to be self-destructive.[3] Rather, we act against our own interests either because we use strategies that we think will help but are in fact counterproductive, or we use 'trade-offs' that end up harming us.

### *Counterproductive strategies*

Baumeister and Scher define counterproductive strategies as ways of pursuing a goal that paradoxically make failure more likely. This is usually because we either under- or overestimate our capacities.

Or we may fail to understand the contingencies or 'rules' that govern certain situations ('No point complaining here') or particular relationships ('Paul likes to be consulted about things well in advance'). We don't foresee that certain things we do will not create the reaction we were hoping for ('I thought I might get a refund or an apology') or will produce an unintended reaction ('I didn't expect he would get so mad').

There is ample evidence that, far from learning from our experience, many of us hold fast to these counterproductive strategies. Among the main culprits are:

- persisting in an obviously failing enterprise
- trying so hard that you 'choke under pressure', and
- wanting too much to be liked.

#### PERSISTENCE: THE PHENOMENON OF 'THROWING GOOD MONEY AFTER BAD'

As with many self-defeating behaviours, overusing a personal strength can work against us.

Take persistence – it is an admirable quality, but persisting in pursuing unachievable goals can use up our precious time, energy and personal resources and prevent us from pursuing other goals that have a chance of success.

Why do we do that?

Well, sometimes it is because we misjudge how difficult something is going to be and overestimate our own powers. But mainly, we become entrapped by the classic gambler's error of 'throwing good money after bad' in the vain hope of 'winning back' the time and effort already invested.

This kind of psychological entrapment can happen in any domain. For example, people are particularly susceptible to entrapment if they volunteer for an impossibly difficult work project – perhaps taking it on despite opposition from colleagues, friends or family. They then become even more vulnerable to persisting in the face of evident failure – although they may try to disguise that failure. In these conditions, giving up is a matter of losing face, tantamount to a public admission of failure and bad judgement.

The same thing can happen when it comes to a young person taking on an impossibly demanding romantic partner. That is why it is so difficult for worried families and friends to know what to do. If they voice too much opposition, they risk making the young person even more committed.

Just being aware of the phenomenon makes it easier to 'catch yourself in the act' and to stop. Going to the trouble of trying to calculate the pros and cons and the probability of success also helps. Setting some limits in advance about how far you are prepared to go, and especially sharing these with somebody else, makes it easier to withdraw.

However, these are strategies that tend to be easier to use in the work domain, rather than in personal relationships.

### TRYING TOO HARD

Trying too hard is most likely to happen when there is a lot of pressure on you to perform well and something important is at stake, including your self-esteem.

People are particularly susceptible to 'choking under pressure' in situations such as sports competitions, examinations, sexual performance and public performances (for example, making a speech or a presentation).[4]

The more pressure you feel, the more you try to ensure success by anxiously monitoring your progress ('Am I succeeding? Or am I failing?'). That self-conscious focus is precisely the problem. The nature of skilled performance is that what was once conscious has become automatic. Conscious thinking disrupts this chain of automatic responses and causes you to stumble. The more you try to control it, the worse you do. You discover, to your dismay, that actually you don't consciously 'know' how to do it.

### WANTING TOO MUCH TO BE LIKED

Sometimes the harder we try to be liked, the more counterproductive it is. This is particularly likely to happen if our efforts to be liked take the form of seeking approval from someone who we perceive to be of higher status than ourselves – more attractive, powerful, popular, or famous. The effort backfires because it is perceived as an attempt to ingratiate – so whatever is said is dismissed as flattery or manipulation.

Trying to 'do favours' as a way of winning approval meets the same fate – particularly if it is seen as an attempt to look good in another person's eyes, or there is an expectation that the favour will be reciprocated. In fact, it reduces the other person's willingness to help at all.

The lesson here is simple.

When you are interacting with somebody who you are in awe of, just be pleasant and ordinary. You can, of course, tell them what you admire about them, if you want to. But do it in a direct, simple and, above all, brief way. No elaborations, no superlatives. Just plain appreciation – which everybody appreciates.

### *Counterproductive 'trade-offs'*

Everything we do brings with it costs and benefits. Sometimes we have to trade one off against the other. This is most likely to happen in situations where we have competing goals.

For example, you want to present a work project you have been working on to a crucial meeting. You know that an important colleague, who has played a lesser role, would like to be involved. So, you include him in the presentation – trading your solo moment of glory for having a good relationship with him.

Similarly, you may trade leisure time for time spent playing with your children, or perhaps the satisfaction of being right for harmonious marital relations. These are fairly benign trade-offs.

But, as Baumeister and Scher point out, we often make very bad bargains indeed. We trade the doubtful benefits of immediate pleasure and avoiding anxiety for the very substantial long-term costs of such behaviours as:

- substance abuse (smoking, alcohol and drugs)
- neglecting our health
- trying too hard to maintain a favourable public image
- self-handicapping.

#### SUBSTANCE ABUSE AND NEGLECTING OUR HEALTH

These are probably the most common and obvious self-destructive behaviours. In the case of smoking, alcohol and drug use, the trade-off is simple. We trade immediate feelings of pleasure for the substantial risks to our health in the long term – and we engage in a great deal of conscious and unconscious self-deception in the process. The immediate benefits are so seductive and certain that we convince ourselves the costs are far off and uncertain, and we dismiss the odds ('Just statistics – I know a man who . . .').

Similarly, with our general health, we don't keep a quarter of the medical appointments we make ourselves – and only half of those made for us by others who care about us. We are equally cavalier about complying with medical advice regarding the treatment or prevention of illnesses.[5]

Why?

Because in the absence of severe or painful symptoms (or sometimes even when they are present), we are willing to trade off the long-term costs of damaging our health, or knocking years off our lives, for the short-term gains of:

- avoidance ('It might hurt too much')
- denial ('These symptoms don't mean anything')
- time ('I am way too busy'), or
- maintaining our daily routine ('It would take too long and disrupt my day').

At the other extreme, we can over-medicate ourselves, endure unnecessary tests, and miss work and social engagements – all because the secret benefit may be the 'secondary gain' we get from playing the invalid – the guarantee of being the focus of care and attention from others.

### TRYING TOO HARD TO MAINTAIN A FAVOURABLE PUBLIC IMAGE

The harder we try to maintain face and avoid making a bad impression, the more vulnerable we are to adopting a style of interaction that is too self-protective or overbearing.

We may protect ourselves from the anxiety of being rejected or looking bad by withdrawing socially and being reluctant to disclose any personal information. (In this way, chronically shy people risk making no impression at all, or being seen as stand-offish.) In other situations, we may disclose too much too soon and risk being seen as too self-centred, or a little weird.

We are most liable to be self-defeating when we are determined to hide a 'shameful' secret, such as being abused by family members, physically or sexually. In such situations, we will trade almost anything – even the balm of friendship and the possibility of help – to keep that secret and maintain an image of 'normality'.

### SELF-HANDICAPPING

Self-handicapping means acting in ways that allow us to excuse failure.

The most common form is either not doing something (such as studying for an exam) or doing something (such as drinking too much the night before an important work task) that will increase the likelihood of failure. We discount the possible failure ('How could I have done well? I did no preparation!), thereby suggesting that if we had made the effort we would have done well; that we are not incompetent, just careless. On the other hand, if we actually succeed, we can present ourselves in a flattering light ('I can't believe I did that well with no effort!), thereby suggesting that if we had, well . . . you know the game.

Win-win?

Well, no.

Because self-handicapping makes failure more likely. And in our anxiety to avoid the implications of failure, we gamble with our real chances of success.

The more external pressure there is to succeed, and the more we privately expect to fail, the greater the temptation to self-handicap. Self-handicapping is often the underlying reason for a chronic pattern of underachievement at school or work, and failing generally to live up to our full potential.

## *Thinking styles: The dysfunctional dozen*

Another tried and trusted way to drive yourself crazy is to engage in certain thinking styles.

Psychologist Aaron Beck, the father of cognitive psychology, worked mainly with people suffering from depression. But, in the course of his work, he identified ten styles of thinking that are dysfunctional for all of us.[6]

1. **'All or nothing' thinking**: You see everything in absolute terms – you are either a complete success or a total failure. One mistake is enough for you to define something as a disaster. As a result, your thinking can be harsh and perfectionistic, hard on yourself – and probably on other people too.
2. **Overgeneralization**: When something bad happens, you immediately conclude that this is now the way things will be permanently ('Well, that's it. That's the end of that'). The words 'always' ('I am always going to screw up') and 'never' ('You never do anything right') come up frequently.

3. **Mental filter**: Your thinking filters out the positive aspects of any situation and zones in on the one negative detail, distorting your perception of the situation. You are often totally unaware of this tendency – but other people are acutely conscious of it and dread your capacity to pour cold water on anything that they suggest or organize.
4. **Disqualifying the positive**: This is another type of mental filtering. You 'read' neutral or positive information as negative, actively discount the positive and end up transforming positive experiences into negative ones ('OK, he did not say it was bad, but the fact that he said nothing means that he must think it is bad. So all the effort was for nothing').
5. **Jumping to conclusions**: You jump to a negative conclusion based on no evidence except your conviction that you 'know' what something means. You believe you can tell what somebody else is thinking ('I know they hate me') and so don't try to look for evidence that this is true, or you base your conclusion on your belief that you can accurately predict the future ('I just know that this is going to happen and it is going to be really bad').
6. **Magnification and minimization**: When something goes wrong, you exaggerate its negative consequences. This is called 'catastrophizing'. You imagine the worst possible outcomes ('The project's gone wrong. I will lose my job. It's the end of my career'), or you minimize your advantages or strengths ('I may be the best-qualified candidate, but I won't get the job. There's no point drawing attention to my achievements').
7. **Emotional reasoning**: You interpret your feelings as facts, assuming that if you feel unloved nobody actually loves you, if you feel anxious there is actual danger, if you feel guilty you have done something wrong, if you feel something can't be done it is indeed objectively impossible.
8. **'Should' statements**: You try to get yourself and other people to do things by issuing a string of 'shoulds'. This has the effect of oppressing and depressing yourself and making others resentful. When you, and they, fail to implement the 'shoulds' (which often happens) you feel demoralized about yourself and disappointed or even bitter about others.

9. **Labelling and mislabelling**: Personal labelling is equating your behaviour with your whole self, saying 'I am hopeless at this' instead of 'I made a mistake'. Mislabelling is when you describe something in an inappropriate and emotionally laden way ('I let you down. I am a horrible person'). You can also apply labelling and mislabelling to other people, and this is a precursor to the stinging personal criticism that can severely undermine relationships.
10. **Personalization**: You nurture the fantasy that to be happy or to feel safe in the world you can or must completely control everything. You therefore feel a crippling sense of guilt when things go wrong – as, of course, they do. This fantasy includes trying to control things and people that at best you can only influence – such as your adult children's lifestyles.

The more stressed we are, the more susceptible we become to one or more of these. Some of us are world-class artistes, mastering all ten styles. The more often we indulge in them, the more they become the automatic 'default' to any setback or stress.

I add to Beck's 'Toxic Ten' our old friends:

11. **Rumination**, and
12. **Worry**.

They underlie many of the dysfunctional thinking styles just described.

## *Sticking with 'crazy-making' behaviour*

Dysfunctional thinking styles leak into our interactions with others, particularly in intimate relationships such as marriage. Not only do we drive ourselves crazy, we drive other people mad too – particularly those we profess to love. In Chapter 2 we looked at John Gottman's work with married couples. He identified the 'Four Horsemen of the Apocalypse' that lead to marital breakdown – personal criticism, contempt, disgust and stonewalling. But, of course, couples have perfected many more 'crazy-making sequences'.

Take a common example, the 'demand-withdraw' pattern. In this pattern, one partner (typically the woman) is making the demands and the other partner (typically the man) is withdrawing (they can also take turns – and, indeed, the same pattern happens in gay and lesbian relationships). This pattern is what therapist Pierre Mornell has labelled 'Passive Men, Wild Women'.[7]

The sequence is often initiated by the woman wanting 'something more' from her husband and conveying this demand directly or covertly (as in deep sighs or pointed silences).

The man perceives this as unnecessary and intrusive 'pressure', and so he withdraws.

This, needless to say, provokes further 'approaches' from the woman.

He retreats even further, finally lapsing into complete silence or passivity.

She then goes wild.

And on it goes. For hours. Weeks. Months. Sometimes for whole lifetimes and across generations.

This is just one of many patterns couples can fall into. The following list is not exhaustive – you can probably think of a few more versions you have noticed in your family and friends.

- One is extravagantly extroverted, the other deeply introverted.
- One is wildly flirtatious, the other is wildly jealous.
- One is hyperassertive, the other a mouse.
- One is over-involved in the relationship, the other not involved enough.
- One expresses every feeling to its limit, the other is equally busy repressing everything.
- One is overly dependent, the other too self-sufficient.
- One is totally risk-averse, the other dauntingly carefree.
- One is always responsible, the other indulgently immature.[8]

We are often drawn romantically to people who have a different and opposite style to our own. But the more extreme the difference, the more likely this will end in grief. Over time, the very characteristic that we first found so attractive, and may have hoped would rub off on us, becomes profoundly irritating and forces us to be an even more extreme version of ourselves. But, by then, the pattern has assumed a life of its own.

The more responsible you become, the more irresponsibly the other behaves.

The more devoted to work the other becomes, the more you are stuck with keeping the relationship going.

All dysfunctional patterns finally resolve themselves into a grim and endless game of each partner alternating between the roles of victim, prosecutor or rescuer.

## *What lies behind self-defeating behaviour*

We get stuck in self-defeating patterns of behaviour for many reasons – including temperament, and previously learned experiences (especially growing up). But, there is one fundamental truth that we need to remind ourselves of on a regular basis: 'You can't be driven crazy without your full cooperation.'

It's worth repeating the important four words here: *Without. Your. Full. Cooperation.*

I stress each of these words because each carries a wealth of meaning. No matter how trying, stressful or difficult the situation in which we find ourselves, no matter how little real power and control we have, the essential characteristic of being a human being is that we can exercise choice. We have a free will, an 'executive self'.

The problem is not that we don't exercise our capacity for choice – we do. The problem is that we often hide from ourselves the actual choices we are making. That is at the core of self-defeating behaviour. We feel like helpless victims when we use counterproductive strategies and 'trade-offs', or get stuck in dysfunctional thinking styles, or suffer through yet another circular round of, 'I wouldn't have to nag, if you responded to my reasonable requests,' or, 'If you didn't nag me, I would respond.'

We are often obscuring from ourselves the hidden choices we are making.

### *The rules of entrapment*

As with many things, the origins of entrapment often lie in our earliest relationships.

Take the example of a child who is reared by a very demanding mother or a hypercritical father. Or the child who grows up in a classic 'role reversal' family, where they have to take responsibility for meeting the psychological needs of a parent who is immature, over-dependent, feckless, or deeply frustrated about how their life has turned out. In such families, the child is given a kind of pseudo power. They are made to feel that they can fulfil parental demands and needs – if they work at it long enough and hard enough.

Children are all too ready to try to please their parents, and so they do try hard. As a consequence, they are often precociously able and responsible. But that power is built on a foundation of inner powerlessness to obtain the love and care they themselves need to grow up. They then bring that 'powerless-power' into adult life. They are on the unconscious lookout for another chance to use it, to achieve in adult life what they could never achieve in childhood. That is why people persist for many years, sometimes for a whole lifetime, in trying to please someone who is not capable of being pleased. Or in trying to obtain love from somebody who is unwilling or incapable of giving it. Or in trying to 'save' somebody who is determined not to be saved.

They become entrapped because the time and energy they invest in this new endeavour becomes fused in their minds with the similar investment they made in childhood, so now there is just too much investment to give up.

The 'wordless blueprints' from childhood come as a series of 'if-then' rules.[9]

The 'if-then' rules that emerge from a loving family work in our favour ('If you love somebody then you get even more love back' 'If you feel vulnerable then it's good to ask for help'). The 'if-then' rules that emerge from unhappy families work against us and maintain self-defeating behaviour ('If I don't please somebody then I will be rejected' 'If I make a mistake then I will be harshly criticized' 'If I disagree with somebody then I will be put down' 'If I don't take responsibility for everything and everybody then the whole thing will fall apart').

Each 'if-then' rule activates a tightly organized pattern of feelings, perceptions, expectations, goals and behavioural responses to new situations. These patterns then become your 'personality signature'.[10]

Hidden inside the 'if-then' rules are the trade-offs you make. The stress and frustration created by using counterproductive strategies, dysfunctional thinking and self-defeating patterns are outweighed by the benefits they deliver. They relieve you of anxiety or guilt. They give you a feeling of temporary control. They shield you from the stress of taking responsibility for your own life, of risking self-disclosure, of trying to solve the problem, or of being wrong. They can shield you from acknowledging that the person you love does not love you, or is mad, sad or bad in a way that you don't want to admit, or acts in ways that have no meaning.

### *The hidden trade-off in rumination and worrying*

The trademark of worrying is 'what if' thinking – imagining the worst. As we have seen already, rumination is the endless, repetitive focusing on negative thoughts and feelings. Both are very self-focused. The more we worry about what might happen, or ruminate on what did happen, the slower we are to grasp what is actually happening.

Both kinds of thinking create a great deal of personal distress.

Susan Nolen-Hoeksema found that the underlying theme of rumination is loss.[11] This may be caused by bad luck, or your own failure, or the failure of other people to live up to expectations. Whereas worry is all about uncertainty ('Will it happen? Or won't it happen?'). Worriers have a deep reluctance to tolerate uncertainty, and so they do the 'work of worrying' to try to control it by anticipating and preparing for the worst. Ruminators have an equally deep reluctance to accept loss. The trouble is that both pay a big price for their sense of control. Ruminators pay the additional price of convincing themselves that they can do nothing to change things.

The solution in both cases is not to underestimate risk or repress the sense of loss. Rather, it is to convert the worry and rumination into an effort to identify any practical action (however small) we can take to reduce the possible risks or alleviate the sense of loss. This includes mentally rehearsing problem-solving actions, and generating other ideas in case our first efforts do not work. It also includes finding effective ways to soothe and distract ourselves from anxiety and depression.

In other words, assessing risk and loss has to be balanced by an equal effort to assess our capacity for handling the situation. The more effort we put into imagining ourselves handling the situation, the more our physiological arousal and stress response will diminish and the more our actual performance will improve – which, in turn, increases the chances of success.

This is one woman's experience of uncovering and challenging her hidden trade-offs.

*Sheila*

Some years ago, Sheila, a successful professional woman and mother of three children then aged five to thirteen, came to see me complaining of stress. She suffered from chronic tension in her neck and shoulders. She slept poorly, often as little as four hours a night. She was often irritable and recently found that she was having frequent arguments 'about nothing'. The thing that stood out about her weekly routine was that virtually every weekend she visited her parents, involving a two-hour trip each way and an overnight stay. She had been doing this since she first moved to Dublin as a student. After she married, she brought her husband and children with her on the trips, but her husband soon got tired of the travelling and opted to stay at home most weekends. She continued to bring the children, but lately the thirteen-year-old was refusing to go. Her husband occasionally complained about her absences but was generally content not to rock the boat as Sheila made no demands on him for help in the house or with the children – 'To make up to him for my being gone at the weekends.'

Sheila explained her frequent trips by telling me that her family had been poor when she was growing up and her mother never tired of telling her of the sacrifices they had made to educate her. As soon as she qualified, she had started giving her parents a regular allowance, and she paid for an extension to their house. On every visit, she brought groceries and gifts and helped her mother with housework and other chores. Her father had health problems, and she liked to take him out 'to give my mother a break'.

Clearly, she was exhausted from this routine, but said, 'I have to do it as Mammy relies on me completely to keep things going.' Then she added, 'Not that anything can make Mammy happy.'

I asked her if she had considered offering to pay for household help.

'Oh, no,' she said, 'Mammy is fiercely independent. She would not let on to the neighbours that she needed help. Anyway, she would not like a stranger in the house.'

Why, I asked, did she not invite her parents to visit her in Dublin?

'Mammy does not like to travel,' she said, adding, 'Anyway, she prefers me to come down.'

I asked Sheila what she wanted to achieve in therapy.

'Learn to manage my stress better.'

And did she think this was really possible in the current set-up?

She looked startled at the question and then said, 'No, I suppose not.'

That, at least, was a start.

Over the course of therapy, Sheila acknowledged the unreasonableness of her mother's demands and uncovered the web of guilt and emotional manipulation that was keeping her trapped in this highly stressful routine. So, her goal became to stop the weekly trips and instead visit her parents once a month and encourage them to visit her in Dublin.

The weeks rolled by and still Sheila did nothing to change things, admitting she was afraid to tell her mother that she would not be coming the next weekend. She worried her mother might stop speaking to her altogether, a tactic she had used frequently in Sheila's childhood. Sheila was quite struck by the intensity of this fear. She marvelled at the fact that she could be assertive in her professional life but could not confront her fear of her formidable mother. She became acutely aware of the self-destructive trade-off she was making – a temporary reduction in anxiety and guilt about her mother for a life full of stress, including a marriage where she felt she could not negotiate a more equal sharing of household and childcare duties.

Then, one day, she arrived triumphant, exclaiming as she came in the door, 'I finally did it! I told her I was not coming this weekend and that from now on I'll be coming only once a month.'

And how did she react?

'That was the most amazing thing,' Sheila said. 'She did not bat an eyelid. She said, "OK. Sure, you were coming down too much, anyway." '

Once Sheila faced down her own fear, the liberating effects spread through her life. She made changes in her marriage and in her work, finding a better balance between her own and other people's needs.

As for her mother, although she was a reluctant traveller, both she and her husband came to visit Sheila regularly. Soon, she was clearly beginning to enjoy these trips, announcing without a trace of irony to Sheila one day, 'I should have done this years ago. But you were always coming down, so I couldn't.'

## *Changing our self-defeating behaviour and making new choices*

However ingrained our self-defeating patterns, we have an inherent capacity to change ourselves.

Here are half a dozen strategies that can give you real control over how you manage your responses to even the most challenging situations.

### *Become aware of the self-defeating 'if-then' rules you are using*

Usually we know when we are behaving in a self-defeating way, but we can't quite figure out why or how. This is because we are not conscious of the 'rules' we impose on ourselves and the 'roles' we occupy in certain relationships.

You can uncover these rules and roles by asking yourself two questions:

- 'What do I *always* do, or *never* do in a particular situation?'
- 'What role do I *always* play or *never* play in a particular relationship?'

Then try breaking that rule, or changing that role. In Sheila's case the rule was, 'I can't say no to my mother,' and the 'role' was 'selfless caretaker' or 'rescuer' – to complement her mother's role as 'prosecutor'. When she broke that rule and changed her role, the situation became open to positive change.

At the very least, you can make yourself less vulnerable to this kind of counterproductive strategy if you set prior limits regarding how far you will go, or how much you will persist in a certain course of action. It then becomes easier to withdraw from the entrapping situation.[12]

### *Learn to substitute alternative and positive 'if-then' rules*

Negative 'if-then' rules are iron rules ('If I do X or don't do Y then I will be rejected / abandoned / a complete failure in life'). So, you need to develop the habit of consciously asking, 'What else positive could I do now?' And then remind yourself that you have a choice about how to respond. Unless you do that, you won't become aware of the positive options.

The more you weaken the old 'if-then' rule, the easier it becomes to create more enabling and flexible versions. For example, if you consciously substitute an old negative 'if-then' rule ('If I disagree with someone important to me then they will react in a punitive way') with a positive 'if-then' rule ('If I tell other people what I honestly think then they will respond with interest'), even if you only do it some of the time, it will gradually pop into your mind as an option with no conscious effort.

The more often you use the new enabling rules, the more you will create a new self – 'Successful Me' – who can do battle with 'Self-Defeating Me'.

### *Manage your negative mood*

Virtually every counterproductive strategy, bad trade-off and dysfunctional pattern of thinking and behaving is made worse by being in a bad mood. Bad mood and negative feelings provoke a strong desire for escape, often at the cost of long-term risks to ourselves. Negative mood drives us back to our most primitive survival strategies ('Oh, just give in. It's easier') and makes it harder to sustain the effort to use our hard-earned new learning ('If I state my case reasonably and stick to my guns calmly, I can achieve my goal here').

Negative mood also increases your focus on yourself. When you feel bad, you become self-obsessed and self-conscious – both of which increase the use of self-defeating behaviours, such as trying too hard to be liked, choking under pressure, or persisting too long in order to save face.

### *Don't overuse your strengths*

The origin of many self-defeating behaviours is not weakness but overuse of a strength.

A high drive for achievement and excellence, the ability to get things done, idealism, conscientiousness, the capacity to care deeply for other people, for forgiveness – all these are admirable qualities. But, when overused, they lead to a host of dysfunctional and self-destructive behaviours: perfectionism, hyper-controlling behaviour, taking on too much, and reckless neglect of self.

When you understand and frame your problem behaviour as the overuse of a strength, it is much easier to motivate yourself to change. Learning to manage your strengths is a more inspiring and energizing endeavour than trying to root out some weakness.

None of us really wants to be 'fixed'; we want to grow into our best selves.

### *Make a resolution and an implementation plan*

Year after year, people try to change themselves, to overcome one self-defeating habit or another. This is the stuff of New Year's resolutions and other regular bouts of self-improvement.

Mostly, we don't succeed.[13]

Despite this, we are nothing if not dogged and full of hope.

Of those of us who fail in our resolutions this year, 60 per cent will make the same resolutions next year. Moreover, we will probably end up making the same resolutions year after year – resolving ten times, on average, to eradicate a particular vice. People who are finally successful typically report making the same resolutions for five years or more before succeeding.

The good news is that, in time, many people succeed in changing self-destructive patterns. And an act of will, of conscious choice, is the essential first step. Making the commitment to change provides a surge of positive feelings and a sense of control and self-efficacy.

For example, just by making a resolution to take more exercise, people immediately rate themselves as more likely to be successful and as feeling more confident in their ability to succeed than they had a week previously. Merely making a phone call to see a psychotherapist produces measurable improvement in distressed individuals. People enjoy that feeling of control – and this, in turn, alleviates feelings of distress and depression.

From previous chapters, you may have an inkling about why it is so hard to change any pattern of behaviour. The very effort to suppress negative thoughts or give something up ('I must not even think of having that cigarette / chocolate / glass of wine') is likely to create the ironic 'white bear' effect, flooding your mind with thoughts of the forbidden fruit. The more stressed and mentally overloaded you are, the more depleted your self-control muscle gets and the harder it is to keep your good resolutions.

You will recall how susceptible we are to being automatically influenced by cues from the environment. We may intend to be reasonable and polite, to eat carefully, to drink in moderation. But once 'in situ', we automatically pick up subtle or not so subtle signals that encourage us to become heated or aggressive, or pile our plate high with food from the buffet, or order another round.

In such situations, our responses and 'choices' bypass conscious control altogether – but it doesn't have to be like this. You can get the automatic system to be your ally in making better choices.

Peter Gollwitzer of New York University has found that the key to successful change and achieving your goal is to harness the power of the automatic system to help change by focusing on implementation rather than intention.[14]

That is not to say that intentions don't count.
They do.

## FORMING INTENTIONS

A strong intention guarantees a better outcome than a weak intention. Keep in mind the following guidelines.

- The more specific the goal, the better ('I am going to say "Let me think about that" before I agree to take on a new responsibility'). Specific goals are easier to plan for, monitor and adapt – that is why 'Do my best' goals ('I will try to think more positively') are generally ineffective.
- Combining a positive element in your intention ('This would make a real difference to my life') and a negative element ('I really have to do this, because it is causing me a lot of grief') also helps.
- Framing your intention as a 'learning goal' ('I am going to learn how to calm my feelings and my body before I discuss a contentious issue') rather than a 'performance' goal ('I am going to see if this helps me to get better at staying calm') is also effective.

Even when you do all the above in framing your intention, the biggest challenge remains – getting started and, once you do, keeping yourself going in the face of distractions from inside (negative feelings and mood) and outside (competing temptations to do something else).

It is not enough to form intentions – however strong, specific, positive and 'learning-oriented' they may be. You also have to form 'implementation intentions'.

## FORMING IMPLEMENTATION INTENTIONS

Gollwitzer defines 'implementation intentions' as pre-deciding *when*, *where* and *how* you are going to pursue your goal, including:

- when, where and how you will get started, and
- when, where and how you will deal with anticipated distractions and temptations.

The most successful formula for making an implementation plan is: 'When/if situation X arises then I will do Y.' You are linking the anticipated opportunities with your desired response. (This process of 'priming' yourself to respond to environmental cues – say, avoiding dessert when eating out – was described in detail in Chapter 9). It is a positive and enabling version of 'if-then' thinking, a benign form of what we used to call 'brainwashing'. Instead of being unconsciously 'controlled' by cues from the environment, you have *consciously* passed control of your behaviour on to the environment and harnessed the power of the automatic system to help you achieve your goal.

Suppose, for example, you are aware that you engage in self-defeating behaviour at work by never speaking up at meetings. Just 'intending' to be more assertive and confident is unlikely to solve that issue. You may intend to speak up at a critical meeting, but 'in situ' you find to your dismay that the discussion is so fast-paced that the opportunity passes you by. Even if you do see an opening, you may be too slow to take advantage of it because you are preoccupied or overcome by anxiety.

That is why you need to pre-decide *when*, *where* and *how* you are going to speak up, including anticipating the likely distractions and temptations, and pre-deciding how you will deal with them. Making 'pre-decisions' about how to act gives you more freedom to think about the many different kinds of responses you *could* make and, most importantly, the response that you most *want* to make in your own interest. Thus, when a good opportunity arises, often for just a fleeting moment, you are ready to take advantage of it and respond in the way you want, rather than in the way that others might be expecting or demanding of you.

Not only will this make you more ready to respond with the desired behaviour, it will spare you the heavy mental processing required for minute-to-minute conscious control of yourself and of the external environment ('Should I speak up now or wait? He's interrupted me as usual, now what am I going to do?).

Research by Gollwitzer and other psychologists shows how effective such implementation plans are in a wide variety of situations.[15]

For example, 66 per cent of students who had formed implementation plans succeeded in completing projects over the Christmas break (a time notorious for distractions and temptations) whereas only 25 per cent of those who did not have implementation plans did so.[16] In a study of women who had all strongly intended to perform regular breast self-examinations, 100 per cent of the women who made implementation plans did do, whereas only 53 per cent of those who did not form such plans did.[17]

Similarly, post-surgery patients who made plans to resume as many activities as possible after surgery were much more likely to succeed than those who merely 'intended' to do so – and these different results could not be accounted for by level of motivation to get better, or by personality.[18]

Self-defeating thinking, behaviour and relationship patterns are like bindweed. They suck up the nutrients, choke off the air and block the light we need in order to grow and flourish.

All of the techniques suggested above can help to clear that bindweed.

They can help you stop cooperating in driving yourself (or other people) crazy in ways that are sapping the positive energy out of your life. They work even better if you follow some of the other guidelines in this book.

For example, building the positive in your life in any of the ways suggested makes you less susceptible to the disruptive effects of negative feelings.

Adopting a mindful style of thinking – an attitude of 'creative uncertainty' – liberates you from self-defeating habits that have become automatic. These orient you to the possibility of seeing new perspectives on what is happening, or understanding the context in a different way.

Ultimately, this all depends on whether you liberate your power to choose to do any of these things. Just as you can choose to drive yourself crazy, you can choose to grow.

As the writer George Eliot put it: 'The strongest principle of growth lies in human choice.'

STRATEGY TEN

# *Embrace the future*

'The best way to predict the future is to create it.'

Peter Drucker
(also attributed to Abraham Lincoln)

# 22. Fearlessly facing the future

What distinguishes the human brain from animal brains is the sheer size of our frontal lobe, which is capable of anticipating, imagining, thinking and planning.

And boy do we make use of this capacity.

Altogether we spend about two hours a day thinking about the future. If Daniel Siegel described the brain as an 'anticipation machine', psychologist Daniel Gilbert goes a step further and says our relish for imagining and trying to predict the future makes us 'part-time residents of tomorrow'.[1] In this sense, 'making future' is the most important work the brain does.[2]

Our brain allows us to imagine how decisions might play out – big decisions (such as who to marry, what career to choose, whether to save or to spend, who to vote for, and who to trust), and small ones (such as where to go on holiday, what to eat, and how to spend an evening). All these decisions are based on how we think we will feel if we make certain choices. By trying to predict the future in this way, we hope to be able to shape and control it – and this need is deeply wired into our brains.

We most crave certainty at times of great crisis. The trouble is, for all the sophistication of the human brain, not only are we not very good at predicting the events of the future, but we can't even predict very accurately how we will feel about things we believe might happen. Of course, we can make a fair stab at imagining how we will feel if we land a great job, get rejected by a lover, or a hammer falls on our toe. But generally, because we are susceptible to a whole host of thinking errors and biases, we are pretty hopeless at getting our predictions right.

In times of crisis and uncertainty, such as we are living through now, we are even more likely to be wrong.

### *Biases and illusions, errors and mental shortcuts*

Psychologist Daniel Kahneman won the Nobel Prize for his work showing how human thinking is characterized by a host of biases, systematic errors and mental shortcuts, or 'rules of thumb', all of which make us poor judges of what will make us happy in the future.[3] Other psychologists, notably Daniel Gilbert, have added further layers of understanding.[4]

This vast and complex research literature could be summarized as follows.

Every prediction we make about the future involves comparing how we are feeling now to:

- how we felt in the past, and
- how we think we will feel in the future.

Sounds simple?

Alas, no.[5]

*Seeing what we expect and want to see*

We like to think our eyes and ears make faithful recordings of what is happening in the present moment.

But, it turns out that we don't so much *see* what is going on as *construct* it in our minds, using a creative mix of:

- what we actually see
- what we expect or want to see, and
- what we already think and feel.

Take the rather extraordinary experiment in which a researcher posing as a tourist, map in hand, stopped people in the street, supposedly looking for directions.[6] As they carefully perused the map, two 'construction workers' (also researchers) carrying a big door between them walked briskly between the 'tourist' and the helpful passer-by, temporarily obscuring their view of each other. This allowed the 'tourist' to slip away unnoticed and be replaced by a completely different person who bore no resemblance to him, and who proceeded to carry on the conversation about the directions. This experiment was repeated many times.

And guess what?

Most people did not notice the substitution.

Why?

Because they were *expecting* to see the same person.

They probably would not have made the error if they had been paying closer attention to the tourist, rather than to the map. But, as we know, a lot of the time our attention does go AWOL. That makes it challenging to predict how we will experience something in the future, since we will be unconsciously comparing it to what we *think* we experienced in the past.

### THE CONFIRMATION BIAS

We pay disproportionate attention to information that confirms what we want to believe, and we neglect contradictory evidence. So, when we celebrate winning a small sum in the lottery using our 'lucky' numbers, we conveniently forget the many times we did not win using the same numbers.

This also works in reverse. We notice every time our beloved does not put out the bin or respond to our passionate embrace, but we fail to register how often they do.

### THE FOCUSING ILLUSION (OR IMPACT BIAS)

As if the confirmation bias were not enough, we also put disproportionate emphasis on whatever draws our attention, thereby exaggerating its impact (positive or negative). This distorts our judgement of how we will react to things.

For example, university students were asked to predict how they would feel a few days after their football team won or lost a big match.[7] Before they made their predictions, one group of students was asked to describe an average day, the other group was not. When they went back to the participants a few days later, the researchers found that those who had first described their average day had predicted more accurately how they would feel about the possible win or loss, whereas the predictions of those who had not done that were wildly exaggerated.

Why were they so wrong?

Because they focused exclusively on one aspect of the future – the team winning (causing ecstasy) or losing (causing depression) – and 'forgot' the impact of the daily hassles that would lessen the ecstasy of winning, or the routine pleasures that would leaven the disappointment of losing.

We routinely make this error when thinking about the future. We overestimate the impact of change.[8] We persuade ourselves that a drop in income, a change in routine, losing weight, or winning the lottery will be the end of life as we know it. But it won't. As with the students, after the initial disappointment or elation, life will go on pretty much as before – with the usual quota of pleasure and pain.

Even when facing deeply adverse changes in our lives, we routinely overestimate their negative impact.

For example, when asked if they would accept a gruelling course of chemotherapy if it would extend their life by three months, no radiotherapists said they would, only 6 per cent of oncologists said they would, and the figure was 10 per cent for healthy people.

But, 42 per cent of current cancer patients said they would.

Dealing with the reality of their illness, they had found that the quality of their lives was much higher than the rest of us, including doctors, would have predicted. Dread at the thought of life with a serious illness or disability leads many of us to make 'living wills', setting out the measures we do or don't want to be taken if we become terminally ill. As some psychologists have observed, 'It is possible that healthy people realize that their preferences will change but nevertheless want to impose their healthy preferences on their future sick selves.'[9]

We make these assessments because we forget about what Gilbert calls our 'psychological immune system'.[10] We don't realize that it is triggered more quickly and effectively when we face serious adversity than when we face ordinary stresses. That is why, paradoxically, we can get so worked up about trivial matters, but turn into models of cool, calm, collected action when real disaster strikes – such as a family illness, an emergency, a natural disaster, a serious crisis at work. At these times we can even summon up our capacity for good humour, to lift the spirits of those around us.

### *Misremembering the past*

Just as we see the present as a mixture of what is happening and what we expect and want to happen, we see the past in much the same way.

To add to the confusion, we include in our memory information we have picked up in the meantime. So, we fill in details that never happened, omit some that did, and include scenes from photos we've looked at or stories we've been told.

This inexact recall is even true of so-called 'flashbulb memories' of highly unusual events.[11]

Take the explosion of the space shuttle Challenger in 1986, shortly after take-off, which was shown live on TV. The following day, Ulrich Neisser of Cornell University gathered accounts from people about where they were and how they found out about the event. He repeated the interviews two and a half years later and compared both sets of accounts. People did indeed claim to have vivid flashbulb memories – but the ones recalled at the later date bore little resemblance to their original accounts. Indeed, a quarter were wrong in every detail, approximately half were wrong on the majority of the details, and just 7 per cent corresponded exactly.[12]

A somewhat similar experiment examining people's recollections of the attack on the World Trade Center in 2001 showed comparable results. Yet those questioned were insistent that their memories of 9/11 were more vivid and accurate than their memories of their routine experiences the day before the attack.[13]

Tali Sharot of University College London has supplied some of the explanation for why this happens. She did fMRI scans on people who had actually been caught in the events of that day as they recalled their experiences, and found that those who had been nearest the collapsing buildings, and who had therefore felt under threat, recalled vividly the 'focal scene' – debris falling, people jumping, the screams, the smell of petrol and smoke – and this was reflected in increased activity in the amygdala. But their recall of peripheral detail was vague – reflected in reduced activity in the part of the brain that remembers the visual details of a scene.[14]

Sharot concluded that what lends flashbulb memories their intensity, and their sense of being imprinted on our brain, is the strength of the associated emotions, particularly fear.

You may recall that neuroscientist LeDoux showed that experiences of threat are laid down with the same neurochemicals that are involved in our 'fight-or-flight' impulses. Even if we are not directly experiencing the threat, our instinct for mirroring the emotional reactions of others (described in Chapter 13) makes us experience real fear.

Flashbulb memories are laid down in order to alert us to the type of situation that might signal great danger or opportunity.

But, they won't help us to predict the future.

## *Getting the future wrong*

For all our brain's incredible power, we are hostages of the present, and our thinking does not wander too far from it.

### THE ANCHORING ILLUSION

This illusion was demonstrated by Daniel Kahneman and Amos Tversky in a series of experiments.[15] For example, they asked people to guess the number of African nations in the UN. Some were asked if the number was less than 10, others if it was greater than 60. Although the suggested starting points were arbitrary, these dictated the size of the final guess.

The group that started with 10 guessed that the correct answer was 25, whereas the group that started with 60 guessed it was 45. Neither group strayed far from the starting point they were given.

In real life, we do much the same thing. We stay anchored to what we are thinking or feeling. This causes us to make some strange decisions.

Suppose you have paid €20 for a concert ticket and, when you get there, you discover you have lost the ticket. You have another €20 in your wallet. Will you buy another ticket? Most people say no.

Now, suppose you are on your way to the concert to buy a ticket, with €40 in your wallet. When you get there, you discover you have lost one of the €20 notes. Would you still buy the ticket? Most people say yes.

In both cases you have lost the same amount of money, or its equivalent value (the ticket), and in both cases you want to go to the concert.

So, why the different outcomes?

Because in the first case you remain anchored in the present and stubbornly persist in comparing the present circumstances to the past ('I had already bought the ticket') rather than to what you want in the future (to hear the concert).

We are even more tightly anchored by our current feelings. We automatically project how we now feel on to the future. In that respect, we are not much more advanced than a four-year-old who declares with unswerving confidence that he wants to be a fireman or to run a sweet shop when he grows up. That's because he cannot imagine any more delightful way of spending his life than riding in a noisy red truck wearing a big helmet, or scoffing sweets all day.

We adults remain just as firmly anchored in the present.

### THE 'HOT–COLD' EMPATHY GAP

When we are in a 'hot' state – hungry, excited, angry, sexually aroused, distressed – we have great difficulty imagining how we will feel in a 'cold' state. This accounts for well-known phenomena such as buying too much food when we are hungry, making reckless promises of love when gripped by lust, saying things we regret in the heat of the moment, and declaring that we will never be happy again when we feel depressed. When we have cooled off, we have even greater difficulty conjuring up the memory of those hot feelings and instead groan aloud, 'Never again.'

Similarly, we routinely underestimate the 'hot' power of social influences and the pressure to conform. We believe that we would have no trouble resisting such pressure and would behave better than those weak-willed people who did not resist the Nazis or stand up for what was right. Unfortunately, a series of experiments have shown that, faced with such pressures, most people do not resist them.

These 'hot–cold' empathy gaps cause us a lot of trouble and make it very hard to predict how we will feel and behave in the near or far future.[16]

### *Why we can't easily correct these thinking biases and errors*

Well, because of another illusion, of course . . .

#### THE ILLUSION OF INTROSPECTION

This is the conviction that we can directly and easily access what is, or was, going on in our minds through a little bout of reflection.

The trouble is, since many of these mental processes are happening below our level of consciousness, we are often unaware of how we are thinking or responding, and so we make up stories to explain ourselves.

For example, in one experiment people were given fifteen pairs of photographs of women and asked which woman from each pair they found more attractive. Later, they were presented with one of their choices and asked to explain why they had made it. But there was a catch. The 'preferred' photo presented was actually one of those they had rejected. Astonishingly, 75 per cent of people did not notice the switch and, moreover, had no trouble coming up with convincing explanations as to why they had found her more attractive.[17]

While we are often unaware of how we are thinking, with the help of our 'interpreter within' we have no trouble inventing an explanation. As a consequence of this tendency, we are often 'strangers to ourselves'.[18]

## *Bring on the experts . . . or maybe not*

We have a touching faith in experts and their ability to predict the future. Yet, the fact remains that experts often get it wrong. The most eminent scientists and commentators of their day declared air and space travel, television and any number of medical developments to be 'impossible', although some sagely took the view that the telephone *might* have some limited use in business but not in social life.

This is the working of Clarke's Law: 'When a distinguished but elderly scientist states that something is possible, he is almost certainly right.

When he states that something is impossible, he is probably wrong.'[19] In the current ferment of dire economic and political predictions, it's well to remember that practically nobody predicted the sudden fall of the Soviet Union. On the other hand, a legion of experts predicted that the Y2K Millennium Bug would cause computer systems to crash, planes to drop from the skies and bring untold chaos to the world.

In 1984 *The Economist* conducted an experiment asking a range of experts – former finance ministers, Oxford economics students, chairmen of multinational companies – as well as a group of London dustmen, to make a range of economic forecasts for the coming ten years. Ten years later, all the forecasts were found to be wildly off the mark, but the dustmen and the chairmen of multinational companies were the least in error.[20]

In his recent book, journalist and writer Dan Gardner trawled through a century of expert predictions.[21] He cites psychologist Philip Tetlock's famous study of predictions.[22] This involved experts from a range of disciplines – political science, economics, journalism – who regularly commented and advised governments and businesses on key trends. He asked 284 of them to make predictions about the future. He repeated the exercise many times over a period of years, thus allowing them to make short- and long-term predictions and also providing a very good sample of their predictive power. In all, he gathered well over 27,000 predictions.

The outcome showed that the experts' predictions were so far off the mark that they might as well have tossed a coin to come up with them. The unimpressive overall performance concealed a wide range in the experts' ability to make accurate predictions. What distinguished the star predictors was their thinking style. Tetlock named the successful predictors 'foxes' and the unsuccessful predictors 'hedgehogs', after an Ancient Greek poem by Archilochus which contrasts the 'fox who knows many things' with the hedgehog who 'knows one big thing'.

The 'hedgehog' experts knew or believed 'one big thing' and, no matter what the issue, their analysis was 'fitted' to that core idea. They shied away from uncertainty and complexity, clinging to their big idea with zeal and utter confidence. Most of us are familiar with 'hedgehogs' in the public and private realm. No matter what the problem, the answer goes back to their big idea ('Bring back religion' 'Back to basics' 'Cut welfare' 'Let the free hand of the market decide' 'Law and order').

The experts who did best were 'foxes'. They 'knew many things' because they made a habit of getting information from many sources, were open-minded and self-critical. They constantly questioned the validity of their conclusions, openly acknowledged when they were wrong, and adjusted their thinking. They acknowledged how difficult or even impossible it was to predict the future, and were much less confident in their predictions. The paradox was that their predictions were the most accurate.

Dan Gardner notes that because 'hedgehogs' have one big easily digestible idea that they present forcefully, they dominate public discourse – talk shows, panel discussions, newspaper columns and bestseller lists. When they occasionally get a prediction right, they get huge attention; when they are wrong (which is most of the time), this is ignored, since something *not* happening is not newsworthy.

Because 'foxes' offer more subtle, nuanced and less dramatic predictions, they get overlooked by the media – even though they are more likely to be right.

Gardner reserves his most damning indictments for economists, quoting IMF economist Prakash Loungani: 'The record of failure to predict recessions is virtually unblemished.'[23] That is not to say that, during times of stability, economists and other experts can't make reasonably accurate predictions by projecting current trends into the immediate future. But they are very poor at foreseeing change. 'Predicting the future by projecting the present is like driving with no hands,' says Gardner. 'It works while you are on a long stretch of straight road but even a gentle curve is trouble, and a sharp turn always ends in a flaming wreck.'[24]

And why?

Because experts are just as susceptible as the rest of us to the errors and biases that afflict thinking – being too anchored in the present, overestimating the likelihood of unusual events and their impact, and projecting current trends on to the future.

We are living in turbulent times and are awash with experts making gloomy predictions about even more terrible times ahead. Normally, most people feel mildly positive about the future, but it is understandable that many people are now fearful.

However, by understanding why our predictions are so often wrong, we can appreciate how many of those experts and commentators are just as fallible. In order to tackle our fears, and to actively work towards creating a better future, the challenge is to cultivate both some positive illusions and a spirit of optimism.

So, my final chapter is about the powerful and practical use of optimism in accompanying us on the road to flourishing.

# 23. In praise of optimism

Psychologists used to think that being in contact with reality was the hallmark of sound mental health. And, to some extent it is. Clearly, if you are seriously deluded about yourself and how the world works, it will create great difficulties. But it turns out that being a little removed from reality is no bad thing.

Shelley Taylor at the University of California, Los Angeles, has changed old assumptions about the optimal level of realism. Influenced by the emerging discoveries about the biases and errors in thinking, Taylor researched their implications for mental health and well-being. She discovered three types of thinking that are typical of most of us:

- a more favourable view of our strengths and talents than is strictly merited by the facts
- an exaggerated feeling of mastery and control over events, and
- an over-optimistic view of the future.

She called these types of thinking 'positive illusions' – to underscore the fact that, unlike mental biases and errors, which imply short-term mistakes in the way we think, these beliefs constitute a more general and enduring way of reacting. Moreover, she found that these illusions are beneficial in multiple ways, making us happier, more contented, more caring, and more productive and creative.[1]

Positive illusions are an example of our positivity bias in action, our attempt to offset the powerful negativity bias. While we respond to threat with immediate short-term mobilization, once we have responded and the crisis is over, our mild positivity bias reasserts itself. We try to minimize the negative by damping down and muting possible threats. Without that capacity, we would be too frightened and intimidated to carry on in life with the confidence and courage it requires.

So, rather than managing our lives in the manner of a scientist or an accountant – gathering information in a non-biased way, combining it in some logical and predictable fashion, and then reaching generally good, accurate conclusions – Taylor found that we gather information about ourselves and the world in a very incomplete way, taking shortcuts and making errors. And yet, the strategy seems to work – we manage to balance being relatively realistic when setting goals with being unrealistically positive when implementing them.[2]

In other words, we keep going.

## *The illusion of being 'above average'*

Like the residents of the fictional Lake Wobegon, most of us think of ourselves as 'above average' – as drivers, problem-solvers, lovers, parents, friends. This, of course, cannot be true – everybody can't be above average. But logic has little to do with it.

When given a list of positive and negative characteristics and asked how they apply to themselves, most people consider them and judiciously conclude that yes, the positive ones are definitely a better fit. Moreover, they regard their own positive traits as rare and distinctive ('I am lucky that I am exceptionally energetic, because I know a lot of people tire more easily') and their negative characteristics as pretty commonplace ('I admit I am impatient. But most people are – and, anyway, patience is overrated').

We also like to think we have made great strides towards something that is important to us ('I am way more open-minded now than I was before'), even when the evidence for improvement is thin on the ground. And just for good measure, we extend our generous assessments to groups that we belong to ('Well, the Lynches were always exceptionally go-getting' 'Can't beat engineers for logical thinking' 'The Irish are friendlier than other nationalities').

If there is any positive information regarding ourselves floating around, we process it rapidly and effectively and have no difficulty recalling it. Not so with negative information, which we tend to dispute – at least, in our own minds ('No matter what she says, I don't really believe I am that bad. Moreover, I am a very complex person, and she couldn't possibly understand me'). Because we are so affected by the negative, when reluctantly forced to accept mild negative feedback about our performance, we feel obliged to internally contest it. Our positive illusions come to the rescue like a house lawyer, arguing the finer points of the feedback or dismissing it as based on faulty evidence and therefore of no great consequence ('OK, I went over budget and may have got the figures wrong, but my great strength is big-picture thinking').

However, in the face of a more severe threat to our self-esteem this rescue is unlikely to be successful.

### *The illusion of control*

Our sense of being in control and the master of our fate is similarly unrealistic.

Numerous experiments show that in situations that are actually determined by chance, we still believe we can control the outcome. We remain stubbornly convinced that, if we personally throw the dice, we can influence how it falls. Invite us to a laboratory for a supposed study of 'learning ability', put us in front of the equivalent of a slot machine and ask us to 'learn' to win as much money as we can, and our illusion of control emerges with a vengeance. Even though the money comes out randomly, we take credit for any wins, believing that we have somehow become skilled at manipulating and controlling the machine. The illusion is boosted if the researcher gives us a chance 'to practise', or if we are put in with a group of other people trying to do the same, with the subtle suggestion that we are competing with each other.

### *Our over-optimistic view of the future*

Most of the time, in the absence of threat (real or imagined), most of us like to believe that things are generally getting better.

We reserve a particularly rosy future for ourselves. We rate our chances of liking the career we choose, doing well in life, and having a gifted child as better than most other people's. We are similarly confident that we are unlikely to have a car accident, be a victim of crime, have trouble finding a job, or get a variety of illnesses. So, our predictions for our future are a creative mix of what we hope, desire and believe will happen.

When confronted with accurate data about the probability of certain negative events arising, we cook the books – we readjust the probabilities in a biased way. When the real probability of the bad things happening is lower than we have guessed, we accept the good news and adjust our estimate downwards ('Oh, I only have a ten per cent chance of dying before I am sixty. Great!'). But when the real probability of something bad happening is higher than we guessed, we ignore or dispute the information ('Well, maybe a third of people eventually get cancer, but of course that is very unlikely to happen to me because . . .'). We either do not adjust our estimate of it happening to us, or we adjust it upwards by just a fraction.

Psychologist Tali Sharot examined what happens in our brains when we perform these mental manoeuvres. She found that our brains are highly selective. We track the 'good news' mismatches between our expectations and the statistical probabilities closely, but have scant regard for the 'bad news' mismatches. That is why we don't learn from experience ('OK, it has rained solidly for two weeks in August for the last three summers, but I think I heard somebody say on the radio that this year will be glorious . . .'). That's how it works for most of us – except for the poor pessimists, who remain relentlessly realistic and stay at home, while we set out for the west of Ireland in August, buoyantly optimistic for yet another year.

## *In praise of optimism*

These three positive illusions work in harmony with each other and, when combined, they have remarkably positive consequences. Clearly, they improve our mood – and, as we know, positive mood makes us better at solving problems, more open to new people and ideas, more likely to help and care for others, more motivated, productive and likely to persist in trying to achieve our goals despite obstacles and setbacks. Positive illusions also encourage us to set higher aspirations and to strive to achieve them. Most importantly, they work as self-fulfilling prophecies.

Of the three positive illusions, the benefits of optimism are most remarkable. Optimists feel happier and more contented with life and cope more effectively.[3] Optimism buffers us from the ordinary stresses of life and also from extreme stress.

For example, mothers who are more optimistic during pregnancy are less likely to get post-partum depression. Women undergoing the stress of fertility treatment do better if they are optimistic. Optimism also helps those caring for relatives suffering from cancer or Alzheimer's to cope with the stress – making them less liable to depression and health problems.

People who are more optimistic make better choices. Not only do they smoke less, but they are also more productive and work more hours per day. They expect to retire later, but they also make a habit of saving.

### *Optimists are healthier, cope better with illness and live longer*

Optimism keeps you healthier, and if you get sick – from *any* disease – it helps you deal more effectively with the illness and, in many cases, to survive longer.

These scientifically robust conclusions have emerged from a recent series of major long-term scientific studies involving large numbers of subjects, and including controls for other factors such as socio-economic status, smoking, drinking and exercise levels. Importantly, these studies have looked not just at the effects of optimism but also at the effects of pessimism and other negative feelings.[4]

One of these studies found that hopelessness not only puts people at a higher risk of heart disease, but it also hastens its progress – whereas optimism has the opposite effect.[5] And if you are already in poor health, a positive mood reduces your risk of dying earlier from your illness, particularly in the case of renal failure and immunodeficiency infections (although not from late-stage cancer).[6]

You might think that one of the few advantages of being a pessimist is that, since you expect the worst, you might be inclined to take care of your health. Not so. Among patients being treated for heart disease, optimists are more successful at lowering their levels of coronary risk by losing weight, eating healthily and taking more exercise. Optimistic HIV-positive gay men were more likely to engage in safe sex practices. On the other hand, pessimists smoke and drink more, engage in other self-defeating behaviours and die younger.[7]

The protective effects of optimism are particularly strong for cardiovascular disease. For example, the largest study yet to investigate whether optimism can reduce mortality from heart disease followed nearly 100,000 women over eight years.[8] It found that the most optimistic women suffered nearly a third fewer deaths due to heart disease than the women who were most pessimistic. Conversely, cynical hostility was associated with an increased risk of death from all causes, including cancer. These relationships held, irrespective of the women's socio-economic status, original health status and lifestyle habits.

Optimism and hostility may influence our bodies directly – most probably by slowing down or accelerating the course of disease processes such as arteriosclerosis – or the effect may be indirect. For example, the study referred to above showed that the optimistic women, even when they smoked, drank and took little exercise, compared to their more pessimistic counterparts coped with stress in healthier ways and built stronger social relationships – itself a buffer from disease.[9]

The effect of optimism on cancer is not as clear cut as it is with heart disease. Studies show that if you get cancer, an optimistic outlook helps you deal more effectively with the psychological impact, and to survive longer.[10] However, what is emerging from all the studies is that while optimism reduces your risk of getting cancer, that may not be enough; the absence of pessimism is just as important. (Recall that the positive and negative emotional systems are independent, and we are capable of feeling both at the same time.) Pessimism, whether it takes the form of hopelessness or cynical hostility, is a significant risk factor for cancer (as it is for heart disease). So, even if you can't bring yourself to be optimistic, it pays to contain and limit the negative.

For example, when it comes to the length of survival times among patients with advanced cancer, it matters more *not* to be pessimistic than to be optimistic. Those who react pessimistically, passively accepting their impending death, actually die sooner than those with a similar prognosis who react optimistically.[11]

So, the two principles of psychological flourishing – constantly and actively building the positive (in this case, optimism) and reducing and containing the negative (in this case, pessimism) – also apply to physical flourishing.

### *Optimism and economic success*

The renowned economist John Maynard Keynes believed that great waves of optimism and pessimism are what drive major economic fluctuations. He went so far as to say that the rational base for major investment decisions amounted to little, and sometimes nothing. Given the precariousness of such a knowledge base, he argued that decisions can only be taken as a result of what he called 'animal spirits' – of a spontaneous urge to act, to do something. He warned that, if these animal spirits are extinguished, and that spontaneous optimism falters, this leaves us overly fearful, with the result that enterprise and innovation falter – although these fears may have as shaky a basis as the exuberance of boom times.

So, while fixing our economic problems and dealing with our massive debts are a critical part of economic recovery, they will not be enough to resuscitate the economy. We also have to revive our 'animal spirits' and cultivate optimism.

Most ordinary people know that. For example, in periods of economic stability we may affect an air of cynicism and mock despair about the state of the country, while feeling privately buffered by optimism that we and our families will be OK. Our optimism makes us feel a bit special, and even exceptional. But, as Tali Sharot shows, the relationship between private and public optimism changes in times of great economic upheaval and our need for a spirit of public optimism and optimistic leadership grows exponentially. We need to feel that things will improve and the general recovery will bring us and everybody else up with it.[12]

We are right in our instincts. Multiple studies consistently identify a key characteristic of effective leadership as the ability to make people feel optimistic about the future and confident about *their* personal contribution to overcoming the challenges ahead. Optimism, far from being the opium of the masses, is critical for sustainable national economic success. This was the conclusion of David Landes, the emeritus professor of history and economics at Harvard. And he should know. In a work of extraordinary scholarship, he set out to discover what makes some countries economically successful and keeps others in poverty.[13]

He highlighted two key cultural determinants of economic success.

- Openness to science and technology – whether once the printing press or now the power of the silicon chip and the Internet.
- Optimism – giving citizens the energy to constantly invent and innovate, to set up new enterprises, and to pick themselves up, time and time again, in the wake of national setbacks and failures.

### *Optimism is a self-fulfilling prophecy*

Perhaps the greatest benefit of optimism is that it is a self-fulfilling prophecy. When we set optimistic expectations for ourselves, we make it more likely that we will make them a reality.

Consider the classic (and ethically dubious) experiment conducted in the 1960s in which teachers were given false information about some of their students. They were told that these students (who had, in fact, been selected at random) had received high scores on a new test of learning readiness and were on the cusp of rapid intellectual growth. Such were the positive expectations created by these 'results' that the teachers spent more time with these students, gave them more detailed feedback and more encouragement in class. By the end of the year, these students scored higher on IQ tests than children who had shown the same IQ scores at the beginning of the year but who were not part of the experiment.[14]

## *Why optimism is vital to positive human functioning*

Imagine that you are a parent and your two-year-old son comes up to you and says, 'Mum, Dad, do you think I will be out of nappies by Christmas?'

If you were to answer completely objectively, you might say, 'Yes, there is a good chance that you will be. But, on the other hand, many young children take until the age of three, and some boys are still not toilet trained by four.'

'So, what about preschool? Do you think I will like that?'

'Oh yes,' you say. 'You probably will like it. It's lots of fun and you will probably make new friends, but there is always the possibility that you will be socially excluded by the other children. You will also get a lot of childhood illnesses, and that will mean you staying home from preschool and Mum having to take time off work, which is a hassle.'

'What about big school, then?'

'Oh, big school is great,' you say. 'You will probably be very good in class because you are intelligent. And you will like the music and art lessons. But, on the other hand, you might be bullied. These things happen.'

'And being a teenager. How will that be?'

'Oh, that will bring lots more freedom. Lots of sports. But, of course, a lot of academic pressure, and the danger of getting in with a bad lot, and drinking too much, and so on. Going out on dates will be lots of fun, though – unless you discover that you are not very popular with the opposite sex for some reason.'

Well, what do you think your two-year-old would do with such a truthful account?

Leap into life with unbounded joy?

Or give up on the toilet training, and wish for a speedy return to the womb?

Of course, you would never say any of that.

Instead, what do you do?

You bring out your trusty positive illusions. Not only will he be out of nappies by Christmas, you tell your child, but preschool, big school and being a teenager will be sources of unalloyed enjoyment, stimulation and affirmation with not a problem in sight. As you paint a glorious picture of a perfect future, not only will your child's eyes light up with delight, you will make it more likely that that picture will become a reality. Encouraged and emboldened, your toddler may indeed be out of nappies by Christmas, and is much more likely to settle enthusiastically into preschool, be a good student at big school, and sail through adolescence with the minimum of crises and angst.

Considering how most parents instinctively present a golden picture of the future to their children gives us a clue about the adaptive function of the three positive illusions. They are there to protect us and help us to thrive.

But, what of the people who hold a 'balanced' view of themselves, who are conscious of their faults and weaknesses and don't exaggerate their strengths? They can readily recall negative information about themselves. They don't believe that they are 'better than average' and their view of themselves is no higher than other people's. They are realistic about how little control they have over many events in their lives. They realize that the future may bring bad as well as good things. These people could be fairly described as unrelentingly objective and realistic – and studies reveal them to be moderately depressed.

It would appear that in a world that is objectively full of threats and random acts of God, with a future that is uncertain and unknowable, our positive illusions not only buffer us against anxiety, stress and despondency, but they also give us the courage to go on. That is why we cling to them most tightly when we feel anxious and under threat, when conditions are uncertain and when something of great importance is at stake. Our illusions are the armour we put on to do battle with the 'slings and arrows of outrageous fortune'.

A dogged realist might say, 'That's all very well, but what if you are so full of positive illusions about yourself and the world that you are delusional? How much is too much?' Like most things in life, the answer is, 'Too much is too much.' Think of being in contact with reality as a continuum, with relentless adherence to objective reality at one extreme and being airily out of touch at the other. Neither extreme brings good outcomes. While it is good to have positive illusions, it is best to aim for having a *slightly* more positive view of yourself, a *slightly* stronger sense of control and mastery and a *moderately* optimistic view of the future than is strictly merited by the facts.

Indeed, moderate optimism is more beneficial than excessive optimism. Extreme optimists smoke more, save less and don't work as hard.[15] At a collective level, extreme optimism can go quickly off the rails, with each over-optimistic decision, while not too harmful in itself (say, a family paying a bit more than they had planned or could afford for a house during the boom), feeding off others in unintended ways. Add the phenomenon of 'group think', and self-interest among those making big decisions about credit supply, financial regulation and public policy. Well, we know where that got us.

What we must do is cultivate a realistic and sustainable optimism.

## *The dynamics of optimism*

While we don't inherit an optimism gene, our basic temperament influences how easy we find it to be optimistic. For example, people high in extroversion are more likely to be optimists, and those high in neuroticism find it correspondingly harder.[16]

Optimism is more than a disposition; it is also a mode of thinking. Renowned psychologist Martin Seligman's work has shown that explanatory style is a key differentiator between optimists and pessimists, particularly when it comes to explaining setbacks and failure.[17]

Optimists explain failure in a characteristic way, seeing setbacks as temporary ('OK, I didn't pass the exam this time, but I will next time'), due to specific conditions ('I didn't study enough' 'I stayed up too late the night before, revising') over which they have some control ('I will approach studying differently next time'). This style of thinking spurs them on to try again, to try harder, and to persevere. Hardly surprising, then, that optimism is often a better predictor of individual success than ability.

Pessimists do the opposite. They explain setbacks as permanent ('Well, that's it: I failed my first-year exams and I won't ever qualify'), internal ('I am hopeless at exams') and over which they have little control ('There's nothing I can do'). This pessimistic explanatory style seems to paralyse and constrict people, making them less productive and creative, and less motivated and active in pursuit of their goals.

Faced with a challenge or setback, optimists spontaneously recall past successes and moments of achievement. This fortifies them, and encourages them to persist and to come up with solutions. Having initiated a course of action, they also spontaneously provide themselves with positive feedback ('I'm getting there' 'One more thing done' 'This is easier than I thought') which, in turn, produces better performance and a greater likelihood of achieving their goal.

Similarly, natural optimists are skilled at handling threat. They recognize the threat but they don't let it leak into every aspect of their thinking. If they feel anxious or overwhelmed, they actively seek out disconfirming evidence of their worst fantasies. Their strategy is to build themselves up, while simultaneously scaling down the threat to get it into manageable proportions. Tellingly, when the situation is uncertain or ambiguous (the most common situation in life), they interpret new information positively – or, at least, give it the benefit of the doubt.

These ways of thinking have the effect of damping down disruptive negative feelings, liberating ingenuity and problem-solving, and motivating confident action.

Faced with uncertainty, pessimists engage in exactly the opposite strategies. They inflate the threat and deflate themselves. They perceive a setback as permanent, due to some fundamental flaw in their make-up – they recall all the other examples of this weakness – and over which they can exercise little control. They compound the situation by generalizing the failure far beyond the context in which it originated ('I lost my job. That means I'm a failure as a husband and father').

This is an example of how optimists' and pessimists' brains process information in different ways.[18] The pessimist's brain pays more attention to negative information. Not only does it have a hyperactive amygdala alert to every possible threat, but there is reduced connectivity between the amygdala and that part of the higher brain that modulates and soothes stress signals. In contrast, the optimist's brain pays more attention to positive information, and there is enhanced connectivity between the higher brain and the amygdala.

The good news is that optimism can be learned. According to Seligman, the skill of disputing negative thinking is at the heart of 'learned optimism'. People with a tendency to pessimism don't do this internal disputing automatically and must learn how to do it. Indeed, learning this skill halves the incidence of depression.[19]

So, we must become like skilled barristers – able to marshal the evidence in defence of a positive outlook, and ferocious at disputing debilitating self-doubt and despondency.

## *The way forward*

### *Learn to be realistically optimistic*

In order to flourish, we must build and sustain an enabling but realistic optimism. Sandra Schneider at the University of South Florida defines being realistically optimistic as maintaining a positive outlook *in the absence of very definite evidence to the contrary*.[20] This last part is crucial, and it depends on remaining open to disconfirming evidence.

We are eternally susceptible to the confirmation bias, considering only the evidence that suits our point of view or narrow self-interest. This is of no great consequence when we are deciding on ordinary day-to-day issues. But it can be fatal when we are contemplating important decisions that involve our own and others' welfare.

Being realistically optimistic means not just being open to negative feedback, but actually soliciting it. Asking 'awkward' questions is always a good strategy, as is including 'awkward' people in your circle of influence. Consult your friends and colleagues with a more pessimistic frame of mind or an opposing viewpoint. This does not mean you have to take their advice. But it does mean that you have to consider it.

In other words, follow the advice in Chapter 22 and be a fox, not a hedgehog.

Realistic optimism means routinely emphasizing possible opportunities and working towards good outcomes *with no guarantee* that these will occur, especially without an effort. That, in turn, means cultivating hope and confidence, and an appetite for challenge.

Some people like to practise 'defensive pessimism' – focusing on the possibility of failure. If you use defensive pessimism to help you deal with a challenge, it will not affect your performance because this strategy still rests on the belief that you will achieve your goal.[21]

But, there is a caveat.

Sometimes we persuade ourselves that if we imagine and expect the worst, this will make it easier to deal with if it happens. It won't. Dread just makes things worse. And the longer we dread something, the worse its impact when it happens.[22]

*Look for what is going right – even when things are going wrong*

As you now know, building the positive is not a passive activity; we have to actively search for what is going right, especially when things are going wrong. We have to build the habit of savouring good things in the moment and being grateful for them. When we are coping with crisis, such practices require mental discipline, as they may seem a distraction from the 'real' work of managing the crisis. But how the real work is handled, and the resources we can mobilize to face a challenge, will be determined in large part by the level of optimism that we draw on.

We also need to learn to drop the debilitating habit of 'social comparisons' – comparing ourselves to people we consider are doing better or worse than us in some respect. While comparing ourselves favourably to others may give us short-term satisfaction, in the long term it promotes an insecure competitiveness.

*Practise looking forward to good things*

When we look forward to an event, we activate the part of our brain that responds to pleasure.[23] The more vividly we imagine it, or the closer to the anticipated event we are, the greater the pleasure. Often these moments of anticipation are as intensely pleasurable as – and sometimes even more pleasurable than – the event itself.

This is what optimists do automatically. Equally, they find it hard to imagine the specifics of possible bad events – these remain mercifully blurry and remote. So, we need to stop giving oxygen to lurid fantasies.

*Give yourself and other people the benefit of the doubt*

Again, this is not a passive but an active habit.

When you embark on anything, you have to consciously expand the range of outcomes that can be defined as positive. If you define the possible positive outcomes too narrowly, and these outcomes fail to materialize, it is hard to stay positive. However, if you include the possibility of learning something useful about yourself and others, of meeting people and having experiences you would otherwise not have had, it is much easier to stay positive and optimistic. Virtually everything we do, whether it works out or not, lends itself to these positive outcomes. The idea is not to deny reality or pretend that bad things are good. Rather, as

Schneider says, it is to search and find 'a perspective that is simultaneously truthful and favourable'.[24]

### *Embrace your fate and choose your future*

One of the quirks in our thinking is that once we choose something, it immediately increases in value for us.

Suppose, as part of a psychological experiment, you are told to imagine going on holiday and asked to rate how much you think you will enjoy different destinations. Imagine you end up saying that two destinations are equally appealing – say, Paris and Rio – and then the researcher pushes you to make a further choice and plump for one of them, so you pick Rio. While you are making those two choices, your brain is scanned each time. Once you make the second choice and finally pick Rio, your brain response will now be more positive for Rio and less positive for Paris than it was the first time around (when they were equally appealing). This rise in positivity once you commit yourself to something was discovered by Sharot in exactly such an experiment.[25]

The same thing happens when the experiment is set up as a choice between negatives. Having being asked to 'choose' between a range of unpleasant afflictions – say, between asthma and migraine – whichever one we end up selecting then becomes the condition we rate as least unpleasant. In other words, when we choose to accept that whatever has happened cannot be changed, it becomes, as Daniel Gilbert puts it, 'inescapably, inevitably and irrevocably ours'.[26] We become committed owners of our fate, and this immediately triggers our psychological immune system. This has a discernible impact on our brains.

In Sharot's experiment, while the prospect of suffering various afflictions has no detectable influence on brain activity the first time subjects' brains are scanned, once they have made a choice, there is increased activity in the connectivity between the amygdala and the higher brain – which allows us to damp down negative overreaction. This is precisely the pattern of activity that accompanies optimistic thinking.

In other words, our incredible ability to adapt to anything that happens, and our capacity to be optimistic, are tightly wired together in the brain. If, however, there is any escape from our fate – be that fate good or bad – we will divert a lot of effort into investigating the alternatives or ruminating about which way to turn. Paradoxically, this makes us less satisfied with our lot.

In one of Gilbert's experiments, students on a photography course were given the choice of keeping one of their two best photographs. Some were told their choice was final, but others were given the option of changing their minds later. When followed up a few days later, the students who had the option of returning their chosen photo liked it less than the students who had had to make an irrevocable choice.

Intuitively, we believe that the freedom to change our minds will make us happier than having to commit ourselves to our choices. This may work well when we are considering buying a sofa. But, when it comes to many of the big decisions in life, our intuition is wrong.[27]

### *Remind yourself of your experiences of managing change*

We need to keep reminding ourselves of our extraordinary capacity to adapt to change. Because we don't generally like change, we underestimate how often it happens and smooth it out of our life narrative, which gives us the illusion of stability. So, when confronted by change again, we are jolted.

Think back over your own life – or, better still, draw a 'lifeline' across a page, with your birth at one end and your death at the other end.

Now, mark out the different stages in your life, each with their high points, low points and transition points. Soon, you will run out of space. Because you will remember that your life was also changed by the high points, low points, transition points and changes in the lives of your family, friends and colleagues. As it also was by the great economic and social changes that have happened during your lifetime. At each point, there was uncertainty. You did not, and could not, know for sure what the future held in store.

Yet, you went on.

You girded your loins and weathered the changes.

And here you are, still standing.

### *Think carefully about what you may regret in your life*

We make a lot of our decisions on the basis of trying to avoid regret. We especially fear that we will regret things if we later find out that there were better alternatives. We are more afraid of accepting bad advice than rejecting good advice, more afraid of making a slightly risky bad choice than opting for the conventional choice.

Ask people to list the things they most regret in the past year or so and they mention 'acts of commission' – doing things that they wished they hadn't. You can probably think of your own list: eating too much at Christmas; that last unwise glass of wine; getting into a foolish argument with a colleague at work; buying the ten-year-old sports car that costs as much to run as a fleet of taxis and spends more time being repaired than on the road; losing your temper with your children; agreeing to join a committee that is now consuming far more time than you expected; and, the all-time favourite, taking on way too many commitments.

But, with a little time to reflect, and looking back on our lives in a more considered way, the things we most regret tend not to be 'acts of commission' but 'acts of omission' – the things we *could* have done but didn't.

We didn't take the good advice to stay in school, or go back to college to get that qualification we always wanted.

We baulked at taking the chance to start our own business, or to change jobs.

We didn't take the time to tell particular people how much we loved them, or how much they had helped us in our lives.

We regret not spending more time with our families and friends, and not relishing to the full the time we did spend with them.

Like many parents, I suspect, when my children were young, I never thought that these glorious years of Transformers and Barbie dolls, of going to amusement parks and on family holidays by the sea, would pass as quickly as they did. But, correspondingly, I have no regrets that we regularly stretched our finances to breaking point to pay for great holidays together as a family every summer.

Why do we regret failure to act more than foolish action?

Because the one reliable consolation in having acted foolishly is that we probably learned something valuable. But what lesson is there in *not* doing something, besides the knowledge that we should have acted?

Fundamentally, we are mistaken about what we will regret, says Gilbert; we do not realize that 'our psychological immune systems can rationalize an excess of courage more easily than an excess of cowardice, we hedge our bets when we should blunder forward'.[28]

The final step to a flourishing life is to cultivate that 'excess of courage' and nurture it with an unrelenting optimism.

I leave the last word to David Landes.[29]

> In this world the optimists have it, not because they are always right, but because they are positive. Even when wrong they are positive, and that is

the way of achievement, correction, improvement and success. Educated eyes-open optimism pays; pessimism can only offer the empty consolation of being right.

The one lesson that emerges is the need to keep trying. No miracles. No perfection. No millennium. No apocalypse. We must cultivate a sceptical faith, avoid dogma, listen and watch well, try to clarify and define ends, the better to choose means.

# Acknowledgements

A book can be a long time in the making. Many people gave me crucial practical, moral and intellectual support during the writing process. If I had the space I would name all of them.

I am greatly indebted to the people who contributed their stories and insights for this book – some named, and others who preferred to remain anonymous. They represent just a small sample of the much larger group of men and women with whom I work regularly and who are my best teachers: Anne Kelleher, Philip Moynagh, Jim O'Hara, Joe Foley, Lucy Dodd, Martin Devilly, Colm Harmon, Tony O'Shea, Bernard Collins, Conn Murray – and many more. I also thank the Psychological Society of Ireland who hosted a public seminar that I held on 'Flourishing under Fire'.

My sincere thanks to my literary agent, Marianne Gunn-O'Connor. From the very first, Marianne has been a vital source of astute, practical advice on every aspect of the project. She offered a very special kind of commitment to this book. Caroline Walsh, Literary Editor of the *Irish Times*, offered generous and unreserved support, as always. Her belief that this book would one day become a reality was often stronger than my own.

The terrific team in Penguin Ireland – Michael McLoughlin, Cliona Lewis and Patricia McVeigh – were always quick and eager to help. Shân Morley Jones's great skill as copy editor left me little work to do in the final stages. Most of all, I was fortunate to work with Patricia Deevy, Editorial Director of Penguin Ireland. Her editorial intelligence, foresight, discretion and determination were crucial to the successful completion of the book and to its final shape.

I want to thank my great friends who encouraged and cheered me on and were always ready to listen to my ideas (and put me right), in particular Gary Joyce, Anne Connolly, Geraldine and Tony O'Daly, Eamon Drea, Marion Creeley, Rita McCormack, Brian Patterson and Ellen McLaughlin. Thanks also go to Barbara Annis, Tania Banotti, Donal de Buitléir, Caroline Bowden, Steve Cheslett, Frances Fitzgerald, Jeannie Grant, Frank Heslin, Mary Higgins, Alice Hockenbury, Maggie Kavalaris,

Helen Keogh, Robin Leeds, Augusta McCabe, Caroline McCamley, Mick McDonagh, Ciarán McGahon, Neena Mehta, Paul Monaghan, Billy Murphy, Cathy O'Brien, Tess O'Connell, Nuala O'Farrell, Paul Quilligan, Pat Quinn, Kevin Rafter, Orlaith Rafter, Grace Smith, Robin Simpson, Mary Stuart and Don Thornhill.

Finally, warmest thanks to the constants in my life: my mother Madge, my brother John and his family, my Barry cousins and Maura Harris. Most of all, thanks to my husband John and children Elly and Jack, who time and again listened with intelligence (and saintly patience) as I tried out my ideas – offering suggestions, reading drafts and providing moral support.

No greater love.

# Notes

## *Part one: What is flourishing?*

### *1. Your instinct to be your best self*

1 Aristotle. Trans. Terence Irwin. 1999. *Nichomachean Ethics*. Second edition. Indianapolis, IN: Hackett Publishing Company, Inc.

2 What I have called connectivity, autonomy and using your valued competencies bear a strong resemblance to what Richard Ryan and Edward Deci of the University of Rochester have identified as the three basic psychological needs essential for self-determination and well-being. See Ryan, R. M. & Deci, E. L. 2000. 'Self-determination theory and the facilitation of intrinsic motivation, social development, and well-being'. *American Psychologist*, 55, 68–78. See also Roberts, L. M., Spreitzer, G., Dutton, J., Quinn, R., Heaphy, E. & Barker, B. 2005. 'How to play to your strengths'. *Harvard Business Review*, Jan, 75–80.

3 Frankl, V. E. 1959/2006. *Man's Search for Meaning*. Boston, MA: Beacon Press, p. 77.

4 See Goleman, D., Boyatzis, R. & McKee, A. 2001 'Primal leadership: The hidden driver of great performance'. *Harvard Business Review*, Dec, 43–51.

5 Waterman, A. S. 1993. 'Two conceptions of happiness: Contrasts of personal expressiveness (eudaimonia) and hedonic enjoyment'. *Journal of Personality and Social Psychology*, 64 (4), 678–91.

6 Quoted in Chatterjee, D. 2003. 'The leadership connection: How relationships renew reality'. *Compass: A Journal of Leadership*. Centre for Public Leadership. Kennedy School, Harvard University, pp. 9–10.

7 Baltes, P. B., Glück, J. & Kunzmann, U. 2005. 'Wisdom: Its structure and function in regulating successful life span development'. In C. R. Snyder & S. J. Lopez (eds). *Handbook of Positive Psychology*. Oxford: OUP, p. 331.

8 For a persuasive and historical account see McMahon, D. 2006. *The Pursuit of Happiness: A History from the Greeks to the Present*. London: Allen Lane.

9 See Beck, U. & Beck-Gernsheim, E. 2001. *Individualization: Institutionalized Individualism and its Social and Political Consequences*. London: Sage Publications.

10 Goleman, D. 1995. *Emotional Intelligence*. New York, NY: Bantam Books.

11 Goleman, D. 1998. *Working with Emotional Intelligence*. New York, NY: Bantam Books.
12 Ibid.
13 Ibid.
14 See Cameron, K. S., Dutton, J. E. & Quinn, R. E. 2003. *Positive Organizational Scholarship*. San Francisco, CA: Berrett-Koehler.
15 Cameron, K. S., Bright, D. & Caza, A. 2004. 'Exploring the relationships between organizational virtuousness and performance'. *American Behavioral Scientist*, 47 (6), 766–90.
16 Kanov, J. M. 2004. 'Compassion in organizational life'. *American Behavioral Scientist*, 47 (6), 808–27.
17 Cameron, K. S. & Caza, A. 2004. 'Introduction: Contributions to the discipline of positive organizational scholarship'. *American Behavioral Scientist*, 47 (6), 731–9.
18 Cameron et al, *Positive Organizational Scholarship*.
19 Buckingham, M. 2005. 'What great managers do'. *Harvard Business Review*, March, 72.
20 See (1) Keyes, C. L. M., Schmotkin, D. & Ryff, C. D. 2002. 'Optimizing well-being: The empirical encounter of two traditions'. *Journal of Personality and Social Psychology*, 82 (6), 1007–22. (2) Keyes, C. L. M. 2002. 'The mental health continuum: From languishing to flourishing in life'. *Journal of Health and Social Behaviour*, 43 (2), 207–22. (3) Keyes, C. L. M. & Lopez, S. J. 2005. 'Towards a science of mental health: Positive directions in diagnosis and intervention'. In C. R. Snyder & S. J. Lopez (eds). *Handbook of Positive Psychology*. Oxford: OUP, pp. 45–59.

## 2. *The magic ratio of positive to negative for a flourishing life*

1 Gottman, J. M. 1994. *What Predicts Divorce? The Relationship Between Marital Processes and Marital Outcomes*. Hillsdale, NJ: Lawrence Erlbaum Associates.
2 Gottman used a complex coding system based on the work of several psychologists, including Paul Ekman's system which can reliably 'read' the human face and can link facial expressions to underlying emotions. See Ekman, P. & Friesen, W. V. 1978. *Facial Action Coding System*. Palo Alto, CA: Consulting Psychologists Press.
3 Gottman ensured that independent sets of coders examined different parts of the data gathered from the couples (verbal, non-verbal and physiological). This prevented the coders developing a preconception or prejudice on the basis of one set of data, and carrying it over to the next. For example, if on

the basis of coding verbal data, a coder formed an impression that a couple were very happy or unhappy, there is a danger that they might carry over this perception to the non-verbal interactions they had to code, that they would interpret them in a way that fitted the view they had already formed.

4 Gottman, *What Predicts Divorce?*, p. 334.

5 See Gottman, J. M. 1998. 'Psychology and the study of marital processes'. *Annual Review of Psychology*, 49, 169–97.

6 Ibid., p. 185.

7 Fredrickson, B. & Losada, M. 2005. M. 'Positive affect and the complex dynamics of human flourishing'. *American Psychologist*, 60 (7), 678–86.

8 Losada, M. 1999. 'The complex dynamics of high performance teams'. *Mathematical and Computer Modelling*, 30 (9-10), 179–92.

9 Fredrickson, B. 2009. *Positivity*. New York, NY: Crown Publishers.

10 Lorenz, E. N. 1993. *The Essence of Chaos*. Seattle, WA: University of Washington Press.

11 Fredrickson and Losada, 'Positive affect'. See also Fredrickson, *Positivity*.

12 Schwartz, R. M., Reynolds, C. F., Thase, M. E., Frank, E., Fasiczka, A. L. & Haaga, D. A. 2002. 'Optimal and normal affect balance in psychotherapy of major depression: Evaluation of the balanced states of mind model'. *Behavioural and Cognitive Psychotherapy*, 30 (4), 439–50.

## *3. Understanding how emotions work*

1 For a more detailed account see (1) Pinker, S. 1997. *How the Mind Works*. New York, NY: Norton. (Paperback edition 1998. London: Penguin.) (2) Goleman, D. 1995. *Emotional Intelligence*. New York, NY: Bantam Books.

2 Philosophers and scientists have spent many centuries trying to distinguish the brain from the mind and I can't do justice to their deliberations here. This is the simplest and quickest of guides. As neuroscientist John Cacioppo points out, everything we feel, think and do, is organized by our central nervous system – the brain, spinal cord and all the associated neural circuitry. But the brain does lots of things, including regulating basic bodily functions like temperature and metabolism. Cognitive psychologist Steven Pinker says that the special status of the brain comes from the *special* thing the brain does – the capacity to process all the information that constantly bombards us from the world outside us and from inside ourselves. That capacity is what allows us to make sense of what we see and hear and allows us to think, feel, choose and act. That capacity we call our 'mind' or our 'consciousness'. So the mind is not the brain, but the special thing the brain does.

3 Once, neuroscientists could only study the brain after a post-mortem. Now, the development of brain imaging techniques reveals the brain as it works, allowing us to observe what happens when somebody feels an emotion, or thinks a thought, or performs an action.
4 For a review of this research see Pinker, *How the Mind Works*.
5 See Siegel, D. J. 2007. *The Mindful Brain*. New York, NY: Norton.
6 Pinker, *How the Mind Works*. Penguin paperback edition, p. 370.
7 Goleman, *Emotional Intelligence*.
8 LeDoux, J. E. 1996. *The Emotional Brain: The Mysterious Underpinnings of Emotional Life*. New York, NY: Simon & Schuster, Inc. See also (1) LeDoux, J. E. 1992. 'Emotion and the limbic system concept'. *Concepts in Neuroscience*, 2, 169–99. (2) LeDoux, J. E. 1993. 'Emotional memory systems in the brain'. *Behavioural Brain Research*, 58 (1-2), 69–79.
9 Goleman, *Emotional Intelligence*, p. 25.
10 LeDoux, *The Emotional Brain*, p. 25.
11 Fredrickson, B. 2009. *Positivity*. New York, NY: Crown Publishers.
12 Of course, the negative and positive systems in the brain and central nervous system are extremely complex. The amygdala and a particular part of the midbrain (the nucleus accumbens) represent the critical connection points, the wellsprings, in these systems – but positive approach reactions and negative avoidance reactions can be activated in many different parts of our central nervous system. For discussion see Cacioppo, J. T., Gardner, W. L. & Berntson, G. G. 1999. 'The affect system has parallel and integrative processing components: Form follows function'. *Journal of Personality and Social Psychology*, 76 (5), 839–55.
13 Taylor, S. E. 2002. *The Tending Instinct*. New York, NY: Henry Holt.
14 See Isen, A. M. 2005. 'A role for neuropsychology in understanding the facilitating influence of positive affect on social behaviour and cognitive processes'. In C. R. Snyder & S. J. Lopez (eds). *Handbook of Positive Psychology*. Oxford: OUP, pp. 528–40.
15 See Fredrickson, B. L. 2001. 'The role of positive emotions in positive psychology: The broaden-and-build theory of positive emotions'. *American Psychologist*, 56, 218–26.
16 This rule was suggested by Nancy Kline, author of *Time to Think*, published in 1999 by Ward Lock, London.
17 See (1) Isen, A. M. & Geva, N. 1987. 'The influence of positive affect on acceptable level of risk: The person with a large canoe has a large worry'. *Organisational Behavior and Human Decision Processes*, 39, 145–54. (2) Isen, A. M., Rosenzweig, A. S. & Young, M. J. 1991. 'The influence of positive

affect on clinical problem-solving'. *Medical Decision Making*, 11, 221–27. (3) Carnevale, P. J. D. & Isen, A. M. 1986. 'The influence of positive affect and visual access on the discovery of integrative solutions in bilateral negotiations'. *Organizational Behavior and Human Decision Processes*, 37, 1-13.

18 Isen et al, 'The influence of positive affect on clinical problem-solving'.

19 Estrada, C. A., Isen, A. M. & Young, M. J. 1994. 'Positive affect improves creative problem solving and influences reported source of practice in physicians'. *Motivation and Emotion*, 18 (4), 285–99.

20 Carnevale, P. J. D. & Isen, A. M. 1986. 'The influence of positive affect and visual access on the discovery of integrative solutions in bilateral negotiations'. *Organizational Behavior and Human Decision Processes*, 37, 1–13.

21 Fredrickson, B. L., Mancuso, R. A., Branigan, C. & Tugade, M .M. 2000. 'The undoing effect of positive emotions'. *Motivation and Emotion*, 24, 237–58.

22 Rosenberg, E. L., Ekman, P., Jiang, W., Babyak, M., Coleman, E., Hanson, M., O'Connor, C., Waugh, R. & Blumenthal, J. A. 2001. 'Linkages between facial expressions of anger and transient myocardial ischemia in men with coronary artery disease'. *Emotion*, 1, 107 15.

## *4. Why negative trumps positive*

1 Miltner, W. H. R., Braun, C. H. & Coles, M. G. H. 1997. 'Event-related brain potentials following incorrect feedback in a time-estimation task: Evidence for a "generic" neural system for error detection'. *Journal of Cognitive Neuroscience*, 9, 788–98.

2 Taylor, S. E. 1991. 'Asymmetrical effects of positive and negative events: The mobilization–minimization hypothesis'. *Psychological Bulletin*, 110 (1), 67–85.

3 Cited in Goleman, D. 1995. *Emotional Intelligence*, New York, NY: Bantam Books, p. 22.

4 Bowlby, J. 1969. *Attachment and Loss: Volume 1. Attachment*. London: Hogarth Press.

5 Baumeister, R. F., Bratslavsky, E., Finkenauer, C. & Vohs, K. D. 2001. 'Bad is stronger than good'. *Review of General Psychology*, 5 (4), 323–70.

6 Rozin, P. & Royzman, E. B. 2001. 'Negativity bias, negativity dominance, and contagion'. *Personality and Social Psychology Review*, 5 (4), 296–320.

7 The research that I will describe in this chapter is a summary of the many hundreds of studies described in the review articles by (1) Taylor, 'Asymmetrical effects of positive and negative events'. (2) Baumeister et al, 'Bad is stronger than good'. (3) Rozin and Royzman, 'Negativity bias, negativity dominance, and contagion. (4) Vaish, A., Grossman, T. & Woodward, A.

2008. 'Not all emotions are created equal: The negativity bias in social-emotional development'. *Psychological Bulletin*, 134 (3), 383–403.

8 Klinger, E., Barda, S. G. & Maxeiner, M. E. 1980. 'Motivational correlates of thought content frequency and commitment'. *Journal of Personality and Social Psychology*, 39 (6), 1222–37.

9 Taylor, 'Asymmetrical effects of positive and negative events'.

10 See (1) Averill, J. R. 1980. 'On the paucity of positive emotions'. In K. Blankstein, P. Pliner & J. Polivy (eds). *Advances in the Study of Communication and Affect. Volume 6. Assessment and Modification of Emotional Behavior*. New York, NY: Plenum, p. 745. (2) Van Goozen, S. & Frijda, N. H. 1993. 'Emotion words used in six European countries'. *European Journal of Social Psychology*, 23, 89–95.

11 Finkenauer, C. & Rime, B. 1998. 'Socially shared emotional experiences vs. emotional experiences kept secret: Differential characteristics and consequences'. *Journal of Social and Clinical Psychology*, 17, 295–318.

12 Vaish et al, 'Not all emotions are created equal'.

13 Hertenstein, M. J. & Campos, J. J. 2001. 'The retention effect of an adult's emotional displays on infant behaviour'. *Child Development*, 75, 595–613.

14 Sorce, J. F., Emde, R. N., Campos, J. J. & Klinnert, M. D. 1985. 'Maternal emotional signalling: Its effects on the visual cliff behaviour of 1-year-olds'. *Developmental Psychology*, 21, 195–200.

15 For a review of this research see Vaish et al, 'Not all emotions are created equal'.

16 Ogilvie, D. M. 1987. 'The undesired self: A neglected variable in personality research'. *Journal of Personality and Social Psychology*, 52 (2), 379–85.

17 Tice, D. M. 1991. 'Esteem protection or enhancement? Self-handicapping motives and attributions differ by trait self-esteem'. *Journal of Personality and Social Psychology*, 60 (5), 711–25.

18 See Huston, T. L. & Vangelisti, A. L. 1991. 'Socioemotional behaviour and satisfaction in marital relationships: A longitudinal study'. *Journal of Personality and Social Psychology*, 61 (5), 721–33.

19 Weiss, R. L., Hops, H. & Patterson, G. R. 1973. 'A framework for conceptualising marital conflict: A technology for altering it, some data for evaluating it'. In L. A. Hamerlynck, L. C. Handy & E. J. Mash (eds). *Behavior Change: Methodology, Concepts and Practice*. Champaign, IL: Research Press, pp. 237–58.

20 Baumeister et al, 'Bad is stronger than good', p. 329.

21 See, for example, Vonokur, A. D. & van Ryn, M. 1993. 'Social support and undermining in close relationships: Their independent effects on the mental health of unemployed persons'. *Journal of Personality and Social Psychology*, 65 (2), 350–59.

22 Cameron, K. S., Dutton, J. E., Quinn, R. E. & Wrzesniewksi, A. 2003. 'Developing a discipline of positive organizational psychology'. In K. S. Cameron, J. E. Dutton & R. E. Quinn (eds). 2003. *Positive Organizational Scholarship*. San Francisco, CA: Berrett-Koehler, pp. 12–13.

23 Kramer, R. M. 1999. 'Trust and distrust in organisations: Emerging perspectives, enduring questions'. *Annual Review of Psychology*, 50, 569–89.

24 Ibid., p. 587.

25 Bolster, B. I. & Springbett, B. M. 1961. 'The reaction of interviewers to favourable and unfavourable information'. *Journal of Applied Psychology*, 45, 97–103.

26 See (1) Kahneman, D. & Tversky, A. 1979. 'Prospect theory: An analysis of decisions under risk'. *Econometrica*, 47, 263–91. (2) Tversky, A. & Kahneman, D. 1991. 'Loss aversion in riskless choice: A reference dependent model'. *The Quarterly Journal of Economics*, 106, 1039–61.

27 See Gilbert, D. 2006. *Stumbling on Happiness*. London: Harper Press.

28 Loewenstein, G. F. & Prelac, D. 1993. 'Preferences for sequences of outcomes'. *Psychological Review*, 100, 91–108.

29 For a review see Vaish et al, 'Not all emotions are created equal'.

30 Matlin, M. W. & Stang, D. J. 1978. *The Pollyanna Principle: Selectivity in Language, Memory and Thought*. Cambridge, MA: Schenkman Publishing Co.

## 5. *Knowing who you really are*

1 James, W. 1890. *The Principles of Psychology. Volume 1*. Cambridge, MA: Harvard University Press.

2 Assagioli, R. 1965/1999. *Psychosynthesis: A Manual of Principles and Techniques*. London: Aquarian/Thorsons. Note: There have been many developments in neuroscience and in all areas of psychology since the 1960s, when Assagioli developed his model, and I have included them in my description.

3 Lawrence, P. R. & Nohria, N. 2002. *Driven: How Human Nature Shapes Our Choices*. San Francisco, CA: Jossey-Bass.

4 See Thomas, A., Chess, S., Birch, H. G. et al. 1963. *Behavioral Individuality in Early Childhood*. New York, NY: New York University Press.

5 LeDoux, J. 1993. 'Emotional memory systems in the brain'. *Behavioural Brain Research*, 58 (1-2), 69–79.

6 Cited in Goleman, D. 1995. *Emotional Intelligence*. New York, NY: Bantam Books, p. 22.

7 Bowlby, J. 1969. *Attachment and Loss: Volume 1. Attachment*. London: Hogarth Press.

8 Collins, W. A., McCoy, E. E., Steinberg, L., Hetherington, E. M. & Bernstein, M. H. 2000. 'Contemporary research and parenting: The case for nature and nurture'. *American Psychologist*, 55 (2), 218–32.
9 For an extended discussion and detailed references see Peterson, C. 2006. *A Primer in Positive Psychology*. New York, NY. Oxford University Press, Inc.
10 Gardner, H. 1983. *Frames of Mind: The Theory of Multiple Intelligences*. New York, NY: Basic Books.
11 Bandura, A. 1982. 'Self-efficacy mechanism in human agency'. *American Psychologist*, 37 (2), 122–47.
12 The spiritual aspect of religious belief is outside the scope of this discussion. My point is that psychological experiences can provide an arena within which individuals can express their spiritual needs or desires, and can be the preferred starting point for spiritual development for many people.
13 See (1) Peterson, C. & Seligman, M. 2004. *Character Strengths and Virtues*. New York, NY: American Psychological Association and Oxford University Press, Inc. (2) Buckingham, M. & Clifton, D. O. 2001. *Now, Discover Your Strengths*. New York, NY: The Free Press.
14 Main, M., Kaplan, N. & Cassidy, J. 1985. 'Security in infancy, childhood, and adulthood: A move to the level of representation'. In I. Bretherton & E. Waters (eds). 'Growing points of attachment theory and research'. *Monographs of the Society for Research in Child Development*, 50 (1-2, serial no. 209), 66–104.
15 Maslow, A. H. 1964. *Religions, Values and Peak Experiences*. New York, NY: Penguin Books.
16 Heaney, S. Commencement Address, University of Pennsylvania, 22 May 2000. *The Penn Current*. University of Pennsylvania, 1 June 2000.
17 Ibid.

## *Part two: Ten strategies to nurture a flourishing life*

### *6. How happiness helps you flourish*

1 Ryan, R. M. & Deci, E. L. 2001. 'On happiness and human potentials: A review of research on hedonic and eudaimonic well-being'. *Annual Review of Psychology*, 52, 141–66.
2 Lyubomirsky, S., King, L. & Diener, E. 2005. 'The benefits of frequent positive affect: Does happiness lead to success?' *Psychological Bulletin*, 131 (6), 803–55.

3 The following sections summarize the results of the studies included in this review. I will include a few specific references. Any reader interested in other specific findings will be able to find further details in the review article.

4 Cohen, S., Doyle, W. J., Turner, R. B., Alper, C. M. & Skoner, D. P. 2003. 'Emotional style and susceptibility to the common cold'. *Psychosomatic Medicine*, 65, 652–7.

5 Cohen, S., Tyrrell, D. & Smith, A. 1991. 'Psychological stress and susceptibility to the common cold'. *New England Journal of Medicine*, 325, 606–12.

6 Marucha, P., Kielcolt-Glaser, J. & Favagehi, M. 1998. 'Mucosal wound healing is impaired by examination stress'. *Psychosomatic Medicine*, 60, 362–5.

7 See (1) Levy, S. M., Lee, J., Bagley, C. & Lippman, M. 1988. 'Survival hazard analysis in first recurrent breast cancer patients: Seven-year follow-up'. *Psychosomatic Medicine*, 50, 520–28. (2) Devins, G. M, Mann. J., Mandin, H. P. & Leonard, C. 1990. 'Psychosocial predictors of survival in end-stage renal disease'. *Journal of Nervous and Mental Disease*, 178, 127–33. (3) Krause, J. S., Sternberg, M., Lottes, S. & Maides, J. 1997. 'Mortality after a spinal cord injury: An 11-year prospective study'. *Archives of Physical Medicine and Rehabilitation*, 78, 815–21.

8 Danner, D. D., Snowdon, D. A. & Friesen, W. V. 2001. 'Positive emotions in early life and longevity: Findings from the nun study'. *Journal of Personality and Social Psychology*, 80 (5), 804–13.

9 Levy, B. R., Slade, M. D., Kunkel, S. R and Kasl, S. V. 2002. 'Longevity increased by positive self-perceptions of aging'. *Journal of Personality and Social Psychology*, 83 (2), 261–70.

10 Harker, L. & Keltner, D. 2001. 'Expressions of positive emotions in women's college yearbook pictures and their relationship to personality and life outcomes across adulthood'. *Journal of Personality and Social Psychology*, 80 (1), 112–24.

11 Diener, E., Nickerson, C., Lucas, R. E. & Sandvik, E. 2002. 'Dispositional affect and job outcomes'. *Social Indicators Research*, 59, 229–59.

12 Barsade, S. G. & Ward, A. J. 2000. 'To your heart's content: A mode of affective diversity in top management teams. *Administrative Science Quarterly*, 45, 802–36.

13 See (1) DeNeve, K. M. & Cooper, H. 1998. 'The happy personality: A meta-analysis of 137 personality traits and subjective well-being'. *Psychological Bulletin*, 124 (2), 197–229. (2) Lyubomirsky et al, 'The benefits of frequent positive affect'.

14 Andrews, F. M. & Withey, F. B. 1976. *Social Indicators of Well-being: Americans' Perceptions of Life Quality*. New York, NY: Plenum.

15 Aspinwall, L. G. 1998. 'Rethinking the role of positive affect in self-regulation'. *Motivation and Emotion*, 22, 1–32.

16 Carver, C. S., Pozo, C., Harris, S. D., Noriega, V., Scheier, M. & Robinson, D. 1993. 'How coping mediates the effect of optimism on distress: A study of women with early stage breast cancer'. *Journal of Personality and Social Psychology*, 65 (2), 375–90.

17 See Seligman, M. E. P, Steen, T. A., Park, N. & Peterson, C. 2005. 'Positive psychology progress: Empirical validation of interventions'. *American Psychologist*, 60, 410–21.

18 Fordyce, M. W. 1983. 'A programme to increase happiness: Further studies. *Journal of Counselling Psychology*, 30, 483–98.

## *7. Discover what* really *makes you happy*

1 This apparently simple measurement of happiness is more valid and reliable than first impressions might suggest. It compares well to more elaborate measurements of happiness, such as a combination of in-depth interviews and reports from your family and friends about how happy they think you are. See Sandvik, E., Diener, E. & Seidlitz, L. 1993. 'Subjective well-being: The convergence and stability of self-report and non-self report measures'. *Journal of Personality*, 61, 317–42.

2 Diener, W., Suh, E. M., Lucas, R. E. & Smith, H. L. 1999. 'Subjective well-being: Three decades of progress'. *Psychological Bulletin*, 125 (2), 276–302.

3 Finzi, E., & Wassermann, E. 2006. 'Treatment of depression with botulinum toxin A: A case series'. *Dermatologic Surgery*, 32, 645–50.

4 Lykken, D. T. 1999. *Happiness: What Studies on Twins Show Us about Nature, Nurture and the Happiness Set Point*. New York, NY: Golden Books.

5 See Sullivan, P. F., Neale, M. C. & Kendler, K. S. 2000. 'Genetic epidemiology of major depression: Review and meta-analysis'. *American Journal of Psychiatry*, 157, 1552–62.

6 This refers to a specific allele (variation) of the 5-HTP gene. See Diener, E. & Biswas-Diener, R. 2008. *Happiness: Unlocking the Mysteries of Psychological Wealth*. Oxford: Blackwell Publishing.

7 Tellegen, A., Lykken, D. T., Bouchard, T. J., Wilcox, K. J., Segal, N. L. & Rich, S. 1988. 'Personality similarity in twins reared apart and together'. *Journal of Personality and Social Psychology*, 54 (6), 1031–9.

8 Haidt, J. 2006. *The Happiness Hypothesis: Putting Ancient Wisdom to the Test of Modern Science*. London: William Heinemann.

9 Costa, P. T. & McCrae, R. R. 1980. 'Influence of extraversion and neuroti-

cism on subjective well-being: Happy and unhappy people'. *Journal of Personality and Social Psychology*, 38 (4), 668–78.

10 Magnus, K. & Diener, E. 1991. 'A longitudinal analysis of personality, life events, and subjective well-being'. Paper presented at the Sixty-third Annual Meeting of the Midwestern Psychological Association, Chicago. May 2–4.

11 Srivastava, S., John, O. P., Gosling, S. D. & Potter, J. 2003. 'Development of personality in early and middle adulthood: Set like plaster or persistent change?' *Journal of Personality and Social Psychology*, 84 (5), 1041–53.

12 See Diener, E., Lucas, R. E. & Oishi, S. 2005. 'Subjective well-being: The science of happiness and life satisfaction'. In C. R. Snyder & S. J. Lopez (eds). *Handbook of Positive Psychology*. Oxford: OUP, pp. 63–73.

13 Oswald, A. & Blanchflower, D. 2008. 'Is well-being U-shaped over the life cycle?' *Social Science & Medicine*, 66 (6), 1733–49.

14 Nolen-Hoeksema, S. & Rusting, C. L. 1999. 'Gender differences in well-being'. In D. Kahneman, E. Diener & N. Schwarz (eds). *Well-being: The Foundations of Hedonic Psychology*. New York, NY: Russell Sage Foundation, pp. 330–53.

15 Gilligan, C. 1982. *In a Different Voice: Psychological Theory and Women's Development*. Cambridge, MA: Harvard University Press.

16 Diener, E., Wolsic, B. & Fugita, F. 1995. 'Physical attractiveness and subjective well-being. *Journal of Personality and Social Psychology*, 69 (1), 120–29.

17 See Lyubomirsky, S. 2007. *The How of Happiness: A New Approach to Getting the Life You Want*. New York, NY: Penguin Books.

18 Mehnert, T., Krauss, H. H., Nadler, R. & Boyd, M. 1990. 'Correlates of life satisfaction in those with disabling conditions'. *Rehabilitation Psychology*, 35, 3–17.

19 See Waite, L. J. & Gallagher, M. 2000. *The Case for Marriage*. New York, NY: Doubleday.

20 Veenhoven, R. and co-workers. 1994. *World Database of Happiness: Correlates of Happiness*. Rotterdam: Erasmus University.

21 Lucas, R. E., Clark, A. E., Georgellis, Y. & Diener, E. 2003. 'Re-examining adaptation and the set point model of happiness: Reactions to changes in marital status'. *Journal of Personality and Social Psychology*, 84 (3), 527–39.

22 Diener, E., Suh, E. M., Lucas, R. E. & Smith, H. L. 1999. 'Subjective well-being: Three decades of progress'. *Psychological Bulletin*, 125 (2), 276–302.

23 DePaulo, B. M. & Morris, W. L. 2005. 'Singles in society and in science'. *Psychological Inquiry*, 16, 57–83.

24 See (1) Feeney, J. A. 1994. 'Attachment styles, communication patterns and satisfaction across the life cycle of marriage'. *Personal Relationships*, 1, 333–48.

(2) Kahneman, D. 2004. 'A survey method for characterising daily life experiences: The day reconstruction method'. *Science*, 306 (5702), 1776–80.

25 See Argyle, M. & Lu, L. 1990. 'The happiness of extraverts'. *Personality and Individual Differences*, 11, 1011–17.

26 Fowler, J. H. & Christakis, N. A. 2008. 'Dynamic spread of happiness in a large social network: Longitudinal analysis over 20 years in the Framingham Heart Study'. *British Medical Journal*, 337, a2338.

27 See Bearman, P. S. & Moody, J. (2004). Suicide and friendships among American adolescents. *American Journal of Public Health*, 94, 89–95.

28 Lucas, R. E., Clark, A. E., Georgellis, Y. & Diener, E. 2004. 'Unemployment alters the set point for life satisfaction'. *Psychological Science*, 15 (1), 8–13.

29 See Peterson, C. 2006. *A Primer in Positive Psychology*. New York, NY: Oxford University Press, Inc.

30 See Putnam, R. D. 2000. *Bowling Alone: The Collapse and Revival of American Community*. New York, NY: Simon & Schuster.

31 Inglehart, R. 1990. *Culture Shift in Advanced Industrial Society*. Princeton, NJ: Princeton University Press.

32 Kahneman, D., Krueger, A. B., Schkade, D., Schwartz, N. & Stone, A. A. 2006. 'Would you be happier if you were rich? A focusing illusion'. *Science*, 312, 1908–10.

33 Diener, E., Sandvik, E., Seidlitz, L. & Diener, M. 1993. 'The relationship between income and subjective well-being: Relative or absolute?' *Social Indicators Research*, 28, 195–223.

34 Brown, R. 1978. 'Divided we fall: An analysis of relations between sections of a factory workforce'. In H. Tajfel (ed). *Differentiation Between Social Groups*. London: Academic Press, pp. 395–429.

35 Argyle, M. 1999. 'Causes and correlates of happiness'. In D. Kahneman, E. Diener & N. Schwarz (eds). *Well-being: The Foundations of Hedonic Psychology*. New York, NY: Russell Sage Foundation, pp. 353–74.

36 Nickerson, C., Schwartz, N., Diener, E. & Kahneman, D. 2003. 'Zeroing in on the dark side of the American Dream: A closer look at the negative consequences of the goal for financial success'. *Psychological Science*, 14, 531–6.

37 Schwartz, B. 2004. *The Paradox of Choice: Why More is Less*. New York, NY: HarperCollins.

38 Brickman, P. & Campbell, D. T. 1971. 'Hedonic relativism and planning the good society'. In M. H. Appley (ed). *Adaptation-level Theory*. New York, NY: Academic Press, pp. 287–302.

39 Aristotle. Trans. Terence Irwin. 1999. *Nichomachean Ethics*. Second edition. Book I, Section 7. Indianapolis, IN: Hackett Publishing Company, Inc.
40 Gilbert, D. 2006. *Stumbling on Happiness*. London: Harper Press, p. 5. Citing philosopher D. Dennett. 1996. *Kinds of Minds*. New York, NY: Basic Books.
41 Lyubomirsky, S., Sheldon, K. M. & Schkade, D. 2005. 'Pursuing happiness: The architecture of sustainable change'. *Review of General Psychology*, 9, 111–31.
42 Lyubomirsky, *The How of Happiness*, p. 20.

## *8. Take on three life projects*

1 Liker, J. 2004. *The Toyota Way: 14 Management Principles from the World's Greatest Manufacturer*. New York, NY: McGraw-Hill.
2 See Locke, E. A. 2005. 'Setting goals for life and happiness'. In C. R. Snyder & S. J. Lopez (eds). *Handbook of Positive Psychology*. Oxford: OUP, pp. 299–312. Note: I have slightly changed the order of the sequence.
3 Pinker, S. 1997. *How the Mind Works*. New York, NY: Norton. Paperback edition 1998. London: Penguin, p. 372.
4 Sheldon, K. M. 2002. 'The self-concordance model of healthy goal striving: When personal goals correctly represent the person'. In E. L. Deci & R. M. Ryan (eds). *Handbook of Self-determination Research*. Rochester, NY: University of Rochester Press, pp. 65–86.
5 See Lyubomirsky, S. 2007. *The How of Happiness: A New Approach to Getting the Life You Want*. New York, NY: Penguin Books.
6 Peterson, C. & Seligman, M. 2004. *Character Strengths and Virtues: A Handbook and Classification*. New York, NY: American Psychological Association and Oxford University Press, Inc.
7 Sheldon, K. M. & Kasser, T. 2001. 'Getting older, getting better? Personal strivings and personality development across the life-course'. *Developmental Psychology*, 37, 491–501.
8 Brickman, P., Janoff-Bulman, R. & Rabinowitz, V. C. 1987. 'Meaning and value'. In C. B. Wortman & R. Sorrentino (eds). *Commitment, Conflict and Caring*. Englewood Cliffs, NJ: Prentice-Hall, pp. 59–105.
9 Brickman, P. & Coates, D. 'Commitment and mental health'. Ibid., pp. 222–309.
10 Sheldon, K. M., Kasser, T., Smith, K. & Share, T. 2002. 'Personal goals and psychological growth: Testing an intervention to enhance goal-attainment and personality integration'. *Journal of Personality*, 70, 5–31.

### *9. What you pay attention to becomes your life*

1 Hallowell, E. 2005. 'Overloaded circuits: Why smart people underperform'. *Harvard Business Review*, Jan, 55–62.

2 Ibid., p. 58.

3 Pinker, S. 1997. *How the Mind Works*. New York, NY: Norton. Paperback edition 1998. London: Penguin, p. 141.

4 Raz, A. & Buhle, J. 2006. 'Typologies of attentional networks'. *Nature Neuroscience*, 7, 367–79.

5 See (1) Baumeister, R. F., Bratslavsky, E., Muraven, M. & Tice, D. 1998. 'Ego depletion: Is the active self a limited resource?' *Journal of Personality and Social Psychology*, 74 (5), 1252–65. (2) Muraven, M., Tice, D. & Baumeister, R. F. 1998. 'Self-control as a limited resource: Regulatory depletion patterns'. *Journal of Personality and Social Psychology*, 74 (3), 774–89.

6 Gilbert, D. T. 1989. 'Thinking lightly about others: Automatic components of the social inference process'. In J. S. Uleman & J. A. Bargh (eds). *Unintended Thought*. New York, NY: Guilford Press, pp. 189–211.

7 Loehr, J. & Schwartz, T. 2003. *The Power of Full Engagement*. New York, NY: The Free Press.

### *10. Rewiring your brain to make the best use of your attention*

1 Siegel, D. J. 2007. *The Mindful Brain*. New York, NY: Norton, pp. 134–5.

2 This phrase is often used as a summary of the classic work of Hebb, D. 1949. *The Organization of Behavior: A Neuropsychological Theory*. New York, NY: Bantam Books.

3 Siegel, *The Mindful Brain*, p. 291.

4 Ibid., p. 5.

5 Ibid., p. 3.

6 Kabat-Zinn, J. 2003. 'Mindfulness-based interventions in context: Past, present and future'. *Clinical Psychology: Science and Practice*, 10 (2), 144–56. See pp. 145–6.

7 See, for example, Davidson, R. J., Kabat-Zinn, J., Schumacher, J., Rosenkranz, M., Muller, D. et al. 2003. 'Alterations in brain and immune function produced by mindfulness meditation'. *Psychosomatic Medicine*, 65 (4), 564–70.

8 For a comprehensive review of this research see the excellent article by Katya Rubia of the Institute of Psychiatry, King's College University, London: Rubia, K. 2009. 'The neurobiology of meditation and its clinical effectiveness in psychiatric disorders'. *Biological Psychology*, 82, 1–11.

9 See Main, M., Kaplan, N. & Cassidy, J. 1985. 'Security in infancy, childhood, and adulthood: A move to the level of representation'. *Monographs of the Society for Research in Child Development*, 50, 1–2.

10 Gilbert, E. 2006. *Eat, Pray, Love*. New York, NY: Penguin Books.

11 Harrison, L., Manosh, R. & Rubia, K. 2004 'Sahaja yoga meditation as a family treatment programme for attention hyperactivity deficit disorder children'. *Journal of Clinical Psychology and Psychiatry*, 9 (4), 479–97.

12 Zylowska, L., Ackerman, D. L., Yang, M. H., Futrell, J. L., Horton, N. L. et al. 2008. 'Mindfulness meditation training in adults and adolescents with ADHD: A feasibility study'. *Journal of Attention Disorders*, 11, 737–46.

13 See (1) Langer, E. 1989. *Mindfulness*. New York, NY: Perseus Books. (2) Langer, E. 1997. *The Power of Mindful Learning*. New York, NY: Perseus Books. (3) Langer, E. 2000. 'Mindful learning'. *Current Directions in Psychological Science*, 9 (6), 220–23. (4) Langer, E. 2005. 'Mindfulness versus positive evaluation'. In C. R. Snyder & S. J. Lopez (eds). *Handbook of Positive Psychology*. Oxford: OUP, pp. 214–30.

14 Langer, 'Mindfulness versus positive evaluation', p. 215.

15 For a review of this literature see Siegel, *The Mindful Brain*.

## *11. The eight-step dance to feeling positive or negative*

1 For reviews of the research literature see (1) Ekman, P. 1992. 'Are there basic emotions?' *Psychological Review*, 99, 550–53. (2) Keltner, D. & Lerner, J. 2010. 'Emotion'. In D. Gilbert, S. Fiske & G. Lindsey (eds). *Handbook of Social Psychology*. Fifth edition. Hoboken, NJ: John Wiley & Sons, Inc, pp. 317–52. (3) Smith, C. & Ellsworth, P. 1985. 'Patterns of cognitive appraisal in emotion'. *Journal of Personality and Social Psychology*, 48 (4), 813–38.

2 See Keltner & Lerner, 'Emotion'.

3 See Ekman, P. 1993. 'Facial expression and emotion'. *American Psychologist*, 48, 384–92.

4 Cacioppo, J. T., Gardner, W. L. & Berntson, G. G. 1999. 'The affect system has parallel and integrative processing components: Form follows function'. *Journal of Personality and Social Psychology*, 76 (5), 839–55. See p. 846.

5 Cacioppo, J. T. & Berntson, G. G. 1994. 'Relationships between attitudes and evaluative space: A critical review with emphasis on the separability of positive and negative substrates'. *Psychological Bulletin*, 115 (3), 401–23.

6 See Siegel, D. J. 2007. *The Mindful Brain*. New York, NY: Norton, pp. 134–5.

7 Langer, E. 2005. 'Mindfulness versus positive evaluation'. In C. R. Snyder & S. J. Lopez (eds). *Handbook of Positive Psychology*. Oxford: OUP, pp. 214–30.

8 Rosenberg, E. L., Ekman, P., Jiang, W., Babyak, M., Coleman, E., Hanson, M., O'Connor, C., Waugh, R. & Blumenthal, J. A. 2001. 'Linkages between facial expressions of anger and transient myocardial ischemia in men with coronary artery disease'. *Emotion*, 1, 107–15.

9 Juslin, P. N. & Laukka, P. 2003. 'Communication of emotions in vocal expressions and music performance: Different channels, same code?' *Psychological Bulletin*, 129 (5), 770–814.

10 Hertenstein, M. J., Keltner, D., App, B., Bulleit, B. A. & Jaskolka, A. R. 2006. 'Touch communicates distinct emotions'. *Emotion*, 6, 528–33.

11 Coan, J. A., Schaefer, H. S. & Davidson, R. J. 2006. 'Lending a hand: Social regulation of the neural response to threat'. *Psychological Science*, 17, 1032–39.

12 Darwin, C. R. 1872/1998. *The Expression of Emotions in Man and Animals*. Third edition. New York, NY: Oxford University Press, Inc.

13 Strack, F., Martin, L. L. & Stepper, S. 1988. 'Inhibiting and facilitating conditions of the human smile: A non-obtrusive test of the facial feedback hypothesis'. *Journal of Personality and Social Psychology*, 54 (5), 768–77.

14 Averill, J. R. 1982. *Anger and Aggression: An Essay on Emotion*. New York, NY: Springer Verlag.

15 Lerner, J. S. & Tiedens, L. Z. 2006. 'Portrait of the angry decision maker: How appraisal tendencies shape anger's influence on cognition'. *Journal of Behavioral Decision Making*, 19 (2), 115–37.

16 Siegel, *The Mindful Brain*, p. 19.

17 Kline, N. 1999. *Time to Think*. London: Ward Lock.

### *12. Identify what you want to achieve – and make it happen*

1 Siegel, D. J. 2007. *The Mindful Brain*. New York, NY: Norton, p. 187.

2 Higgins, E. T., Grant, H. & Shah, J. 1999. 'Self-regulation and quality of life: Emotional and non-emotional life experiences'. In D. Kahneman, E. Diener & N. Schwartz (eds). *Well-being: The Foundations of Hedonic Psychology*. New York, NY: Russell Sage Foundation, pp. 244–66.

3 See (1) Elliot, A. J. & Church, M. A. 1997. 'A hierarchical model of approach and avoidance achievement motivation'. *Journal of Personality and Social Psychology*, 72 (1), 218–32. (2) Elliot, A. J. & Sheldon, K. M. 1997. 'Avoidance achievement motivation: A personal goals analysis'. *Journal of Personality and Social Psychology*, 73 (1), 171–85. (3) Elliot, A. J., Sheldon, K. M. & Church, M. A. 1997. 'Avoidance of personal goals and subjective well-being'. *Personality and Social Psychology Bulletin*, 23, 915–27.

4 Isen, A. M., Daubman, K. A. & Nowicki, G. P. 1987. 'Positive affect facilitates creative problem solving'. *Journal of Personality and Social Psychology*, 52 (6), 1122–31.
5 Lazarus, R. S. 1991. *Emotion and Adaptation*. New York, NY: Oxford University Press, Inc.
6 Wegner, D. M. 1994. 'Ironic processes of mental control'. *Psychological Review*, 101 (1), 34–52.
7 Ibid., p. 39.
8 See Brown, R. & Gilman, A. 1960. 'The pronouns of power and solidarity'. In T. A. Sebeok (ed). *Style in Language*. Cambridge, MA: MIT Press, pp. 253–76.
9 Peterson, C. & Seligman, M. 2004. *Character Strengths and Virtues*. New York, NY: American Psychological Association and Oxford University Press, Inc.
10 Buckingham, M. & Clifton, D. O. 2001. *Now, Discover Your Strengths*. New York, NY: The Free Press.

## *13. Mood matters*

1 Morris, W. N. 1999. 'The mood system'. In D. Kahneman, E. Diener & N. Schwarz (eds). *Well-being: The Foundations of Hedonic Psychology*. New York, NY: Russell Sage Foundation, pp. 169–89.
2 Ambady, N. & Gray, H. M. 2002. 'On being sad and mistaken: Mood effects on the accuracy of thin-slice judgments'. *Journal of Personality and Social Psychology*, 83 (4), 947–61.
3 Smith, S. M. & Petty, R. E. 1995. 'Personality moderators of mood congruency effects on cognition: The role of self-esteem and negative mood regulation'. *Journal of Personality and Social Psychology*, 68 (6), 1092–1107.
4 Lount, R. B. Jr. 2010. 'The impact of positive mood on trust in interpersonal and intergroup interactions'. *Journal of Personality and Social Psychology*, 98 (3), 420–33.
5 For an excellent review of this research literature see Goleman, D., Boyatzis, R. & McKee, A. 2002. *Primal Leadership: Realizing the Power of Emotional Intelligence*. Boston, MA: Harvard Business School Press.
6 Neumann, R. & Strack, F. 2000. 'Mood contagion: The automatic transfer of mood between persons'. *Journal of Personality and Social Psychology*, 79 (2), 211–23.
7 Friedman, H. & Riggio, R. 1981. 'Effect of individual differences in nonverbal expressiveness on transmission of emotion'. *Journal of Nonverbal Behavior*, 6, 32–58.

8 See Rizzolatti, G. & Craighero, L. 2004. 'The mirror-neuron system'. *Annual Review of Neuroscience*, 27, 169–92.

9 See (1) Fadiga, L., Fogassi, L., Pavesi, G. & Rizzolatti, G. 1995. 'Motor facilitation during action observation: A magnetic stimulation study'. *Journal of Neurophysiology*, 73 (6), 2608–11. (2) Gallese, V., Fadiga, L., Fogassi, L. & Rizzolatti, G. 1996. 'Action recognition in the premotor cortex'. *Brain*, 119 (2), 593–609. (3) Iacoboni, M. et al. 1999. 'Cortical mechanisms of human imitation'. *Science*, 286 (5449), 2526–8. For a discussion of research on mirroring see Winerman, L. 2005. 'The mind's mirror'. *Monitor on Psychology*, 36 (9), 48 & ff.

10 McClintock, M. 1971. 'Menstrual synchrony and suppression'. *Nature*, 229 (5282), 244–5.

11 Levenson, R.W. & Ruef, A. M. 1997. 'Physiological aspects of emotional knowledge'. In W. Ickes (ed). *Empathic Accuracy*. New York, NY: Guilford Press, pp. 44–73.

12 See Totterdell, P. 2000. 'Catching mood and hitting runs: Mood linkage and subjective performance in professional sports teams'. *Journal of Applied Psychology*, 85 (6), 848–59.

13 Bartel, C. A. & Saavedra, R. 2000. 'The collective construction of work group moods'. *Administrative Science Quarterly*, 45 (2), 197–231.

14 For a review see Brief, A. P. & Weiss, H. M. 2002. 'Organisational behaviour: Affect in the workplace'. *Annual Review of Psychology*, 53 (1), 279–307.

15 Schneider, B. & Bowen, D. E. 1995. *Winning the Service Game*. Boston, MA: Harvard Business School Press.

16 For an excellent review of this literature and a discussion of leader behaviour see Goleman et al, *Primal Leadership*.

17 See George, J. M. 2000. 'Emotions and leadership'. *Human Relations*, 53 (8), 1027–55.

18 Schein, E. D. 1999. *The Corporate Culture Survival Guide*. San Francisco, CA: Jossey-Bass, Inc.

19 For a review of this research see Goleman et al, *Primal Leadership*.

20 Kelner, S. P., Rivers, C. A. & O'Connell, K. H. 1996. *Managerial Style as a Behavioral Predictor of Organizational Climate*. Boston, MA: McBer & Company.

### *14. How to manage your mood*

1 Norris, F. H. & Kaniasty, K. 1996. 'Received and perceived social support in times of stress: A test of the social support deterioration deterrence model'. *Journal of Personality and Social Psychology*, 71 (3), 498–511.

2 See Emmons, R. A. & Crumpler, C. A. 2000. 'Gratitude as human strength: Appraising the evidence'. *Journal of Social and Clinical Psychology*, 19, 56–69.
3 Emmons, R. A. & Shelton, C. M. 2005. 'Gratitude and the science of positive psychology'. In C. R. Snyder & S. J. Lopez (eds). *Handbook of Positive Psychology*. Oxford: OUP, pp. 459–71. See p. 465.
4 Emmons & Shelton, 'Gratitude and the science of positive psychology'.
5 Csikszentmihalyi, M. 1999. 'If we are so rich, why aren't we happy?' *American Psychologist*, 54 (10), 821–7.
6 Miller, T. 1995. *How to Want What You Have*. New York, NY: Henry Holt and Company.
7 Ransford, H. E. & Palisi, B. J. 1996. 'Aerobic exercise, subjective health and psychological well-being within age and gender subgroups'. *Social Science and Medicine*, 42, 1555–9.
8 Lyubomirsky, S., Tkach, C. & Sheldon, K. M. 2004. 'Pursuing sustained happiness through random acts of kindness and counting one's blessings: Tests of two six-week interventions'. Unpublished raw data. Cited in Lyubomirsky, S., Sheldon, K. M. & Schkade, D. 2005. 'Pursuing happiness: The architecture of sustainable change'. *Review of General Psychology*, 9 (2), 111–31.

## *15. The joy of losing yourself in everything you do*

1 Csikszentmihalyi, M. 1992. *Flow: The Psychology of Happiness*. London: Rider & Co.
2 See Nakamura J. & Csikszentmihalyi, M. 2005. 'The concept of flow'. In C. R. Snyder & S. J. Lopez (eds). *Handbook of Positive Psychology*. Oxford: OUP, pp. 89–105.
3 Csikszentmihalyi, *Flow*, pp. 39–40.
4 Brickman, P. 1987. 'Commitment'. In C. B. Wortman & R. Sorrentino (eds). *Commitment, Conflict and Caring*. Englewood Cliffs, NJ: Prentice-Hall, pp. 145–221.
5 For a review of the evidence of the effects of TV see Putnam, R. D. 2000. *Bowling Alone: The Collapse and Revival of American Community*. New York, NY: Simon & Schuster.
6 Brickman, 'Commitment'.
7 Nakamura, J. & Csikszentmihalyi, M. 2003. 'The construction of meaning through vital engagement'. In C. L. M. Keyes & J. Haidy (eds). *Flourishing: Positive Psychology and the Life Well-lived*. Washington, DC: American Psychological Association.

8 Wrzesniewski, A., McCauley, C. R., Rozin, P. & Schwartz, 1997. 'Jobs, careers, and callings: People's relations to their work'. *Journal of Research in Personality*, 31, 21–33.

9 Gardner, H., Csikszentmihalyi, M. & Damon, W. 2001. *Good Work: When Excellence and Ethics Meet*. New York, NY: Basic Books.

## *16. The crucial importance of making sense of your life*

1 This observation by the philosopher Kierkegaard is cited in Langer, E. 2005. 'Mindfulness versus positive evaluation'. In C. R. Snyder & S. J. Lopez (eds). *Handbook of Positive Psychology*. Oxford: OUP, pp. 214–30. See p. 221.

2 See (1) Baumeister, R. 1991. *Meanings of Life*. New York, NY: Guilford Press. (2) Baumeister, R. & Vohs, K. 2005. 'The pursuit of meaningfulness in life'. In C. R. Snyder & S. J. Lopez (eds). *Handbook of Positive Psychology*. Oxford: OUP, pp. 608–18.

3 See Vallacher, R. R. & Wegner, D. M. 1985. *A Theory of Action Identification*. Hillsdale NJ: Lawrence Erlbaum Publishers.

4 Pinker, S. 1997. *How the Mind Works*. New York, NY: Norton. Paperback edition 1998. London: Penguin, p. 563.

5 Csikszentmihalyi, M. 1992. *Flow: The Psychology of Happiness*. London: Rider & Co., p. 217.

6 See (1) Gazzaniga, M. S. 1985. *The Social Brain*. New York, NY: Basic Books. (2) Gazzaniga, M. S. 1993. 'Brain mechanisms and conscious experience'. In *Experimental and Theoretical Studies of Consciousness*. Ciba Foundation Symposia Series, no. 174. Chichester: Wiley, pp. 247–62.

7 Vallacher, R. R. & Wegner, D. M. 1987. 'What do people think they're doing: Action identification and human behaviour'. *Psychological Review*, 94, 3–15.

8 Seligman, M. E. P. & Maier, S. F. 1967. 'Failure to escape traumatic shock'. *Journal of Experimental Psychology*, 74, 1–9.

9 Baumeister, *Meanings of Life*.

10 Haidt, J. 2006. *The Happiness Hypothesis: Putting Ancient Wisdom to the Test of Modern Science*. London: William Heinemann.

11 Baumeister, *Meanings of Life*.

12 Guidano, V. F. 1999. 'Self-observation in constructivist psychotherapy'. In R. A. Neimeyer & M. J. Mahoney (eds). *Constructivism in Psychotherapy*. Washington, DC: American Psychological Association, pp. 155–68.

13 See McClelland, D. 1998. 'Identifying competencies with behavioural-event interviews'. *Psychological Science*, 9, 331–9.

14 Dickman, R. 2003. 'The four elements of every successful story'. *Reflections*. Society for Organisational Learning and the Massachusetts Institute of Technology, 4, 351–6.

15 Neimeyer, R. A. 2000. 'Narrative disruptions in the construction of self'. In R. A. Neimeyer & M. J. Mahoney (eds). *Constructions of Disorder*. Washington, DC: American Psychological Association, pp. 207–41.

## *17. Good stress, bad stress*

1 Lazarus, R. S. & Folkman, S. 1984. *Stress Appraisal and Coping*. New York, NY: Springer Verlag.

2 See Holmes, T. H. & Rahe, R. H. 1967. 'The social readjustment rating scale'. *Journal of Psychosomatic Research*, 11, 213–18.

3 Segerstrom, S. C. & Miller, G. E. 2004. 'Psychological stress and the human immune system: A meta-analytic study of 30 years of inquiry'. *Psychological Bulletin*, 130 (4), 601–30.

4 Suinn, R. M. 2001. 'The terrible twos – anger and anxiety'. *American Psychologist*, 56 (1), 27–36.

5 Folkman, S. & Lazarus, R. S. 1980. 'An analysis of coping in a middle-aged community sample'. *Journal of Health and Social Behaviour*, 21, 219–39.

6 Folkman, S. & Moskowitz, J. T. 2004. 'Coping: Pitfalls and promise'. *Annual Review of Psychology*, 55, 745–74.

7 Taylor, S. E. et al. 2000. 'Biobehavioral responses to stress in females: Tend-and-befriend, not fight or-flight'. *Psychological Review*, 107 (3), 411–29.

8 See, for example, Gur, R. C., Gur, R. E, Obrist, W. D., Hungerbuhler, J. P., Younkin, D., Rosen, A. D., Skolnick, B. E. & Reivich, M. 1982. 'Sex and handedness differences in cerebral blood flow during rest and cognitive activity'. *Science*, 217, 659–61.

9 Maercker, A. & Zoellner, T. 2004. 'The Janus face of self-perceived growth: Toward a two-component model of post-traumatic growth'. *Psychological Inquiry*, 15 (1), 41–8.

10 Scheier, M. F., Carver, C. S. & Bridges, M. W. 2001. 'Optimism, as the myth, and psychological well-being'. In E. C. Chang (ed). *Optimism and Pessimism: Implications for a Theory, Research, and Practice*. Washington, DC: American Psychological Association, pp. 189–216.

11 Taylor, S. E. & Armor, D. A. 1996. 'Positive illusions and coping with adversity'. *Journal of Personality*, 64 (4), 873–98.

12 Costa, P. T. & McCrae, R. R. 1985. *The NEO Personality Inventory Manual*. Odessa: Psychological Assessment Resources.

13 Kobasa, S. C. 1979. 'Stressful life events and health: An enquiry into hardiness'. *Journal of Personality and Social Psychology*, 37 (1), 1–11.

### *18. How to handle unruly emotions*

1 See, for example, (1) Stanton, A. L., Danoff-Burg, S., Cameron, C. L., Bishop, M. M., Collins, C. A. et al. 2000. 'Emotionally-expressive coping predicts psychological and physical adjustments to breast cancer'. *Journal of Consulting and Clinical Psychology*, 68, 875–82. (2) Stanton, A. L., Parsa, A. & Austenfeld, J. L. 2005. 'The adaptive potential of coping through emotional approach'. In C. R. Snyder & S. J. Lopez (eds). *Handbook of Positive Psychology*. Oxford: OUP, pp. 148–58.

2 See, for example, (1) Nolen-Hoeksema, S. 2000. 'The role of rumination in depressive disorders and mixed anxiety/depressive symptoms'. *Journal of Abnormal Psychology*, 109, 505–11. (2) Nolen-Hoeksema, S., Wisco, B. E. & Lyubomirsky, S. 2008. 'Rethinking rumination'. *Perspectives on Psychological Science*, 3 (5), 400–24. (3) Ray, R. D., Gross, J. J. & Wilhelm, F. H. 2008. 'All in the mind's eye: Anger, rumination and reappraisal'. *Journal of Personality and Social Psychology*, 94 (1), 133–45.

3 See, for example, Davis, R. N. & Nolen-Hoeksema, S. 2000. 'Cognitive inflexibility among ruminators and nonruminators'. *Cognitive Therapy and Research*, 24, 699–711.

4 See, for example, Joormann, J. 2006. 'Differential effects of rumination and dysphoria on the inhibition of irrelevant emotional material: Evidence from a negative priming task'. *Cognitive Therapy and Research*, 30, 149–60.

5 Waugh, C. E., Wager, T. D., Fredrickson, B. L., Noll, D. C. & Taylor, S. F. 2008. 'The neural correlates of trait resilience when anticipating and recovering from threat'. *Social Cognitive and Affective Neuroscience*, 3 (4), 322–32.

6 Ibid., p. 330.

7 See Watkins, E. 2008. 'Constructive and unconstructive repetitive thought'. *Psychological Bulletin*, 134 (2), 163–206.

8 Segal, A., Williams, J. M. G. & Teasdale, J. D. 2002. *Mindfulness-based Cognitive Therapy for Depression: A New Approach to Preventing Relapse*. New York, NY: Guilford.

9 Goleman, D. 1995. *Emotional Intelligence*. New York, NY: Bantam Books, p. 14.

10 See (1) Lerner, J. S. & Tiedens, L. Z. 2006. 'Portrait of the angry decision maker: How appraisal tendencies shape anger's influence on cognition'. *Journal of Behavioral Decision Making*, 19 (2), 115–37. (2) Beck, A. T. 1976. *Cognitive*

*Therapy and the Emotional Disorders*. New York, NY: International Universities Press.

11 For a review see Rosenberg, E. L., Ekman, P., Jiang, W., Babyak, M., Coleman, E., Hanson, M., O'Connor, C., Waugh, R. & Blumenthal, J. A. 2001. 'Linkages between facial expressions of anger and transient myocardial ischemia in men with coronary artery disease'. *Emotion*, 1, 107–15.

12 See Weinberger, D. A. & Davidson, M. N. 1994. 'Styles of inhibiting emotional expression: Distinguishing repressive coping from impression management'. *Journal of Personality*, 62 (4), 587–613.

13 Weinberger, D. A., Schwartz, G. E. & Davidson, R. J. 1979. 'Low-anxious, high-anxious, and repressive coping styles: Psychometric patterns and behavioural and physiological response to stress'. *Journal of Abnormal Psychology*, 88 (4), 369–80.

14 Hariri, A. R., Bookheimer, S.Y. & Mazziotta, J. C. 2000. 'Modulating emotional responses: Effects of a neocortical network on the limbic system'. *Neuroport: For Rapid Communication of Neuroscience Research*, 11 (1), 43–8.

15 Davidson, R. J. 2000. 'Affective style, psychopathology, and resilience: Brain mechanisms and plasticity'. *American Psychologist*, 55 (11), 1196–1214.

16 Fredrickson, B. L., Mancuso, R. A., Branigan, C. & Tugade, M. M. 2000. 'The undoing effect of positive emotions'. *Motivation and Emotion*, 24, 237–58.

## *19. Flourishing under fire*

1 See Tedeschi, R. G. & Calhoun, L. G. 2004. 'Posttraumatic growth: Conceptual foundations and empirical evidence'. *Psychological Inquiry*, 15, 1–18.

2 Masten, A. S. 2001. 'Ordinary magic: Resilience processes in development'. *American Psychologist*, 56 (3), 227–38.

3 Tedeschi & Calhoun, 'Posttraumatic growth: Conceptual foundations and empirical evidence'.

4 See Kübler-Ross, E. 1969. *On Death and Dying*. New York, NY: Macmillan.

5 Horowitz, M. J. 1986. *Stress Response Syndromes*. Northville, NJ: Jason Aronson, Inc.

6 McAdams, D. P. 1993. *The Stories We Live By: Personal Myths and the Making of the Self*. New York, NY: Morrow.

7 See (1) McAdams, D. P., Reynolds, J., Lewis, M., Patten, A. H. & Bowman, P. J. 2001. 'When bad things turn good and good things turn bad: Sequences of redemption and contamination in life narrative and their relation to the psychosocial adaptation in midlife adults and in students'. *Personality and*

*Social Psychology Bulletin*, 27, 474–85. (2) McAdams, D. P. 2001. 'The psychology of life stories'. *Review of General Psychology*, 5 (2), 100–22.

8 Pals, J. L. & McAdams, D. 2004. 'The transformed self: A narrative understanding of posttraumatic growth'. *Psychological Inquiry*, 15 (1), 65–9. See p. 65.

9 Ibid., p. 66.

10 Ibid.

11 McAdams et al, 'When bad things turn good and good things turn bad', p. 474.

12 Tomkins, S. S. 1987. 'Script theory'. In J. Arnoff, A. I. Rabin & R. A. Zucker (eds). *The Emergence of Personality*. New York, NY: Springer Verlag, pp. 147–216.

## *20. The path to growth and wisdom*

1 Frankl, V. E. 1959/2006. *Man's Search for Meaning*. Boston, MA: Beacon Press, p. 77.

2 Taylor, S. 1983. 'Adjustment to threatening life events: A theory of cognitive adaptation'. *American Psychologist*, 38, 1161–73.

3 Affleck, G., Tennen, H., Croog, S. & Levine, S. 1987. 'Causal attribution, perceived benefits, and morbidity after a heart attack: An eight-year study'. *Journal of Consulting and Clinical Psychology*, 55, 29–35.

4 Lehman, D. R., Wortman, C. B. & Williams, A. F. 1987. 'Long-term effects of losing a spouse or child in a motor vehicle crash'. *Journal of Personality and Social Psychology*, 52 (1), 218–31.

5 Ehrenreich, B. 2009. *Bright-Sided: How Positive Thinking is Undermining America*. New York, NY: Picador USA.

6 This quotation from Rabbi Kushner is from J. Viorst. 1986. *Necessary Losses*. New York, NY: Fawcett. It was quoted in R. G. Tedeschi & L. G. Calhoun. 2004. 'Posttraumatic growth: Conceptual foundations and empirical evidence'. *Psychological Inquiry*, 15, 1–18. See p. 10.

7 See (1) Niederhoffer, K. G. & Pennebaker, J. W. 2005. 'Sharing one's story'. In C. R. Snyder & S. J. Lopez (eds). *Handbook of Positive Psychology*. Oxford: OUP, pp. 573–83. (2) Pals, J. L. & McAdams, D. 2004. 'The transformed Self: A narrative understanding of posttraumatic growth'. *Psychological Inquiry*, 15 (1), 65–9. (3) Neimeyer, R. A. 2004. 'Fostering post-traumatic growth: A narrative elaboration'. *Psychological Inquiry*, 15 (1), 53–9.

8 Lyubomirsky, S., Sousa, L. & Dickerhoof, R. 2006. 'The costs and benefits of writing, talking, and thinking about life's triumphs and defeats'. *Journal of Personality and Social Psychology*, 90 (4), 692–708.

9 Ibid.

10 Niederhoffer & Pennebaker, 'Sharing one's story', p. 577.
11 Smyth, J. M. 1998. 'Written emotional expression: Effect sizes, outcome types, and moderating variable'. *Journal of Consulting and Clinical Psychology*, 66, 174–84.
12 Frankl, *Man's Search for Meaning*, p. 72.
13 Brickman, P. 1987. 'Commitment'. In C. B. Wortman & R. Sorrentino (eds). *Commitment, Conflict and Caring*. Englewood Cliffs, NJ: Prentice-Hall, pp. 145–221.
14 Chodoff, P., Friedman, S. B. & Hamburg, D. A. 1964. 'Stress defenses and coping behaviour: Observations in parents and children with malignant disease'. *American Journal of Psychiatry*, 36, 463–76.
15 Tedeschi, R. G. & Calhoun, L. G. 2004. 'Posttraumatic growth: Conceptual foundations and empirical evidence'. *Psychological Inquiry*, 15, 1–18.
16 Melvyn Bragg's Channel Four interview with Dennis Potter was broadcast on 5 April 1994. On 12 September 2007 the *Guardian* newspaper published an edited transcript and put an extract from the broadcast on its website, the source for this quote.

## 21. *You can't be driven crazy without your full cooperation*

1 Williamson, M. 1992. *A Return to Love: Reflections on the Principles of a Course in Miracles*. New York, NY: HarperCollins, pp. 190–91.
2 In the interest of attributing full credit to the person who originally coined this great phrase, I have trawled through all my books and also Googled the phrase but, alas, have been unable to trace its source.
3 Baumeister, R. F. & Scher, S. J. 1988. 'Self-defeating behaviour patterns among normal individuals: Review and analysis of common self-destructive tendencies'. *Psychological Bulletin*, 104 (1), 3–22.
4 Baumeister, R. F. 1984. 'Choking under pressure: Self-consciousness and paradoxical effects of incentives on skilful performance'. *Journal of Personality and Social Psychology*, 46 (3), 610–20.
5 See Sackett, D. L. & Snow, J. C. 1979. 'The magnitude of compliance and non-compliance'. In R. B. Haynes, D. W. Taylor & D. L. Sackett (eds). *Compliance in Health-care*. Baltimore, MD: Johns Hopkins University Press, pp. 11–22.
6 See (1) Beck, A. T. 1976. *Cognitive Therapy and the Emotional Disorders*. New York, NY: International Universities Press. (2) Burns, D. D. 1999. *Feeling Good: The New Mood therapy*. New York, NY: Avon Books.
7 Mornell, P. 1979. *Passive Men, Wild Women*. New York, NY: Ballantine Books. Cited in A. Christensen. 1988. 'Dysfunctional interaction patterns in couples'. In

P. Noller & M. A. Fitzpatrick (eds). *Perspectives on Marital Interaction: Monographs in the Social Psychology of Language I.* Clevedon: Multilingual Matters, pp. 31–53.

8 See Christensen, 'Dysfunctional interaction patterns in couples'.

9 Baldwin, M. W. 1997. 'Relational schemas as a source of if-then inference procedures'. *Review of General Psychology*, 1, 326–35.

10 Mischel, W. & Shoda, Y. 1995. 'A cognitive-affective system theory of personality: Reconceptualising situations, dispositions, dynamics, and invariance in personality structure'. *Psychological Review*, 102, 246–68.

11 Nolen-Hoeksema, S., Wisco, B. E. & Lyubomirsky, S. 2008. 'Rethinking rumination'. *Perspectives on Psychological Science*, 3 (5), 400–24.

12 Brockner, J., Shaw, M. C. & Rubin, J. Z. 1979. 'Factors affecting withdrawal from an escalating conflict: Quitting before it's too late'. *Journal of Experimental Social Psychology*, 15, 492–503.

13 See Polivy, J. & Herman, C. P. 2002. 'If at first you don't succeed: False hopes of self-change'. *American Psychologist*, 57, 677–89.

14 Gollwitzer, P. M. 1999. 'Implementation intentions: Strong effects of simple plans'. *American Psychologist*, 54, 493–503.

15 Gollwitzer, P. M. & Sheeran, P. 2006. 'Implementation intentions and goal achievement: A meta-analysis of effects and processes'. *Experimental Social Psychology*, 38, 69–119.

16 Gollwitzer, P. M. & Brandstatter, V. 1997. 'Implementation intentions and effective goal pursuit'. *Journal of Personality and Social Psychology*, 73 (1), 186–99.

17 Orbell, S., Hodgkins, S. & Shreeran, P. 1997. 'Implementation intentions and the theory of planned behaviour'. *Personality and Social Psychology*, 23, 945–54.

18 Orbell, S. & Sheeran, P. 2000. 'Motivational and volitional processes in action initiation: A field study of implementation intentions'. *Journal of Applied Social Psychology*, 30, 780–97.

## 22. *Fearlessly facing the future*

1 See Klinger, E. & Cox, W. M. 1987–8. 'Dimensions of thoughts in everyday life'. *Imagination, Cognition and Personality*, 7 (2), 105–28. Cited in Gilbert, D. 2006. *Stumbling on Happiness*. London: Harper Press, p. 16.

2 Gilbert, *Stumbling on Happiness*, p. 5. Citing philosopher D. Dennett. 1996. *Kinds of Minds*. New York, NY: Basic Books.

3 See Kahneman, D. 1999. 'Objective happiness'. In D. Kahneman, E. Diener & N. Schwarz. (eds). *Well-being: The Foundations of Hedonic Psychology*. New York, NY: Russell Sage Foundation, pp. 3–25.

4 For a review of this research see (1) Gilbert, *Stumbling on Happiness*. (2) Loewenstein, G. & Schkade, D. 1999. 'Wouldn't it be nice? Predicting future feelings.' In Kahneman et al, *Well-being: The Foundations of Hedonic Psychology*, pp. 85–109. (3) Wilson, T. D. & Gilbert, D. T. 2003. 'Affective Forecasting'. In M. P. Zanna (ed). *Advances in Experimental Social Psychology*. Volume 35. New York, NY: Academic Press, pp. 345–411. (4) Taylor, S. E. 1983. 'Adjustment to threatening events: A theory of cognitive adaptation'. *American Psychologist*, 38, 1161–73.

5 See Gilbert, *Stumbling on Happiness*.

6 See Simons, D. J. & Levin, D. T. 1998. 'Failure to detect changes to people in a real-world interaction'. *Psychonomic Bulletin and Review*, 5, 644–49.

7 Wilson, T. D. 2000. 'Focalism: A source of durability bias in affective forecasting'. *Journal of Personality and Social Psychology*, 78 (5), 821–36.

8 See (1) Loewenstein & Schkade, 'Wouldn't it be nice?' (2) Wilson & Gilbert, 'Affective Forecasting'. (3) Taylor, 'Adjustment to threatening events'.

9 Loewenstein & Schkade, 'Wouldn't it be nice?', p. 92.

10 Gilbert, *Stumbling on Happiness*, p. 162.

11 Brown, R. & Kulik, J. 1977. 'Flashbulb memories'. *Cognition*, 5, 73–99.

12 Neisser, U. & Harsch, N. 1992. 'Phantom flashbulbs'. In E. Winograd & U. Neisser (eds). *Affect and Accuracy in Recall: Studies of 'flashbulb' Memories*. New York, NY: Cambridge University Press, pp. 9–32.

13 Talarico, J. M. & Rubin, D. C. 2003. 'Confidence, not consistency, characterises flashbulb memories'. *Psychological Science*, 14, 455–61.

14 Sharot, T. 2007. 'How personal experience modulates the neural circuitry of memories of September 11'. *Proceedings of the National Academy of Sciences*, 104 (1), 389–94.

15 Tversky, A. & Kahneman, D. 1974. 'Judgment under uncertainty: Heuristics and biases'. *Science*, 185, 1124–31.

16 Loewenstein & Schkade, 'Wouldn't it be nice?'

17 Johansson, P., Hall, L., Silkstrom, S. & Olsson, A. 2005. 'Failure to detect mismatches between intention and outcome in a simple decision task'. *Science*, 310 (5745), 116–19.

18 See Wilson, T. D. 2002. *Strangers to Ourselves: Discovering the Adaptive Unconscious*. Cambridge, MA: Belknap Press.

19 Clarke, A. C. 1963. *Profiles of the Future*. New York, NY: Bantam Books, p. 14. Cited in Gilbert, *Stumbling on Happiness*, p. 112.

20 See *The Economist*, 3 June 1995.

21 Gardner, D. 2011. *Future Babble: Why Expert Predictions Fail and Why We Believe Them Anyway*. London: Virgin Books.

22 See Tetlock, P. 2005. *Expert Political Judgment*. Princeton, NJ: Princeton University Press.

23 Loungani, P. IMF Working Paper WP/00/77. Cited in Gardner, *Future Babble*, p. 13.

24 Gardner, *Future Babble*, p. 95.

## 23. In praise of optimism

1 Taylor, S. E. & Brown, J. D. 1988. 'Illusion and well-being: A social psychological perspective on mental health'. *Psychological Bulletin*, 103 (2), 193–210. Note: Taylor based her conclusions both on her own substantial research and the work of many other psychologists.

2 Taylor, S. E. & Gollwitzer, P. M. 1995. 'Effects of mindset on positive illusions'. *Journal of Personality and Social Psychology*, 69 (2), 213–26.

3 For a general review of this research see (1) Seligman, M. E. 1991. *Learned Optimism*. New York, NY: Knopf. (2) Sharot, T. 2011. *The Optimism Bias: A Tour of the Irrationally Positive Brain*. New York, NY: Pantheon Books. (3) Carver, C. S. & Scheier, M. F. 2005. 'Engagement, disengagement, coping and catastrophe'. In A. J. Elliot & C. S. Dweck (eds). *Handbook of Competence and Motivation*. New York, NY: Guilford, pp. 527–47.

4 For a general review see Rasmussen, H., Scheier, M. & Greenhouse, J. 2009. 'Optimism and physical health: A meta-analytic review'. *Annals of Behavioral Medicine*, 37, 239–56.

5 Giltay, E., Gelenijnse, J., Zitman, F., Hoekstra, T. & Schouten, E. 2004. 'Dispositional optimism and all-cause and cardiovascular mortality in a prospective cohort of elderly Dutch men and women'. *Archives of General Psychiatry*, 61, 1126–35.

6 Chida, Y. & Steptoe, A. 2008. 'Positive psychological well-being and mortality: A quantitative review of prospective observational studies'. *Psychosomatic Medicine*, 70, 741–56.

7 Giltay et al, 'Dispositional optimism'.

8 Tindle, H., Chang, Y. F., Kuller, L., Manson, J. E., Robinson, J. G., Rosal, M. C., Siegle, G. J. & Matthews, K. A. 2009. 'Optimism, cynical hostility, and incident coronary heart disease and mortality in the Women's Health Initiative'. *Circulation*, 120, 656–62.

9 Ibid.

10 Carver, C. S., Pozo, C., Harris, S. D., Noriega, V., Scheier, M. F., Robinson, D. S., Ketcham, A. S., Moffat, F. L. & Clark, K.C. 1993. 'How coping medi-

ates the effect of optimism on distress: A study of women with early stage breast cancer'. *Journal of Personality and Social Psychology*, 65 (2), 375–90.

11 See Carver & Scheier, 'Engagement, disengagement, coping and catastrophe'.

12 Sharot, *The Optimism Bias*.

13 Landes, D. 1998. *The Wealth and Poverty of Nations*. London: Abacus.

14 Rosenthal, R. & Jacobson, L. 1992. *Pygmalion in the Classroom*. New York, NY: Irvington Publishers.

15 Puri, M. & Robinson, D. T. 2007. 'Optimism and economic choice'. *Journal of Financial Economics*, 86 (1), 71–99.

16 For discussion see (1) Sharot, *The Optimism Bias*. (2) Carver & Scheier, 'Engagement, disengagement, coping and catastrophe'.

17 Seligman, *Learned Optimism*.

18 See Sharot, *The Optimism Bias*.

19 Seligman, M. E. P. 2005. 'Positive psychology, positive prevention, and positive therapy'. In C. R. Snyder & S. J. Lopez (eds). *Handbook of Positive Psychology*. Oxford: OUP, pp. 3–13.

20 Schneider, S. L. 2001. 'In search of realistic optimism'. *American Psychologist*, 56 (3), 250–63.

21 Norem, J. K. & Illingsworth, K. S. S. 1993. 'Strategy-dependent effects of reflecting on self and tasks: Some implications of optimism and defensive estimates'. *Journal of Personality and Social Psychology*, 65 (4), 822–35.

22 See Sharot, *The Optimism Bias*.

23 Ibid.

24 Schneider, 'In search of realistic optimism', p. 254.

25 Sharot, T., De Martino, B. & Dolan, R. J. 2009. 'How choice reveals and shapes expected hedonic reaction'. *Journal of Neuroscience*, 29 (12), 3760–65.

26 See (1) Gilbert, D. 2006. *Stumbling on Happiness*. London: Harper Press, p. 183. (2) Frey, D. et al. 1983. 'Re-evaluation of decision alternatives dependant upon the reversibility of a decision and the passage of time'. *European Journal of Social Psychology*, 14, 447–50.

27 Gilbert, D. T. & Ebert, J. E. J. 2002. 'Decisions and revisions: The affective forecasting of changeable outcomes'. *Journal of Personality and Social Psychology*, 82 (4), 503–14.

28 Gilbert, *Stumbling on Happiness*, p. 179.

29 Landes, *The Wealth and Poverty of Nations*, pp. 523–4.

# Index